'TEN PER CENT AND NO SURRENDER'

'Ten Per Cent and No Surrender'

THE PRESTON STRIKE, 1853–1854

H.I. DUTTON
Lecturer in Economic History, Lancaster University

J.E. KING
Lecturer in Economics, Lancaster University

CAMBRIDGE UNIVERSITY PRESS
Cambridge
London   New York   New Rochelle
Melbourne   Sydney

CAMBRIDGE UNIVERSITY PRESS
Cambridge, New York, Melbourne, Madrid, Cape Town, Singapore, São Paulo

Cambridge University Press
The Edinburgh Building, Cambridge CB2 8RU, UK

Published in the United States of America by Cambridge University Press, New York

www.cambridge.org
Information on this title: www.cambridge.org/9780521236201

© Cambridge University Press 1981

This publication is in copyright. Subject to statutory exception
and to the provisions of relevant collective licensing agreements,
no reproduction of any part may take place without the written
permission of Cambridge University Press.

First published 1981
This digitally printed version 2008

A catalogue record for this publication is available from the British Library

ISBN 978-0-521-23620-1 hardback
ISBN 978-0-521-07257-1 paperback

Contents

	Preface	*page*	vii
	Prologue		1
1	Industry and Unions		6
2	Ten Per Cent (5 June–14 October 1853)		27
3	The Operatives		46
4	The Masters		77
5	Locked Out (15 October 1853–9 February 1854)		94
6	Council and Bench		116
7	Guardians of the Poor		137
8	Lord Palmerston		149
9	The Press		163
10	Defeat (10 February–13 May 1854)		177
11	Posterity		195
	Epilogue		205
	Notes		209
	Bibliography		251
	Index		262

Preface

Our greatest debt is to the men who compiled the scrapbooks on the Preston strike (now held by the Lancashire County Records Office) which first aroused our interest in the dispute. One, Henry Ashworth, was a cotton manufacturer and a bitter enemy of the strikers. The other was a cotton operative, almost certainly George Cowell, the leader of the Preston weavers throughout the strike. Without the foresight of these two men, ironically on opposite sides in 1853—4, this book would never have been written.

By far the most important source has been the comprehensive reports of the strike in the national, provincial and (above all) the local press. In this respect we have been extremely, perhaps uniquely, fortunate: unsurpassed in detail, rarely challenged as to accuracy, careful to distinguish fact from opinion, the reporting of the Preston strike in many ways puts the modern press to shame.

Moving forward more than a century, we must record our thanks to John Foster, Jean King, David Reid and John Saville. Librarians at Blackburn, Burnley, Lancaster, Manchester, Preston and Stockport were most helpful, as were the staff of the British Library, the British Museum, the Public Records Office, the Royal Society of Arts and (especially) the Lancashire County Records Office in Preston. We would also like to thank the Lancashire Evening Post and the Lancashire County Records Office for permitting us to use the unique illustrations for this book. We are also extremely grateful to Hilary Dutton and Wendy Höpfl for typing the final manuscript and to Richard Charnley for taking the photographs.

Some readers may have forgotten the (pre-decimal) days of real money, when there were four farthings to a penny, twelve pence to a shilling and twenty shillings to a pound. We have not provided decimal conversions in the text, but have used the contemporary abbreviations: 'd' for pence, and 's' for shillings. The apparently tiny sums at stake in the strike may be placed in perspective if it is remembered that, in 1853, 10s (or 50p) would buy the services of a weaver for a week.

Local government boundaries were transformed in 1973, when ancient Lancashire was partitioned and the new metropolitan counties of Greater Manchester and Merseyside came into existence. Like the county cricket authorities, we have taken no notice of these changes. We do, however, apologise to residents of Stockport (formerly Cheshire), Glossop (once Derbyshire) and any other such towns for occasionally treating them all as Lancastrians.

1981   H.I.D.
J.E.K.

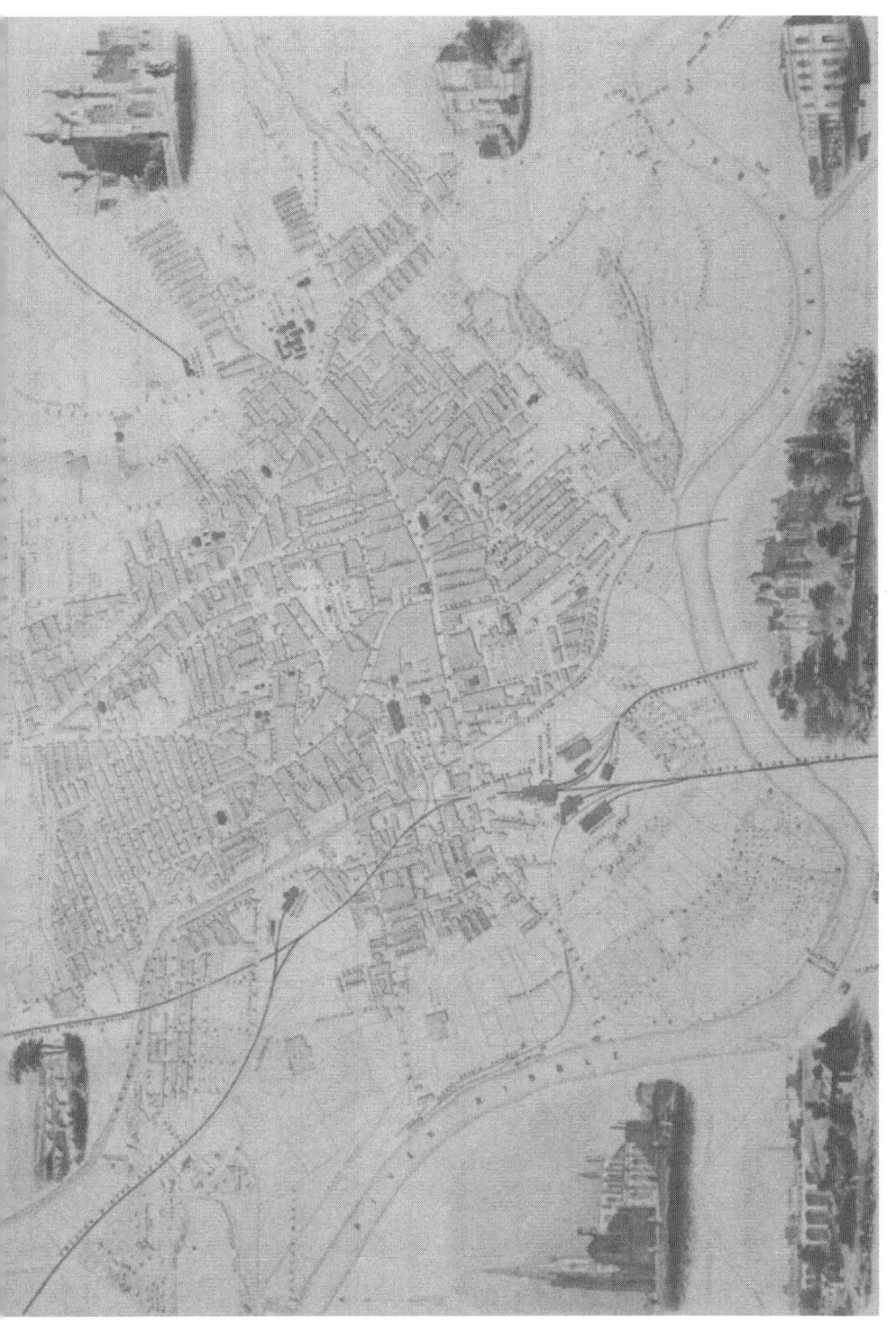

1853 Street Map of Preston

Prologue

On the afternoon of Saturday 11 March 1854, the cotton operatives of Preston marched in their thousands through the rolling countryside of the Darwen valley, south-east of the town. At their head were two bands; just behind the musicians, the vanguard were carrying banners. 'A Fair Day's Wage For A Fair Day's Work', could be read on one; 'Peace, Law, And Order', on another. 'Cursed Is He That Defraudeth The Labourer of His Wages', said a third. The key to the procession was found on a banner inscribed 'Ten Per Cent And No Surrender'. The marchers had been locked out for almost five months, ever since their employers closed down the mills rather than pay a ten per cent increase in wages. The procession reached the railway station at Hoghton, midway between Preston and Blackburn and in sight of the impressive Tudor ruins of Hoghton Tower, a popular picnic site for day-trippers.

The Preston millhands had come here to reaffirm to the world their solidarity and their determination, and to express their gratitude to the factory operatives of Blackburn, who had been their most loyal supporters during the 21 weeks of the lock-out. The landlord of the Railway Hotel had lent them a meadow for the occasion. Laughing and joking, the operatives filed into the field. Proceedings got under way with a song:

> You may see of a truth that the people are not dead,
> Though 'twas said that they died long ago;
> But we've risen from our sleep, a holiday to keep,
> Determined to work under price no more.
>   CHORUS
> So we've put by the reed-hook and the comb,
> And hung up the shuttle on the loom;
> And we'll never be content
> 'Till we get the ten per cent,
> In spite of their let well alone.

Then someone climbed onto an overturned cart to address the crowd. This was John Cheetham, an Oldham man, a veteran Chartist and trade unionist whose turbulent radicalism had brought him into contact with the law on more than one occasion. This time he was calm and composed. 'Friends,' he began, 'we are met here today because a portion of the authorities of Preston have thought fit to prohibit our meetings in the borough. But we intend to keep the peace, and have no desire to come in collision with any party. Our object in assembling today is to make known the rights and claims of labour, and I believe this meeting will make a great impression on the country.'

Cheetham stepped down. His place was taken by James Young, another Oldham man, a cardroom hand and Chartist. 'We are here', he told an attentive audience, 'to protest against the injustice, the tyranny, and the oppression which the manufacturers of this country have practised upon their operatives for a great number of years. It is my duty to caution the card-room hands among you to be peaceable and orderly. You must throw nothing in the way of the authorities of Preston to enable them to cause an outbreak or riot.' This brought an immediate response from the turnouts. Their bitter resentment against the authorities, who had made no secret of their sympathy with the millowners, was tempered by fears of provocation and entrapment. Plain-clothes policemen were active in the town, seeking to lead astray the more impressionable of the operatives. So far they had failed. As the murmurings of the crowd died away, Young continued:

The card-room hands have suffered as much injustice and persecution as any branch of industry upon the face of the earth. Considering the labour we have to perform, and the unhealthy atmosphere in which we are employed, we must be united for the protection of our wages from the avaricious and unprincipled aggressions of capital. I have looked into the statement of wages which the manufacturers of Preston have been paying to their card-room hands. I find individuals working for 6s.6d per week. I find men stripping and grinding for 8s. and 9s., when in Ashton, Manchester, Bolton and Oldham they receive 16s. or 12s. for the same labour.

All Lancashire believed wages in Preston to be miserably low, and the cotton operatives of the entire county saw Preston's cause as their own. Each week they raised £3,000 or more to assist in the struggle. 'I exhort you', Young exclaimed, 'show that you are determined to relieve labour from the thraldom of capital, that you know the rights of labour, and are determined to protect those rights, no matter how great may be the amount of persecution the employing classes bring to bear against you.' He walked away, to thunderous applause.

Next on the impromptu rostrum was James Waddington, a Preston weaver, who had been deeply involved in the campaign since October. He was soon to be arrested for his part in frustrating the millowners' plans to import blackleg labour. 'We have been struggling for the ten per cent for 29 weeks', he declared, 'and our ardour is not in the least diminished. This vast assembly indicates the firmness of our determination to carry out the object in view.' The crowd roared its approval. They began the struggle back in the summer of 1853, and it was a rash of small strikes in August which precipitated the lock-out. 'When I look round upon the thousands and tens of thousands who have walked five or six miles to be present here', Waddington continued, 'it tells me that the sooner the manufacturers of Preston give the ten per cent, the better it will be for all parties.' He was forced to pause until the cheering subsided. 'During the last week or two, the manufacturers have been trying to dampen the spirits of the people of Preston. They have been importing people from the south, from Ireland, and from all parts of the country where they could find a union bastille and where they could persuade the guardians to turn the people out.' Since the end of February the masters had travelled as far afield as Bradford and Belfast recruiting 'knobsticks' from the workhouses, those hated symbols of the New Poor Law. 'The papers tell us that Horrockses have 900 hands at work', Waddington remarked, to cries of 'Eh?' and 'It's a lie!'. 'But I know that Mr Miller is dissatisfied with what he has, but does not know how to get rid of them. All I regret is, that the masters do not have 900 apiece of such hands.' Thomas Miller was the proprietor of Horrockses and Miller, the largest firm in Preston. He was chairman of the masters' association, and the operatives' most bitter enemy. But the knobsticks were inexperienced and incompetent; they presented no threat. 'While this is going on', Waddington said, to renewed cheering, 'our committee have removed a larger number of skilled hands than ever, and five of these are worth more than fifty of such as the associated masters have brought into the town.'

Waddington was unable to go on, for the air was again full of music. The Blackburn operatives were arriving, marching behind their banners and with three bands at their head. They had won the ten per cent back in the summer, and had been at work in the mills all morning. Their arrival was greeted by deafening cheers, which all but drowned the music. Not to be outdone by the newcomers, the Preston bands started up in competition, and a friendly but energetic contest began between the rival musicians. Speakers waiting to address the meeting stood by helplessly, and were forced to rush and seize the instruments before proceedings could continue. By now the crowd was so vast that many were beyond the reach of any speaker's voice, and turned instead to dancing and other amusements.

One of the Blackburn contingent stood up to compliment the people of Preston on their strict observance of peace, law and order. No great orator, he made way for the young Stockport weaver, Luke Wood. Still in his mid-twenties, Wood was already a seasoned campaigner, having played a prominent role in the successful ten per cent strike in his home town in the previous year. 'During the Stockport strike,' he recalled, 'the people of Blackburn assembled on Rishton Moor. That meeting had its effect in the proper quarter, and I have no doubt this meeting will have its effect in the proper quarter too.' Wood stepped down, not knowing that he too would be arrested within a fortnight. His place was taken by Robert Worswick of Padiham, who told the enthusiastic crowd:

I regard this monster meeting as a demonstrative proof that the working classes feel that their employers have for years been infringing the rights of labour. That you have walked six miles to be present shows the interest you take in this movement. I believe that if you had had 20 miles to walk instead of six, you would not have stayed away. This shows that the noble-hearted men and women of Preston are not going to act the part of a Judas and sell the interests of the working classes of this country. I believe that you are resolved that, rather than succumb, you will die groaning 'Ten Per Cent, and No Surrender'.

The Prestonians roared their approval. Until recently they had been scorned by operatives in other towns as docile and cowardly, willing to accept low wages and drag down the living standards of more militant districts. This time, they had decided, it would be different.

Wallace Beevers, from the township of Brooksbottom, near Bury, was the next to speak. 'I have been informed', he told them, 'that the reason the Blackburn people were late in their arrival is that, after leaving work, they stopped to pay in their subscriptions for Preston.' So they had, to the tune of £660. 'I admire them for their foresight', he continued, 'and I hope the Prestonians will take encouragement from the generous spirit thus manifested towards them. And the people of Blackburn tell me that if you want more money, you have only to ask and you shall have it.' Great cheering greeted this news, and heralded the final speaker.

This was Mortimer Grimshaw, the Thunderer of Lancashire. The son of a notable radical active in the early years of the century, Grimshaw had once been himself a weaver. He was now a full-time agitator, whose rhetorical skills were renowned throughout the county. He, too, would soon run foul of the law. 'We are assembled today', he commenced his powerful harangue, 'to reinaugurate the labour movement. I believe it is possible now, not only to concentrate the veritable working classes of this country into one mighty union, but to enrol under our banners all who depend on wages for a livelihood.' This allusion to the Chartist Ernest Jones's ambitious plans for a great 'Mass Movement', coordinating strikes across the length and breadth of the kingdom, was endorsed by many in the audience. 'It has been declared to the world that this is a question of mastership', Grimshaw said, referring now to the views of the Preston manufacturers. They regarded trade unions as a form of dictation, and considered claims for wage increases to be an unwarranted interference with the conduct of their businesses. 'This assertion is without foundation', he declared. 'We have no desire whatever to manage or control the affairs of the employers. All we want is the right to live by our labour, to be paid that which is our due, to enter the mills free men and women, so long as we are prepared to do our duty as workpeople. What we claim is the right to be masters of ourselves, to resist all petty tyranny and oppression, to hold the right of private judgement, and to speak the free sentiments of our minds. And so far we intend to be masters.' This brought renewed cheering. 'Men and women of Lancashire! Now is the time to free yourselves from the iron grasp of your oppressors. I ask the Blackburnians: is Preston to be subdued for want of your money?' The Blackburn operatives responded at once. 'No; methinks I hear the whole of Lancashire exclaiming that the operatives of Preston must never be allowed to go in short of the full ten per cent.'

Grimshaw stepped down from the platform, to tumultuous applause. It was now six o'clock. The light was fading fast, and the cold March wind had begun to whistle through the bare branches of the trees. The meeting ended in good heart. Led by their bands, the operatives of Preston and Blackburn set off for home. Participants in one of the greatest industrial battles of their generation, they would return to Hoghton in even greater numbers next day, and would continue the struggle for another seven weeks before admitting defeat.[1]

1 Industry and Unions

> In eighteen forty-seven, my boys
> I am sorry for to say,
> They took from us the ten per cent,
> Without so much delay
> And now we want it back again,
> Our masters in a pout,
> Said they would not grant it us,
> So we're everyone locked out.

In the 1720s, Defoe described Preston as a fine town. 'Here's no manufacture,' he writes, 'the town is full of attorneys, proctors and notaries.'[1] Half a century or so later, Preston remained a 'beautiful town, built of brick ... with neat streets and fine walks', but as Rev. William MacRitchie noted, cotton had become the principal industry.[2] When Eric Svedenstierna, the Swedish industrial spy, visited Preston in 1802–3 he considered it to be one of the 'most considerable [of] several manufacturing towns in Northern Lancashire.'[3] And by 1821 Marmaduke Tulket reckoned it had grown into the second largest 'emporium for the cotton spinning and manufacturing businesses'.[4] William Cobbett, who stood as Preston's radical candidate in the 1826 election,[5] never visited the town during his northern tours of 1830 and 1832 and although he recollects the 'pretty girls ... who spat upon the "individual" of the Derby family',[6] he passes no comment on the growth of industry of the town itself. By the early 1840s though, Preston was 'conspicuous ... for the prosperity of its trade and manufacture',[7] and for the growth of its working population. In 1801 Preston's population was 12,174. It had more than doubled by 1821 and between 1831 and 1841 grew on average 5% per annum. In 1841 the population stood at 50,887 and by 1851 it had increased a further 37% to 69,542.[8]

This rapid increase in population, in a town which in 1851 measured one and a half miles from east to west and one mile from north to south, predictably created living conditions significantly different from those observed by Defoe a century or more earlier. The spacious and elegant living of the attorneys, proctors and notaries had now largely given way to a town overcrowded with factory operatives, living in appalling conditions. When Engels toured England in the early 1840s, he noted that nearly all Lancashire towns:

of thirty, fifty, seventy to ninety thousand inhabitants, are almost wholly working-people's districts, interspersed only with factories, a few thoroughfares lined with shops and a few lanes along which the gardens and houses of the manufacturers are scattered like villas. The towns themselves are badly and irregularly built with foul courts, lanes and back alleys, reeking of coal smoke, and especially dingy from the originally bright red brick, turned black with time ... Cellar dwellings are general here; wherever it is in any way possible, these subterranean dens are constructed, and a very considerable portion of the population dwells in them.[9]

That Preston's death rate at this time was alleged to have been the highest in the United Kingdom[10] merely confirms Engels's view that Preston was one of the most squalid towns he had visited.

The changing conditions within Preston can be explained entirely by the growth of the cotton industry. In the mid eighteenth century cotton products were a mixture of linen warp and cotton weft — known as fustian — and were produced by domestic workers who worked up the material distributed by merchants and fustian manufacturers. At this time a considerable proportion of the population of Lancashire, the West Riding and Cheshire were dependent upon the textile trade, although many were able to supplement earnings — and perhaps the quality of life — by working on the land. Children usually prepared and cleaned the raw cotton whilst the women spun the yarn on a hand-wheel and the men wove the cotton on the loom. The productivity of spinning was generally low and one weaver often required four spinners to be kept regularly employed. With the invention of Kay's flying shuttle, which had become widely adopted in the 1760s, the unbalance between weaving and spinning became more serious and yarn consequently scarce. This shortage was gradually overcome as the spinning inventions of Hargreaves, Arkwright and Crompton were taken up in the 1770s and 1780s. Unlike the woollen industry, which hitherto had been England's staple textile trade, cotton was more susceptible to technological change of this kind. Demand for light tough washable fabrics increased with changing tastes and with the growth of markets in warmer parts of the trading world. The supply of raw cotton was also more responsive and it increased rapidly when the invention of the cotton gin encouraged the development of plantations in North America. Compared with wool, cotton was a tough pliable material and less likely to break when twisted and attenuated by the actions of the early machines.[11] These technical and market advantages soon made cotton Britain's premier manufacturing industry and by 1802, in terms of value added, cotton had outpaced the woollen industry. In 1815 cotton exports were valued at £28.3m (40% of British exports) and by 1850 the value of cotton exports reached £71.4m.[12]

This expansion coincided with several significant changes within the industry: the emergence of factory production; the relocation of production from rural to urban areas; further technological change; and an increasingly large proportion of the labour force divorced from owning the means of production.[13]

The growth of factories in the late eighteenth century was fairly rapid, although domestic production and mechanical power were not mutually exclusive. Water wheels provided most of the power and the early jennies and hand mules were largely employed in small workshops in rural areas. After the cancellation of Arkwright's patent in 1785 the water-frame spread through the industry and spinning emerged as a factory process. Of the 900 factories known to exist in 1797, 300 were roller spinning on the Arkwright frame and 600 were mule spinning.[14] Mule factories were generally smaller, but by 1812 were the most significant in terms of spindles: 4m mule spindles, compared with 300 water-frames and 155,000 jenny spindles. Steam power at this time was still in its infancy, and did not begin to overtake water as the major source of power until the late 1820s, when factories were increasingly located in urban areas.[15] In the early 1820s a 60hp cotton mill was considered large and, since a Pennine stream could generate up to 400hp,[16] country mills in Lancashire disappeared slowly.[17] By 1838, though, 1,819 cotton factories employed some 1,641 steam engines with a total horse-power of 46,826. Sixty-five per cent of these factories were concentrated on the Lancashire coalfields and only 1.1% of the total horse-power was provided by water.

On the weaving side of the industry, the factory system was slow to develop, even though weaving was, in the early nineteenth century, the single largest manufacturing sector in the British economy.[18] Occasionally, large handloom manufacturers employed more operatives than the factory spinning lords,[19] and handloom weaving sheds, which represented the transitional stage between the domestic system and power driven weaving, often had upwards of 20 handlooms.[20] But these relatively large concerns accounted only for a small proportion of the industry's output. Most output was still organized on the traditional putting out system, where production was largely unmechanized and where weavers worked up the cloth in their own homes. In the 1790s approximately 180,000 were employed in this way, and although Cartwright had invented the power loom in 1795 it was slow to be taken up; labour was abundant and the skills required for weaving plain cloth easily learnt, whilst the capital cost of a pair of looms was as low as £5. Consequently, with technological change in the spinning sector displacing labour, and with the increased demand for cotton goods raising relative wages, labour from agriculture and other textile trades such as wool, linen and sailcloth began to move into weaving. Technological change in the weaving sector was not profitable until the 1820s and even then was adopted by manufacturers only when the economy was in an expansionary phase, as in 1823–5 and 1833–5. In 1819 only 14–15,000 power looms were in operation.[21] By 1830 the number had increased to 80,000 and although there were still 225,000 handloom weavers,[22] many of these, especially in urban areas, were increasingly specializing in fancy goods, that part of the trade where power looms had yet to make any impression. Investment in power looms came almost exclusively from spinning masters, who already had power supplies, factory space, experienced mechanics and managerial expertise to tend the now more technically developed machines.[23] The relative decline in spinning profits after 1835[24] also induced spinners to integrate the weaving process and explains why power looms were first located outside of the old weaving districts of northern Lancashire.

The introduction of power loom weaving and the steady, but slow, diffusion of the new self-acting spinning technology in the 1830s brought a change in the structure of the industry. Before the 1820s, spinning factories and weaving sheds were generally quite separate, but once spinning masters began investing in the power loom, firms increasingly combined both processes on the same site. Between 1825 and 1840 integrated firms grew rapidly[25] and were only checked by the inability of power looms to work fine yarn and by the increased export of yarn after 1832. By 1841 approximately one-third of Lancashire cotton factories were of the combined type. Of the 975 firms operating in 1841, 321 combined spinning and weaving; 470 spun coarse yarn; 80 fine yarn; and 104 manufactured cloth on the power loom.[26] By 1850, the zenith of the integrated firm, 38% of Lancashire firms were combined and these employed 81.8% of the total number of looms, 55.7% of the total number of spindles and 62.6% of the industry's labour force.[27]

This process of vertical integration tended to alter the ratio of fixed and working capital, and increased the absolute level of investment.[28] Combined firms were on average larger than single-process firms and generally employed more labour, machinery and steam power. Estimates for a large mill in the 1780s and 1790s indicated a cost of £5,000,[29] whereas in the 1830s a large combined firm could cost anything up to £80,000. In 1841 the total fixed capital employed in spinning and weaving in Lancashire amounted to £14.6m, an average of £15,000 per firm. But large firms did not dominate the industry, which remained competitive throughout the first half of the nineteenth century. Barriers to entry were low and the small and medium[30] single-process firms retained their numerical dominance in the market. In fact the distribution of assets between small and large firms remained much the same as it had been at the end of the Napoleonic wars.[31] In a period when partnership and family connections ensured that ownership and control went hand in hand, there were obvious managerial and financial[32] limits to growth, and large firms rarely expanded to employ more than 1,000 operatives. Economies of large scale production in the industry were often uncertain, and efficiency depended on the speed with which new technology was adopted, rather than the size of the firm itself. Up to the 1850s, and possibly beyond, small and large combined and single-process firms happily co-existed. In 1850 the representative spinning factory in Lancashire operated 11,800 spindles and employed 108 hands. In weaving the representative firm operated 163 power looms with 100 hands, whilst the representative combined firm operated 330 looms and 17,800 spindles, and employed 310 operatives.[33]

The changing nature of the cotton industry was reflected in the growth of Preston, which by 1851 was essentially a single-industry town.[34] In the eighteenth century Preston was an important market town comparatively isolated from the growing industrial enclaves of Lancashire. Located at the lowest bridge point on the Ribble, it developed as a centre of communications and as a base for distributing the agricultural products of the Fylde. Linen was the staple manufacture, and although it progressed in the late seventeenth century it never developed into an industry of any importance. In the eighteenth century Preston remained a sleepy administrative and aristocratic town. Nor was this somnolent atmosphere greatly disturbed by the building of the first cotton mill in 1777 by Messrs Collinson and Watson. Preston did not begin to develop as a cotton town until John Horrocks erected his Yard Factory in 1792. According to one local historian this unquestionably 'gave the chief impetus, which, in little more than half a century, converted the quiet aristocratic town, of about 6,000 or 7,000 inhabitants, into a busy hive of industry'.[35] Indeed, within the next ten years another four spinning mills were erected; two by Horrocks (1796, 1797), one by Messrs Ainsworth & Co. (1796) and one by Messrs Riley & Paley (1802). In 1799 the House of Correction was converted for this purpose.

The Napoleonic wars, which increased demand, and technological change, which progressively reduced the price of cotton goods,[36] clearly explain the increase in the number of cotton mills built in towns such as Ashton, Stockport, Oldham, Burnley and Blackburn, but the growth in Preston was relatively slow. By 1802 only seven mills were in operation. Undoubtedly cotton was a coming trade, but, as Dr Aikin observed in 1795, Preston was mainly 'a sort of mart for the Lancashire linens, and sheetings are still sold here; but of late the cotton branches have obtained possession'.[37] Most of this change was due to John Horrocks, who by 1811 operated possibly the greatest number of spindles (100–110,000) in the world,[38] and by 1816 the firm employed 7,000 hands.[39] Horrocks, who died in 1804 leaving £150,000, was in fact *the* cotton industry in Preston.

After the Napoleonic wars the natural geographical advantages of Preston became more important. Situated on the edge of the Fylde, Lancashire's main agricultural district, local manufacturers were provided with an abundant supply of cheap labour which kept wages down.[40] Since labour costs constituted roughly 30% of total expenses of production, Preston manufacturers gained an unearned competitive advantage. With the onset of the agricultural depression after 1813 and with wheat prices falling almost continuously to 1835,[41] the movement of rural migrants into urban areas intensified. In 1851 70% of Preston's adult population came from outside its boundaries and 40% of these from places less than ten miles distant.[42] As Preston concentrated on the production of coarse low quality cotton goods, the inflow of an untrained agricultural labour force did not pose serious problems with regard to learning new skills. The ready supply of cheap food also enabled manufacturers to keep money wages down, compared with their rivals (though real wages may have been the same) and the availability of cheap building materials and low land values merely reinforced these advantages. Preston's relative isolation did have its costs. It was almost 30 miles from Manchester, the chief marketing centre, and was not near a coal field. On the whole, though, Preston was favourably located and did gain from its position.

The growth of cotton in Preston in the immediate post-war years was not rapid. Between 1802 and 1820 only a further nine mills were built. Horrocks and Miller, who joined in partnership in 1809,[43] remained the largest producer, employing some 63% of the town's total 236hp in their eight factories.[44] Messrs Ainsworth, Catterall & Co., the second largest, employed 45hp, whilst Swainson and Birley, established in 1808,[45] was the larger of the two combined firms with 35hp. At the time of the 1836 spinners' strike, however, the number of mills had increased to 42, employing 1,200hp. Ashworth estimated a total capital of £800,000: £550,000 working and £250,000 fixed. Approximately 20% of the population were employed in primary cotton production; 6,100 were power loom weavers and cardroom hands, 1,320 piecers, 660 spinners and 420 were overlookers and engineers.

The early 1830s was the period of most significant growth when measured in terms of the number of mills built. Statistics for the number of new mills for the period 1820—36 do not exist, but growth was almost certainly concentrated in the period 1833—6. The boom of 1825 undoubtedly induced entry into the industry but, down to 1832, the value of output (national) did not greatly increase and profit margins generally fell. The volume of output increased each year as firms attempted to spread overhead costs and began to utilize the excess power supplies installed in 1825.[46] Combined firms also emerged in this period as profits were relatively higher in the manufacturing sector of the industry. In the early 1830s conditions improved. Demand and profits increased and, with power supplies fully utilized, new investment took place. Between 1835 and 1838 the cotton industry experienced a 50 per cent increase in horsepower. This subsequently increased capacity, and in the period up to the 1841—2 depression prices and profits came under pressure and marginal firms left the industry.[47] In Preston the number of mills appears to have remained the same, although it is quite possible that new entrants forced out the unprofitable ones. When Leonard Horner surveyed Lancashire textile firms in 1841 he estimated that Preston had 42 mills.[48] Of these 15 were single spinning firms employing 529hp (all steam) and 2,527 operatives. Combined firms had now increased from 2 in 1820 to 15 employing 1,258hp and 6,639 hands. This section of the industry included two of the largest firms in the cotton industry. Horrockses and Miller with a full capacity of 1,422 hands and 250hp was the largest one-site employer in Lancashire.[49] Three mills were weaving by power loom only, five doubling yarn and four were not running. Employment statistics exist for only 30 of the 42 mills, but these were probably the largest. In 1841 20% of Preston's population were employed in these 30 mills; 707 spinners, 1,725 piecers, 7,495 power loom weavers, cardroom hands and reelers, and 523 were overlookers, packers and engineers.[50]

The main period of growth for Preston's cotton industry was, then, probably concentrated in the early and mid 1830s, with 'semi-reserve capacity' allowing further expansion of output and employment in the following years.[51]

The partial adoption of the self actor after the 1836 strike and the growth of combined firms helped maintain profits when prices and demand were falling. Power looms were also extensively installed in the boom of 1833–6. Horrockses, who first introduced the loom in the early 1820s, had 764 in operation by 1836.[52] Entry into the industry over the period seems to have been fairly easy and small firms managed to compete effectively, perhaps through the purchase of second-hand machinery. In Preston the large firms were generally the old firms which had grown in the years of high profits before and during the Napoleonic wars.[53] Horrockses and Miller, Ainsworth, Swainson and Birley, Birley Bros and the Paleys tended to dominate the town[54] though they did not preclude others from growing.

After the 1842 depression the cotton industry quickly revived and continued to expand until 1846, when depression again set in. In 1847, when a shortage of raw cotton supplies led to increased prices and when demand in foreign markets slackened, many Lancashire mills either shut down or worked short time.[55] In Preston 15 mills were working short time, some five days and some three, whilst five small mills were closed down. By now the number of mills had increased to 46,[56] employing a total of 2,783hp and 13,950 hands. In the next few years the industry experienced a remarkable boom, induced both by domestic demand[57] and by demand from industrialized and primary product countries. Low rates of interest added to the urge for investment, and technological change minimized the problems created by relatively inelastic supplies of raw cotton.[58] In the year ending October 1851, 73 new factories were built in Lancashire, many of them in and around the Preston area.[59] This expansion continued into the following year when a further 84 mills were erected. Over this period 9,875hp was added[60] and it is little wonder that Horner, the northern factory inspector, was forced to conclude that 'at no period during the last 17 years that I have been officially acquainted with the manufacturing districts of Lancashire have I known such general prosperity, the activity in every branch is extraordinary ... [and] new mills are going up everywhere'.[61] Preston more than shared in this boom and by 1852 the number of firms had increased to 64[62] and horse-power to 3,500. In all, 1,100,000 spindles were in operation and capable of producing 800,000lb of Number 32 yarn weekly, whilst the 2,000 power looms could weave up to 90,000 pieces of Indian shirtings weekly.[63] Estimates of the number of operatives varied between 21,000 and 25,000, approximately 30% of the total population.

This expansion in Preston's productive capacity can largely be explained by the growth of two overseas markets: India and China.[64] Since the 1830s there

13   *Industry and Unions*

had been a steady shift in the distribution of cotton cloth exports throughout the world. As Europe and the United States began to develop import-substituting industries, British exports of cotton piece goods — by value 75% of total cotton exports — switched into India and China. Both markets developed rapidly, and by the early 1850s India was the world's main importer of cotton goods. In 1830 India imported 52m yards, in 1840 145m and by 1850 314m yards, amounting to 23 per cent of British cotton exports.[65] Trade with China, though less important in terms of volume, grew rapidly after the boost given by the 1842 Treaty of Nanking. In 1840 China imported 13m yards of cotton cloth; by 1850 this had increased to 73m yards, and represented 5% of British cotton exports.[66]

Both markets were of crucial importance for Preston, whose manufacturers concentrated on grey and white cotton shirtings and whose spinners largely produced yarn of coarser counts.[67] Fancy goods such as Balasore handkerchiefs were a speciality of the town but the production of plain goods remained unquestionably the main output. Since this branch of the trade was always more susceptible to the automatic technology of the self actor and the power loom, productivity gains were generally passed on through lower prices to feed the burgeoning demand of consumers in low-income countries. But whilst India and China provided growing markets Preston's fortunes depended heavily on the economic and political conditions prevailing in each country. Specializing in low quality goods for fairly restricted markets which often experienced violent fluctuations in demand had its costs. In 1853 exports to China fell off dramatically, both in volume and in value. Exports fell from 98m yards in 1853 to 41m in 1854: in value terms this meant a drop of £700,000.[68]

Internal rebellion was the reason for this decline in demand. Ever since the Treaty of Nanking and the subsequent privileges gained by the French and Americans, Chinese isolationism had been steadily eroded by Western influence. The concessions made to the British in 1842 were considered by Chinese nationalists as humiliating, and the toleration of Catholic and Protestant religions acted as a springboard for anti-Manchu feeling which had persisted underground in South China for many years. Initially the insurrection was a religious movement, based on Protestant doctrines, and involved the denunciation of Buddhist and Taoist cults and the destruction of images in public temples. When Chinese officials failed in their attempt to arrest the leaders, the movement became committed to overthrowing the Ch'ing dynasty. This new revolutionary force, known as the Taiping, had immediate military success and almost captured Peking. Further insurrectionary movements, though quite opposed to the Taiping's Christianity, now emerged. In September 1853 the Small Sword Society seized the main port of Shanghai and remained there until April 1854 when they were eventually driven out by joint British and American forces.[69] The occupation of China's main port clearly disrupted trade and, since Lancashire's cotton industry was in the process of expanding capacity, stockpiling and falling profits were the inevitable result. That the Preston operatives

14   *Ten Per Cent and No Surrender*

should choose this time to demand a ten per cent wage increase was, as many contemporaries insisted, extremely unfortunate.

Despite the growth of the factory system, the labour force in the cotton industry was, up until the 1830s, dominated by handworkers. In 1830 the number of handloom weavers (240,000) still exceeded the number of factory spinners and power loom weavers (185,000), and it was perhaps only after the mid 1830s that the factory worker really came of age.[70] By 1844-6 the number of factory spinners had increased to 190,000 and power loom weavers to 150,000 and, in 1853, about 90% of the labour force (335,000) was employed in the factory.[71] Ancillary trades such as dyeing and calico printing remained almost the only significant processes carried on outside the factory.[72]

The factory labour force itself was dominated by women and, before the 1830s, by children. In 1816 adult males accounted for only 17.7% of the labour force, whilst roughly 40% were children under the age of 18.[73] At Horrockses, Miller & Co. (1816), Preston's largest concern, 73% of the labour force were under the age of 18.[74] But with the diminished employment of parish apprentices and the growth of factory legislation the employment of children decreased. Between 1835 and 1838 children under 14 fell from 13.2% to 4.75% of total employment. By 1850 the factory labour force consisted of: 4.6% children under 14, 11.2% males between 13 and 18, 28% males over 18 and 55.8% women over the age of 13.[75] The average age of the adult factory worker was also fairly low, and fell even further towards the middle of the century. Older men and women tended to leave the factory for other occupations, since peak earnings were generally achieved between the ages of 20 and 30.[76]

The increasing employment of women also altered the occupational structure of the factory. In the highly varied domestic system of the eighteenth and early nineteenth century, weaving was carried out by men, spinning by women and the preparation and finishing processes usually by children. With the emergence of factory spinning these roles changed. Spinning became the preserve of men as water-frame factories spread, whilst mules, which required greater physical strength to operate, made spinning almost entirely an adult male occupation.[77] Throstle spinning, which produced the warp, was the exception, being entirely the province of women. When the self actor was introduced from about 1830 the male monopoly of spinning weft began to weaken as a higher proportion of women were employed as minders, although it was still dominated by young adult males.[78] In weaving, which by 1833 was the single largest occupational group in the factories, the introduction of the power loom allowed a far greater proportion of women to move into the mills, adult male weavers being more inclined to cling to the independent handloom tradition. In Stockport in 1841 55% of the factory weavers were women, 60% in 1851, and 65% by 1861.[79]

The changing structure of the industry also determined the growth and nature of unionism in both spinning and weaving.[80] The emergence of factory work,

15   *Industry and Unions*

rigidly controlled by the clock and the driving discipline of the machine, soon sharpened the distinction between work and leisure and between masters and their operatives. Within the confines of the mill the operatives could easily identify their masters, just as they could now identify their own interests. Harsh discipline, the systematic use of fines, corporal punishment, the threat of dismissal and excessively long hours belie the notion that factory workers were like 'elves at play'.[81] Yet the degree to which factory workers were able to organize themselves into unions varied considerably between occupations and over time. Cardroom hands, whose position in the production process provided them with the capacity to disrupt the whole trade, appear to have had no formal union until the 1830s, and then it was of a very limited geographical coverage and lifespan. The power loom weavers' unions did not emerge on any scale until the 1840s, and the piecers, who were supervised and controlled by the spinners, were generally prevented from joining the spinners' union except on a casual basis, and then never had any significant power.[82] Within the factory the mule spinners were, until the 1840s, the only effectively organized section of the labour force.[83]

Some of the first spinners' unions of the 1790s adopted the pattern of unionism developed by weavers from the mid eighteenth century: mule spinning was at first, if not for long, a domestic occupation and since many of the spinners were former handloom weavers they carried with them an inherited tradition of organization.[84] The early weavers' trade societies generally grew out of meetings in public houses, in shop unions — especially in the towns[85] — and were closely associated with Friendly Societies, which provided insurance against sickness, old age and death and later camouflage from the Combination Laws. These unions were informal and expressed the natural links between men working in the same trade.[86] They were organized locally and reflected the particular skills and status of the craft; fine weavers in Bolton and Bury, smallware weavers in Stockport and Manchester and the velveteen fustian trade in Oldham.[87] Each trade in each area developed its own union, and remained autonomous and sectionalist, concerned almost exclusively with the preservation of traditional skills. They achieved this largely by controlling entry, restricting apprenticeship and controlling the quality and length of cloth, whilst wages were standardized and determined by custom. Weavers were generally less concerned with short term wage bargaining and negotiation. Their 'occasional disputes with their employers resembled rather family differences than conflicts between distinct social classes'.[88]

Weavers' associations were not formally continuous. They usually appeared in depressed years, when weavers sought to enforce entry controls and customary wages, as in 1757–8 and 1777–8.[89] In the 1780s, when the spread of innovations in the spinning sector increased the output of yarn, the old trade societies found it difficult to maintain control over entry, especially in the sections of the trade dominated by widely dispersed outworking. In these years

— the golden age of the weaver — an amazing increase in the number of weavers, especially in the south east of Lancashire, brought in an ever-increasing number of unqualified 'illegal men', particularly in the fustian part of the trade. And when wages and employment began to fluctuate — often violently — during the early years of the Napoleonic wars, the protection that weavers' unions offered seriously diminished. Weavers, desperate for work, continued to produce during recessions and simply depressed their wages further.[90] The type of association which nurtured organization amongst the early journeymen and amongst the skilled weavers of the late eighteenth century became outmoded. Exclusiveness and sectionalism largely dissolved under the compelling force of large numbers and poverty and, as it did so, weavers responded to their worsening plight by forming a general or federated association, through which they appealed to Parliament to secure a minimum wage and Boards of Arbitration.

The formation of the General Association in 1799 was a move in a new direction to enforce the old wage legislation of the Tudors and Stuarts.[91] The Association, which was directed from Bolton, federated 14 local unions mainly in south Lancashire. A general committee was formed, and a petition for legislation on wages and apprenticeship was signed by 23,000. The Combination Acts of 1799–1800 appear to have resulted in the dissolution of the formal organization, although contact was maintained throughout the weaving districts by its secretary, James Holcroft of Bolton. In 1800 Parliament passed the Cotton Arbitration Act, which the weavers used extensively, but rejected the vast petitions of 1808, 1809, 1811 and 1816–19 calling for a minimum wage, a tax on machinery and the prohibition of the export of yarn. The full-scale strikes in England in 1808 and 1818 and in Scotland in 1812 were no more successful, but they indicate that the weavers' organization was widespread, if limited and rudimentary. Local unions, especially for skilled weavers, were evidently easy to organize. Some, like the smallware weavers, gingham and shirting weavers and bed-quilt weavers, maintained a continuous and fairly effective organization through to the late 1820s and early 1830s. The General Association, which required efficient co-ordination over wide areas, was far more difficult to sustain, particularly since the weavers' commitment generally varied inversely with the conditions of trade.

The absence of formal organization does not, of course, mean that the delegates of local unions did not meet on an informal basis. The speed with which they could combine themselves when trade was depressed shows that the weavers had a capacity for collective action. In south Lancashire, around Manchester, Bolton, Bury and Ashton, processions, marches and itinerant delegates kept towns in contact and, although the contact with northern districts around Preston and Blackburn was intermittent,[92] weavers were able to react fairly quickly when it was needed. After 1818 though, active union organization between weaving areas virtually ceased. Attempts to rekindle a permanent general weavers' union in Manchester and Bolton after the repeal of the Combination Laws failed, and a similar attempt in 1831 drew only a handful of weavers to the meeting.[93] By this time the poverty and distress of the handloom weavers had become acute. The influx of demobbed soldiers and Irish immigrants, together with wage cutting and over-production, had made handloom weaving little more than the 'last refuge of the unsuccessful'.[94] The indiscriminate tide of progress had made their craft an anachronism. Political rather than industrial means now became the weavers' main preoccupation.[95]

Although the first mule spinners' unions were modelled on the weavers' societies of the eighteenth century, the spinners soon developed their own type of organization to suit the needs of the factory environment, where the sharp division between capital and labour made exploitation more obvious.[96] During and after the 1790s, unions sprang up under the guise of Friendly Societies throughout much of Lancashire. Most of these were local and short-lived,[97] but by the end of the Napoleonic wars the spinners possessed, despite the Combination Laws and the frequent arrest of their leaders, one of the strongest and most menacing workers' organizations. Most mule-spinning district societies probably had close to 100% organization[98] in their factory towns.[99] Local associations found in Manchester, Stockport, Oldham and Bolton were autonomous like the weavers' societies; they made their own rules, appointed their own committees, and rotated their officials to prevent incipient 'professionalism' and to create a veil of anonymity, as a safeguard against victimization and arrest. Entry fees and weekly contributions were high. In Manchester the Societies' acceptance fee was 10s (10s 6d for spinners who had learnt to spin elsewhere), weekly contributions 7d, and sometimes extra weekly levies of 3s 6d were imposed.[100] Unlike the weavers, the spinners were able to sustain their sectionalism by effectively controlling entry into the craft. They employed and paid their piecers who, in the early nineteenth century, were often the spinners' own children or close relatives, and controlled through a system of seniority the speed at which piecers could become spinners themselves.[101] Women, although members of the unions formed in the early 1790s when spinning was a domestic and rural occupation, were prohibited from joining the mule spinners' union. By 1829 there were no females in the Manchester unions – the strongest ones – and at the 1829 Isle of Man conference they were urged by the spinners to form their own union. Piecers were also excluded until the late 1820s, and only admitted to the union then because the spinners feared they might take work from unemployed spinners.[102]

The spinners' privileged and exclusive position contrasts sharply with the position of the handloom weavers. Spinners were the highest-paid factory operatives[103] and tended, as a result, to be more more aggressive and opportunistic. Whereas weavers would strike in depressions in a desperate defensive reaction to wage cuts, spinners generally went on strike in periods of prosperity, as in 1810, 1818, 1823–4 and in 1834–6.[104] They developed an effective delegate system and used this to keep local unions in touch, to channel financial aid from one town to another, and to manage the rolling strike, where selected groups of operatives would strike in turn whilst supported from the contribution of those still at work. This tactic was originally applied within a district, then between districts, and eventually between different types of spinners over the whole spinning region. Spinners used this method to bring country wages up to the rates paid in Manchester, as in 1810 and 1824, to defend the position of high wage areas, or simply to increase wages all round as in 1818. The equalization of wages remained the spinners' main objective, especially when the adoption of larger mules introduced wage disparities, displaced spinners and increased the number of piecers.

Though the spinners' strikes were largely unsuccessful, their management, if only on a temporary basis, was impressive. In the four-month strike of 1810, when 30,000 operatives were involved, £17,000 was distributed in strike pay; and in the two-month 1818 strike, involving 20,000 operatives, the spinners raised £4,500.[105] In 1810, 1825 and 1829 attempts were also made to establish a federation, to overcome the difficulty posed by local unions striking out of turn: this exhausted funds and often made some local unions inactive for short periods. The two early attempts at 'institutionalizing well-established inter-union co-operation' were unable to overcome the traditional autonomy of local unions.[106] The Grand General Union of 1829 (a depressed year) was part of a defensive campaign (uncharacteristic of spinners) against wage reductions. But its attempt to combine all spinners within the UK also collapsed when the call for a general strike of spinners in 1830 ended in a fiasco, and when the Ashton turnout of 1830–1 failed. Spinners who were concerned with their own local problems soon became disillusioned, and no further attempts at forming federations were made until the early 1840s.

The early 1830s were bad years for spinners. Trade was depressed, unemployment high and the successive strike failures in 1829–33 had weakened union membership and finances. The wider adoption of the larger mules weakened the spinners' ability to regulate the supply of labour and the introduction of the self actor, which required less skill and strength and brought more young male minders and women into the factory, slowly undermined the 'unilateral and unequivocal' authority of the mule spinner.[107] In these years, grand schemes for a general federation of trades' unions became the rage and Owen's Grand National of 1834 linked unions with the radical and socialist movements. The spinners remained distant. They had already attempted, without much success, to unite different trades. The Philanthropic Society of 1818 soon disintegrated, as did another Manchester-based confederal body in 1826. The 1829 Grand National Association for the Protection of Labour, inspired by John Doherty's belief that a union of unions would secure workers their political and economic rights, was well supported by the spinners, but when the Lancashire unions refused to support strikes in the Midlands during 1832 it collapsed. Thereafter, the spinners became disenchanted with wider unions, realizing that they were unlikely to yield the financial aid they expected. Spinners were not represented in Owen's Grand National, and expressed no interest in joining the National Association of United Trades for the Protection of Labour formed in 1845.[108]

Many thousands of cotton operatives took part in the strike of 1842, and in all the major manufacturing centres production ceased for a while. The strikers' aims were mixed, some being interested only in resisting the wage reductions threatened by the masters, others urging a continuation of the turnout until the People's Charter had become the law of the land, converting it in effect to a revolutionary general strike.[109] The stand taken by the Manchester power loom weavers' union serves to illustrate the complexity of motives, hopes and fears during the strike. Represented at the crucial trades' delegate meeting in August by their president, the ardent Chartist Daniel Donovan, the Manchester weavers decided to strike for the Charter *only* if the manufacturers refused to restore the wage rates prevailing in 1840.[110]

After 1842 the appeal of Chartism and political activity declined, and, as trade improved, revived unions began to experiment with different forms of organization. Mule spinners began to allow self-actor minders into their unions, and although some were later expelled (as at Bolton and Ashton),[111] in the mid 1840s strike circulars were often addressed to the 'Operative Spinners, Self-acting Minders, Twiners and Rovers of Lancashire, Cheshire, Yorkshire and Derbyshire'. By 1853 the spinners possessed an Amalgamated Association of Cotton Operative Spinners with a 'more or less permanent organization'[112] and considerable funds. The development of unionism among the factory weavers was slower. The occupation was dominated by women, who had little experience of organization and lacked the self-confidence which the (male) spinners derived from recruiting and controlling their assistants.[113] Although the weavers were more militant than the spinners in the late 1840s, their unions remained local, informal and short lived. The collapse of the Plug strike destroyed the General Association of Power Loom Weavers of Great Britain and Ireland set up in 1840, and its revival in 1846 was only temporary.[114] Before 1853 the weavers' organizations were informal and intermittent.

Because power loom weavers were unable to control entry they remained more interested than spinners in standard wage lists.[115] Spinners could hope to control wages by restricting the supply of labour, whereas weavers had to rely almost entirely on negotiating piece rates for particular types of cloth. In the eighteenth century, when technological change was relatively slow and the types of yarn and cloth limited, wages were determined largely by tradition and custom within a particular district. But with more rapid technological change and the growing range of products, it became increasingly difficult to enforce the customary standard rate of payment for a certain quality of yarn and cloth, especially since piece rates were negotiated at the mill level. As wage differentials for identical work widened, demands for a uniform wage list intensified.[116] Though these lists became more important in the 1840s they have a long history.

One is reported in Manchester in 1769 and another in 1798. The first district wage list for factory spinners came into existence in 1813 at Bolton, and lists were enforced at Rochdale between 1819 and 1829.[117] There is less evidence for list agitation in the late 1830s, but weaving lists were later drawn up by ad hoc committees in Ashton and Burnley (1843), Stockport (1844) and Oldham (1846).[118] By the mid nineteenth century the demand for a standard price list was the weavers' main preoccupation, and even the spinners, who were gradually losing their power over entry, were coming to see such lists as crucial.[119] In 1853 the Blackburn weavers negotiated the famous List which later, extended in operation throughout north Lancashire, came to be known as the 'Cotton Operatives' Charter'.[120]

These lists were very complicated and were best administered by men like Ned Whittle, secretary of the Blackburn weavers and active in the Preston strike, who was noted 'as a sound, profound and wonderfully proficient mathematician'.[121] Lists required skilled union leaders and a permanent organization to ensure that they were enforced. Equally, they required employers to formalize their own collective associations and to nominate skilled negotiators. Indeed, the extension of piece work and wage lists was perhaps the 'strongest influence towards the acceptance of collective bargaining' in the mid nineteenth century.[122] Employers' associations had, like the early unions, existed since the mid eighteenth century, but with the rise of spinning unions they became more formidable. As early as 1803 the master spinners in and around Manchester raised a £20,000 fighting fund to defeat the spinners' union[123] and in 1808, 1818 and throughout the 1820s employers extensively used the lock-out tactic to counter the effect of the rolling strike. They frequently blacklisted those who were active in disputes and allegedly provoked conflict in depressions in an attempt to exhaust union funds at little cost to themselves.

Most employers' associations, though, fluctuated with the strength of the unions. Only when their position was seriously challenged were employers able to forget their own differences. Even then, it was difficult for them to organize on any enduring basis. Some employers of handloom weavers supported claims for minimum wages to forestall competition from small masters paying low wages.[124] A few even contributed towards strike funds. Large spinners would likewise support strikes at mills employing more advanced technology – such as long mules where piece rates were generally reduced – and sometimes where they had a chance of capturing a competitor's market.[125] The bonds and fines which masters imposed on themselves suggests that collective action was difficult without a continued threat from organized labour. Consequently, there is very little evidence of a continuous and permanent employers' association in the first half of the nineteenth century. Among the oldest, in 1853, were the Preston Masters' Association, with a rather chequered history going back continuously no further than the great strike of 1836, and the Stockport association, set up in 1840 to establish uniformity of wages throughout the town and intermittently ever since.¹²⁶ The rash of newly-formed employers' associations which sprang up in 1853 testifies to the difficulties inherent in maintaining organization in periods of industrial peace.¹²⁷

By midcentury, the desire for industrial peace and price stability ultimately led, in some areas, to the establishment of negotiating machinery. In the newly-developed centres such as Preston, though, the millowners remained uncompromisingly aggressive. 'The cotton lords of Preston', said the Ashton Chartist Alexander Challenger in 1842, 'are the greatest tyrants in the country. It is well known that they grind their workmen down more than any other persons, getting their work done cheaper, and therefore they can undersell their neighbours.' Challenger was hardly an unbiased witness: he was using 'a great deal of vulgar language, calling the masters many vulgar names', in an attempt to persuade the Preston operatives to join the general strike.¹²⁸ But his allegations had a great deal of substance to them. A decade later an outside observer, James Lowe, noted that the abundant supply of labour to the local industry 'gives the employing class an immense power of control over the employed', so that strikes occurred in Preston only when discontent 'has become very general and very extreme throughout other parts of the district', and were invariably unsuccessful.¹²⁹ Similar complaints were to be made by the Preston operatives themselves in 1848, and their shameful reputation for docility and willingness to tolerate low pay would exert a significant influence on the ten per cent campaign five years later.

The tranquillity of Preston industry was not unbroken. In 1808 the presence of the military was required at a meeting of handloom weavers on the Preston Moor, and great alarm was occasioned in 1818 when the weavers paraded through the streets to demand higher wages. The country-wide weavers' riots of 1826 against the introduction of power looms passed Preston by, though as a precaution one large mill was 'converted into a kind of fortress, and armed with cannon. Small arms were likewise provided for the workmen, to defend the establishment, and large quantities of paving stones were stowed upon the roof and in the upper stories.' In 1831 the same factory was damaged in the course of riots over the introduction of improved machinery. The Preston House of Correction was threatened by the rioters, and later fortified to prevent further attacks.¹³⁰ Less dramatically, a spinners' union was active in the town in 1814, and again in 1823,¹³¹ while much interest was taken in the wider movements for general unionism in the late 1820s and early 1830s.¹³² Between 1834 and 1837, too, there is evidence of a local union of power loom weavers.¹³³

As early as the 1820s the Masters' Association in Preston was regarded as one of the strongest in Lancashire.¹³⁴ Before 1836, according to Henry Ashworth, it was a rule in many of the mills to refuse employment to union members. In that year the Preston spinners' union was revitalized by delegates from Bolton, and all the town's 660 spinners threatened a strike to obtain the

Bolton list of prices. The Masters' Association offered an advance of ten per cent, which went a long way towards the Bolton rates, but insisted upon the spinners' withdrawal from their union. The ensuing turnout was as much in defence of the right to union membership as in prosecution of the wage claim. After two months of growing distress the manufacturers repeated their offer of a ten per cent increase, but now demanded a written declaration from their hands 'to the effect that they would not, at any future time, whilst in their service, become members of any Union or combination of workmen'. Over the next month the strike crumbled, its collapse hastened by the employment of knobsticks from neighbouring towns, and the introduction of a handful of self-acting mules.[135]

This crushing defeat subdued the spinners' union, without destroying it. The police continued to keep a close watch on the union, especially in 1841 when wages were reduced three times in rapid succession, to ensure that sedition and machine-breaking were not discussed.[136] The Masters' Association, too, continued to operate, being particularly active in 1839.[137] Most of the Preston mills turned out in the strike of August 1842, when several rioting strikers were killed in a clash with the military in Lune Street. The deaths brought a rapid end to the strike in Preston, and (along with the rest of north Lancashire) the town was unrepresented at the important meeting of trades' delegates in Manchester which declared for the Charter. Nonetheless it was found necessary to send policemen to the meetings of the spinners' union at the end of the month, when a decision against a renewed turnout for higher wages was taken only after a protracted debate.[138]

When trade revived in 1844 it was the power loom weavers who took the first initiative, meeting in September 'after the example of other towns' to petition the manufacturers for the restoration of the ten per cent cut from their wages in 1842. Their memorial claimed – and this was to be a recurrent theme – that the millowners had promised an advance in wages as soon as conditions improved. The next few weeks saw a number of strikes by weavers in support of their claim.[139] The weavers also collected signatures for a trades' petition to Parliament against proposed changes in the law of Master and Servant.[140] The spinners, who had secured an advance in 1844, returned with a further wage demand in the following summer and met with almost immediate success.[141] Encouraged by this victory, in November 1845 the spinners invited their masters to a tea party at the Corn Exchange. Ostensibly a purely social gathering, the party was interpreted by most of the manufacturers as an attempt to reopen the question of the Bolton price list, and they stayed away. One who did attend, John Paley Junior, claimed the authority of the employers as a whole in refusing to countenance the Bolton list.[142]

Among the weavers, then, there is evidence of at least intermittent union activity in the mid 1840s, occasionally involving contact with weavers in other towns.[143] As for the Preston spinners, there is little doubt that their organization functioned continuously (if sometimes in a low key) from 1836 onwards, almost certainly as part of a Lancashire-wide federation. Probably it was the movement for Factory Reform which did more than anything else to reinforce contacts between the operatives throughout the manufacturing districts, and also to weaken the sectional barriers which divided the various occupational groups. Here was a question of vital importance to all who worked in cotton factories, on which continuous vigilance was required. In Preston agitation on the Ten Hours question began in the 1830s, and was almost continuous from 1844 right down to 1853. It was conducted by a Short Time Committee dominated not by middle-class sympathizers (as in some other towns) but by the factory operatives themselves.[144] Most of the leaders of the strike of 1853–4 had been active Factory Reformers.

The immediate origins of the ten per cent campaign of 1853 are to be found in the commercial crisis of 1846–8.[145] The first signs that trade was languishing came in August 1846, when the Blackburn masters' association gave notice of the introduction of a four-day week, and the Preston association met to consider a similar proposal;[146] two months later, having heard reports from manufacturers in other towns, the Manchester millowners decided to implement short-time working.[147] Early in 1847 conditions in Preston had deteriorated drastically. In the first quarter of the year the local Poor Law Union relieved twice as many paupers as in the first three months of 1846.[148] By May soup kitchens had been opened,[149] 1,000 of the town's 14,000 cotton operatives had been laid off, and a further 5,000 were on short time (working mainly four days a week instead of six, with earnings reduced accordingly).[150] Conditions improved slightly in the summer months, but by the autumn trade was as depressed as ever. At the end of October one in six of the population was receiving outdoor relief, quite apart from those in the workhouses,[151] and the soup kitchens reopened. They were badly needed, as the editor of the *Preston Guardian* confirmed:

We have consulted those who call at hundreds of the poor people's houses every week, such as collectors for burial societies and collectors of rent, and they affirm that the people were never so reduced to poverty and utter destitution as at present. They are leaving their separate dwellings, and two or three families are squeezing into a single cottage or becoming lodgers. Their all is gone; furniture sold to subsist upon; clothing and bedding all worn out.[152]

Two local manufacturers, Joseph Gillow and Robert Gardner, suspended payments.[153] In Blackburn 200 operatives marched to the nearby village of Feniscowles to plead for three days' work a week, but were refused: 'as the men returned home, the pangs of hunger urged them to pluck turnips from the fields by the wayside, which the poor creatures ate with relish, strewing the tops on the highway'.[154]

The operatives saw short-time working as a painful but necessary, and above all temporary, expedient. Reductions in wages, which bitter experience had taught them to expect in depressed times, were neither necessary nor (for all the masters' promises) temporary. The anticipation of wage cuts led the weavers to revive their union organization. By the end of 1846 there were energetic unions of power loom weavers in Blackburn and Darwen, and also a country-wide federation based on Oldham.[155] The Preston union, which had been recruiting actively for some months, issued its manifesto in December under the signature of its secretary, Richard Marsden, a former handloom weaver and a prominent Chartist. Calling upon all weavers to take up membership, the manifesto appealed also to the millowners 'to prevent the English workman from sinking to the level of the Irish serf'.[156] Stockport manufacturers paid higher wages than those in Preston, Marsden wrote later.[157] But competitive wage reduction between the two centres would prove self-defeating, for it would destroy the manufacturers' own home market: 'we only sink labour lower still, till at length the power of the operatives to purchase clothing, or food sufficient is at an end, and we come to rely solely upon foreign trade'.[158]

Such arguments had no appeal for the millowners, whose financial straits demanded immediate solutions. In May 1847 a strike at one Preston mill, against a 5% reduction, ended when the employer concerned, William Ainsworth, promised to restore the cut when trade improved.[159] The Blackburn weavers' union was locked in a protracted dispute with Hopwood & Co., which ended (after £2,261 had been spent in strike pay) only when five of his fellow manufacturers agreed to serve as arbitrators.[160] Further strikes soon broke out in Blackburn and Darwen,[161] and in August the Spinners' Federation called for a Lancashire-wide strike of fixed duration to clear the market of the accumulated stocks of unsold cotton goods.[162] William Ainsworth announced in September a further five per cent reduction, and other Preston masters were expected to follow suit.[163] The cuts, as a spinners' deputation told the Prime Minister, Lord John Russell, were 'likely to become general'.[164] In October the Preston weavers called a meeting to protest against reductions proposed by John Paley Junior, the current mayor of Preston. After delegates from Darwen had addressed them, in a Temperance Hall 'crowded almost to suffocation', the weavers resolved to build up a fund which would provide six shillings a week for those forced to strike in defence of their wage rates. But Edward Swinglehurst, chairman of the meeting, expressed the general mood when he declared that 'everything that can be done should be adopted before a strike is resorted to, which indeed is the last thing that ought to be thought about'.[165]

Little came of the resolution, and wage reductions continued to spread. A major obstacle in the way of the unions was the hostility of the masters to the organization of their hands. Introducing a resolution at a meeting in support of the National Association of United Trades, Richard Marsden regretted the necessity for him to do so. He would have called upon someone else, he said to cheers, 'had he not been aware that they were for the most part so bound down by their employers, that very few dare take part in that meeting'.[166] In January

1848 Marsden organized an eventful meeting of weavers in the course of which one speaker accused an unnamed employer (probably John Goodair) of threatening to send spies to the hall and to reduce the wages of any of his hands observed to be there; Marsden attacked another manufacturer, John Hawkins, for promising to dismiss any of his operatives similarly detected; one Jack Moss, said to be Goodair's spy, was ejected from the hall; and a harrowing tale was told of the late William Crankshaw, who had been sacked by Goodair for attending a previous meeting and had died soon afterwards.[167] Clearly intimidation, real or imagined, was rife.

Despite the fear of victimization, a number of strikes broke out in Preston in reaction to the reductions. At Thomas Naylor's mill the turnout resulted in the halving of the proposed reductions: instead of 11s 8d for an eleven-hour day, Naylor's weavers now earned 9s 6d or 10s for ten hours.[168] The weavers — principally girls — at Richard Threlfall's mill also struck, organizing processions through the streets and begging for 'loans'. Their handbills claimed that 'Threlfall himself acknowledged to us that it was a robbery, but he must follow others', a statement which Threlfall indignantly denied. Unable to fill the Temperance Hall, the strikers appealed for support at meetings in the Craven Heifer Inn. Little was forthcoming; they were soon forced to submit, several dozen strikers being victimized.[169] Their defeat marked the end of the strikes in Preston. Even in militant Blackburn, where strikes continued as late as August, failure was inevitable. All over Lancashire, wages were being forced down — probably by an average of ten per cent.[170]

Preston had not been in the vanguard of the resistance to the reductions. 'Imitate the spirit of the operatives of Blackburn and Darwen', urged John Bowman, appealing for funds for Threlfall's strikers. 'I was in Blackburn a week last Sunday, and called on the weavers' committee, to see if they were willing to assist us, but I found them rather backward, for they look upon Preston as about one of the rottenest places, as regards standing up against a reduction in our wages.'[171] John Nottingham complained that 'it has been a pretext with the masters in Ashton, in order to reduce wages, to say that they cannot sell their cloth with the Preston manufacturers, because they pay less wages than them'.[172] The willingness of the Preston operatives to accept low wages, complained of in 1842, was to play an important part in their mobilization in 1853. In 1848 Bowman could do little more than declare, unhappily, 'I have been a factory operative fourteen years, and every year I have found myself in the receipt of less wages.'[173] A month later the defeated weavers met in the Craven Heifer to hear a number of speakers, including Richard Marsden, call for the formation of a permanent union to resist *further* wage cuts. The degree of militancy among the audience — themselves presumably less passive than the majority who were absent from the meeting — was unwittingly revealed by one speaker. He urged affiliation to the National Association of United Trades, 'who would, if strikes were necessary, send an agent down to conduct them so that the workpeople would not need to take any part, but only to attend at the weekend for the purpose of receiving their remuneration'.[174]

The operatives believed that the employers had undertaken to restore the reductions as soon as trade improved.[175] For their part the masters denied that any firm commitment had been made. Early in 1849, when the worst of the depression was over, the Stockport masters' association refused their operatives' request for an advance in wages.[176] There were several local strikes in Preston at this time, with wages apparently involved in most of them.[177] At the end of February a public meeting of weavers agreed to circularize the masters for the restoration of the ten per cent, but the spinners, acting on the advice of their federation, decided in March to defer their wage demands until the legality of the relay system had been determined.[178] It was not until August that the spinners returned to the wages question, when they petitioned the masters for a ten per cent advance.[179]

Neither weavers nor spinners met with much success, and George Cowell later reported the failure of repeated applications to individual employers for the return of the ten per cent in the next three years.[180] 1850 and 1851 were quiet years in the Preston cotton industry. With the exception of a few isolated disputes[181] the operatives' unions seem to have lain dormant until the spring of 1852, when a drawn-out dispute affecting winders at Radcliffe coincided with a strike of weavers at Threlfall's mill in Preston. The weavers were able to attract 350 people to a meeting in support of the two strikes, but it was still necessary for a delegate from the iron trades to suggest 'that committees should be formed of hands from each factory in the town, for the purpose of checking encroachments upon their labour'.[182] Evidently the weavers' union of 1846–8 had faded from the scene.

2 Ten Per Cent

5 June 1853–14 October 1853

> In Preston it's reported,
>   The Mills are going to close,
> There's eight and thirty Masters' names
>   Posted on the walls;
> But when our holiday do come,
>   With mirth and glee we'll pass,
> Unt'll the Masters do give in
>   Unto the working class.

By the end of 1852 the return of general prosperity could no longer be doubted. It was increasingly embodied in bricks and mortar, as new mills rose up around Preston and plans for more were announced (prompting the town's bricklayers to strike for higher winter wages).[1] The Bolton millowner Henry Ashworth noted an increasing scarcity of labour,[2] and an anonymous observer in Preston grew concerned: 'While so many new factories in the town and neighbourhood are nearing completion, and so many looms in the present ones are resting for want of hands, it seems a natural inquiry — "where are we to go for a supply?".'[3] He suggested a return to the Poor Law Board's discredited policy of recruiting workers from the low-wage agricultural areas of the south.[4] The operatives had other ideas. They began to see the boom as an ideal opportunity to secure the restoration of their ten per cent.

In the spring of 1853 there developed throughout the country a movement for higher wages, which brought increases to a variety of trades. The Manchester brickmakers struck in January, followed in February by masons and joiners at Ashton, and by farm labourers near Salisbury. March saw strikes in several Liverpool crafts, in the Batley and Dewsbury woollen mills, and on the land in Oxfordshire. In April boys struck at a Liverpool engine works and a shipyard at Birkenhead, and strikes broke out among waggonwrights and bricklayers at South Shields, seamen at Ipswich, Liverpool shoemakers, brickmakers and joiners at Wigan, and the joiners of Sunderland and Hartlepool.[5] Generally, though, strikes were not needed. The *Burnley Mentor* wrote:

We are happy to be informed that in our town the carpenters and joiners have demanded, and to the honour of the masters, be it known, have obtained an advance of two shillings per week in their wages. The plasterers and painters are also in negotiation with their employers for a like increase in pay; and they are, we believe, in a position to ensure their own success. This is cheering, and shews that the beneficial effects of prosperity in trade are not confined to one class. We trust that labour in every department will soon enjoy a higher remuneration, from the voluntary and generous concessions of employers themselves.[6]

To stimulate the generosity of the cotton masters, the operatives began to organize their own agitation for higher wages. Late in January the spinners of Bolton, Leigh and Chorley petitioned the employers for an increase of ten per cent, citing two years of prosperity as proof of their ability to pay. One master did so, the rest delaying their reply until the next meeting of the local masters' association, whose offer of a five per cent advance was accepted by the spinners on 3 February.[7] A week later spinners employed by Richard Bashall at the village of Walton, near Preston, accepted his offer of a five per cent increase, in response to their claim for ten.[8] In the same week weavers at a mill in Manchester turned out in pursuit of higher wages. For the moment, this would remain an isolated incident. 'The cotton districts have been remarkably free from strikes for some considerable time past, until this arose', commented the *Preston Guardian*.[9] Conflict on a large scale was not to begin for almost four months.

When the storm did finally break, it was in Stockport. Here, on 11 March, the weavers gathered in the Lyceum to support a memorial to the masters calling for an advance. The respected Stockport radical shopkeeper and one-time weaver, George Cooper, expressed his amazement that the wages question had been dormant for so long. While the manufacturers had been making enormous profits, the operatives 'had been too much asleep to their own interests, and had also neglected the interests of that trade by which they gained their bread'. J.B. Horsfall, a victimized weaver from Royton, now a bookseller and publisher, insisted that an increase was fully justified. 'The newspapers tell us that trade is most abundant, profits large, and the operatives fully employed and content. If this really be so, I contend that this prosperity and this abundance ought to be diffused through every grade of society, and that the powerloom weavers ought to enjoy a portion of it.' Stockport, he alleged, was among the lowest-paid towns in the area, earnings there being ten, fifteen, or even twenty per cent below such towns as Heywood, Bury and Blackburn. 'At present, the position of Stockport retarded the advance in other towns.' Throughout the districts, accused Mortimer Grimshaw of Great Harwood, 'Stockport was pointed out as having stained itself amongst the list of manufacturing towns because it was paying the lowest rate of wages'. Duly admonished, the Stockport weavers agreed to 'throw off the stain of reproach' by pressing their claims for higher wages, and to appoint a committee to raise funds for the organization of the struggle. There was, as yet, no thought of striking; 'respectful deputations' and 'courteous appeals' to the masters would suffice.[10]

The Preston millowners now became alarmed, and hastily revived their own organization. Meeting in secret at the Bull Inn on 18 March, the Preston Master Spinners Association established a committee whose directions were to be binding upon the members, and agreed in principle to a levy. A fortnight later the Association approved an initial levy of five shillings per horse-power (which would raise several hundred pounds), and resolved that each member should demand a 'discharge note' from all spinners seeking employment, to aid the identification and possible blacklisting of activists.[11] That the masters' concern was warranted became clear in the first week in April, when the Preston spinners issued a circular to the employers asserting the prosperity of trade as grounds for increased wages.[12]

If the Preston masters looked set to resist the campaign, the response of the Stockport employers was only a little more encouraging for the operatives. They offered, 'when trade mended', to pay the average of the wages given in thirty-five cotton districts in Lancashire and Cheshire, but warned that this, far from justifying an increase, would probably require a *reduction* for the weavers of Stockport. When the operatives met in the Lyceum on 1 April this contention was greeted with incredulity. The weavers decided to meet the masters on their own ground, and set up a committee of six men to collect information on the wages actually paid in other towns.[13] Three weeks later they reported to a further meeting that wages in Stockport lagged eight per cent behind the average paid in thirty other centres, and no less than twelve and a half per cent behind towns within a ten-mile radius of Manchester.[14] This appears to have embarrassed the employers who, early in May, announced their refusal to recognize the operatives' committee: in future they would deal only with representatives of their own hands, mill by mill.[15]

Unrest was now spreading. While the Bolton spinners had settled for five per cent, the agitation continued in nearby towns. Several thousand spinners struck work in Ashton late in April on a different issue, the violation by the masters of the Ten Hours Act.[16] A turnout of spinners at a small mill in Blackburn was soon settled, but the evidence which this provided of a more general discontent was no doubt one factor behind the decision of the Blackburn masters' association to grant a five per cent increase to all spinners at the end of the month.[17] On 4 May a meeting of weavers' delegates from the Blackburn mills agreed to petition the masters for the restoration of the ten per cent which they had lost in 1847. After two weeks of reflection the millowners refused. A further delegate meeting was called, and a strike began to appear likely.[18]

In Stockport four thousand operatives packed the cattle market on 27 May, their patience all but exhausted. This time George Cooper's tone was distinctly menacing: 'I warn the employers to remember the approach of the schoolmaster from Ashton in 1842. That holy week was the labourer's holiday. By that holiday, I think the schoolmaster administered a lesson to the manufacturers in this district, which would never be forgotten.' (This was a reference to the 1842 strike,[19] which had provided lessons of a particularly violent kind.) There were three options open to the Stockport masters, Cooper continued. They could pay wages equal to the average of those prevailing within a ten-mile radius of

Manchester; they could agree to a simple ten per cent increase; or they could go to arbitration. They had six days to reply,[20] but no reply came. On 5 June a meeting of weavers' delegates from all the major cotton towns approved the demand for an unconditional increase of ten per cent. Four days later the striking operatives paraded through the streets of Stockport, waiting to be joined by those whose notice was expiring hour by hour.[21] Battle had been joined in the first great dispute of the ten per cent campaign.

For the next two days the Stockport strikers paraded noisily, but peacefully, through the streets. The masters' association met on Monday 13 June, resolved to refuse their demands and adjourned until Wednesday. The same day the strikers held a large open-air meeting at which one of their leaders, William Chadwick, claimed that the ten per cent had already been won in Preston, as in Bolton, where the local MP had been among the first to agree the increase.[22] This was purely wishful thinking as far as Preston was concerned, but several Bolton millowners had indeed conceded the ten per cent, and the remainder were generally expected soon to follow suit.[23] Next day another open-air meeting agreed to the establishment of a large committee to scour the manufacturing districts in search of financial support for the Stockport operatives, on which business they promptly departed. It became apparent how necessary their mission was when on 16 June the masters' association published a proclamation reaffirming their stand. The cut made in 1848, they explained, was imposed only after they had discovered themselves to be paying thirteen per cent more than the average paid by their competitors in other towns, and followed increases granted in 1844 and 1845. Moreover, they had not promised to restore the ten per cent when trade improved: this would be possible only as and when wages were increased elsewhere in the industry. They had now repeated their calculations, and were prepared to offer five per cent to the mule spinners, and eight per cent to the throstle-spinners — but nothing to the weavers. By the end of the first week of the strike only two members of the association had broken ranks. The rest stood firm.[24]

The Stockport delegates lost no time in publicizing their cause, and in appealing for contributions. Everywhere they went, the agitation was growing. At Accrington, where they were promised the proceeds of a weekly levy of a penny per loom, they found that the local weavers were demanding the ten per cent on their own account but were awaiting the outcome of the Stockport dispute before pressing the claim.[25] In Burnley both the spinners and the weavers were involved.[26] The Blackburn weavers were also hoping for victory at Stockport. Here the twisters and drawers were already on strike in search of a modest twenty-five per cent increase. There was a turnout of loomers at the large mill of Messrs Feilden and Jackson, and when the firm responded by introducing blacklegs it provoked the weavers to come out in sympathy. This dispute developed political overtones. The Feildens were pillars of the Blackburn Liberal party, and were bitter enemies of the Tory Hornby family (themselves large, and paternalistic, millowners). The arch-Tory *Blackburn Standard* gleefully reported that the strikers' slogans included cries of 'Hornby for ever – he's the man for us!' and 'Let's set up an orange flag!' Strikes were also breaking out in nearby Darwen.[27]

In Preston the weavers finally followed the example of the town's spinners, holding their first mass meeting on 9 June in the Temperance Hall. The recent delegate meeting at Bolton, they were told, had firmly rejected any notion of a five per cent increase. From now on, their motto was 'Ten per cent, and no surrender'. As yet, feeling was less intense in Preston than in other areas. The secretary of the impromptu weavers' committee declared that he would rather see twelve months of agitation than a one-month strike, and the chairman, George Ainsworth, disavowed all ideas of striking for the ten per cent.[28] These pacific sentiments were reinforced by the principal speaker, George Cowell. A local weaver, Cowell was to become the leader of the Preston strike and for the next year would spend almost every waking hour in that capacity. For the moment, he was confident of a peaceful settlement. 'I and one or two friends,' he said 'having read a circular sent out from Blackburn upon the subject, have resolved to see if we cannot arouse the operatives of Preston to bestir themselves with a view to obtaining an advance of wages in common with the other towns and districts.' That an increase was due, he argued, could not be denied. Wages in Preston were twenty per cent lower than in Oldham, where the weavers had a permanent union. The cost of living was rising and the manufacturers, who had pledged universal prosperity as a result of Free Trade, had failed to carry out their promises.

Cowell obtained endorsement for the text of a circular to the Preston masters, which pointed to the flourishing state of trade as a justification for granting the ten per cent. The meeting agreed to set up a committee, one delegate from each mill, to organize deputations to individual masters in order to solicit the increase.[29] The need for the Preston operatives to 'bestir themselves' was forcefully stated by the Stockport delegation who attended the next weavers' meeting on 15 June. 'How are we to meet the Preston manufacturers in the market', the Stockport masters were asking, 'whilst they pay so much less than ourselves? Unless you can pull them up, we cannot advance you.' Similar complaints had been made against Preston in 1848. This time, steps would be taken to put the matter right.[30]

The immediate priority, though, was to ensure the success of the struggle at Stockport. Delegates from seventeen towns met there on Sunday 19 June and agreed to continue at work, sustaining their contributions to the Stockport turn-outs, until the issue was decided. Any premature strike action in other towns would merely divert attention (and subscriptions) from Stockport, whose victory was rightly seen as an essential condition for advances elsewhere.[31] Events in Blackburn soon posed a threat to this strategy. On Tuesday the Blackburn masters' association published their decision (apparently taken five days earlier) not merely to resist demands for the ten per cent, but to give notice of a general lock-out commencing on 9 July. This stern resolution, prompted by the isolated strikes of loomers and others which were already under way, at once provoked further strikes by weavers at three important mills. Delegates from Stockport had to hurry across to Blackburn to urge a return to work, their recommendation being firmly endorsed by the local weavers' committee.[32] Eventually their advice was taken, but the loomers' strike continued, throwing 300 weavers out of work. The masters' lock-out notices remained in force, although their determination must have been weakened by the news that Hornby, who was not a member of the association, had offered to pay the ten per cent to his loomers if other employers would follow suit.[33]

In Stockport large open-air meetings of the turnouts were held almost every day. The masters' association, which had resumed its recognition of the operatives' committee on the eve of the strike, met a delegation on 20 June but refused to modify its stand. Fourteen thousand hands were now out, and all the principal mills were closed. Many of the strikers were leaving town to seek work in other districts, a process accelerated by the efforts of certain employers from Colne who began actively recruiting spinners in Stockport. On the 22nd, in an interesting (though this time orderly) reversal of the great 'lesson' of 1842, the strikers organized a procession from Stockport to Ashton and Stalybridge, to whip up support there.[34] Money was now trickling in, a couple of hundred pounds being raised in the second week of the dispute. By far the largest contribution (some £82) came from Blackburn, while significant sums were sent from Darwen, Bolton and Oldham.[35] Weekly meetings were being organized in Darwen, and growing activity was reported in Padiham and Burnley.[36]

The 43 mills in Preston contributed only £10, no more than was raised by workers at five mills in the much smaller centre of Clitheroe. When the Preston weavers held their third meeting in the Temperance Hall on 23 June, the Stockport delegate James Bentley complained that the thousand weavers at Messrs Horrockses & Miller had contributed a miserly 1s 3½d! (The true object of Bentley's concern became apparent when a few days later he absconded with the Preston subscriptions, apparently to America.) Fund-raising in Preston was not without hazards of a different sort, as two collectors who had visited the 'Big Factory' of Messrs Swainson and Birley could testify. They had been seized by the mill manager 'and a few of his minions', held for two hours, and then prosecuted for assault. Undeterred, the meeting voted a levy of twopence per loom in support of Stockport. The ten per cent agitation in Preston itself was meeting with only limited success, the operatives' deputations being 'rudely repulsed' by many masters. Messrs Napier and Goodair, George Cowell's own employers, had however paid five per cent *more* than had been taken off in 1848, two other firms had agreed to pay the ten per cent, and conditional promises had been received from a few more.[37]

In Stockport local opinion was beginning to rally round the strikers. Eight hundred shopkeepers, whose own business was suffering as a result of the dispute, petitioned the masters' association to urge them, since trade was good, to settle on the operatives' terms. The mayor and the chief magistrate, having vainly attempted to reopen negotiations between the parties, eventually succeeded, and on Saturday 25 June the masters' association met a six-man delegation from the strikers. But the meeting was fruitless. The six operatives (two each from the weavers', spinners' and cardroom hands' committees) argued for a flat ten per cent increase on the Stockport list of piecework prices, while the employers simply repeated their offer of a county average. On 25 June the masters' association, seeing no prospect of a rapid settlement, adjourned for a fortnight, while the strikers continued to call for ten per cent 'and no surrender'. On the 28th the first strike pay was distributed, a meagre 1s 10½d for the weavers and (surprisingly) only 1s 7d for the spinners. At the end of June there was complete deadlock. Out of 52 mills in Stockport, only 15 or 16 had paid the ten per cent; these were mainly small concerns, and only four were members of the masters' association. Rumours were circulating of a meeting in Manchester of manufacturers from various districts, at which an industry-wide lock-out had been discussed.[38] There was some truth in this rumour, though it was — as yet — greatly exaggerated.

Strike fever was meanwhile continuing to rage across the country. Early in May 'nearly all the trades in South Wales' began to agitate for increased wages, striking work when advances were refused; shipbuilders in South Shields followed suit. In June turnouts were in progress at Swansea (masons and shoemakers), Cardigan (ships' carpenters), and Liverpool (cotton porters and brickmakers' carriers). During July bricklayers engaged in the construction of the new Houses of Parliament struck work, as did the Leeds carpenters, Blackfriars corkcutters, Dowlais miners, Southwark dockers, London cab-drivers, Linlithgow shoemakers, gardeners at Dalkeith Palace, and even the Hull police.[39] Strikes were now spreading to the heart of the cotton belt. In May miners and plumbers at Wigan and brickmakers at Stockport came out; in June it was the turn of quarrymen at Burnley and Padiham, carpenters at Ashton, and (by collective resignation) a large section of the Manchester police force. July saw disputes involving miners at Ashton and Oldham, shoemakers at Bolton, and the night-soil men employed by Manchester corporation.[40] The contagion started to spread through the cotton industry itself as isolated strikes began in Glossop, Bury and Accrington, where there was extensive disorder. Finally it reached Manchester, where strikes broke out in a large number of mills in June. On 2 July, a month's notice having expired, there began a protracted turnout of some two thousand Manchester dyers and bleachers, who claimed to have had no wage increase for twenty years.[41]

Millowners generally were becoming increasingly alarmed. Their fears were voiced by an anonymous manufacturer who wrote to the *Manchester Guardian* early in July, urging his fellow masters to resist the operatives' 'exorbitant demands'. 'I think it quite time', he declared, 'for the mill occupiers and owners to associate themselves, and at once make a stand against the encroachments of their workpeople.' The recent success of the engineering lock-out demonstrated what might be done.[42] On 7 July the Manchester Spinners' and Manufacturers' Association was established, with the aim of drawing up a standard list of piecework prices. No time was lost in extending the employers' organization to the industry as a whole. On 11 July representatives of 360 firms from a number of towns met in Manchester to co-ordinate resistance to 'unreasonable demands, such as are now being made by the associated bodies of mill hands, because concessions to such demands would be most injurious to employers, and to the trade generally'. Under the chairmanship of Robert Birley, a prominent Manchester employer, they agreed to set up local masters' associations in each town and to form a central association, with a view to adopting standard price lists in every district.[43] Concerned lest they be picked off one by one by the united operatives, the masters had now themselves united. Their organization was to prove a decisive factor in the eventual outcome at Preston.

The course of the Stockport strike was not significantly affected by these developments. In fine weather the strikers met each day in Stringer's Fields, after which they amused themselves by singing, dancing, and other innocent pursuits. The masters' association stood firm on its refusal to pay the ten per cent, and declined to meet a deputation to discuss the state of trade. The exodus of operatives to other towns continued — itself suggestive of strong demand for labour elsewhere — reviving unhappy memories of 1842, when walls of empty houses had been daubed with the slogan, 'Stockport to let'.[44] Delegates spoke at meetings in Blackburn, Darwen, Haslingden, Burnley, Padiham and Preston. In the first week of July £628 was raised for the Stockport weavers of which Blackburn's share, £180 obtained from a levy of 3d per loom and from contributions by craft unions and local shopkeepers, was by far the largest. The striking weavers received 2s each, making a grand total of 3s 6d over the four weeks of the strike; their helpers were paid a further 1s; and the spinners had to be content with 1s 1d.[45]

Little progress was being made outside Stockport. At Blackburn the loomers did indeed secure a ten per cent increase and returned to work, but the weavers were less successful. A meeting between five members of the weavers' committee and a similar number of employers' representatives achieved nothing, despite the former's claim — a strange one in every way — that wages in Blackburn were lower than in Preston. On 13 July the Blackburn operatives, led by two bands, paraded through the streets behind a flag inscribed 'ten per cent'.[46] Next day two thousand Preston weavers assembled in Chadwick's Orchard, that 'convenient arena for the exhibition of the oratorical prowess of all manner of enthusiastic patriots, real or pretended, local or national, from the "honourable member" soliciting a renewal of public confidence to the humbler exponent of the virtues of "teetotalism", the mysteries of Mormonism, or the blessings of free trade'. Once a beautiful fruit-garden, the Orchard was now 'merely about two or three acres of very valuable building land, situated near the centre of the town [where] ... little meets the eye except crumbling walls and broken railings enclosing areas of doubtful sanitary reputation'.[47] An open-air venue had been chosen since the Temperance Hall was now too small to hold the numbers involved in the agitation, and the Mayor had denied them the use of the (more spacious) Corn Exchange. They heard George Cowell introduce a new address to the masters, copies of which were to be sent to the press, to local MPs, and later to the government. The petition repeated earlier assertions that trade was sufficiently prosperous to warrant the restoration of the ten per cent, and offered to submit to arbitration on this question. Cowell attacked the meeting of manufacturers in Manchester, and for the first time allowed himself to hint that strike action might, in the last resort, be called for.[48]

The second week of July saw a further improvement in the financial position of the Stockport strikers. Blackburn contributed £260 to the total subscription of £856, which allowed payments of 2s 6d to the weavers and 2s to the spinners. Some additional relief was provided by the Oddfellows, who supplied their striking members with twelve pounds of flour, twenty pounds of potatoes and a pound of bacon weekly, as a loan to be repaid at the end of the dispute.[49] Stockport remained calm, despite press reports of intimidation. Whilst successfully defending a girl accused of molesting a blackleg, W.P. Roberts[50] forced the arresting constable to admit that he had never known any turnout as peaceful as the present one; no serious arrests had been necessary. An important victory was achieved on 23 July when two large firms conceded the ten per cent. Next day the Rev. J.H.C. Wright filled his church to capacity when he preached a special sermon for the operatives. On the 25th Henry Coppock, an influential local businessman, proposed that arbitration be invoked to settle the question of wages in Stockport in comparison with earnings in other towns. The masters' association, sensing that its position was crumbling, agreed to this suggestion but the strikers' attitude hardened. They refused even to consider wage comparisons, and would now accept nothing but an unconditional ten per cent.[51]

Agitation was gathering pace. Weekly subscriptions grew, first to almost £900 and then to £1,541. At Burnley there was a levy of 1d per loom, while at Padiham it was increased to 2d. The Blackburn levy was raised to 4d and then 6d. Accrington was collecting 3d per loom, and augmenting the amount thus raised by a boycott of shopkeepers who refused to contribute. By 29 July the *Stockport Advertiser* felt that the end was near, and the very next day the masters' association agreed to pay the ten per cent to the spinners and cardroom hands, who promptly returned to work. The weavers, who had been offered only five per cent, adamantly refused to compromise, and on Saturday 6 August the employers, accepting the inevitable, made the ten per cent increase universal. The Stockport strike, which had lasted almost two months, was over.[52]

News of the victory led to great rejoicing as far away as Padiham, where the operatives, accompanied by a large contingent from Burnley, paraded through the streets in celebration.⁵³ For their part the Stockport masters accepted defeat gracefully, some even giving their operatives 'a liberal gratuity to spend in some enjoyment before resuming labour'. Relations were eased by the knowledge that the strikers had conducted themselves in a remarkably orderly and peaceful way (the crime rate having actually declined in the course of the strike). The operatives allowed themselves the luxury of burning the latest issue of the *Manchester Guardian* — detested for its opposition to their cause — at their victory meeting. Otherwise they celebrated by asking the Rev. Wright to preach them a second sermon, which attracted a 'vast multitude' to his church. A final mass meeting endorsed a vote of thanks to Wright, to the mayor, and even to the superindendent of the borough police, for their assistance during the strike.⁵⁴

The Stockport victory gave an immediate and substantial boost to the morale of the operatives in other towns. At Blackburn success had appeared increasingly likely since 22 July, when Hornby again laid down the gauntlet to his fellow manufacturers. This time he announced the payment of an immediate five per cent increase. If other firms in the town followed his lead, he would pay the remaining five per cent; if they did not, he would reluctantly withdraw the advance at the end of the year.⁵⁵ Within a few days three more masters had granted a five per cent increase,⁵⁶ and pressure mounted on the others. The weavers stepped up the campaign, holding weekly meetings. Negotiations reopened in the second week of August. After several meetings between the two parties, a settlement was finally reached on 18 August when the employers conceded a ten per cent advance upon the newly-agreed standard list of piecework prices. The operatives, having achieved their aims without the need for a strike, celebrated with a victory parade to Blakey Moor and decided upon a final levy of one penny per loom to cover expenses.⁵⁷

The ten per cent could not now be long withheld from operatives in other parts of North East Lancashire. A week later the Accrington masters followed the example of Blackburn, and gains were reported in Haslingden.⁵⁸ In Burnley there were deeply felt grievances, as the secretary of the weavers' committee explained:

so far from the weavers of this town being better paid than others, there is no place of equal importance where they have been as badly treated during the last few years of comparative commercial prosperity. Hardly a month has passed without reductions in some shape or other. Couple the above, with the fact, that in a great majority of cases, a weaver cannot mention wages without running the risk of losing his employment, we think all reasonable men will agree that no class can be found, who would suffer the like wrongs without endeavouring to get from under the yoke.⁵⁹

Here, too, weekly mass meetings kept up the pressure until, on 20 August, the masters capitulated. Led by a dozen bands, 25,000 operatives from Burnley, Padiham, Colne, and the surrounding villages marched through Burnley in celebration, and concluded their proceedings by passing a vote of thanks to the masters. Although isolated strikes continued, the *Burnley Advertiser* was well satisfied: 'We are happy in being able to say that the agitation upon the ten per cent question may now be looked upon as finally settled — at least so far as Burnley is concerned.'[60] This assessment was to prove distinctly optimistic.

Elsewhere less progress was being made. The strikes at cotton mills in Manchester, in which the piecers appear to have played the leading part, began to fizzle out, but the dyers' and bleachers' dispute became increasingly bitter. The masters started to introduce blackleg labour, provoking the strikers into a violent reaction which culminated in an assault on the senior partner at one firm.[61] At Wigan the millowners were conceding nothing, while at Settle, deep in the upper valley of the Ribble, 300 weavers struck on 29 August for the ten per cent.[62] Two days later weavers at a small firm in Bolton (where the issue had, in general, been settled several weeks earlier) were forced to take the same step.[63] The real problem, though, was at Preston. If the operatives here were unable to exact the ten per cent, there was a distinct danger that it would be taken back in other towns.

In Preston itself life continued much as before. Some 15,000 people gathered to watch the exploits of 'Steeple Jack', otherwise known as James Duncan Wright. Attired as a sailor, his approach heralded by two bands and two pieces of cannon, Wright climbed the chimney of Swainson and Birley's 'Big Factory' and descended in ten seconds on a pulley to the valley 500 yards away.[64] Factory excursions to the coast provided further relief from the pressures of the agitation. Throughout August parties of operatives from the various mills boarded special trains for Blackpool, Fleetwood or Liverpool to enjoy a day at the sea. When the hands employed by Horrockses and Miller travelled to Fleetwood on 6 August, their journey began with a procession through the streets of Preston, pausing at the residences of Thomas Miller (the owner of the firm) and his brother Henry, where the band played 'The Fine Old English Gentleman'.[65]

Yet there was no doubt that tension was mounting. Henry Wilkinson, who had chaired the weavers' meeting on 14 July, was dismissed as a result, as was a young woman collector. One employer, Miles Rodgett, provoked a strike by threatening to *cut* wages unless productivity increased. Still anxious to avoid trouble, Cowell urged the strikers to return to work and to sue Rodgett for breach of contract if the proposed reductions were implemented.[66] Both the spinners and the cardroom hands were actively campaigning for the ten per cent. The weavers now met every Thursday in the Orchard, marching there through the streets with bands. Edward Swinglehurst, the veteran of the 1847 agitation, began to take an active part in the movement. The immediate energies of the weavers were devoted to the collection of subscriptions for Stockport. On 5 August collectors at Horrockses were seized by the police (acting on instructions from Thomas Miller), charged with begging, and locked up for the night. The magistrates, evidently embarrassed by the case, freed the operatives next day and reprimanded the policemen concerned. The latter were subsequently (though unsuccessfully) sued for unlawful arrest, with the assistance of the weavers' committee. When the weavers met on 11 August to discuss the implications of the Stockport triumph, George Cowell launched into the first of many bitter attacks on Miller, who, he claimed, had said in Manchester that all the mills in Lancashire should be closed in order to starve the Stockport strikers into submission. (Miller indignantly denied the charge, which Cowell later withdrew.) But the operatives' defiance remained verbal: they agreed to persist with deputations to the masters, and to refrain for the present from strike action.[67]

Despite their pacific intentions, they began to prepare for the worst. On 14 August Cowell attended a meeting of weavers' delegates in Stockport, and secured a promise of support from other districts if a strike should be needed at Preston.[68] The Preston committee began to have difficulty in restraining the rank and file. 'Stimulated by the recent example of Stockport, the operatives generally throughout Preston seem impatient of a holiday', as Cowell put it. Weavers employed by Edward Edge struck work on the 15th and immediately obtained the ten per cent. Next day weavers at John Swainson's worsted mill in Leighton Street turned out, while Cowell had to persuade strikers at two further mills to return to work.

No fewer than ten thousand people packed the Orchard on 18 August to hear Cowell report the successful outcome of the Blackburn agitation. The masters' response in Preston remained patchy. Cheers greeted the announcement that Messrs Swainson and Birley's 'Big Factory' had paid the ten per cent. Messrs J. and A. Leigh had agreed to pay if the majority of Preston masters would do the same, while Richard Threlfall had offered *twenty* per cent if other firms followed suit. Horrockses had also conceded, though not before time. 'Almost every manufacturer in Preston,' said Cowell, 'when asked for the ten per cent, had pointed to Messrs Horrockses & Miller, as paying notoriously low wages, and declared that if that firm would give an advance, they were ready to do the same.' Some resistance remained. Humber Brothers had offered less than five per cent, while Birley Brothers had offered a seven per cent increase which would leave their operatives no better off than those in Blackburn had been before the ten per cent was won there. As for John Hawkins, this 'very stubborn gentleman' had come up with the 'extremely funny dodge' of offering to cut the wages of his tacklers and award the proceeds to the weavers! Again Cowell appealed for there to be no strike until the committee decided; if they were patient, strike pay would be forthcoming. A levy of one penny per loom was agreed to meet contingencies.[69]

On 19 August the *Preston Guardian* sent a reporter to inquire of the spinners' and weavers' committees as to the results of their efforts. The spinners claimed complete success at ten firms and offers of five to seven and a half per cent at other mills, while the weavers reported that the 16 largest firms had agreed to pay the full ten per cent. The *Guardian* was optimistic: 'reviewing both lists, there seems to be little doubt but that matters will be amicably arranged, and the good feeling which has so long existed between employers and employed will still be continued'.[70]

Doubt was cast on these reports when the spinners met at the Temperance Hall on 22 August. George Cowell, making a rare appearance at a meeting of spinners, denied that most masters had in fact agreed to pay the ten per cent to their weavers. John Sergeant, from the chair, clearly did not regard the millowners' response as satisfactory. 'I detest strikes,' he declared, 'but no other course is open to us.' The masters should beware: if they were forced to turn out, the spinners would demand not ten but twenty per cent before returning to work. This hint that the spinners' demands were increasing as their impatience grew was reinforced by their secretary, Michael Gallaher, who secured approval of a resolution calling for the ten per cent 'combined with an equalisation or a standard list of prices, so that each operative might have a better chance of receiving a fair day's wage for a fair day's work'. In 1853 this was fighting talk. The Preston spinners would be supported in their stand by other districts. Delegates from the leading centres of the cotton industry, meeting in Preston just the previous day, had resolved that Preston should demand a ten per cent increase upon the *highest* rate paid in the town, followed by the equalization of wages in all mills at that rate.[71]

When the weavers next met, on 25 August, Cowell angrily defended himself from Thomas Miller's recent charge that he was a self-interested, 'noisy agitator'. He had been agitating for ten weeks, Cowell replied, and had done nothing else for the past fortnight; he had received a total of thirty shillings for his pains. Too many masters continued to refuse the weavers' demands. Less ambitious than those of the spinners, these had now crystallized into the simple but effective slogan, 'ten per cent and no surrender'. The weekly levy was increased to threepence per loom.[72] A day later 380 women weavers at Birley Brothers turned out.[73] Twisters at one firm and rovers at another, having left work without notice on their employers' refusal to pay the ten per cent, were ordered back to work by the magistrates on pain of imprisonment under the Master and Servant legislation.[74]

Despite reports that only five firms were still holding out,[75] it was now obvious that the issue was far from settled. Another meeting of weavers' delegates, this time at Bolton on 28 August, reaffirmed its support for Preston. By the beginning of September the spinners at five mills were serving their notice prior to turning out. Weavers at four mills were already on strike, and were laid off at two others on account of strikes by cardroom hands. At John Swainson's Leighton Street mill the striking weavers were being paid six shillings a week, and their assistants three shillings, by the committee. £112 had been collected in Preston in the last week of August, and funds were being augmented by the proceeds of a twopence per loom levy in Blackburn.[76]

One of the main Preston thoroughfares, Friargate, was the scene of the first disturbances of the campaign, on 12 September, when a crowd of operatives hooted and jeered hands (employed by John Hawkins) who had refused to pay the levy to the union. Five youths were arrested in the fracas, and eventually received prison sentences of six weeks or three months.[77] But there was no serious disorder, and few were prepared for what came next. The Preston Masters' Association had been keeping a very low profile. Its activity back in March had been kept a closely guarded secret, and was not in fact revealed until the end of the year. Exactly what part the Association played during the summer months remains unclear, but it is certain that a large majority of firms in Preston and the surrounding villages did agree to pay the ten per cent, leaving only eight (at most, ten) in dispute. These were, apparently, supported by the Association to the extent of 9d per loom, and ½d per pound of yarn, per week, financed by a levy.[78] The Masters' Association had not, however, played any visible role in the struggle before its first public act: the surprise announcement, on 15 September, that a general lock-out would begin one month later.[79]

Thirty-five firms[80] signed the association's manifesto, addressed to 'the operatives of Preston and the neighbourhood':

> A month has now elapsed since the Associated Masters of Preston and the Neighbourhood, yielding to the request of the operatives employed in their respective mills, and after a full consideration of the circumstances of each particular case, agreed to give an advance upon the then rate of wages.
>
> Notwithstanding this concession, and the wish thereby shown on their part to settle the question in a liberal manner, the masters regret to find, that the operatives have put themselves under the guidance of a designing and irresponsible body, who, having no connexion with this town, nor settled position anywhere, but living upon the earnings of the industrious operatives, interfere, for their own purpose and interest, with the relation between master and servant, create where it does not exist, and foster and perpetuate where it unhappily does, a feeling of dissatisfaction and estrangement, and in a spirit of assumption, arrogate to themselves the right to determine, and dictate to the operatives the means of enforcing the conditions upon which they shall be PERMITTED to labour.
>
> To this spirit of tyranny and dictation the masters can no longer submit, in justice either to the operatives or to themselves; hence they are reluctantly compelled to accept the only alternative left: to close their mills until those now on strike are prepared to resume their work, and a better understanding is established between the employer and the employed.
>
> In adopting this course they are fully sensible of the serious evils, moral and social, which must attend it, and which the sad experience of 1836 must painfully recall to the recollection of many. They feel, however, that the responsibility is not theirs: it rests with those who have recklessly created the difficulty, and forced this decision upon them.[81]

The masters told the *Preston Pilot* that they had been meeting employers in other towns, and expected the lock-out to spread throughout the county, as in 1836. The essential issue was one of mastery, not wages. In a succinct statement of their position, the *Pilot* reported that the masters 'feel determined to break down the union of the operatives'.[82] Their own union was intended to be indestructible. Each member of the association had pledged himself to forfeit a bond of no less than £5,000 upon failure to abide by its policy and decisions. The defections which had so weakened the Stockport millowners were not to be tolerated in Preston.[83]

The operatives assembled that evening in a mood of defiance. Their usual bands were unable to play until they reached the Orchard, as the magistrates had earlier that day issued a proclamation prohibiting all processions. Cowell's first target was the bench, and especially the severity of the recent sentences imposed on 'comparative children'. He blamed the disturbances on the plans of the masters to entrap them (police provocation was to be a recurring complaint in the course of the dispute). Cowell refused to be intimidated by the prospect of a lock-out. The weavers of Preston would go to work in Blackburn by train, he declared. Sufficient subscriptions would be forthcoming from other districts to allow relief to those who remained at six shillings per week for up to a year. The Queen's speech to Parliament had boasted that trade was prosperous, and the weavers intended to get their share. 'The masters have no excuse for resisting, save that they are not going to be beaten by the weavers. This is the whole of their argument, and it is now a struggle between Capital and Labour.'[84]

The weavers' delegates now met every Sunday in Preston. On 18 September seventy delegates, representing several dozen manufacturing towns and districts, agreed to raise funds sufficient to support the weavers, winders and loomers already on strike at the rate of 6s per week, and to pay 3s to the tenters (weavers' assistants). Delegates from other towns increasingly stopped over in Preston to address mass meetings. On the morning of Monday 19 September two thousand operatives, in the main those who were already on strike, gathered in the Marsh to hear Cowell and Swinglehurst. They were supported by John Mathews from Heywood,[85] Thomas Rhodes, one of the leaders of the Stockport strike, and William Walton, who had been prominent in the Blackburn agitation. Walton stressed the anxiety of the Blackburn masters that wages be increased in Preston to allow them to compete. Swinglehurst, who, with Cowell, had already been on a speaking tour throughout the area, endorsed Walton's views from first-hand experience. 'I rode in a railway carriage with a manufacturer who said we ought to bring Preston masters up — that we are right in so doing; and every manufacturer about Blackburn, Darwen and elsewhere speaks the same sentiments.'[86]

A larger meeting for those still at work had been called for that evening in the Orchard, but a sudden change of plan was required when it became known that the magistrates had issued a further proclamation forbidding all open-air assemblies after sunset. Now that the nights were drawing in this placed a serious obstacle in the way of the main channel of communication between the leaders and the mass of the operatives, and it drew severe criticism from the delegates who spoke at a hastily rearranged meeting in the Temperance Hall. This gathering is notable for Mortimer Grimshaw's first public appearance in Preston. He took the opportunity of advocating the construction of co-operative mills, like those operating successfully at Padiham, as a long term answer to the masters' challenge. The idea soon caught on, though at first with a more limited perspective. At the next delegate meeting a committee of five was set up, with the task of drafting a prospectus for a co-operative mill to provide work for those who, it was expected, would be victimized in the course of the dispute. From now on 'co-operative self-employment' was to figure prominently (if in the end abortively) in the operatives' thinking.[87]

On 22 September the weavers met again in the Temperance Hall. George Cowell hinted at a conspiracy among the millowners. It had been suggested, he said, that the Stockport employers had conceded the ten per cent only as a tactical move, 'in order that the battle-ground might be Preston, because Preston manufacturers think in their own mind that they can accomplish what the Stockport manufacturers could not do'. In this they were mistaken, despite reports that 'the workpeople of Preston are more chicken-hearted, more humble and docile, more flexible to the wishes of their masters than the workpeople of any other district; in other words, we are represented in other towns and districts to be a most rotten portion of the operative community'. (The charge had been levelled against the Stockport weavers, and echoed the sentiments expressed in Preston itself in 1848.) The Preston masters could still opt for a peaceful settlement, Cowell observed. He called on them to open negotiations, with an independent person of stature acting as 'umpire'. Either of the two Preston MPs, R. Townley Parker and Sir George Strickland, or the Vicar, the Rev. J.O. Parr, would be entirely acceptable to the operatives. After two further mass meetings, the weavers wrote on 26 September to Thomas Miller and William Ainsworth, demanding that the Masters' Association either begin negotiations or agree to arbitration. Four days later the masters replied with a curt refusal to consider either course, just as they had, the previous day, dismissed the appeal of the spinners' committee to open discussions.[88]

At the end of September the outlook was distinctly stormy, and not just at Preston. In Wigan 7,000 or more factory operatives, acting on their own initiative and with the cardroom hands in the vanguard, had just struck work for the ten per cent. They were following the example of the Wigan miners, who had turned out to obtain their second advance of 2d in the shilling within four months.[89] Developments in North East Lancashire were even more menacing. Although the Burnley masters had agreed late in August to pay the ten per cent, sporadic strikes continued to break out there; at one mill several hundred hands struck to support the demands of just four warpers.[90] The Colne weavers' committee was forced to resolve that no turnouts should commence without its approval, which would be granted only after negotiations had failed.[91] A masters' association was formally constituted at Burnley on 17 September, buttressed by a £2,000 bond. Rumours grew that a lock-out was under consideration, and that it would embrace Bury, Bacup and other nearby towns.[92] On 1 October the Burnley masters announced that a lock-out would indeed begin on the 28th, to force a return to work at Messrs Slater and Pollard's mill; the weavers remained defiant. Within days, the millowners of Padiham, Bacup and the Rossendale valley declared that they would join the lock-out.[93]

Exactly what had gone wrong here remains obscure. The *Burnley Advertiser* appeared as bewildered as anyone:

> It is stated, for instance, that the masters who refuse compliance with the demands made upon them, are insolent and overbearing in their interviews with the deputations appointed to wait upon them, and refuse to listen to their representations. On the other hand it is said that the operatives are unreasonable in their demands, and that they are led by misguided men, whose language is oft-times abusive and violent.[94]

Its rival, the *Burnley Mentor*, hinted that the masters were having second thoughts about the ten per cent, when it wrote that 'to us it appears somewhat remarkable that the Burnley manufacturers cannot afford to pay as high wages as those paid in other towns in Lancashire'.[95] Perhaps a clue is provided by the intention of the weavers, expressed early in August, to demand an equalization of wages, according to the prices given by the six largest firms in the town, *after* the ten per cent had been won.[96] Possibly here, too, it was now seen as a question of 'mastery'. Whatever the causes of the escalating conflict in North East Lancashire, its effects were obvious and, from the viewpoint of the Preston operatives, extremely undesirable. It was not just a question of diverting attention from their own cause. Tens of thousands of operatives were soon to be thrown out of work, and would be unable (however willing) to contribute their subscriptions to aid the Preston struggle.

In Preston the weavers were meeting almost daily, and their delegates visited the various cotton towns to promote the cause and solicit subscriptions. Henry Fellowes, who took the chair at many of the Preston meetings, became a seasoned traveller. His itinerary twice took in his native Lancaster, a small town remote from the heart of the industry, where in the first week of October little more than £1 had been collected for Preston. Other districts were much more generous, raising in that week £1,054 — a total exceeding that subscribed to Stockport in all but one week of the general turnout there.[97] Back in Preston, delegates from a number of local craft societies met on 7 October to affirm their solidarity with the cotton operatives. The bulk of the subscriptions were now required to support those already on strike, occasioning a bizarre and tragic accident on 4 October when 2–3,000 cardroom hands queued in an upstairs room at the Corporation Arms to receive their pay: the floor collapsed, killing one operative and injuring fifty. A paper war broke out, with rival placards covering the walls of the town. The more poetic of the operatives now began to compose ballads in support of the ten per cent. Printed and sold around the town, these provided an additional means of promoting the movement, not to mention a useful supplement to strike pay. The magistrates aroused further antagonism when, early in October, they prohibited the singing of these ballads in the streets.[98]

Irritation of a more substantial nature resulted from the news that Horrockses' overlookers had, on 5 October, declared their independence of 'the union', calling for mediation and mutual compromise. In conjunction with clergymen and other respectable middle-class citizens, they arranged a meeting for the next evening to discuss means of averting the lock-out. About 150 overlookers were expected at the Pole Street school. In the event, no less than 2,000 people arrived, the great majority of them weavers who had come direct (and uninvited) from their own assembly in the Temperance Hall. The chairman, a local teetotaller by the name of Henry Bradley, called for the dissolution of the operatives' committees and their replacement by unco-ordinated representations to the masters, mill by mill. Two overlookers and the Revs. S.F. Page and William Walling supported Bradley, only to be greeted by 'the most violent demonstrations of dissent', and the overlookers' proposals were defeated by an immense majority.[99] Undeterred by this setback, the 'anti-strike committee' (as it was widely known) met in less turbulent circumstances on 8 October, and issued a placard which roundly condemned the operatives. 'Various acts of insubordination and dictation in the Mills proved the existence of an evil spirit', it was asserted; the operatives' demands were excessive, and the spinners' appeal (in their placard of 1 October) for the equalization of wages itself amounted to 'dictation'.[100]

October 8th saw the first and only public expression of dissent at a mass meeting of weavers. Henry Newsham, himself employed as a weaver at Horrockses, bravely stood up in front of 4,000 operatives in the Orchard 'to prove that strikes were wrong in principle, and that they never did and never would do any good to the working classes of this country'. Newsham's speech was greeted with loud groans and hisses, one sardonic voice in the crowd suggesting that his real motive was to secure himself a tackler's job at Horrockses. His views were rebutted by all four of the delegates who had preceded him on the rostrum (an overturned cart). Challenged by the weavers' committee to a more detailed debate on the following Monday (10 October) Newsham accepted. He failed to appear at the appointed time because, as he subsequently explained, he believed (not without reason) that he would not have received a fair hearing. Another diversion was provided by John Catterall's claim that Horrockses' hands had abandoned the struggle, which forced the weavers' committee to call a special meeting for the operatives concerned to deny the allegation. Cowell angrily described Catterall, the secretary of the 'anti-strike committee', as a minion of the masters.[101] On 11 October the Pole Street school was the scene of another (and this time undisturbed) meeting 'purporting', as the *Preston Pilot* somewhat cynically put it, 'to be one of the operatives who object to the strike', but dominated by Bradley, Walling and Catterall. Next day a deputation approached the Masters' Association, only to be told, rather brusquely, that the dispute was not their concern.[102]

Two days before the lock-out was due to commence the local clergy convened another meeting, under the chairmanship of the Vicar. A number of reverend gentlemen attended, along with the editors of the two principal local newspapers, several other prominent citizens, and George Cowell's employer, John Goodair, who was not personally involved in the lock-out. Cowell himself was present, on behalf of the weavers' committee. Of those invited, only three failed to appear: two Roman Catholic priests, who regretted their inability to intervene in secular affairs, and the chairman of the Preston Masters' Association, Thomas Miller. The Vicar repeated his belief that the operatives must make concessions, and was supported by the Rev. John Clay,[103] chaplain to the Preston House of Correction. John Catterall called for mediation, while Cowell defended the weavers' refusal to compromise on the ten per cent. Inevitably, given the absence of Miller, nothing concrete came out of the conference. Miller's refusal to attend drew bitter condemnation from Cowell at the weavers' meeting that evening. Thomas Miller's father came to Preston as a poor handloom weaver, Cowell asserted (wrongly, as it happens), yet his son was too proud to talk to the operatives and was determined to crush their union by locking out his hands. He could finance the construction of churches; he was building a large new mill; and he was in the process of buying himself a country estate. Yet he paid wages 15 or 20 per cent less than his neighbours. It was true that Miller *had* paid the ten per cent (even slightly more), but only because he would otherwise have been unable to retain his hands. 'I once worked for Mr Miller,' Cowell said with feeling, 'and I have no hesitation in saying that I will not work for that firm again, under the present rules, and under the system of tyranny which is practised there.'[104]

As the prospect of a peaceful settlement receded, the weavers pressed on with their plans for co-operative mills. Their delegate meeting on 9 October approved the prospectus drawn up by Swinglehurst and the other members of the subcommittee appointed for that purpose.[105] The Oldham delegate John Cheetham waxed lyrical on the possibilities of co-operation. If, he calculated, four million of the six million adult males in the country contributed 1d per week, this would amount after 60 years at compound interest to no less than £3,471,129,995 18s 4d, 'which sum would buy up all the property in the kingdom'! On a more practical note, Cowell announced that the committee would provide financial assistance for weavers who wished to move to Blackburn.[106] William Walton repeated his claim that the operatives had the full support of the masters in his town. When the Preston masters went to Blackburn to appeal for assistance, he reported, 'some of the masters in that town had threatened to kick their a—s out of the mills if they came there again'.[107]

On Friday 14 October more than 10,000 operatives, many of whom must have left work early, thronged the Marsh to hear speeches by Cowell, Swinglehurst and the Blackburn delegate William Brown. At the conclusion of the proceedings Cowell proposed three cheers for Queen Victoria and the Royal Family. Next morning the lock-out officially began.[108]

3 The Operatives

> Swinglehurst, Cowell, and Fellowes, our advocates so bold,
> With threats no man can frighten them, nor bribe them with their gold;
> The masters cry, 'To prison the rascals should be sent';
> But THEY do swear by all that's good, they shall pay the Ten per Cent.

Without doubt the most prominent among the leaders of the turnouts were George Cowell and Mortimer Grimshaw. Relatively little is known of their background. Grimshaw came from Great Harwood, and it was probably here that his father had played an eloquent part in radical politics earlier in the century.[1] The younger Grimshaw, involved in the ten per cent campaign at Stockport as early as March 1853,[2] had already achieved a certain reputation for his activities in the 'Jacobin village' of Royton, outside Oldham. In 1852—3 he served as secretary of the Royton Short Time Committee, campaigning for the enforcement and strengthening of the Factory Acts. In 1852, as editor of the *Royton Vindicator* (an anti-Whig election broadsheet) he justified tactical alliances by the Chartist movement with the Tories against the Whigs, and attacked the victimization of political activists at a local mill.[3] Evidently a similar fate had befallen Grimshaw himself a few years earlier. A weaver by trade, he regarded himself as black listed at every mill in Lancashire 'because of his independence of mind'.[4] Exactly how he earned his living remained obscure, inevitably laying him open to the charge (frequently made during the Preston strike) of being a self-interested professional agitator.

Such allegations did Grimshaw less than justice. In the case of George Cowell, they were patently absurd. 'Cowell is a Preston weaver,' wrote the local journalist Charles Hardwick, 'yet, though I am a native, and pretty well known to the working classes of the town, I never heard of such a man before the commencement of the "strike"! Indeed, had Cowell been merely a "professional agitator" or "spouting demagogue", the struggle could not have lasted half the time it did.'[5] Unlike Grimshaw, Cowell was a local man, born within six miles of the town and resident in Preston itself since the late 1830s; he was a Methodist and a staunch teetotaller.[6] Cowell had worked as a weaver for Horrockses.[7] In the summer of 1853 he was employed by Messrs Napier and Goodair, to which concern he intended to return at the conclusion of the dispute.[8] Cowell was not, as Hardwick implies, a complete stranger to working-class politics, having participated in a variety of radical movements in previous years. In 1848 he had played a prominent part in the Chartist movement in North Lancashire, chairing the important camp meeting at Brindle in April of that year.[9] Unlike many Cowell remained a Chartist in 1849,[10] when he also appeared on the same Ten Hours platform as Oastler, Fielden and Rayner Stephens and represented Preston at the Manchester delegate conference of Factory Reformers. He spoke at two further Ten Hours meetings in Preston during 1850.[11] A year later he addressed a Blackburn audience on the plight of Hungarian nationalist refugees,[12] and in the 1852 election campaign questioned the candidates on the separation of church and state, the law of entail and primogeniture, and on the franchise, the ballot, and the property qualification for MPs.[13] His choice of the last group of issues suggests that Cowell maintained his support for the People's Charter, support which became evident in the course of the Preston strike.[14]

Politically Cowell and Grimshaw had much in common, but in style and personality they were very different. Both contemporary and modern commentators have emphasized their differences, invariably to Grimshaw's disadvantage. 'Cowell was undoubtedly a man of integrity,' wrote Anne Smith a few years ago, 'while his colleague Grimshaw was equally clearly a ranting demagogue.'[15] There is some truth in this appraisal. Certainly it was Grimshaw, not Cowell, who at the climax of the strike had to be warned by the weavers' chairman to moderate his language.[16] It was Grimshaw again who apparently aroused such antagonism among a section of the Warrington operatives that he was unable to address a meeting there.[17] And no-one at all would have dreamed of calling Cowell the 'Thunderer of Lancashire'.

But the contrast can be overdrawn. Hardwick was more perceptive when he compared Cowell and Grimshaw with the two great bourgeois radicals of mid-Victorian England. He wrote at the end of the strike:

These two men were the Cobden and Bright of this 'Labour League' ... The parallel holds good in several respects. Their temperaments to some extent assimilate. Cowell was generally calm and logical in his style of address. After all, he appealed more to the intellect and judgement of his audience, such as it was, than to their passions ... George Cowell is rather below the middle height. His forehead is ample, and the expression of his countenance thoughtful and benevolent. He is a man of very limited scholastic education, but he appears to possess calm, steady resolution, coupled with a powerful and somewhat active brain. With early cultivation, he would doubtless have distinguished himself in a more 'respectable' arena than the one generally occupied by the 'stump orator' ... Mortimer Grimshaw is a bigger man, very much marked with the small-pox. He was well known by his white hat, which, I suppose, he wore after the fashion of Hunt and Cobbett, to indicate the depth of his 'Radical' propensities. As John Bright plants his elevated fist firmly in advance, whilst eloquently expounding the doctrines of the Peace Society, so Mortimer Grimshaw advocates liberty to the oppressed 'factory slaves' with a dogmatical invective ... more worthy of a Russian despot than an English patriot. I do not assert that he is insincere. Maliciously impugning an adversary's motives is the height of folly to my mind, and the worst of all arguments. He appears to me to be an enthusiast, and that the warmth of his feelings, when excited, overpowers his judgement.[18]

George Cowell addressing a meeting of factory operatives in the Orchard, from the *Illustrated London News*, 12 November 1853.

If Cowell's clear head and iron self-control were invaluable to the turnouts, so too were Grimshaw's passion and fire. Like Cobden and Bright they complemented each other, to produce a formidable partnership.

For the duration of the strike, at least, they were full-time agitators. Grimshaw, whose involvement at Preston began late in September 1853, had spoken at more than 60 public meetings in the town by the following May. He had travelled throughout Lancashire, reaching as far afield as Sheffield and Bradford.

The Operatives

"THE TEN PER CENT, AND NO SURRENDER!"

Mortimer Grimshaw, as depicted by the *People's Paper*, 4 February 1854.

Cowell's life was even more hectic. In the twelve months beginning in June 1853 he spoke at 91 mass meetings in Preston, not to mention more than 30 delegate meetings in the town and countless other gatherings across the manufacturing districts. He toured Crewe, the Potteries and Birmingham; paid four visits to the London trades, and a further journey to the metropolis to address the abortive Society of Arts conference; spoke, during separate trips, at Glasgow and Carlisle; and attended Ernest Jones's Labour Parliament on one of many visits to Manchester. Attacked by placards and in the press, he replied by broadsheet and letter. When plain-clothes policemen appeared intent on provoking disorder he complained in person to the mayor and superintendent of police.[19] When the *Manchester Guardian* published allegations of fraud in the administration of strike relief, he visited the editor to protest.[20] Small wonder that, as Dickens's reporter noted, the strain began to show. 'The feverish and anxious expression of the eyes', James Lowe concluded his description of "Cowler", 'tells of sleepless nights and of constant agitation.'[21]

For one of Cowell's closest associates, the pressures proved too great. Edward Swinglehurst, who had spoken at almost all of the weavers' meetings in the late summer and early autumn of 1853, taking the chair on many occasions, took to his bed for the winter. When he recovered sufficiently to resume his place in the agitation in February 1854, it was with diminished vigour. Swinglehurst was an old campaigner. 'I have been connected with agitations for the last thirty years', he once announced, proudly (much to Henry Ashworth's annoyance).[22] His early life was spent as a linen weaver in the Yorkshire village of Bentham. Around 1827 he moved to Kendal, where he played an active and controversial part in the local trade union and co-operative movement,[23] and represented the town at the 1834 temperance conference.[24] A Chartist from the very beginning of the movement, Swinglehurst remained an active reformer after his move to Preston in 1840 with his family (one son was named Henry Hunt!). Apart from a brief period of disillusion in 1844, Swinglehurst's loyalty to the People's Charter was unswerving.[25] In Preston he became, like so many working-class radicals of the period, a bookseller. He seems to have been more prosperous than most, for he maintained the same premises for over a decade, in which time he saw two of his three sons established in respectable and lucrative middle-class professions (one, indeed, was in 1853 employed as an agent by the Manchester Chamber of Commerce).[26] By 1850 Edward Swinglehurst had become the elder statesman of working-class radicalism in Preston. Weavers' trade agitations, Chartism, the Ten Hours movement, Hungarian nationalism, opposition to the construction of a union workhouse in Preston, all were issues which saw him deeply involved.[27] And in the early stages of the ten per cent campaign, before his health gave way, Swinglehurst played a role second only to George Cowell.

Although less prominent than Swinglehurst, several of the leading Preston activists were involved in the same popular movements. Among the weavers, Robert Baxendale had appeared on the Ten Hours platform in 1849–50, and intervened in the election campaign two years later on the issues of primogeniture and Hungarian nationalism.[28] Thomas Daly had been a Factory Reformer, and took the chair at a meeting called in 1852 to solicit support for striking winders at Radcliffe.[29] Pryce Humphreys was in his twenty-seventh year as a weaver, many of them spent in Manchester, and could draw on his memories of a score of previous strikes.[30] John Bowman had been an enthusiastic Factory Reformer, and was active in the unsuccessful wages agitation in 1848–9. He remained sufficiently respectable to serve on the (predominantly middle-class) committee established in Preston in connection with the Great Exhibition of 1851. This experience proved invaluable during the strike: he served as one of the secretaries to the weavers' committee, and was sent on several missions to London.[31]

The spinners did not lack men of similar calibre. John Sergeant had been a mainstay of the local Short Time Committee, on whose behalf he organised support for the sympathetic Sir George Strickland in the 1852 election, with his fellow spinner Robert Richardson.[32] Robert Greenough, another frequent visitor to London during the strike, was also a Factory Reformer.[33] In contrast the spinners' secretary Michael Gallaher was a schoolmaster; 'a man of learning', in Cowell's words, who 'has had a college education; but yet, notwithstanding that, he knows what it is to work between a pair of spinning wheels'.[34] At the end of the strike Gallaher was succeeded as secretary by the young Thomas Banks,[35] already a veteran of the Ten Hours agitation, where he had worked with William Parkinson, now an inn-keeper but still a staunch ally of the spinners.[36]

At the weavers' meetings the chair was taken, as often as not, by James Waddington. 'The chair itself was a myth,' Hardwick recalled, 'or rather a polite fiction, as Mr. W. simply stood amongst the other occupants of the cart, undistinguished by either insignia or position. His opening address presented a capital specimen of what I term the medium phasis of the rich dialect of Lancashire ... Take a "stickful", as a printer would say, by way of a specimen:—

'Well, friends, what dun yo think? They (I meean t'press) nah co us delicates "stump orators"! They sen we goa about maunting t'stump an' meeking speeches; an we do it o' for t'brass as yo give us. We'll, it's a terrible deal yo give us, to be sure. (Loud laughter.) They sen we're lazy fellows, an to idle to wark. (Laughter) I should think I know what wark is as weel as some on 'um; an I'll tell yo what, it's t'fost time I ever went aut a "stumping" it; and it's t'hardest wark I ever did i' moy life afore. It'll never do for lazy chaps, I con tell yo. (Loud cheering.) I don't care ha soon I give o'er; an when we're settled this, you waynt catch me going aut on t'stump agean so soon, I know!'[37]

Waddington's sentiments would have been shared by the scores of Preston operatives who took to 'stump oratory' in quest of the ten per cent. They were echoed, no doubt, by such weavers as Henry Fellowes and James Whalley, by the spinners George Richmond, John Gardner, Giles Howarth and George Eccles, the throstle-spinners James Postlethwaite and H.B. Wadman, and by John Bibby from the cardroom, about whom (and a host of others) nothing is recorded apart from their occasional speeches in the Orchard or on the Marsh. Their anonymity is ill-deserved.[38]

The appearance of a woman on the platform was evidently a rare event, and always sufficient to disconcert the gentlemen of the press. Often it was felt unseemly to report the names of the ladies concerned. Of those not thus condemned to oblivion, Mrs Cooper and the sisters-in-law Ann and Margaret Fletcher were no mean orators. On one occasion, at Glossop, one of the Fletchers made the fiery Grimshaw seem moderate and restrained as she savaged 'the grinding capitalists, men who had risen from the dunghill'.[39] At Blackburn there was a flourishing women's committee,[40] but in general (and in spite of their massive numerical preponderance among the turnouts) women played a very subordinate role in the entire ten per cent campaign. Their fundamental ambition was to secure the right *not* to work. 'Married females', the *Ten Hours Advocate* had urged in 1846, 'would be much better occupied in performing the domestic duties of the household, than following the never-tiring motion of machinery. We therefore hope the day is not distant, when the husband will be able to provide for his wife and family, without sending the former to endure the drudgery of a cotton mill.'[41] 'It is a disgrace to an Englishman', Margaret Fletcher told an enthusiastic audience in the Orchard in November 1853, 'to allow his wife to go out to work. Let the women look after our rights, it is high time we look to ourselves. We have let the men manage our affairs long enough, and a pretty position they have brought us to.' (Laughter and cheers.) The Fletchers then achieved the adoption of a resolution pledging the married women of Preston not to go to work 'until their husbands are fully and fairly remunerated for their labour'.[42] This was partly just a shrewd application of the laws of supply and demand. 'Let the labour market be thinned', Margaret Fletcher urged the operatives of Bolton, by the withdrawal of married women, thus allowing the wages of their husbands to rise.[43] But there was more to it than that. In an era when families were large, and when work began at six in the morning and ended twelve hours later, any advocate of the rights of women could see distinct advantages in domesticity.

Once the weavers had decided to concentrate their energies and their funds on Preston, delegates from other towns began to play an increasingly prominent part in the dispute. Several of the heroes of the Stockport strike made frequent journeys north of the Ribble. Thomas Rhodes, still in his early twenties, was voted onto the weavers' Executive Committee and appeared regularly in the Orchard.[44] Luke Wood, only a little older, had chaired the great meeting to celebrate the successful conclusion of the Stockport campaign, and often served in a similar capacity in Preston. In all probability Wood was an active Chartist,[45] along with William Chadwick, who in 1848 had been sentenced to six months for seditious conspiracy.[46] Another of the Stockport men, Thomas Smith, was a supporter of Busfield Ferrand's Labour League, chairing one of its meetings in his home town. Smith was older than Rhodes and Wood, and had possibly been involved in the Ten Hours agitation as early as 1835.[47]

Due to their town's enormous contributions to the strike funds, the Blackburn delegates were always afforded special respect in Preston. William Brown, who appeared on the platform nearly 30 times during the strike, was the chairman of the Blackburn Short Time Committee,[48] while the mechanic Benjamin Harbury had been associated with Cowell and Swinglehurst in organizing support for Kossuth in 1851.[49] Nothing is known of the background of such energetic Blackburn men as Robert Walker, William Walton, John Lang, Thomas Edmundson, or even the secretary of the local weavers' union, Edward Whittle.

Whittle was no orator, but an administrator and negotiator of great ability. Robert Worswick, of Padiham, was

a capital specimen of another style. He does the low comedy, and does it well, too ... He is a singularly enthusiastic, but good-humoured fellow. He complimented the lasses on their appearance, made jokes, told humorous anecdotes, declared his 'head, heart and hands' were all true to the cause, and finished off in a complete paroxysm of virtuous determination to sacrifice his life in the cause. He flourished his arms in the air as wildly and rapidly as the sails of a 'peg', or wooden windmill, in a gale of wind. He danced and jumped with an enthusiasm more fanatically outrageous than an Eastern dervish, and finished off by exclaiming, amidst the laughter of his audience, with a singular mixture of energy and good humour: 'I don't care what comes or goas, I'll ne'er surrender. I'm alus thinking about it neet an day. I dream about it. I know it's our just reets, and we'll hev it yet. I'll ne'er give in if yo do. I've med up my mind fer t'wost. I'm determined to hev it or to dee, shaughting ten pu'zent and noa surrender!' Then, bringing the whole of his force to bear for a single effort, he clasped his hands, threw up his arms, and screaming at the top of his voice, 'Ten pu'zent! *ten pu'zent!* TEN PU'ZENT, and noa surrender!' fell back into the cart.[50]

The Oldham delegates took life altogether more seriously. John Cheetham, once described by Swinglehurst as the operatives' Disraeli, was a Chartist of long standing, who had been arrested in 1842. In 1848 he was charged with conspiracy after having led a crowd of 200 to Royton to close the mills and ensure support for a demonstration in Manchester on behalf of the Irish nationalist John Mitchel. By 1852 he was active in the Ten Hours movement at Royton.[51] John Mills, an Oldham spinner, was also a Factory Reformer.[52] Another Oldham man, Kinder Smith, became chairman of the weavers' Executive Committee, and handled the weekly delegate meetings in the Cockpit with a skill, or so Swinglehurst maintained, 'not surpassed by the Speaker of the House of Commons'. Charles Hardwick recalled,

Mr. Smith is not an old man, though at a little distance his mild, placid expression and somewhat bald forehead might leave that impression upon a stranger. The provincial *patois* of his district is strongly marked in his speech. He is not always very fluent in his address, but he seems to possess, for a man of his station, good shrewd sense, and an inflexible determination to conduct the assemblies conducted to his charge with the most scrupulous decorum.

In the late 1840s a Chartist and a Factory Reformer, Kinder Smith had been active in the attempt by the Oldham radicals to resist the incorporation of the town, thereby retaining their control of the local police.[53]

J.B. Horsfall came from Royton, where he had served as secretary of the weavers' association, and had been dismissed from his job in consequence. After a spell in Warrington, Horsfall had returned to Royton, only to find himself and his sisters blacklisted by the manufacturers. He, too, became a bookseller and printer, publishing a working-men's paper, the *Factory Operative's Guide*. He participated in the Ten Hours movement and acted as secretary of the Royton Chartists, who used his premises for their meetings. A vice-chairman of the Labour League, Horsfall rarely appeared on the public platform, but during the Preston strike he handled much of the weavers' correspondence, printed their balance sheets, and audited the accounts.[54] His fellow auditor John

Mathews, of Heywood, was sent by the weavers' committee on a number of missions to London. Mathews had represented Bury at the Chartist National Assembly in 1848, and like Horsfall was active in the Labour League.[55]

These men must have been conscious, if only dimly, that they were witnessing the beginning of a social transition in which the class confrontation of the Chartist period was fading into the more harmonious social relations characteristic of mid-Victorian Britain. In their classic history of trade unionism Sidney and Beatrice Webb encapsulated the process in the titles of their chapters. As they saw it, 'The Revolutionary Period' (1829–42) was followed by 'The New Spirit and the New Model' (1843–60).[56] For a later writer, the change was a more gradual and continuous one, in which 'the temper of radicalism softened as it settled comfortably into a soothing cultural ambience . . . middle class liberalism and the Left had common origins and shared many values, aspirations and assumptions. These historical affinities have made it difficult for the Left to maintain its ideological independence.' On this view the 1850s and 1860s provide a case study in the loss of working-class independence: the political radicals and union militants of an earlier generation slowly succumbed to the hegemony over ideas and culture of an ascendant bourgeoisie.[57]

Many historians have assailed the Webbs's analysis as over-simplified, emphasizing instead the essential continuity in trade union development throughout the 19th century and discounting both the supposed revolutionary fervour of the second quarter of the century and the alleged passive conformity of subsequent decades.[58] It is necessary to go back only eleven years to realise that, at least for Lancashire, the Webbs were not so wide of the mark. The 'Plug Riots' of 1842 were in essence a massive general strike which brought production to a halt across vast areas of the Midlands and the North, amid considerable violence and widespread civil commotion.[59] Moreover, the strike had distinct revolutionary overtones, culminating in a meeting of trades' delegates in Manchester which resolved to continue the strike until the People's Charter became the law of the land.[60] The ten per cent campaign of 1853–4 could not have been more dissimilar. Two minor riots in the course of a year, the military conspicuous by its absence, not a single fatality, moderate and respectable leadership which commanded the grudging admiration of even the most hostile middle-class observers, demands which never went beyond the narrowly economic: even in its greatest industrial dispute the tranquillity of 'the age of equipoise' was largely undisturbed. In little more than a decade a remarkable transformation had taken place.

Yet some doubt remains. Can the firebrands of 1842 really have mellowed so much, so rapidly? Had yesterday's Chartists genuinely accepted their subordinate place in a newly consolidated 'viable class society'? Outward conformity is not always a reliable indication of inner conviction, nor social pacifism the only alternative to social insurrection. In their language, if not their actions, the leaders of the Preston strike were still a long way from assimilation into 'a culture that presupposed middle-class pre-eminence'.[61] The working classes, said the South Lancashire Chartist delegates in 1842, had been reduced 'to a worse than Egyptian state of bondage'.[62] Such phrases were the stock in trade of the Orchard orators eleven years later. The manufacturers were still 'those things in human shape called "masters"', as Cowell put it.[63] Cowell was quite willing to share a platform with the Chartist leader Ernest Jones, and to espouse Jones's political convictions. 'The trades' unions will never be able to alter the state of things', Cowell told an enthusiastic Oldham audience in November, 'unless they take up the political question and embrace the political movement (Cheers). Nothing but the People's Charter, I believe, will elevate the condition of the people, or ever succeed in emancipating them from the yoke of the factory tyrants. I exhort all the Trades and working men henceforth to struggle for the Charter (Great applause).'[64]

If the operatives' sights had been lowered, their aspirations dampened, it was much more for practical than for ideological reasons. Chartism had lost whatever attractions it might once have had for the working people of Preston.[65] A revolutionary general strike had been doomed to failure in 1842; now it would have been suicidal. Better to strive for attainable goals, even if they fell far short of what they felt might legitimately be demanded. Cowell was willing to declare his support for political reform. But as he told a Chartist questioner at a London meeting, he was *not* prepared to introduce political questions into the ten per cent campaign, for this would guarantee failure.[66] There was, in fact, a poignant and inescapable contradiction in the turnouts' attitude to the mighty struggle in which they were engaged. They rejected the values and norms of the ruling class — and in local terms, at least, the Preston millowners were nothing if not that. But they were forced by the realities of the situation in which they found themselves to act as if they accepted the relations of dominance which those values upheld, seeking only the palliative of higher wages.

Nowhere is this ambivalence more vividly revealed than in the economic arguments which the delegates propounded. Whether political economy was *deliberately* vulgarized as a weapon in the class struggle remains contentious.[67] That it was thus used there is no question. Wages depend on supply and demand, the operatives learned from all sides. What could be more stupid than to suppose that they could be improved by trades unions or strikes? Even the sympathetic *Preston Guardian* was saddened to find that the turnouts 'have but little knowledge of Trade, and none at all of the principles of Political Economy'. There were a few believers, like the 'factory operative of 40 years' standing' who wrote, in the same issue: 'I believe that the laws which regulate labour and wages are as immutable and unalterable, by force or compulsion, as the laws which regulate the heavenly bodies.'[68] Presumably George Cowell was not counted among the faithful. 'When the working classes begin to want more money,' he complained bitterly, 'they are taunted about their ignorance. These political economists, however, will fail to convince you that 18s a week is preferable to 20s ... Political economy! What is it? The doctrine of buying cheap and selling dear — a doctrine utterly irreconcilable with the divine precept "Do unto others as you would that they should do unto you." The sooner we can rout political economy from the world, the better it will be for the working classes of this country.'[69] But it was Cowell who, only a month before, had attacked the Manchester School on quite different grounds: 'the free traders advocate the principle of selling in the dearest market and buying in the cheapest. Factory operatives have nothing but our labour to sell, and we wish to dispose of it to the best advantage.'[70]

Possibly this can be explained as a rather effective debating point. 'There has been a combination of masters in Manchester,' Grimshaw said scornfully in January 1854, 'and they are all Protectionists now ... There are no longer any political economists, it appears.'[71] It was more difficult for Mrs Fletcher to escape embarrassment when accused of contradicting herself: attacking political economy on the one hand, and applying it (in her 'thinning the market' speech) on the other.[72] Equally, when the weavers' delegate meeting set up an emigration fund which they regarded as an integral part of their activities, their initiative is capable of more than one interpretation.[73] Was it simply a tactical ploy designed to frighten the masters (in which it evidently succeeded)? Was it aimed more at relieving a little human suffering, while reducing the burden of numbers to be supported from the strike fund? Or did it imply an unspoken belief that wages were after all dependent on supply and demand, and that the laws of political economy must be accepted and manipulated in their favour? What too were the delegates doing when, time after time, they insisted that trade was flourishing to a far greater degree than the masters would allow? Were they simply playing the manufacturers at their own propaganda game? Or were they acknowledging a mutual subordination to the iron hand of the world market? Perhaps they themselves did not know.

Only rarely did there emerge a coherent alternative to orthodox economic ideas. Under the influence of the obscure and penniless German refugee Karl Marx, Ernest Jones preached a rough and ready theory of surplus value,[74] but few were aware of it and even fewer understood. When William Newton visited Preston in April 1854 his lecture was announced by placards headed 'Labour is the Source of All Wealth', but his economics were woolly and his inspiration came from Adam Smith, Malthus, Ricardo and John Stuart Mill.[75] John Mathews identified himself with a quite different school of political economy in his attacks on Free Trade. The working men did not want the manufacturers to clothe the backs of people across the seas, he argued, for so long as they did that they must destroy the home markets.[76] Cobbett had taken much the same line in his *Perish Commerce!*, and similar arguments had been deduced by the Ricardian Socialists from their underconsumptionist analyses of economic crises. Higher wages at home meant stronger demand and less dependence on foreign markets; Say's Law was the Achilles' heel of classical economics.[77]

Along with Grimshaw and J.B. Horsfall, Mathews was an active supporter of the Lancashire, Yorkshire and Cheshire Labour League. Established in London at the beginning of 1853, this organization was originally known simply as the Labour League. It was the brainchild of Samuel Kydd, in 1848 a prominent Chartist and now secretary to the celebrated Tory Factory Reformer Richard Oastler.[78] The objects of the League bore a striking resemblance to those of the National Association of United Trades, from whose short-lived journal its name had been borrowed. They included the arbitration of industrial disputes by local 'Boards of Trade'; Factory Reform; the abolition of Truck; the repeal of the detested New Poor Law; and — here was the rub — a return to the protection of domestic industry.[79] Although the eleventh and final section of its manifesto asserted that 'the Labour League cannot, under any circumstances, be identified with any political party', it was in fact the organ of the Tory—radical protectionist faction, among whom Oastler and the former MP William Busfield Ferrand[80] figured prominently. For once the Chartists and the Manchester School were in agreement: the League was, in Ernest Jones's words, 'a new protectionist trick'.[81] Its appeal is not difficult to understand, especially when embellished by such advocates as Grimshaw. 'I am not in favour of a bread tax,' he told an attentive audience at Accrington, 'which is a one-sided protection for the benefit only of the landowner. I am for *every* class being protected, the labourer *not excepted*, as has heretofore been the case.' Political economy, on the other hand, was 'at war with Christianity'.[82] It was in such terms that Ferrand, along with Oastler and that High Tory turned insurrectionist, the Rev. J. Rayner Stephens, had supported the Ten Hours movement. In the autumn of 1853 the League moved north, with Ferrand now at its head, and held a series of well-attended meetings in a number of cotton towns (though not, apparently, in Preston), before fading from view.[83] Its influence over such men as Grimshaw, Mathews and Horsfall — all associates of the League's arch-enemy Ernest Jones — testifies to the confusion which afflicted the more politically-conscious operatives in the period of Chartist decline.

The turnouts' support for co-operative production is no easier to interpret than their attitude towards political economy. A thriving cooperative mill at Padiham was often held up as a paradigm of what might be achieved, and rarely did the operatives meet without being urged to follow this example. Concrete proposals were being discussed by the weavers' delegates as early as September 1853. During the dispute itself there was no time to pursue the project in any detail, but at the end of the strike considerable energy was devoted (if ultimately in vain) to drawing up a prospectus and raising funds. The original plan had the modest aim (shared by the Manchester dyers after their defeat, and by no means unusual at the time) of providing work for those who would be dismissed and blacklisted in the course of the strike. A number of victims of the Burnley lockout were indeed employed in this way. Attitudes hardened along with the masters' intransigence, and co-operative production came increasingly to be seen as a means of transforming society as a whole. The weavers' final address echoed sentiments expressed time and again by many of the delegates over the previous six months: 'there is another way of striking — a strike that shall strike down the employers by making the operatives their own employers. This shall be our next strike, and we hope every working man will strike in this way, until the name of employer is *stricken* out of the English language.'[84] The spinners' parting shot was similarly worded.[85]

This concept of a classless society freely based on mutual aid and 'cooperative self-employment' dated back at least to the Owenite days of the 1830s. Grimshaw's vision of a 'New Regenerated Preston'[86] was neither stupid nor ignoble. But its implications were, by the 1850s, fraught with ambiguity. Two of the three Preston newspapers, both bitter enemies of the turnouts, gave their cautious approval to cooperation, but as an embodiment of that ultimate symbol of mid-Victorian respectability, Self-Help.[87] Cooperation also formed an important part of the Christian Socialists' 'particular version of feudal socialism ... an hierarchic Community in which every man knew his social status; one in which those in high places both recognised and practised the duties and obligations which they owed to their fellow men'. This was merely to replace one form of 'Egyptian bondage' with other, much older, chains.[88] Support of a quite different kind came from John Baynes, an enlightened Blackburn manufacturer. He supported co-operation as the best means of promoting social peace. It would instruct the operatives in the laws of political economy, and allow the formation of 'a middle class of manufacturers, composed of associated workmen, forming a connecting link between the private manufacturers and the operatives ... this middle class of manufacturers would form a breakwater, and prevent, to a great extent, those collisions between Labour and Capital, which it has been our lot to witness so frequently during the past years.'[89]

It was his perception of precisely these dangers that had prompted Ernest Jones's vigorous opposition to co-operation, and his insistence that political power alone could secure the emancipation of labour.[90] His conversion to the co-operative principle, which took place during the Preston strike and must have been a consequence of it, is a tribute to the influence of the turnouts. Jones's intervention in the ten per cent campaign began at the end of October when he undertook a two-week tour of the manufacturing districts, urging support for Preston and enlisting recruits for the National Charter Association. In Manchester he was accompanied by John Teer, secretary of the dyers' union, while at Warrington J.B. Horsfall and Mortimer Grimshaw shared his platform. Jones arrived in Preston on 4 November. Unable to hire a hall, he went to the Marsh to address a crowd variously estimated at twelve and fifteen thousand operatives.

Inevitably Swinglehurst took the chair, while Cowell and Mathews moved the vote of thanks. (This was the same Mathews, be it noted, who was actively promoting the 'old Tory arbitration trick' masquerading as the Labour League!) Cowell met up with Jones again a week later, at Oldham, on the eve of the issue of Jones's *People's Paper* which launched his ambitious scheme for a Parliament of Labour.[91]

Before leaving London for the North, Jones had pointed to the wider implications of the lock-out, and by the time he reached Preston he was advocating a mass movement of organised labour to support the turnouts. His ideas soon found concrete expression in an editorial written for the *People's Paper* while he was still in Lancashire.

What I would recommend and urge, is this: make your organisation national at once, let mass meetings be called simultaneously in every town of the kingdom, and, at each of these an organisation be formed in connection with a great central committee (the existing Trades Unions in these towns might form the component parts of the whole, uniting their several bodies into one amalgamated committee of all trades in each district): at each of these meetings let an organised system for raising regular weekly subscriptions be adopted; where the towns are large, let them be divided into wards for that purpose.

There was nothing particularly controversial about Jones's organizational proposals, which were indeed already being implemented in many parts of the country. More novel was his advocacy of a 'Parliament of Labour': 'Let a mighty delegation from all trades assemble in the centre of action, in Lancashire, in Manchester, and remain sitting until the victory is obtained ... At a crisis like this, the ears of the world hang more on the words of the humblest of those delegates than on those of the coroneted senators of the loftiest House.' This was the Chartist Convention in a different guise, and with more limited pretensions — which were nevertheless to include, besides publicizing the cause of the Preston turnouts, supervising the conduct of their dispute.[92]

The Labour Parliament soon obtained the valuable endorsement of Grimshaw,[93] and a vote of confidence from the card room hands of Stockport.[94] Cowell's feelings were mixed. He remained a convinced Chartist, but he could not agree to diffuse the massive popular support built up around the ten per cent campaign, however noble the cause. Why not remain on strike until the Charter is achieved, he was asked at one of the large London meetings. His answer was deliberate: 'I might perhaps be inclined to go as far politically as [his questioner] — for the Charter, if you like — but, until the ten per cent is secured, I think everything else should be kept out of the question.'[95] Others were less diffident. The London trades were quick to repudiate any association with Jones and his plans. Delegates from the Manchester-based committee established to organize the first meeting of the Labour Parliament came to the weavers' delegate meeting on 29 January. After a debate in which Cowell seems to have remained silent, and Grimshaw found himself in a small minority, they were turned away without an opportunity to speak.[96] At Blackburn Edward Whittle resolutely opposed the schemes of that 'notorious political character' Ernest Jones, and

Wallace Beevers 'recommended the Manchester agitators to stay at home and mind their own business'. Thomas Rhodes concurred: 'The only "parliament" we want is the 10% parliament that now meets in the Cockpit, at Preston.'[97]

The Labour Parliament finally assembled in Manchester in the second and third weeks of March 1854, with messages of support from Louis Blanc, Victor Hugo, Proudhon and Marx. It approved an ambitious and minutely detailed constitution providing for the collection of a 'national labour revenue' in the form of a weekly levy graduated according to earnings. The funds of this 'mass movement' were to be applied in strike finance, in the purchase of land for individual or collective cultivation, and in the establishment of cooperative factories and workshops. The Parliament itself was to function as the supreme authority of the movement; between sittings, power would be vested in a small elected executive.[98] As Jones's biographer observes, 'the whole plan was wildly unpractical and utopian, and the final programme of the Labour Parliament ... is a document which belongs to 1834 rather than 1854'.[99]

Utopian or not, it continued to attract the support at least of a minority of the weavers' delegates and some of the cardroom hands (the spinners remained entirely uninvolved). Jones's views on co-operative production were now extremely close to those of the turnouts, and the donation of £172 recently received from the Mass Movement Committee[100] must have dispelled a few doubts. The exact nature of the relationship between the Labour Parliament and the Preston strike remains somewhat mysterious. Its programme, as reproduced in the *People's Paper*, concludes with 47 signatures. Along with Jones, Marx and Louis Blanc are John Teer, James Brierly of the Manchester Cotton Skin Dyers, M'Quire, Young and Smith of the 'Cardroom Hands of Lancashire, Cheshire, etc.', and seven names from Preston: Cowell, Grimshaw, Mathews, Pryce Humphreys (again the victim of misspelling), John MacLean, Wallace Beevers and the totally unknown John Westray.[101] The Parliament's meetings were open to the press, and the Manchester papers provide independent confirmation of the presence, for some of the sessions, of all but Mathews (who would hardly have missed such an occasion) and the elusive Westray. Whether they represented anyone except themselves is less certain. On 10 March Cowell and MacLean were reported as saying that 'fears were at one time entertained by some of the lockouts at Preston that the operations of the labour parliament would interfere seriously with the position of affairs at Preston; but when they returned they should disabuse the minds of any one who so thought, for they believed the services of the labour parliament would be of the greatest advantage to the working classes'.[102]

Evidently they met with little success, for only two days later Jones was refused permission to speak at the great Hoghton meeting when 'several of the operatives' committee objected to his taking any part in the proceedings, being resolved to keep the wages question apart from all others.'[103] This slight drew an immediate apology from John MacLean, apparently acting on behalf of the

Amalgamated Committee. On the following Wednesday Grimshaw and Beevers (whose conversion to support for the 'Manchester agitators' had taken less than a month) visited the Parliament and, like Cowell before them, were elected 'honorary delegates'.[104] Their involvement drew the immediate censure of the weavers' delegates, who resolved 'that no member of the Executive or Propagandist Committees be allowed to interfere with the "mass movement" . . . that the Central Committee, representing the Power Loom Weavers of the main districts, do not countenance or recognise the "mass movement" or its proceedings'.[105] As the Labour Parliament had already concluded its first (and only) session, this brusque statement marked the end of the affair.

It was a curious episode. Here we have Cowell, a man of universally recognized moderation and good sense, deeply (if uneasily) involved in a 'mad illegal Chartist scheme'. Here we have Mathews, the pillar of the Labour League, enmeshed with one of its most bitter adversaries. The weavers' most respected leaders are censured by their own committee, itself at odds with the Amalgamated Committee on which it was strongly represented. Yet those who fought against association with the Labour Parliament did so, in the main, for pragmatic rather than ideological reasons; less because they disagreed with its principles, than because they doubted its practicality. The hesitations and contradictions which the Labour Parliament exposed provide a further illustration of the difficulties facing any radical working man in the early 1850's. 'One distinct phase of the English labor movement had wrought itself out through thought and action and disillusionment,' writes the most perceptive observer of the period, 'and those whose necessities had fashioned it found themselves without a workable theory or policy, but with problems only less pressing for solution than in the years just behind them. The next two decades were to be for English workmen a critical period of transition and adjustment.'[106] The road they were eventually to take would lead them first to tactical alliances with middle-class reformers, then to implicit acceptance of bourgeois values and ideas, and finally to class collaboration and Lib-Labism. In 1854 there were still many, like Horsfall, Mathews and Grimshaw, who 'preferred Tories to Whigs'.[107] The long journey had barely begun.

If the operatives' politics were confused, their organization was remarkably effective. With the exception of the spinners, there was little in the way of formal trade unionism in the cotton industry in the early summer of 1853, and rapid improvization was called for. Here the Stockport strike was the crucial event, in which past experience was drawn on, old contacts revived, and new links forged. In Stockport itself committees representing the weavers, spinners and cardroom hands had sprung up. To render assistance to the strikers, committees were organized — or where they already existed were expanded and strengthened — in towns and villages throughout the region. These in turn sent delegates to those regular meetings which were, as the masters recognized only too clearly, embryonic trade unions in all but name. From this point developments were rapid. In mid-September, only a fortnight after a meeting of Bacup weavers had called for the foundation of a 'National Association of Factory Operatives and Power Loom Weavers', their Manchester colleagues were pledging themselves to join the 'Power Loom Weavers' Association of North and South Lancashire', a body whose origins were clearly recent in the extreme.[108] Six months later Edward Whittle, secretary of the Blackburn weavers, was already using the language of the modern trade union bureaucrat when he castigated a Chartist speaker who 'came here without the sanction of any of the operatives' committees',[109] a serious breach of union protocol.

Despite the eventual triumphant success, the mobilization of support for the Stockport turnouts revealed just how rudimentary prior organization had been. Compared with the vast sums which were to flow into Preston, the Stockport operatives were on iron rations. Documentation is sparse, but fragmentary press reports suggest that the weavers were paid less than 2s weekly in the early stages of the strike, and could have received no more than 3s 4d at the end (when subscriptions from other towns reached their peak). Over the seven or eight weeks of the dispute the *total* payments to the weavers cannot have exceeded 14s, at best one-fifth of their normal earnings for such a period. The cardroom hands subsisted on barely one third as much, while the spinners — and this casts doubt on the allegedly superior quality of their organization — were actually paid less than the weavers.[110] What was encouraging for the strikers, and deeply worrying for the millowners, was the extremely rapid growth of support as the strike proceeded. From a wholly inadequate £282 in the last week of June, contributions rose to the more satisfactory sum of £1,541 by the end (though the collections for Preston would soon be more than double this figure). To judge by the list of contributors, the operatives' organizations now encompassed almost all the cotton towns. Manchester, with battles of its own to fight, came at the bottom of the list; Rochdale and Wigan (the latter already set on the stubbornly independent course which was to lead it to disaster) were altogether absent. Only a tenth of the total had come from those Stockport operatives who had remained at work. Astonishingly, Blackburn alone supplied more than one quarter, and its close neighbours (Accrington, Darwen, Clitheroe and Great Harwood) another sixth.[111]

The organization of the Preston strike was simply an extended and refined version of the model which had served so well at Stockport. In Preston itself there were separate committees of weavers, spinners, cardroom hands and throstle-spinners. Each held its own mass meetings (the weavers more frequently than the others), collected funds on its own account, and organized its own relief payments.[112] Subscriptions collected in other towns were brought in person by the local delegates, who met to exercise collective supervision over the conduct of the dispute and the administration of the strike funds. The weavers' Sunday delegate meeting in the Cockpit became an established part of Preston life, while the spinners' delegates seem to have moved from town to town. The cardroom hands and throstle-spinners, about whom much less is known, operated on similar lines, if rather less effectively.

The various committees worked closely together, while retaining their separate identities. For the most part there was no sign of that tension between the different occupations which could sometimes be observed later in the century. Nor did the spinners — easily the highest-paid group of any size in the industry — display their accustomed aloofness. The great open-air meetings were open to all, and on occasion a spinner would appear on the weavers' platform and *vice versa*. Spinners and weavers would travel together to London to solicit support, and in times of crisis (especially at the first sign of blackleg labour) they would work together without distinction. Sectional interests and inhibitions were cast aside in the common cause, at least until the closing stages of the strike when defeat loomed large. The issue at stake must have acted as a powerful unifying influence, for 'ten per cent and no surrender' applied to all, irrespective of earnings or status. The employers unwittingly helped to cement unity. While the Stockport masters had attempted to isolate the weavers, and had failed, the Preston manufacturers refused to consider such tactics, even when the spinners weakened sufficiently to propose a compromise.[113] More than anything, though, the weavers earned the respect of their fellow turnouts. In Cowell and Grimshaw they had the two finest orators of all, men whose names would become synonymous with Preston. And they had evolved, in a matter of weeks, an organization of surprising efficiency.

The cardroom hands and throstle-spinners, on the other hand, found organization very difficult. The protracted strike at Wigan diverted attention and subscriptions away from Preston, for in Wigan the cardroom hands were (unusually) in the forefront. Only Blackburn and, to a lesser extent, Ashton raised significant sums for the almost 2,000 cardroom hands involved in the Preston dispute, and it required sustained and generous assistance from supporters outside the industry to finance the slow growth of relief payments, from a maximum of 3s 6d in November to as much as 4s 6d by April.[114] The throstle-spinners, who numbered just over four hundred, were even more heavily dependent on outside support.[115]

Even before the start of the lock-out, the weavers' weekly income exceeded £1,000. By early November this had doubled, and did not fall significantly below £2,000 until the very end of the strike some six months later. This was equivalent to the wages of perhaps 4,000 weavers.[116] It was sufficient to allow weekly relief payments first of 4s and then of 5s (virtually half-pay) to over seven thousand weavers and associated trades, and 2s or 2s 6d to several hundred assistants. Just over one-tenth of the weavers' expenditure was financed by levies on those Preston mills unaffected by the lock-out. Of the remainder, the overwhelming bulk came from the weavers of the other manufacturing towns. As in the Stockport strike, little assistance was forthcoming from Manchester, and none from Wigan. The operatives of Bury, Bacup, Burnley, Padiham and Rossendale, first engaged and then defeated in lockouts of their own, could offer little support. By the end of the strike Stockport had contributed nearly £7,000, Ashton and Darwen over £3,000, and Oldham £2,400, with Hyde, Glossop, Stalybridge, Church, Accrington and Great Harwood all well into four figures. Pride of place went, once more, to Blackburn, where it was a poor week indeed when less than £600 was collected for Preston. At the end Blackburn's accumulated contribution amounted to over £18,000, almost one-third of the total.[117]

There is no easy explanation for Blackburn's leading role. For a time in the late 1840s it had been noted for its working-class radicalism, marked by W.P. Roberts's Chartist candidature in the general election of 1847 and the (temporary) strength of trade unionism in the depression of 1846–8.[118] But by 1853 its inhabitants, still prone to riot, were aroused more easily by Irishmen or Whig–Tory rivalry than anything else. Wages were not, by the standards of the industry generally, either especially high or extremely low, though it is possible that three-and-four-loom operation was quite advanced (giving a minority of weavers very high piecework earnings). Of much greater importance were the peculiarities of the local manufacturers. Divided, vacillating and ultimately conciliatory, the Blackburn masters posed no threat to the organization of their hands, and kept them at work throughout the dispute. Perhaps, too, an accident of personality played a part. In Edward Whittle, 'the compiler of the Blackburn lists', 'our calculator Hume', the Blackburn weavers possessed an administrator of remarkable talents. Here was a man who, had he been born two generations later, would undoubtedly have taken his place in the procession of labour leaders whose careers led them 'from workmen's cottage to Windsor Castle'. Whatever the reasons, Blackburn was without doubt the linch-pin of the weavers' organization.

While the weavers occupied the centre of the stage, the achievements of the spinners were barely less impressive. Each week they collected between £600 and £700, allowing the unbroken payment of 7s to the 800 or so spinners, and lesser but still regular amounts to rather more than 2,000 piecers and bobbiners. In a number of towns spinners' and minders' associations organized the subscriptions, while towards the end of the strike the assistance was acknowledged of a 'Central Association' with substantial funds of its own. The latter body was also the probable owner of the mysterious 'inexhaustible box' which was drawn on increasingly heavily in April and May 1854. Of the individual towns, Blackburn once again headed the subscription list with Stockport and Bolton not far behind.[119]

For the most part the operatives' money was freely given and scrupulously accounted for. That a few were at best reluctant subscribers is evident from the occasional convictions of collectors for intimidation, and the cryptic references in the published balance sheets to the fate awaiting those who refused to pay. 'If that roller coverer at Eccles Mill [in Blackburn] does not pay up next week,' reads a typical item in the card-room hands' weekly report, 'Punch will pay him a visit ... If those few snobs from Rochdale do not pay next week, Punch will visit them.'[120] One Blackburn weaver claimed to have lost his job for objecting to the weekly levy, after his work-mates had threatened to strike for his dismissal.[121] Sanctions were normally of a gentler kind:

> To publish names we do not like,
> Then lads and lasses pay to those on strike,
> If you don't we this tell you,
> That Punch he will speak ill of you. (Ashton)

and

> Within these walls there are two girls
> Who will not pay their copper,
> One of their names is Ann Web [sic],
> And the other is Ann Rutter. (Chorley – Stump Mill)[122]

It is difficult to believe that small minorities were intimidating large majorities, still less sending them to Coventry. The great majority of those who contributed must have done so freely, often enthusiastically.

Nor was their trust abused. One or two cases of defalcation came to light, involving individuals who simply failed to arrive in Preston with the moneys charged to their care. These isolated cases were so ruthlessly exposed by a largely hostile press that it is unlikely that any more were concealed. Administrative expenses were not disproportionately high. In the weavers' case, just over 5% of their total income was spent on organization, and was minutely itemized. Printing and postage charges absorbed the greater part, understandably when 17,000 copies of an 8-page balance sheet had to be distributed every week. Quite a number of delegates, devoting all their energies to the campaign, had in effect become full-time employees of the weavers' committee, from which they drew their income. When the treasurer received £1 per week, however, and the secretary 15s (probably for hours which would have been illegal if worked in any cotton mill), it is unlikely that anyone grew rich at the operatives' expense.

By far the greatest part of the funds which sustained the Preston turnouts came from the operatives throughout the manufacturing districts. Their contributions were augmented from a variety of sources, including subscriptions from the general public. Preston itself was divided into 24 districts. The weekly visits of the collectors to shops and taverns produced £40 to £60 on each occasion, every individual sixpence being painstakingly accounted for and itemized in the balance sheets of the Amalgamated Committee. This body, set up in August on the initiative of the Preston craft societies, consisted of delegates from the weavers, spinners, and other cotton operatives, augmented by four delegates representing local craftsmen and small traders. Its joint secretaries were John MacLean, who had played an active part in the Preston shoemakers' agitation earlier in 1853,[123] and William Crook, a tradesman who was to stand (unsuccessfully) for the council as 'the poor man's friend'.[124]

By the beginning of 1854 the Amalgamated Committee was disbursing upwards of £600 weekly. Though middle-class contributions were welcomed, and indeed actively solicited, the committee's exertions were directed largely towards the craft unions, who revealed in their response a degree of solidarity which goes against the notion that the mid-Victorian 'labour aristocracy' was essentially inward-looking, sectional, and selfish. As might be expected, the Preston trade societies were in the forefront. On 16 October they issued a placard declaring their support for the turnouts and engaging in a bitter polemic against the mill-owners. Moral support was soon complemented by financial assistance, and contributions came from the Preston branches of the Amalgamated Society of Engineers (ASE), the cabinet makers, coachmakers, blacksmiths, moulders, carpenters and joiners, steam engine makers and tailors, while the Preston shoemakers collected money from their society's branches throughout the country. Individual activists gathered subscriptions among their workmates, and cash flowed in from the building sites, foundries, railway workshops, sawmills and tanneries, not to mention the office of the *Preston Guardian*. Even 'a Weaver turned Navvy' contributed his half-crown.[125]

Collectors besieged the general public of the cotton towns, raising substantial sums from tradesmen who, dependent for their livelihood on working-class custom, gave either gladly or grudgingly, but often with little choice in the matter. Glossop may serve as an example. Here the collectors divided the town into districts and canvassed every shopkeeper. 'At their weekly meetings they announce the names of persons who refuse to contribute,' the *Manchester Examiner* reported indignantly, 'who are represented as enemies to the working-classes.' Under the powerful threat of 'exclusive dealing', the Glossop tradespeople dipped into their pockets in large numbers. When attempts were made to 'bring ministers of the gospel under the same bondage', an Independent pastor took on the combined might of the operatives' delegates, Grimshaw and the redoubtable Mrs Fletcher among them, to denounce the 'tyranny' of the boycott.[126] Here, too — unusually — the local friendly societies made regular contributions.[127]

Among the larger provincial centres, big public meetings were arranged in Manchester, which housed the headquarters of a number of national unions. Speakers included the northern organiser of the ASE, W. Hemm, and the influential secretary of the stonemasons' society, Richard Harnott, who committed his union to a donation of £116. Smaller amounts came from the calico printers' engravers, glass cutters, moulders, printers, mechanics, millwrights, waggon makers, silk smallware weavers, and joiners.[128] The Liverpool Trades' Guardians Association had been active in the campaign for the Combination of Workmen Bill, and supported the Manchester dyers during their ill-fated strike.[129] Now the Trades' Guardians organized collections for the Preston turnouts among the Liverpool trades, drawing on the generosity of the shipwrights, tailors, tinplate men and railway workers. The whitesmiths raffled a number of bedsteads on behalf of the strikers, and a benefit concert was arranged.[130] Another concert took place under the auspices of a committee representing the Sheffield metal

The Operatives

trades,[131] while a 'theatrical performance' was put on by the Hanley potters.[132] Both committees also collected regular subscriptions, as did similar bodies in Birmingham, Derby, Nottingham and Bristol. In February 1854 the Bristol trades' committee raised £33 by means of a benefit performance at Cooke's circus.[133]

Smaller towns played their part. Meetings in support of the turnouts were held at Halifax and Barnsley.[134] Railway employees at Ashford organized a fund-raising ball, while their colleagues in Brighton made regular contributions and arranged a public meeting with the assistance of W. Conningham, the same 'gentleman of fortune' who had lent his support to the ASE during the great engineering lock-out of 1852.[135] From Newton Abbot to Stockton-on-Tees, from Norwich to Chippenham, branches of the ASE itself featured in the balance sheets. A multitude of provincial craft societies responded to the call. The shoemakers of Barnsley, Stafford, Bristol, Cambridge, and Bedford; the iron-moulders of Ipswich, Stockton and Bridgwater; the blacksmiths of Smethwick and Gloucester; the coachmakers of Wolverhampton, Bolton, Bedford, Leicester and Derby; the tailors of Bradford, Newcastle, Cambridge and Bristol: the Preston operatives gratefully acknowledged their aid. Tinplate workers in Belfast, shipwrights on the Wear, flint glass makers at York, the Lace Trades' Society of Radford, near Nottingham, bricklayers at Bristol and Hull, even the 'non-society boilermakers' of Swindon and Portsea, all collected. From Newcastle, assistance arrived from the Society of Philanthropic Coopers; from Birmingham, the Iron Wire Drawers lent their support; from Stoke, the men at the railway station contributed.[136]

North of the border, committees flourished in tiny Galashiels and Hawick, while the Edinburgh Society of Typefounders drew on its funds.[137] Relatively little in the way of financial assistance came from Glasgow, for the Scottish cotton operatives had troubles of their own. The Glasgow weavers spent the autumn fighting a series of strikes to press their own wage demands, while the spinners were distracted by a lengthy (though partial) lock-out which began just after Christmas. Cowell's visit at the end of December attracted considerable sympathy, but it was not until Easter 1854 that the Glasgow trades' delegates could turn their undivided attention to collecting for Preston.[138] Support came from even further afield, in the form of donations from well-wishers in Fall River, Massachusetts, and from members of the Amalgamated Engineers in Canada and Rio de Janeiro.[139]

But, outside the manufacturing districts, it was London which provided the most valuable assistance, both moral and pecuniary. The metropolis was, of course, the undisputed focus of the country's political and constitutional affairs. Since the decline of Chartism, with its deep roots in the manufacturing areas of the north, the leading role of London in English radicalism had increased still further. Above all, if the complex, fragmented web of trade unionism could be said to have a geographical centre, then it was to be found on the Thames. Excepting only the cotton operatives and coal miners, the overwhelming majority of trade unionists in the 1850s were craftsmen. And London contained not only the headquarters of the greatest of all the craft unions, the ASE, but easily the largest single concentration of skilled tradesmen in the nation.

There were in London four groupings which took up the cause of Preston: two factions comprising the rump of the Chartist movement; the National Association of United Trades for the Protection of Labour (NAUT); and the Metropolitan Trades' Delegates. The differences between these bodies reflected divisions over emphasis and tactics rather than fundamental principles, but they were sufficient to encourage each to intervene independently. Chartism, if only a shadow of its former self, remained in 1853 (especially in London) very much a living entity. Bronterre O'Brien, with Feargus O'Connor perhaps the most famous of all the Chartist leaders, had settled in Soho, where his dedicated followers remained active into the final quarter of the century. The Chartist mainstream was represented by the National Charter Association, now under the unquestioned control of Ernest Jones. Jones and O'Brien had become bitter personal enemies, O'Brien's jealousy of the success of the *People's Paper* having much to do with the feud between them.[140]

The NAUT had 'preached economic heresy' since its formation in 1845, asserting the need for a national federation of trades unions to assist each other in strikes and lock-outs, promote arbitration, develop cooperative production, and initiate legislation favourable to the interests of labour. Its president was the celebrated Radical MP for Finsbury and latter-day John Wilkes, Thomas Slingsby Duncombe. Unable to secure the affiliation of any significant number of craft societies, the NAUT was nevertheless not without influence. Its sympathizers were active in Preston in the later 1840's, and in 1850–1 the Association organised the defence of striking Wolverhampton tinplate workers who had been charged with criminal conspiracy. Early in 1853 it waged an energetic (if eventually unsuccessful) campaign to amend the law so as to prevent similar prosecutions in future disputes.[141]

If the craft unions remained aloof from both the Chartists and the NAUT, they were by no means isolated from each other. 'The organization of the London Trades was in fact nearly continuous, at any rate from the period just after the Napoleonic Wars.'[142] From 1848 their organization had been known as the Metropolitan Trades' Delegates, at whose meetings 'were promulgated doctrines as much at variance with middle-class conceptions as those of Chartists or Socialists'. In 1849 the Delegates had advocated nationalization of the land as the only solution for unemployment, as well as manhood suffrage and the establishment of local 'boards of trade' (on the French pattern) to arbitrate in industrial disputes. Three years later they called for a return to the protection of domestic industry, while one of their most distinguished members, William Newton of the ASE, lectured on 'Labour, the legitimate source of all wealth'.

The Operatives

In the same year, 1852, Newton stood for Parliament in Tower Hamlets, perhaps 'the first independent labour candidacy' in British history. His platform, while revealing Newton's 'fourfold character of Chartist, Christian Socialist, trade unionist and Liberal', was close enough to that of the Chartists to win the virtual endorsement of the ultra-purist Ernest Jones.[143]

In the early months of 1852 the Delegates came to the aid of the ASE in its momentous battle with the engineering employers.[144] The lock-out threw out of work not only members of the Society but also labourers and several thousand skilled men who were not ASE members. The labourers were in effect left to fend for themselves, but the non-Society craftsmen, as potential blacklegs, had to be supported by the union. With the active support of the Metropolitan Trades' Delegates some £5,000 was contributed by other societies,[145] but this did not prevent a crushing defeat for the ASE. The Trades' Delegates were sufficiently impressed by the affair to resolve 'that in consequence of the rapid succession of industrial disputes, this meeting is of the opinion that a federation of the trades of Britain, for deliberation on trades matters, is necessary to prevent a recurrence of similar disastrous events'.[146] Although nothing concrete came of the Delegates' decision, its theme was close enough to the platform of the NAUT to indicate that the two bodies, though organizationally distinct, had much in common.

To the London craft societies, events at Preston must have appeared as an unwelcome but almost exact replica of the great engineering lock-out. The manufacturers' tactic — a sympathetic lock-out — was identical, and their aim — the suppression of trade unionism — was similar. Barely a fortnight after the lock-out began the executive committee of the ASE voted £50 to the strike fund, and the small typefounders' union agreed on a weekly levy, evidently without knowing how to forward the proceeds to Preston. In anticipation of similar decisions, and to avoid further uncertainty, the Metropolitan Trades' Delegates began a series of weekly meetings at the Bell Inn which were to continue for over seven months.[147] By the middle of November the NAUT, too, had issued a manifesto urging support for the Preston turnouts and using the dispute as further proof of the need for a general federation of the trades. Probably the National Association was behind the 'committee and friends of the Preston operatives' whose meeting on 20 November was addressed by George Cowell, on the first of several visits to London. Cowell visited the Metropolitan Trades' Delegates on the following Thursday, having attended an abortive public meeting in Finsbury the day before. The meeting, chaired by Charles Sturgeon of the NAUT, was abandoned when it attracted only a few dozen people. Its failure, blamed on dense fog, was perhaps also indicative of the NAUT's inability to marshal the London unions in the face of the successful efforts of the Trades' Delegates.[148]

During November Cowell seems to have spent about ten days in London.[149] On the 30th he returned to Finsbury for a meeting convened by the Chartist 'committee in aid of the Preston operatives', where he shared the platform with Ernest Jones, James Finlen and Bronterre O'Brien.[150] After a brief trip to Lancashire, Cowell came south again with John Mathews to address a large public meeting in the National Hall in Holborn. By now three of the four groups supporting Preston — the NAUT, the Delegates and the O'Brienites — had coalesced. Sturgeon took the chair, and speakers included his associate William Peel (secretary of the NAUT), G.W. Prideaux of the Metropolitan Trades Delegates, and O'Brien, whose advocacy of communism seems to have outraged no-one.[151] This time Mathews, accompanied by John Bowman, stopped in London to visit the Delegates, whose ranks were now swollen by the affiliation of the NAUT.[152] The latter organization had evidently taken offence at Ernest Jones's proposed 'Mass Movement', and now actively distanced themselves from Jones. F. Green, an executive member of the NAUT and current chairman of the Trades' Delegates, disclaimed any connection with Jones, whose *People's Paper* had until recently carried a weekly column under his signature.[153] His colleague William Peel was equally forthright, and

warned the delegates and all industrial associations to beware of political adventurers, and not to be misled by the cry of a labour movement which, whatever might be its real merits, was quite out of place at the present time, and especially in connection with a movement which had solely for its object the rendering of moral and pecuniary aid to the Preston operatives.[154]

In London, if not in the north, Jones was now increasingly isolated.

By the first week in January the Delegates were handling upwards of £200 each week. Their accounts, faithfully recorded in *Reynolds' Newspaper*, read like a directory of the London craft societies. Carpenters and joiners at several large building sites took up regular collections, while joiners' societies based at such taverns as the Running Horse, the Blue Coat Boy and the Warwick Arms passed the hat round every week, or voted donations from their accumulated funds. Other contributors included the enigmatically titled brass cock finishers, along with cabinet makers, block-coopers, tinplate workers, smiths, stove makers, engineers, masons, painters, silver spoon makers, tailors, silk hatters, shoemakers, compositors, bookbinders, cigar makers, coachsmiths, umbrella and parasol weavers, gilders, wheelwrights, mat weavers, upholsterers, paper stainers, printing machine managers, pattern and model makers, curriers, zinc workers, lithographic printers, ships' caulkers and bricklayers.[155] With the help of the cabmen, collecting boxes were placed in more than 100 London inns.[156] Late in January a theatrical benefit was held at the Drury Lane Theatre, graced by the presence of 'two or three Members of Parliament, and several barristers of eminence'.[157] By April the Delegates had dispatched over £2,000 to Preston, and a similar sum, obtained through their efforts, had been sent direct to the Amalgamated Committee.[158]

All in all the Amalgamated Committee received a total of £12,143 during the dispute, or slightly less than one eighth of all the money collected by the turnouts. Its largest single source of income – some £1,600 – was the public (as opposed to the organised trades) of Preston itself. The ASE contributed almost as much: £720 (including a single donation of £500) voted by the central executive of the union, with a further £826 from its various branches. Carpenters and joiners raised a total of £627. Not far behind came the shipwrights (£508), printing trades (£448), stonemasons (£439), iron moulders (£309), boilermakers (£300), boot- and shoemakers (£233), tailors (£232), coachmakers (£224), and a host of minor trades. Of the provincial cities, the Manchester committee raised slightly less than £900, Liverpool nearly £500, Sheffield £285 and Bristol and the Potteries almost £200 each. A little over one-tenth of the Amalgamated Committee's income was consumed by administrative expenses, the great bulk in connection with the printing of placards and balance sheets. The remainder, almost £11,000, was made over to the four operatives' committees. Nearly one third (£3,074) went to the weavers; in relation to their numbers, the spinners' £2,204 was surprisingly considerably larger. Reckoning proportionally, though, the lion's share went to the cardroom hands and the throstle-spinners, whose own financial resources were exceedingly meagre. Almost a half of the cardroom hands' total expenditure of £9,904 was financed by the Amalgamated Committee (who provided £4,642), and well over a third of the throstle-spinners' (£915 out of £2,476).[159] For the weavers and spinners the trades had provided more of a moral impetus; for the other groups, their assistance was a financial lifeline.

Nº 1 of the PRESTON LOCK-OUT ILLUSTRATED

"WELL MASTER, YOU MUST COMPELL THE OTHER HAIR PEOPLE FOR WITH ME AND GOOD MAKE AN EXCHANGE WITH THOSE KNOBSTICKS WILL NEVAIR DO I MUST SEND THEM BACK A GAIN WHERE THEY COME FROM"

"WILL MANAGER"

"I AM COMMING FOR THE LARGE FIRM Mr THOU GRINDER TIME IS UP OF THE POOR"

A BOX FULL OF NEW KNOBSTICKS
THEY COST FIVE SHILLINGS CARRAGE

MANAGER   Mr LARGE FIRM

Nº 2 THE PRESTON LOCK-OUT
ILLUSTRATIONS TO BE
CONTINUED.

THE SKILLED HANDS OR LOCK-OUTS   RECRUITING SERGANT AT B's FACTORY NORTH ROAD

4 The Masters

> Have you not heard the news of late,
> About some mighty men so great,
> I mean the swells of Fishergate,
> > The Cotton Lords of Preston.
> They are a set of stingy Blades,
> They've lock'd up all their Mills and Shades,
> So now we've nothing else to do,
> But come a singing songs for you,
> So with our ballads we've come out,
> To tramp the country round about,
> And try if we cannot live without,
> > The Cotton Lords of Preston.

The millowners of Preston were distinguished chiefly by their individual and collective mediocrity. Other cotton towns could boast their Cobdens, their Brights, their Ashworths, their Fieldens: men with a reputation extending beyond the view of their factory chimneys, noted for achievements in fields other than the spinning of yarn and the amassing of great wealth. Proud Preston, once the home of Horrocks and Arkwright, still produced fortunes but no longer celebrities. Apart from Charles Swainson's unsuccessful candidature in 1841, even the Parliamentary representation of the borough had been left for outsiders to contest. Only two of its citizens in this period found their way (at any length) into print. One was the prison chaplain, and the other a wholesale cheese merchant.[1]

Most important of the Preston employers was Thomas Miller, sole proprietor of the great concern known as Horrockses, Miller and Co., and easily the richest man in Preston. Chairman of the Masters' Association throughout the dispute, Miller was the son of a small manufacturer from Bolton who had come to work for the Horrockses at the turn of the century, and had married the sister of John and Samuel Horrocks, whose partner he soon became. As the firm grew the Horrockses gradually loosened their connection with it, and the elder Miller's influence became increasingly pronounced. Born in 1811, his son Thomas was educated in Manchester and Paris. He too married a Horrocks, and took over command of the firm (which now employed some 2,000 hands) on his father's death in 1840.

Like his father, Thomas Miller played the part expected of him in the government and administration of justice in Preston, serving as a borough and county magistrate and as an alderman. These responsibilities apart, Miller was not especially prominent in public life. He rarely spoke at public meetings, and seems to have had no Parliamentary ambitions. His political allegiance lay with the conservative wing of the Liberal party, and in the general election of 1852 he had sponsored the candidature of C.P. Grenfell. He had actively opposed the Ten Hours Act of 1847 — a rare display of direct political involvement — and conspicuously failed to support the more radical Sir George Strickland, who was immensely popular with the operatives for his vigorous advocacy of Factory Reform.

Thomas Miller aroused conflicting emotions. 'Mr. Miller was both by personal bearing and education a gentleman', the *Preston Guardian* was to write in an obituary which was no less fulsome than the occasion demanded.

The son of a man who had risen from the people, he had none of those unpleasant traits of character which are too commonly attributed to the cotton lords of Lancashire. Of simple and retiring habits, with a thoroughly English love for his home, and with that taste for the fine arts which marks the person of refined nature, he was one of those men who would adorn any rank of life.

In 1853 the weavers took a rather less charitable view of a man who, in George Cowell's words, 'had become notorious for screwing down the operatives in his employ', paying miserly wages and maintaining harsh discipline in his mills. That Miller was a stern and self-righteous man is suggested by his (infrequent) public utterances during the strike, and also by a curious incident in his past. In 1845 he had refused the opportunity to become mayor. A year later he would willingly have accepted the office, but was now denied it through a devious manoeuvre by which the Preston Tories achieved the re-election of John Paley Junior, thereby securing his appointment as a magistrate. The embittered Miller vowed never to accept the mayoralty, and adhered to his decision for the rest of his life, despite several subsequent approaches. In Thomas Miller the operatives had a stubborn and unforgiving opponent.[2]

The secretary of the Masters' Association for much of the dispute was Miller's friend and neighbour, William Ainsworth. Four years older than Miller, Ainsworth was the son of an established cotton manufacturer. Unable, as a Unitarian, to penetrate the religious barrier surrounding Oxford and Cambridge, he was sent to Glasgow University, and returned to Preston with the intention of practising law. After spending some time articled to a local solicitor, Ainsworth was persuaded by his father to join the family business. This was one of the biggest concerns in Preston, employing in 1853 some 800 hands.

William Ainsworth sat on both borough and county benches, and had served for several years as a municipal councillor. In recent years he had become increasingly conservative in outlook. Previously he had been a Free Trade zealot, Factory Reformer, founder of the Preston Operative Reform Association, and even (in 1848) a supporter of Joseph Hume's 'little Charter' movement. In the Parliamentary election of 1852, however, he plumped for C.P. Grenfell, spurning Strickland whom he had nominated for election in 1841 and again in 1847. William Ainsworth's drift to the right had little effect on relations with his hands, for these had always been stormy, with frequent turnouts and the invariable prosecution of the strikers. His apparent manipulation of the Town Council in the strange case of the magisterial appointment of Miles Rodgett and Edward Hollins only served to increase the unpopularity of this 'Louis Napoleon of Preston'.[3]

Between them, Miller and Ainsworth dominated the Masters' Association, the other large manufacturers being content to leave the dispute in their hands. Very little is known about the majority of the Preston masters. Three of the Association's largest member firms were controlled by two Tory dynasties, the Swainsons and the Birleys. The former were in their third generation as cotton lords, and Charles Swainson (of the second generation) had been the last millowner to attempt a Parliamentary career (he was defeated in 1841). The Birleys, for their part, represented the Kirkham branch of a large landed family whose connections, by marriage, included both the Swainsons and the Hornbys of Blackburn (themselves millowners of considerable status). Hugh Hornby Birley, notorious for his part in the Peterloo massacre, was also a relative.[4]

Like the Swainsons and Birleys, the Paley family, proprietors of perhaps the third largest enterprise in Preston, were active Tories and deeply involved in local affairs. John Paley Senior, in 1853 an octogenarian (though still an alderman and magistrate), was a self-made man whose rise in the world might have been taken from the works of Samuel Smiles. Beginning his working life as an apprentice wheelwright and joiner in Pateley Bridge, he crossed the Pennines in 1792, working as a joiner for John Horrocks. Seven years later he opened a small engineering works. 'There being at that time no foundry in Preston, Mr. Paley not unfrequently [sic] walked to Wigan, carrying a model and bringing back in the same way the casting required.' Soon he built his own factory and, with assistance from John Horrocks, branched out into cotton spinning. Truly he was 'the architect of his own fortune, raising himself from the humble rank of an artizan to that of a wealthy employer of labour; from the joiner's bench to the highest office in the municipality'. John Paley Junior, whose tussles with Thomas Miller have been noted, found time to combine management of the family business with a wide range of municipal duties; he was also a deputy lieutenant of Lancashire.[5]

John and William Humber, owners of one of the largest firms in Preston, and sons of a local corn merchant, were Tories too.[6] John Humber served for a time as secretary to the Association. John Hawkins, also a leading millowner, was a Liberal of radical inclinations, long a supporter of Strickland and in earlier days an advocate of Free Trade. This did not prevent his being hooted in his own mill in the tense summer months of 1853.[7] George Smith had begun life as a piecer before helping to manage his father's warehouses and finally becoming a manufacturer. He too was a Liberal, whose earlier radicalism (like that of his friend William Ainsworth) had become somewhat attenuated.[8] C.R. Jacson, son of one of Horrocks's partners and owner of Horrocks, Jacson and Co., was a Tory Anglican. He had recently joined John Paley Junior as a deputy lieutenant of the county, and also served as a member of its General Finance Committee. 'He does not care much for cotton,' according to a later description, 'and never particularly worshipped it'.[9] In this respect, at least, he was exceptional.

Outside the Masters' Association stood Joseph Gillow, a small manufacturer and leader of the town's Roman Catholic community. Gillow was a devoted supporter of Sir George Strickland, whose candidacy he had secured in the election of 1847 against opposition from the more 'Whiggish' of the Preston Liberals.[10] The Factory Reformer Robert Gardner, pioneer of the celebrated short-time experiment in the 1840s, also stood aloof from the Association.[11] Easily the most prominent figure among the non-members, however, was John Goodair. Goodair was not quite the 'manufacturer who had risen from the working classes' that his former employee George Cowell had made him out to be. He was in fact the son of a London cotton merchant who risked his capital in spinning ventures in Stockport and Chorley, lost it, and returned to the metropolis. The thirteen-year-old John Goodair stayed behind. After attending Stockport and Chorley Grammar Schools, he worked for a time as a warper in the latter town, moving to Preston in 1838 as manager of a silk and gingham works. Six years later he set up on his own account in the cotton trade, and 'by his untiring industry and almost superhuman exertions' expanded the business until it ranked second only to Horrockses and Miller in the hierarchy of Preston cotton manufacturing. Goodair was an Anglican, a recognized authority on the cotton industry, and since 1847 a borough councillor. In politics he was a Liberal, and had chaired Sir George Strickland's election committee in 1852. As the ten per cent dispute began, he was helping his son Richard to expand his own cotton business.[12]

The associated masters of Preston numbered in their ranks radical Liberals and traditional Tories, dedicated Free Traders and erstwhile Protectionists, Nonconformists and Anglicans. Political wrangling and religious debate were not allowed to intrude upon the serious business of dealing with a workforce in revolt. In their conception of the ten per cent campaign the millowners never wavered. They simply drew upon the ideology of their class, a compendium of economic laws, moral values and plain hard-headed common sense which cut across all political and personal barriers to give them a unity of purpose and an unfaltering belief in the righteousness of their cause. When the Earl of Derby visited Bury in November he met the local manufacturers, who 'talked often of the strike, which had partly reached them: their tone respecting it was that of the most invincible determination to win, without either anger against, or compassion for, their opponents.'[13] As at Bury, so in Preston.

The most detailed public statement of the masters' position appeared after the defeat of the turnouts, in the form of the *Final Report* of the Manufacturers' Defence Fund. In it the millowners regretted that the operatives had failed to learn from the bitter experience of their 1836 defeat. 'By the results of this strike, and the events which shortly followed, they had it practically proved to them that the regulation of the price of labour was as little in the power of the employer, as in that of the employed.' After the defeat of the turnouts, in the normal course of trade, the laws of supply and demand had given them higher wages. Similarly, market pressures had pushed up the earnings of all classes of hands since the wage reductions of 1847. Thus, even if the rates prevailing in 1853 were not the equilibrium ones, 'the facts here detailed prove that, without any violent or artificial interference, the inexorable law of mercantile economy would have – perhaps insensibly, but unerringly – adjusted any material inequality, more certainly and effectually than the most favourable combination'.

As trade improved early in 1853, the masters claimed, the ten per cent had been restored. Then the unions 'sought to raise the minimum earnings to the current maximum rates; thus abandoning the original conditions of peace'. The operatives were willing to accept the wage increases already conceded, but the union leaders would not permit it. 'No alternative was left to the employers but to protect themselves from this dictation – to meet conspiracy by combination – and to show that, so long as they maintained their establishments, they were determined to be masters of their own property.' The defence of their rights had cost the Preston masters some £165,000, but the burden on the operatives was much heavier. They had forfeited the ten per cent; employment opportunities had declined, because of the waste of capital, the cessation of new investment, and the introduction of labour-saving machinery; new hands had been introduced; 'and last, though not least', came 'the alienation of those kindly sentiments of mutual regard which ought always to exist between persons whose interests are so closely connected as those of the employers and the operatives in the cotton trade'. The blame for all this lay with the delegates: 'by the tyranny and machinery of secret combination, they have forced 26,000 persons ... to place themselves in ungrateful antagonism to the very establishments on whose prosperity they solely depend for their subsistence'.[14]

In earlier statements the manufacturers had given more details of their grievances. They were concerned that the operatives, organized into a powerful union stretching 'from London to Glasgow', were intent on a general (and extremely costly) levelling-up of wages.[15] Even more disquieting was the apparent collapse of their authority inside their mills. At one establishment, in the summer of 1853, the secretary of the spinners' union had called to demand the dismissal of an overlooker. Another firm was threatened with a strike to secure the reinstatement of a dismissed overlooker. When the hands at a third mill struck against the sacking of an operative for alleged idleness, they 'brought an itinerant band of music outside the mill, and danced and played in ridicule and defiance of their employers'.[16] John Hawkins (he who was hooted in his own mill) produced an impressive list of grievances. His hands refused him permission to train dressers; read press accounts of the Stockport strike while at work; and physically assaulted overlookers and weavers who refused to subscribe to the relief of the Stockport turnouts. In the manufacturers' eyes this insubordination was 'subversive of all good order and discipline in their establishments'.[17] Many of them, no doubt, agreed with Henry Ashworth that more than the smooth running of the mills was at stake. For Ashworth, incidents such as these posed a threat to discipline 'alike in public establishments and private families'. By assailing the right of the individual to do what he wished with his own, it could have only one result — Communism.[18]

Employers' complaints about the 'dictation' of trade unions were as common in this period[19] as operatives' grievances about the despotism of their masters (if less well founded). 'Depend on it,' Richard Cobden had told his brother in 1842, 'nothing can be got by fraternising with trades unions. They are founded upon principles of brutal tyranny and [even worse!] monopoly. I would rather live under a Dey [Bey?] of Algiers than a Trades Committee.'[20] In the same — admittedly tempestuous — year Cobden's colleague in the Anti-Corn Law League, W. Cooke Taylor, had gone even further. 'I have on various occasions received abundant evidence', he wrote, 'that the tyranny of Trades Unions is not a shade less cruel or less unscrupulous than that of Robespierre and the Jacobins.'[21]

For 1853 this was a bit strong: even Mortimer Grimshaw was not advocating the use of the guillotine (not in public, anyway). In their own public utterances during the strike, both Cobden and John Bright were unusually circumspect. Neither produced a forthright denunciation of the turnouts, Cobden using the dispute as evidence of the need for more education, and Bright losing himself in a maze of circumlocutions.[22] In a private letter to Ashworth, though, Cobden attacked the delegates' 'refusal to give to men the right of individual action and judgement in a matter affecting their own subsistence'. This he saw (and underlined) as *'the worst of all tyranny'*.[23] 'Why is Free Trade in Labour not to be allowed also?' asked the Wilmslow manufacturer Samuel Robinson, in his (generally) accurately-titled *Friendly Letters* to his operatives. Were the delegates not responsible for 'a regular system of coercion and intimidation?'[24] The millowners concluded, with Henry Ashworth, that both they and the operatives must be defended from 'the mischievous interference and terrorism of Trades' Unions'.[25]

Interference from third parties, however well-intentioned, was no more to be tolerated. Charles Dickens found this surprising. 'Gentlemen are found in great manufacturing towns, ready enough to extol imbecile mediation with dangerous madmen abroad', he complained after his visit to Preston early in 1854. 'Can none of them be brought to think of authorised mediation and explanation at home?'[26] For the most part, they could not. 'Arbitration, so much recommended, can do nothing in disputes of this kind.' This was Bright's verdict on the Preston strike, which merely rehearsed arguments put forward by the Preston masters themselves.

> It is not necessary, nor is it possible that wages should be the same in all towns in Lancashire, or even in all the mills in Preston – differences in size and perfection in machinery – in speed – in quality of cotton worked, in quality of preparation, that is, in carding, roving etc., in fineness of yarn spun or cloth woven – all this affects wages earned, and no person living could come to any conclusion [on] questions of this kind. How absurd to think of arbitrating the price of corn; it is equally so when wages are in dispute.[27]

In short, the employers' case was broadly this. The interests of masters and men were identical. There was no rational basis for conflict between capital and labour, because neither one could survive without the co-operation of the other. Wages depended on the impersonal and irresistible laws of supply and demand, and were best left to the higgling of the market. Interference by the state in their operation was unthinkable; interference by organized bodies of workers was either futile or (an ambiguity never fully resolved) damaging to the operatives themselves. Within the mills the writ of the master must run supreme. Unions were at best the construction of ignorant and misguided men, at worst the creatures of unscrupulous agitators. They invariably oppressed the helpless individual operative, who suffered from their tyranny no less than his master. It was the moral duty of the employer, as well as his right, to resist their dictation by whatever means proved necessary, even if this entailed – *in extremis* – resorting to a defensive combination of his own.

There were certain inconsistencies in this position. The manufacturers' own campaign against the Corn Laws was still fresh in the minds of many, who remembered how vigorously the millowners themselves had agitated. One letter to the *Burnley Mentor* bore the following sardonic heading: ' "Agitation is the only means in your power. It will crown your efforts with glory, and be a blessing to the country at large" Richard Cobden'.[28] More serious was the apparent contradiction between the rugged individualism of the manufacturers' political economy, on the one hand, and the blatant collectivism of their masters' association, on the other. They defended themselves against the charge of hypocrisy with a repeated and almost desperate insistence that *their* combination was an act of self-defence. William Bashall Junior was doubtless sincere when he proclaimed that 'having a great objection to unions of all sorts, I did not join the Masters' Association until after my weavers turned out and insisted upon being paid a higher rate of wages than was paid by other parties'.[29] Another Preston employer (anonymous, but probably a Birley) was less convincing when he claimed, in a letter to *The Times*, that the Masters' Association in the town had been reorganized only *after* the commencement of the Stockport strike. It is difficult to regard this as anything other than a deliberate lie.[30]

Amidst the bluster there lurked some more positive ideas concerning the relationship between employer and employed. In his *Friendly Letters* Robinson cited with approval Sir Thomas Talfourd's pronouncement at Stafford Assizes: 'If I were asked what is the great want of English Society, I would say in one word, the want is the *want of sympathy*.' Sympathy might best be fostered, many believed, and scheming agitators rendered impotent, by a comprehensive paternalism of the kind advocated by such dissimilar mid-Victorian notables as Hugh Tremenheere and Edwin Chadwick.[31] The case was put most eloquently by Sir J.P. Kay-Shuttleworth in January 1854.

> Every master must look to the sewerage of his factory village; he must improve his cottages; make his schools models of order and intelligence; diligently work his benefit societies, savings banks, and annuity clubs; provide for the education of the young men and women in evening schools; promote the healthful recreation of all his dependents [a telling term]; and give constant, earnest and practical proofs of the presiding influence of his sympathy and intelligence. Before such a system socialism will disappear like a mist before the sun.

To avoid any misunderstanding, Kay-Shuttleworth made it clear that he was referring to 'that form of socialism which manifests itself in the trades' unions'.[32]

Some of the larger Preston millowners had began to put these ideas into practice. Right up to the Cotton Famine, for example, Horrockses and Miller guaranteed employment for their hands, whatever the state of trade, and 'a situation under that firm was considered as equivalent to a life-long provision for its holders'. Life-long indeed, for retiring operatives with long service were granted pensions.[33] In the 1840s Paul Catterall opened an evening school with eight teachers, in addition to a mill Chapel and mill Sunday School, libraries and hot and cold baths for his adult hands. The prison chaplain John Clay was rapturous.

> I desire to express my sense of the immense benefits which *do*, and must, follow, such measures as those of Messrs. Catterall. The operative in their employment must be blind indeed if he do not see that his masters' welfare and his own are bound together. A happy effect must be wrought on the sentiments of all parties, when employers and employed, acting in mutual reliance on each other, through the busy week, 'meet in the House of God as friends', on the Sabbath.[34]

Other Preston manufacturers had begun to follow suit.[35]

Both Miller and Catterall were members of the Masters' Association. Added significance is given to their views by the fact that they were shared by John Goodair, the most important of the manufacturers who remained outside the Association and refused to join the lock-out. Goodair was no friend of trade unions. In 1848 he had been denounced at a public meeting of operatives for threatening to dismiss any of his hands who joined the (short-lived) weavers' union. In his defence against the charge — in which he claimed only to dissuade his operatives from membership, rather than forbidding it — Goodair revealed the existence of a curious system for resolving grievances in his mill. If a weaver felt he had been fined unfairly, he could submit his case to arbitration by two parties, one chosen by himself and one by Goodair. Evidently 'noisy agitators' were excluded from the system.[36]

Goodair's views were expressed at much greater length in his pamphlet,

The Masters

Strikes Prevented, which appeared later in 1854.[37] Significantly, the frontispiece contained the same statement by Justice Talfourd which Samuel Robinson had cited. 'The main cause' of strikes, Goodair believed, 'is a want of cordial feeling — the absence, in fact, of a good understanding between the parties to the labour contract.' This is largely the fault of the *employer*, for neglecting the educational and moral development of his operatives. 'What wonder if they take the hands of self-elected leaders as blind as themselves, who lead them, perhaps unwittingly, into snares and pitfalls. It is *our* duty to lead them, and if we do not perform it, the consequences will recoil upon ourselves.' The master should choose his overlookers and tacklers with care, and pay his hands on Friday, rather than Saturday, so that the money goes home to the family, not straight into the alehouse. He should set up sick clubs in his mill to foster 'habits of mutual assistance and sympathy between the operatives themselves', for 'it is plain to every one that operatives who have acquired habits of saving are much more likely to be well-conducted, and to recognise the responsibility of property, than those who live from hand to mouth'. (And, of course, they will be less likely to strike.) Above all else, education is important, since 'the great desideratum now wanted in the factories is intelligent labour'. Goodair used his mill fines (symbol of industrial authority!) to endow a library in the mill, run by the operatives themselves (subject to his right of veto). He organized and chaired operatives' discussion groups on political economy, and on the conduct and discipline of the mill. Far from threatening discipline, this produced cordial feeling between himself and his hands, served to prevent strikes, and (it is implied) rendered unions quite superfluous.

In 1853, if not in 1848, Goodair was genuinely popular among the operatives at large. The irony is that his underlying philosophy, with its insistence upon a harmony of interests within which the operative must be content to remain subordinate to his omniscient master, differed very little from that of the despised members of the Masters' Association. Only the detailed implementation of this perspective marked out Goodair as more 'enlightened' than his competitors. So little information has survived concerning the other Preston firms which worked throughout the dispute that it will probably never be known whether such enlightened measures were typical. In all probability they were not, though (as will shortly be seen) paternalism of a more traditional kind played an important role in events at Blackburn.

In matters of political economy Goodair was entirely orthodox. Quite the reverse was true of Joseph Gillow who, in two remarkable letters to the local press in December 1853,[38] denounced 'the grasping eagerness of employers to extend their business far beyond any reasonable bounds'. This, he suggested, was the source of over-production and hence of trade depression, and the ten per cent should be paid as a stimulus to purchasing power. (Gillow's views were no doubt the product of his own bitter experience in the slump of 1847—8, when he had found himself on the very edge of bankruptcy.)[39] He rounded off his exposition of an underconsumptionism more popular in radical working-class circles than amongst cotton masters with a call for legislation against employers' associations!

It was well that no such statute existed, for by 1853 organizations of employers in the cotton trade had a considerable history. Their history, however, was a rather intermittent one. The Preston association had to be revived early in 1853. That no association was functioning in Manchester at the beginning of the ten per cent campaign is suggested by the appearance in the press of letters from employers proposing the foundation of just such an organization, which was duly established early in July 1853. The almost simultaneous meeting of masters from the entire county attracted 350 millowners, who agreed to the formation of a central federation and, significantly, of local associations in each town.[40] The masters' associations of Burnley, Todmorden and Ashton (the latter including the substantial hinterland of Stalybridge, Dukinfield, Hyde and Glossop) were not formally constituted until September.[41]

In Preston the masters declared that the revival of their Association was a purely defensive reaction to the growing indiscipline and excessive demands of their hands in the early summer of 1853. From the special correspondent of the *Times*, sent to Preston in November, came a detailed refutation of this claim which, if he was correct, was a deliberate fabrication. The Preston Masters' Association, he reported, had operated continuously since 1836, co-ordinating the wage cuts of 1839, 1842 and 1847, and had met twice in March of 1853, well before (according to the masters' own account) their hands had formed a union. By the end of that month the Association had a committee, whose directions were to be binding upon the members; agreement had been reached upon a levy of five shillings per horse-power employed; and a rule had been fixed requiring a discharge note from all spinners seeking employment.[42]

Some of the material in the *Times* report is so detailed that its authenticity is hard to doubt,[43] but its unqualified portrayal of the Masters' Association as the aggressor is less firmly established. The spinners' union at least was very active early in 1853, in other towns if not in Preston, and especially in Bolton, whence the Preston millowners had good reason to anticipate trouble. And there is no direct evidence of the Association's role in 1842 or 1847. Possibly the frequency with which Ainsworth took the lead in reducing wages, and thereby provoking strikes,[44] indicates that he was acting as the trail-blazer for other firms, but it may equally reflect nothing more than the size of his firm and its prominence in the minds of local reporters. It is hardly a substantial basis on which to rest a conclusion that the Masters' Association had acted in concert throughout. No evidence has been uncovered of any public statement by the Association between 1836 and 1853, nor of any intervention by it in, for example, the rash of strikes which broke out in 1849.[45] Moreover, the problems of internal discipline from which the Association was to suffer – and about which more will be said below

The Masters

– point against the *Times*'s insinuation of a continuous organizational unity among the manufacturers.

It is unlikely that this question will ever be resolved with any certainty. As was often observed at the time, the masters functioned behind closed doors, telling the outside world as little as possible about their operations. Samuel Kydd cited the founder of political economy, no less, on this subject. Adam Smith had written:

> We rarely hear of the combinations of masters, though frequently of those of workmen. But whoever imagines, upon this account, that masters rarely combine, is as ignorant of the world as of the subject. Masters are always and everywhere in a sort of tacit, but constant and uniform combination, not to raise the wages of labour above their actual rate. To violate this combination is every where a most unpopular action, and a sort of reproach to a master among his neighbours and equals. We seldom, indeed, hear of this combination, because it is the usual, and one may say, the natural state of things which nobody ever hears of.[46]

Preston was still a small town, in area if not in population, and one in which the manufacturers must have been in almost continuous contact with each other. Most of them lived in the select central residential district bounded by Fishergate and Fishergate Hill to the north, the River Ribble to the south, West Cliff to the east and Oxford Street to the west. Here were the residences of Daniel Arkwright (Bushall Place), John Clayton and John Paley Junior (Fishergate), Hugh Dawson Junior and Miles Rodgett Junior (West Cliff), J. Furness and William McGuffog (Spring Bank), Joseph Gillow (Frenchwood Street), Adam Leigh, John Paley Senior and Richard Threlfall (Ribblesdale Place), James Leigh (Cross Street), James Seed (Starkie Street), William Shaw (Oxford Street) and Edward Swainson (Fishergate Hill).[47]

The focal point of Preston society lay at the centre of this area. Even today Winckley Square is a calm and elegant oasis in a bustling town. Here in 1854 lived Thomas Miller (at No. 4), John Swainson Junior (No. 6), William Birley (No. 7), Miller's brother Henry (No. 9), William Ainsworth (No. 10), John Humber (No. 11), Paul Catterall and James German (No. 13). They lived well. A contemporary account describes the Square as 'a large parallelogram, with enclosed gardens in the centre, similar to the "squares" of London. In point of extent and picturesque beauty, this provincial *"rus in urbe"* might successfully compete with many in the metropolis. It is ornamented by some of the handsomest [sic] buildings in the town', including Ainsworth's 'Italian Villa' and Miller's 'newly-erected mansion', with a statue of Peel in the gardens.[48] The Square also housed the Literary and Philosophical Institution and the 'Winckley Club House', or 'Gentleman's News Room'.[49] Together with the Theatre and the churches of the town centre, this was where the Preston millocracy gathered in their leisure hours. They met, too, in the performance of their public duties as magistrates, councillors and guardians of the poor.[50] Liberal politics were dominated by manufacturers and the Tory caucus heavily influenced by the cotton lords, who crossed swords at the public meetings at which were discussed the burning issues of the day. Material interests also brought them together. No fewer than 29 manufacturers were partners in the Preston Banking Company.[51]

All in all, it was almost impossible to be a cotton manufacturer in a town like Preston without rubbing shoulders with one's peers, and it is not difficult to see how Smith's 'tacit, but constant and uniform combination' could so easily have formed part of the fabric of everyday life. There is, moreover, some specific evidence to this effect. Whether or not they functioned as an employers' association in the sense in which the term is commonly understood today, the Preston masters (like those in every cotton town) associated with each other in an organized way on a wide range of questions of common concern. Free Trade was, of course, a mainly Liberal issue which had divided the millowners along party lines, but the tenacity and resolution of its advocates suggests that the Anti-Corn Law League may well have played a significant part in fostering contacts among masters throughout the area. It may be suspected also that the threat of a return to protection supposedly posed by the Derby administration in 1852, which brought about the temporary resurrection of the League, aroused the concern of Peelite Tories as well as Whig manufacturers.[52] Less divisive, and if anything even more protracted, was the question of Factory Reform. With but few honourable exceptions the Preston millowners met, lobbied and petitioned against statutory restrictions on the hours of labour.[53] As with the operatives, so with their masters: the Ten Hours issue encouraged organization when the question of wages lay dormant.

Against this background, the precise history of employers' organizations in general, and the Preston Masters' Association in particular, loses much of its importance. There is no need for a leather-bound minute book to reveal that the millowners never entirely lost contact with each other, any more than a formal constitution is required before allowing a sporadic existence, throughout the 1840s and 1850s, to some sort of union among the various classes of factory hands. In both cases 1853 saw the revival of old connections, and the refashioning of old associations, rather than anything radically new.

In both cases, too — but most obviously for the manufacturers — there was a crucial precedent for them to consider. Along with London, the North West had been the centre of the engineering lock-out in 1852, and the strongest bastion of the federated employers. Preston itself was only indirectly affected. None of the town's engineering workshops had closed, the *Preston Chronicle* reported laconically. 'The only steps that have been taken have been intimations given by the principal machinists and iron-founders that all members of the "amalgamated society of engineers and mechanics" are to quit that body or be discharged from their employment.'[54] South Lancashire was the centre of the employers' resistance, and it was here that their determination brought what appeared at the time to be a resounding victory. The similarities between the origins of the engineering conflict (with its roots in union 'dictation' and 'tyranny') and the millowners' reaction to the ten per cent campaign are obvious, and were widely noted at the time.[55] There was a personal connection too. Henry Whitworth, of the Manchester law firm of Whitworth and Richardson, had played a leading role in the organization of the engineering employers' associations, and it was to the same partnership that the administration of the Masters' Defence Fund was now entrusted.

Like the master engineers, the cotton manufacturers did not maintain a continuous formal association after the successful conclusion of their struggle, so that very little information has survived about the central federation, based in Manchester. Many tantalizing questions simply cannot be answered. Did the local Manchester association play the leading role in the formation of the county-wide federation, or was the city chosen as the venue for its transactions simply because of its central position? If the latter, which town or towns supplied the moving spirits? Did the Stockport masters receive any assistance from the federation in the 1853 strike, or did they (as seems more likely) fight alone? Was the crucial decision to lock out the Preston operatives taken centrally, or by the Preston Masters' Association on its own initiative? Who, then, chose Preston as the 'decisive battleground': masters or men? What guarantees of financial support, if any, did the Preston masters receive in September? Why was it not until the end of the year that such support was forthcoming (or, at least, publicized)? Were the lock-outs in Wigan, Burnley, Bacup, Bury and elsewhere planned from Manchester, or were they the result of autonomous decisions by the millowners of each district? There are gaps in the information concerning the operatives' side of the confrontation, which have to be filled by inference. As regards the employers, even inference is often impossible.

One thing is certain, and that is the degree of mutual mistrust displayed by the manufacturers. It was natural enough for competitors — which, after all, is what they were — to be suspicious of each other, and it was in all probability not only the turnouts who speculated as to the motives of those employers who encouraged others to close their mills. Standards of commercial conduct were not high. The self-righteous Quaker Henry Ashworth, for example, was in the habit of buying secret information about his competitors, and had once hired a tackler at a Preston mill as a paid informer.[56] Calculated dishonesty apart, the manufacturers were constantly concerned that their common front could not be maintained in the face of the pressures on individual firms to break ranks. Many a combination of Lancashire coal-owners, for example, had disintegrated in this way.[57] To avoid this possibility the manufacturers resorted to a bonding system which threatened heavy financial penalties against defectors. This was no innovation: in 1833 the woollen manufacturers of Leeds agreed in principle to a bond 'binding the subscribers in a heavy penalty not to employ any persons who were in the Trades' Union, or who would not abandon that Union'. Insufficient signatures were obtained, so the bond was inoperative, but the same system was used (with evident success) in the engineering dispute. Outside Preston, bonds were employed in 1853 by masters' associations in Ashton, Wigan (£500), Burnley (£2,000) and Bacup (£5,000).[58]

In ideological terms the bond was something of an embarrassment to the manufacturers. Its introduction did little to support their case against the interfering and tyrannical unions of the operatives, as Lord Justice Campbell rather acidly observed in 1855 when he declared the system to be contrary to public policy.

There must be entire reciprocity between liberty to the masters and liberty to the men; and it seemed to him that a decision in favour of this bond would establish a principle upon which the fantastic and mischievous notion of a 'labour parliament' might be realised, for regulating the wages and the hours of labour in every branch of trade all over the empire. The most disastrous consequences would follow, therefore, to masters and men, and to the whole community.[59]

This case involved a Wigan employer who had reopened his mill against the instructions of the local masters' association. It reached the Queen's Bench a full eighteen months after the incident itself, and seems to have been the only one of its kind. Whether other masters were prepared to disregard their undertakings in the anticipation that bonds would later be declared unlawful must remain a matter for conjecture. Certainly the bond was threatened with great effect in January 1854, forcing the Preston manufacturer John Swainson to revoke his decision to reach agreement with the weavers.[60] On the other hand it is possible that a few small firms defected from the Preston Masters' Association undeterred (and apparently unmenaced) by the prospect of financial retribution.[61]

More firms locked out their hands in October than had signed the Masters' Association proclamation in the previous month. Only one of these definitely joined the Association, thereby (presumably) accepting the bond: this was the medium-sized concern of Sharples and Wilding. Three more may be inferred to have followed the same course. Two of these were very small (G. Corry and W. Shaw), the third being the large Farington concern of Bashall and Boardman.[62] Of greater interest are those manufacturers who participated in the lockout without at any point — so far as can be ascertained — accepting membership of the Masters' Association. One was Hugh Dawson, with whom the weavers enjoyed a fluctuating and often turbulent relationship throughout.[63] Gratrix Brothers' quarrel with the operatives seems to have hinged entirely on the question of wages, and when this was settled (in February) their mill reopened to mutual satisfaction.[64] The motives of Edward Hollins were more complex. He claimed to have paid the ten per cent and then to have locked out his hands because 'it would have been dishonourable, if not dishonest' not to have done so. Honour was, one assumes, eventually satisfied, for his Royal Sovereign Mill resumed work at the same time as that of Gratrix Brothers.[65] The much smaller Derby Street mill of William Seed, locked up in October, reopened in January by agreement with the operatives.[66] There may well have been other firms, including some large ones, which took an equally independent line.[67]

Many firms, indeed, refused to have anything at all to do with the lock-out. By far the largest of these was, of course, Napier and Goodair. Two substantial flax-spinners, German and Petty and Hincksman and Furness, worked throughout the dispute, as did R. Gardner's and John Cooper's rather smaller firms. The remaining non-members were all small mills, ranging from 30 hp (Slater and Smith) through 20hp (R. Goodair – John's son, J. Williamson), to 10 or so (J. Anyon, W. Boys, J. Calvert, John Gardner, R. Miller and – probably – W. Paley). They share no obvious common characteristic except their size. John Cooper was a Tory, who had played a leading role in the Factory Reform movement in the 1840s.[68] R. Gardner was almost certainly the Robert Gardner whose unilateral introduction of an eleven-hour day in 1844 had given the Ten Hours' Campaign a welcome impetus. J. Anyon was probably his former book-keeper.[69] Councillor Samuel Smith, of Slater and Smith, was a Methodist preacher who had begun life as a tallow chandler and soap merchant; a Liberal, he is known not to have favoured the weavers' union.[70] William Paley was a Tory councillor and in all likelihood a relative of the two Johns,[71] though whether R. Miller had any connection with Thomas cannot be established. All that can safely be concluded is that men of a variety of persuasions found the actions of the Masters' Association unnecessary, morally distasteful or (most telling of all?) commercially unpalatable, and kept their mills running.

With one exception (Napier and Goodair), these were not particularly important firms, and their non-involvement in the lock-out could have had only a marginal effect on its prospects of success. Much more damaging to the Preston masters was the total absence of support from the manufacturers of Blackburn. The Blackburn millowners had conceded the ten per cent without undue reluctance. They were almost alone among the cotton lords of Lancashire in both standing aloof from the Manchester federation and making no threatening noises to their operatives in the autumn of 1853. They were the very last to reduce wages in the following year, and permitted their hands to provide easily the greatest source of moral and financial backing for the Preston turnouts. At the time many believed that this was all part of a conspiracy to steal markets from Preston, while others were convinced that the Blackburn employers, worried about being undercut by their low-wage competitors to the west, were anxious for the Preston strikers to succeed.[72] There may be an element of truth in both these arguments, but they overlook the most important single determinant of the Blackburn masters' behaviour: their extreme disunity. The cotton lords of Preston divided fairly evenly between Tories and Liberals. Elections were keenly contested, and up to 1841 (but, significantly, no later), there were complaints of victimization by millowners of operatives who had voted against the approved candidate.[73] But for Preston masters, politics were more of a pastime than an obsession. None of them had political ambitions of his own, and conflicts at the hustings never turned into acrimonious personal feuds.

In Blackburn, however, this is precisely what happened. William Feilden of Feniscowles was the scion of an old and prolific family. Early in the century he set up as a cotton manufacturer in Blackburn. The borough having been awarded two seats by the Reform Act of 1832, Feilden entered Parliament as a Tory and held the seat until his retirement 15 years later. Meanwhile the Hornbys of Kirkham (who were related to the Feildens by marriage) had also entered the cotton industry in Blackburn. In 1841 John Hornby defeated the sitting Whig to join Feilden as the second Tory member for the borough. He held the seat in 1847, in an election characterized by an unprecedented absence of rioting. When Parliament was again dissolved in 1852 the poll was topped by the local manufacturer James Pilkington, a Liberal Free Trader who had entered Parliament in 1847. Pilkington's 'Liberal-Conservative' colleague William Eccles, himself a manufacturer, defeated Hornby for second place. The Tories now brought a petition alleging that Eccles had bribed voters — an unthinkable abuse of which they themselves were of course quite innocent! — and he was unseated. For the by-election in March 1853, John Hornby retired from politics and his brother William Henry took up the Tory standard. His adversary was one Montague Joseph Feilden, younger son of the late Sir William, and a Liberal. After a campaign which was violent even by Blackburn standards, and which aroused the condemnation of the outside world, Feilden won the election by 631 votes to 574.[74]

In this northern Eatanswill, politics were only a little less vicious at the municipal level.[75] More significantly, electoral conflict spilled over into the mills. Voters could be bribed, intimidated, even assaulted, but they also had to be *persuaded* that the rival candidates (each of them a cotton manufacturer) had their interests at heart. The Blackburn masters, then, were forced to bid against each other, not merely for the labour services but also for the loyalty and affection of their operatives. Thus in Blackburn, unlike Preston, the millowners dominated the Ten Hours movement, which no master of substance felt able to ignore (let alone to oppose).[76] Hornby's deliberately provocative display of benevolence on the wages front[77] fits neatly into the same pattern. Here were cotton lords for whom commercial calculation was *not* the over-riding consideration, for whom political power and electoral influence, the esteem and gratitude of the factory operatives, were more important than profits.[78]

In September 1853 the Operative Conservatives of Blackburn took over the town in a mass tribute to Hornby, who provided an excursion to Blackpool for the Tory operatives, and a ball and banquet on their return. Acknowledging the presentation of a silver candelabrum (inscribed to him as 'the well-tried, FAITHFUL AND CONSTANT FRIEND OF THE WORKING-CLASSES'), Hornby congratulated the operatives on the achievement of the ten per cent. 'If

The Masters

I have been the means of bringing about the settlement of this all-important question', he told them.

> I feel I have done a great good, not only to the employers, but also to the employed ... Is there anything illegal in working men associating together to prevent a dropping of their wages, or rather, is there any more evil in working men doing that than in the masters assembling together, and forming an association to prevent an advance of wages? (Cheers). You have your own interests to look after both in the House of Commons and out of it, and I for one should support any act which you might request to be passed to protect you from the attacks of tyrannical masters (Hear, and renewed cheering).[79]

Inevitably Montague Feilden was cited, by name, as one of the tyrannical masters. Small wonder that the Liberal Blackburn manufacturers had no stomach for a confrontation with their operatives.

5 Locked Out

15 October 1853–9 February 1854

We're on strike, we're on strike, for a full ten per cent,
We're made up our minds, and we'll never relent;
Up, up, with your voice, let it go through the land,
We're on strike, we're on strike, almost every hand.

The lock-out involved a large majority of the mills, but it was by no means universal. Of the 35 signatories to the Masters' Association's original proclamation, eight were already shut through strikes, 23 closed on 15 October, and the remaining four were under notice to follow suit within the next week or so. A further six concerns, which had not been parties to the original decision, joined the lock-out, while rather more than a dozen firms remained aloof.[1]

At least 80% of the town's productive capacity had closed. According to one initial report, those firms engaged in the lock-out possessed a total of almost 2,400 horse-power, though this is an underestimate due to the absence of figures for several firms (including at least two large ones) in such outlying areas as Fishwick, Walton, Farington and Lostock. The independents were operating almost 600 horsepower.[2] Estimates of the number of operatives involved varied wildly. Rather more than 14,000 hands were receiving strike relief.[3] This cannot be taken as a reliable guide to the numbers involved in the dispute, if only because there is evidence that the operatives employed at one large mill received no assistance whatever in the early stages of the dispute.[4] At the other extreme is a press report that between 20,000 and 25,000 hands were locked out, with a total loss in wages of £10–£11,000 per week, while 5,000 (with a weekly wage bill of £2,500) remained at work.[5] At the end of the dispute Henry Ashworth put the numbers locked out at about 17,000,[6] but he was taken to task by the Rev. John Clay. The prison chaplain supplied his own estimates of the numbers involved, and these are probably the most accurate available. Totalling 18,000, there were 6,200 males and 11,800 females. Of the males, according to Clay, two-thirds were adults, and most of the remainder were youths aged between 13 and 17. Rather more than half of the females were adult women, teenage girls accounting for nearly all the rest. Very few children, of either sex, were involved in the dispute.[7]

The operatives were not merely convinced of the justice of their cause; they believed no less firmly that the masters were perfectly able to pay the ten per cent. Was not the country as prosperous as ever it had been? Was it not true that the cotton industry was booming? By the autumn of 1853 an affirmative response to the first question now required some qualification, while the second could only be answered in the negative. In the second half of the year Stock Exchange prices fell by an average of 15%,[8] and interest rates doubled.[9] These symptoms of nervousness, occasioned in part by increasing tension between Russia and Turkey, did little to interrupt the progress of the British economy as a whole, for which 1854 was to see the peak of the boom. But the cotton industry was out of phase with general economic conditions. Investment in new mills continued to increase, but this necessarily reflected decisions taken earlier, in more favourable circumstances. In the third and fourth quarters of 1853 the cotton market deteriorated rapidly, with a sharp decline in yarn and cloth prices and a slump in profits.[10] At Henry Ashworth's New Eagly Mill near Bolton, which was undisturbed by strikes, the rate of return on capital had been 14.6% in the year ending June 1853; in the next twelve months, it was only 4.7%.[11] Preston was particularly affected by the disruption of its important Far Eastern trade brought on by political turmoil in China. Equally ominously, from the operatives' point of view, a wet summer had ruined the harvest and induced a substantial and continuous increase in food prices.[12]

These developments had important implications for the outcome of the Preston dispute, as independent commentators began to realise. A week before the start of the lock-out the *Preston Chronicle* pointed to political instability overseas, upheavals in the money markets, rising food prices and the onset of winter as proof that now was not a good time for a turnout.[13] A few days later the local clergy 'urged the gloomy prospects of commercial affairs as a reason for the operatives' seeking an early settlement of their differences, if even at a sacrifice of some of their demands'.[14] The *Chronicle* returned to its theme on 15 October. The turnout was poorly timed, like the unsuccessful strikes of 1826 and 1836: all had come 'at the close of a long career of prosperity'.[15] 'It has become almost an axiom,' the *Blackburn Standard* reflected, 'that strikes never take place until we are on the eve of a panic or a famine. A more unsuitable opportunity could not have occurred than the present.'[16] Unsuitable it may have been, for the operatives; things were different for the masters. From their point of view:

the men have made one of the greatest mistakes it was possible for them to make. Their warehouses are glutted. They have 20 weeks' stocks on hand. The China market is closed. There are goods enough in the Indian seas without purchasers, to supply the markets, when the trade is opened, for months. They say that they were never in a better position for fighting the question than now.[17]

And so it was to prove, as output was curtailed, and short time introduced, throughout the industry.

The full extent of the depression did not become apparent for some time, and the operatives began the lock-out in a spirit of buoyant optimism. The magistrates' prohibition of open-air meetings applied only after sunset. During the hours of daylight the operatives, no longer confined to the mills, could assemble without hindrance. On Monday 17 October a vast crowd, estimated to number between 20,000 and 35,000 people, gathered in the Marsh to roar their disapproval of the (pitifully insignificant) 'anti-strike committee'. Even the spinners, numerically much weaker than the weavers, attracted 5,000 to the Orchard three days later. Delegates were dispatched to Birmingham, Sheffield, Liverpool and the Potteries, and later to Glasgow and Plymouth, to seek aid in their struggle against what Swinglehurst now called 'the poltroons, the base scoundrels, called manufacturers'. Enthusiasm was so intense that on Thursday evening a large crowd assembled at the Temperance Hall even though no meeting had been announced, and had to disperse in disappointment. The rash of placards continued unabated. The Preston craft societies issued their own, which compared the cotton operatives' leaders favourably with the notorious Anti-Corn Law agitators of the previous decade. On the 18th Cowell published a reasoned and detailed statement of the weavers' case. Union had been forced on them when the masters had victimized members of the original deputations: 'good experience had taught us the folly of pursuing those claims in isolated bodies'. The early strikes could have been avoided, Cowell repeated, had the committee been consulted by the masters in advance.[18]

Faith in the possibility of a negotiated settlement died hard. Facing an audience of 10,000 on 22 October, a Manchester millwright by the name of Braham cited the disastrous outcome of the engineering lock-out the previous year as a demonstration of the need for mediation. He called upon the mayor to organize discussions between operatives and masters, claiming that this might be the only means of averting a revolution! His proposal drew the support of the Stockport delegate Thomas Rhodes. Despite some opposition, and even though the assembly had just declared its 'unalterable resolve' to hold out for an unconditional ten per cent, it was approved by acclamation.[19] William Walton wrote to the ageing radical Joseph Hume and evinced a reply which deplored strikes, condemned the conduct of the masters, and suggested that recourse to arbitration might end the dispute.[20] The retiring mayor, Peter Catterall, had other ideas; he refused to intervene.[21]

This rebuff only strengthened the turnouts' resolve. James Postlethwaite, the leader of the throstle-spinners, whose financial plight was dire, had expressed his determination to die in the field rather than submit. Cowell responded to rumours that an industry-wide lock-out was under consideration with the angry assertion that such a step would make revolution inevitable. If arbitration were not accepted – R. Townley Parker MP might serve in this capacity – then 'they would give the manufacturers of Preston such a flogging as they never had in their lives'.[22] A flogging of sorts was meted out on 1 November when the operatives seized the opportunity to inflict a crushing defeat on those masters seeking re-election to the Town Council. Though this had little effect on the composition of the council, which continued to be dominated by the cotton masters and their allies, it was a gratifying moral victory for the operatives.[23]

Materially, the struggle was more arduous. Some took Cowell's advice and moved to Blackburn, where they readily found work (albeit only by displacing less skilled or less healthy operatives there).[24] The great majority, though, were now dependent on the relief payments organized by the various committees. The spinners, whose organization was most effective and had substantial financial reserves, received the largest weekly payments, though it was little enough by comparison with their earnings while at work. Huge sums were subscribed by weavers in other towns. Blackburn and Stockport collected a weekly levy of 6d per loom, or close to 10% of a weaver's earnings.[25] Those Preston weavers still at work contributed 1s per loom,[26] while even the surviving handloom weavers provided assistance.[27] Cowell suggested that members of sick clubs apply to them for loans.[28] Excitement was aroused by the rumour that a donation of £500 had been received from 'a gentleman from London'. According to some reports, the donor was Sir John Tyrell, Tory MP for North Essex and a long-standing enemy of the manufacturers and their Anti-Corn Law League. The story, which circulated as far away as Stockport, turned out to be a hoax.[29] Despite all their efforts, the weavers were forced to reduce their weekly payments to 4s, though, as Cowell reminded them, this was very much more than the Stockport strikers had received.[30] For some it would have been more than welcome: the hapless throstle-spinners somehow subsisted on 1s per week.[31]

On 2 November the masters issued their first public statement since the beginning of the lock-out. This took the form of a placard purporting to give details of events at the half dozen firms where, in the summer months, disputes had occurred. One of the firms concerned, Messrs Birley Brothers, wrote to the *Times* to support the association's statement. The demand at this firm, it was alleged, was for an advance of 12½%. Since Birley Bros already paid well, there were grounds for suspecting that it was to be used as the standard for the proposed 'equalization' — in practice, levelling up — of wages throughout Preston. The firm had offered an increase as near to 10% as was possible: ¾d on a piece-rate of 8d, which would have left the firm's several hundred weavers £1 6s 11d *in total* below the ten per cent (a matter of ¾d per week each). At two other mills the spinners had demanded not ten per cent, but fifteen, and there was a record of unrest and union 'interference' at a number of others.[32]

Richard Ashworth, of Bamber Bridge, had joined the lock-out, but was not a member of the Masters' Association. At the beginning of November he announced his intention to reopen his mill, paying the ten per cent to his spinners and card-room hands, but offering nothing to his weavers, who in consequence stayed out.[33] The Association itself took a much harder line when it met, for the first time since the lock-out began, on 4 November. Referring to the deterioration in trade, and to the interference of 'mischievous and irresponsible parties who have been the cause of all the distress brought upon the town', it declared that the recent wage increases (allegedly agreed by the Association on 19 August) could no longer be sustained. The mills would not reopen until the masters were satisfied that 'the operatives are prepared to emancipate themselves from the dictation of parties who have an interest in prolonging the unfortunate dispute between the employers and the employed'. When they *did* reopen, it would be at the rates paid on 1 March. Demonstrating its belief that an early end to the lock-out was unlikely, the Association adjourned for four weeks.[34] Reductions in wages in many mills, the final abandonment of the ten per cent, and the dissolution of the operatives' unions: these were now the conditions for ending the lock-out. No-one – least of all the masters – expected that they would be accepted. A war of attrition now began.

The conflict had already spread to North East Lancashire. Although the strikers at Slater and Pollard's in Burnley had returned to work in the hope of a settlement, the masters would have none of it, and the lock-out there began, as announced, on 28 October. Fifty-eight mills in Burnley and Padiham were closed, and 12,000 hands found themselves out of work.[35] The issue had now become crystal clear: the mills would reopen only if the operatives pledged themselves to discontinue their subscriptions to Preston.[36] Only a division of opinion in the masters' association at Accrington prevented a lockout there.[37] In Bacup and the Rossendale valley a similar closure had commenced eight days earlier. Again, the masters demanded an end to their operatives' support for the Preston turnouts.[38] By the end of October 183 mills in Preston, Burnley, Padiham, Bacup and Wigan were idle, and 47,000 operatives at leisure.[39]

The Manchester masters met on 31 October and resolved to withdraw, from 3 December, all advances in wages made during the year, under threat of a lock-out. The operatives, who were in no position to resist, gave way peacefully.[40] A week later the Glossop manufacturers issued a similar pronouncement.[41] The strike of dyers and bleachers in Manchester was at last nearing defeat. Early in November the masters had recruited 1,200 blacklegs, and it appeared likely that only 400 of the original 1,600 strikers could hope for re-engagement.[42] As one dispute ended, another began. The Bury millowners gave notice on 25 October that a lock-out would begin on 10 November to prevent subscriptions to Preston, and more than 6,000 hands were duly turned out of the mills.[43]

The most dramatic single incident of the entire ten per cent campaign occurred at Wigan. Having struck without the support of other towns, the Wigan operatives were thrown entirely onto their own slender resources.[44] Hunger, together with the proximity of thousands of turbulent colliers (themselves on strike for several weeks past), finally precipitated a full-scale riot. Friday was market day in Wigan. 28 October was also the date of the autumn cattle fair, and the busy streets were even more crowded than usual with loitering strikers. In the afternoon hundreds of miners gathered expectantly outside the Royal Hotel in the Market Place, where the coal-owners were meeting, hoping that an offer of higher pay would be forthcoming. When, instead, they learned of the decision to open the pits at pre-strike prices, the strikers hooted, jeered and jostled the owners as they left the hotel. It was now 5.30 pm. The police appeared — all eleven of them — and promptly beat a hasty retreat. The crowd attacked the hotel, breaking a large number of outside windows. At 6.30 the mayor telegraphed to Preston for military assistance, having already dispatched a special locomotive to summon help. After a brief lull the crowd reassembled at about nine in the evening, with cotton operatives now in the majority. This time they broke into the Royal Hotel and stormed through the streets, breaking windows and ransacking the houses of two prominent millowners before dispersing (about midnight) upon the arrival of the troops.[45] Three days later the army was again called into action when striking colliers (on this occasion without the support of the factory operatives) attacked 120 Welsh blacklegs at Lord Crawford's pit. Shots were fired, one collier being injured.[46]

The Wigan riots horrified middle-class opinion.

Mills are closed, loiterers fill the streets, itinerant orators address and inflame gaping crowds, the tradesmen see more beggars than customers, the honest millhands are dreary and desolate, the streets are filled with military to preserve the public peace, riot is rife, blood is shed, and disorder reigns where for months and years there has been a singular union of liberty, peace and order.[47]

This was not a fair description of conditions in other towns, and least of all in Preston. Here the weavers' leaders appealed for calm, and attributed the Wigan riots to provocation.[48] The Recorder of Preston, T.B. Addison, repeatedly complimented the operatives on their peaceful demeanour, comparing their conduct most favourably with the disorderly and violent days of 1842.[49] The Rev. Clay paid tribute to the strikers' 'self-restraint, good temper and cheerfulness; their patience and resolution in pursuit of their object; their fidelity and devotion to what they believed a just cause'. Investigating the effects of the dispute on the crime rate in Preston with his usual tireless energy, he discovered an increase in crime among young boys, but a significant drop in convictions of adult males and an even greater decline among women. This he explained by the salutary effects of the lock-out on the liquor trade. The Preston operatives were heavy drinkers, but financial privation reduced spending on alcohol by no less than £1,000 a week (equivalent to about one quarter of the total weekly disbursements of all the operatives' committees!). Weekly consumption of spirits fell by 300 gallons, and of beer by 200 barrels. This accounted for the virtual halving of convictions for drunkenness, assault, and similar offences of intoxication.[50] But the orderliness of the turnouts had other sources. The maintenance of strike relief to so many thousands for so long represented a major advance on the destitution suffered in previous strikes; especially among the young, it must have removed a major temptation to theft and riotousness. The appeals of the delegates for the preservation of order, repeated with an obvious sincerity doubted not even by their fiercest opponents and intensified at times of special stress, also played their part. In an unusually perceptive editorial, one newspaper criticized the Preston masters for their intemperate attacks on the agitators. Leaders tend to render trade movements responsible, it observed; if Wigan had possessed a man like George Cowell the riots would probably never have occurred.[51]

If the turnouts had neither the money for drink nor the inclination for rioting, just how did they spend their unaccustomed leisure? Only a small minority — which may nevertheless have run into hundreds — was actively engaged in the furtherance of the campaign. Many turned to education, no longer deterred by the prospect of weary hours in ill-lit schoolrooms after an arduous day of toil. Cowell appealed to the clergy to throw open their schools, and some at least responded. The Rev. Clay's daughter, with some of her friends, took a daily class of 35 girls.[52] To judge by the outpouring of ballads and songs, many more must have been engaged full-time in advanced literary and musical activities. Others welcomed the opportunity to spend time with their young children; material hardship did not prevent the infant mortality rate from declining during the dispute.[53]

In its early stages, in fact, the lock-out provided a most enjoyable relief from the daily grind. One balladeer expressed his feelings in blank verse:

> The fields they are green and fragrant are the flowers,
> And the birds sweetly warble their tunes,
> These things we'll enjoy while we hold our holiday,
> 'Twill be pleasanter than piecing up our ends.[54]

An unlikely description of grimy Preston, perhaps, but Charles Dickens's reporter found himself 'astonished' as he left the station on arriving from London, 'to perceive that the atmosphere, instead of being thick and smoky, is as clear here as the air upon Hampstead Heath'. Such was the effect of the closing of the mills. Waiting for a meeting of weavers to begin, he found himself in an enormous playground: 'play is going on upon the Marsh with a vengeance; "kiss in the ring" is being briskly carried on; the sterner sort of lads are engaged in leap-frog or football. There are few symptoms of care and contention here ... '[55] Games of another sort were being played, as the eminently Victorian Rev. Clay noted with great concern:

The fact of 9 or 10,000 young persons of opposite sexes living, for more than six months, in total and unaccustomed idleness – and with few or no restraints upon their inclination to associate – must have been fraught with evil consequences; and it is but too certain that many young women, unprotected by watchful parents and their own good principles, have been led or forced into immorality to an extent quite sufficient to mark the Preston strike with a *stigma* which the most triumphant success could never have wiped away, and which must greatly embitter the consciousness of failure.[56]

Deprived of their beer, the operatives could still enjoy sex and football.

In mid-November a curious flaw was revealed in the weavers' otherwise impeccable organization, when Rodgett Bros of Moon's Mill managed to reopen at 1 March prices. For some unknown reason the operatives employed by

Bashall's of Farington were excluded from the relief payments made to the turnouts at all the other affected mills. Late in October they not surprisingly offered to return to work, but the company, bound firmly to the Masters' Association, had no option but to refuse. This left Rodgett Bros, which did not belong to the association, with an ample source of willing recruits.[57]

This, though, was an isolated incident, and in general November saw no change in the extent of the lock-out. The operatives now settled into a routine which changed but little over the next six months. The weavers would gather in the Orchard or on the Marsh every Saturday, allowing their leaders to gauge their feelings before the delegate meeting the next day. Another big meeting would be held on Monday, at which the operatives could learn of the continued growth of support for their cause, and hear about the progress of disputes in other towns. Relief payments would be spread over Tuesday and Wednesday,[58] and there might be a further mass meeting on Thursday or Friday before the cycle repeated itself. One Wednesday the town crier, whose services were invariably used to announce the meetings, became carried away in his enthusiasm; a crowd gathered in the Orchard entirely without the knowledge of the weavers' committee, who had to be hastily summoned from their makeshift office in Murphy's Temperance Hotel.[59]

Support continued to grow. In the second week of November no less than £2,600 was distributed to slightly more than 14,000 turnouts, at the rate of 7s for spinners, 4s for weavers, and 2s 6d for the cardroom hands. The Preston craft societies issued a further manifesto, addressed this time to 'the inhabitants of the United Kingdom'; 'the white slaves of Preston', it asserted, were no less worthy of support than the black slaves of the Americas.[60] On 17 November Cowell travelled to London, where he addressed a meeting of delegates from the various craft societies in the capital, and obtained the support of the National Association of United Trades.[61] A ball was held in Lancaster, at which John Mathews and George Richmond gave recitations from Shakespeare and Burns.[62] Rhodes, Wood and Chadwick, who had played such an important part in the Stockport strike, divided their time between visits to Preston and fund-raising activities in their own town. These activities were not entirely without incident. There were reports of intimidation of operatives who refused to pay their subscriptions, and one meeting ended in uproar when George Cooper ('the George Cowell of Stockport') declared that the Preston cause was hopeless, and urged an end to the collections.[63] Cooper's advice was ignored, and Stockport continued as the second largest single contributor to the Preston weavers' fund.

By far the largest sums came from Blackburn: £860, or one-third of the total, in the second week of November. Delegates from Blackburn were regular visitors to Preston. The Blackburn operatives realised that success in the dispute there would in the long run prove critical to their own prospects of retaining the ten per cent, about which they were obviously anxious. On the one hand William Brown assured the Preston turnouts, amid cheers and laughter, that 'the Blackburn manufacturers encouraged them to preserve in this struggle – saying, in effect, "Go on, lads, while we get all their best customers." '[64] On the other hand, they were nervous lest the lock-out might even now spread to Blackburn, and had set up a 'detective committee' to watch out for any attempt by the Preston masters to enlist support in their own town.[65] On Wednesday 16 November – market day in Blackburn, which had its own thriving Cotton Exchange – the rumoured arrival of some Preston manufacturers sparked off disturbances in the centre of the town. Turnouts from Preston, who had been searching trains and buses for signs of the masters, were joined at dusk by local operatives on their way home from work. A crowd of more than 5,000 besieged the Bull Hotel, where the Blackburn masters' association generally met, and sent in an inspection party to look for millowners from Preston. The search proved to be abortive. A foreman in the employ of Paul Catterall of Preston was discovered and attacked, as too (presumably in error) was an innocuous Preston tailor, but the manufacturers themselves could not be found.[66] Local opinion held Preston people responsible for the disturbances, but the Preston masters themselves, petitioning the government for protection, exonerated them and put the blame on the unruly operatives of Blackburn.[67] Certainly such disturbances were nothing unusual for Blackburn, where every election occasioned a major riot,[68] and this time little damage was done. If the Preston masters *had* been hoping for a sympathetic lock-out in Blackburn – and, as Cowell acidly observed, they could have had no other business there[69] – they were to be disappointed.[70]

The Preston weavers themselves had petitioned Palmerston earlier in the month, warning him of the inevitable threat to public order if the lock-out continued much longer, but obtained only a tardy and non-committal reply.[71] When the contents of the petition became known, the Masters' Association issued a statement defending their stand. They pointed to the wage increases which they had already paid since 1847, and to the reduction in hours of work (from 69 per week to 60) which had taken place. Since the original strikes had begun in the highest-paid mills, they had good reason to fear that the operatives' real intention was to level up wages, picking off the masters one by one.[72] The Association met again on 1 December. By now the weekly subscriptions to the turnouts had reached £3,000; and as the *Preston Guardian* observed, 'there can be little doubt that the pecuniary assistance rendered to the cause of the operatives has taken the masters a little by surprise'.[73] While reaffirming the conditions they had decided upon a month earlier, the masters now decided to test the operatives' solidarity by announcing their intention to receive applications for employment, each day at the respective mills. If sufficient numbers showed themselves willing to return on the Association's terms, the mills would reopen for normal working; if not, the lock-out would continue.[74]

This gambit was to prove an almost total failure. Meanwhile, November had brought a crushing defeat for the locked-out operatives at Burnley and Padiham.

Subscriptions from other towns were being channelled to Preston, and appeals for help from North East Lancashire could not be answered. The most that the Burnley weavers' committee could manage was the distribution of small quantities of (oat) meal; cash relief amounted to no more than 2d per operative over the entire duration of the lock-out. Most of the turnouts were forced to rely on middle-class charity (which was never needed at Preston) to alleviate their distress.[75] The depression continued to worsen. 'The majority of masters who have closed their mills', the *Blackburn Standard* observed, 'would have been compelled, if they had not chosen that alternative, to work short time. With about 200 mills shut, stocks do not appear to have seriously diminished.'[76]

Assured of victory, the Burnley masters resolved on 19 November to reopen their mills nine days later. Their announcement was a chilling expression of capitalist class consciousness in triumph:

TO THE OPERATIVES OF BURNLEY AND THE NEIGHBOURHOOD.

In consequence of extensive combinations of the workpeople employed in the cotton mills of this district, we were, some months ago, compelled, in self-defence, to form a masters' association, not for the purpose of regulating wages — to do which, permanently, we believe to be out of the power of any association, either of masters or men — but simply to annul the action of the union of workpeople, and to prevent the masters from being obliged, one at a time, to yield to ever increasing demands and encroachments, which would, in the end, have brought ruin on both parties.

To meet the acts of the trades' union — to put an end to the subscriptions for the support of turnouts — to show, that for the future, combined efforts would not be allowed to be brought to bear upon individuals, or even upon single towns — in consequence of certain acts of insubordination and violence, on the part of some workpeople — and also to escape serious losses from badness of trade, the masters' association resolved to stop their mills on the 28th October.

The depression in trade still continues and even grows worse, but as we knew that many of the operatives would, at an early period, have been glad to rid themselves of the trammels of the union, as we think it probable, that opinions more in accordance with our own, may have spread during the suspension of employment, and as we feel anxious if possible, to prevent the severe destitution which must be the consequence of a protracted stoppage, we have resolved at the risk of loss to ourselves, to give the opportunity of resuming work, to those who think this unpleasant contest has lasted long enough.

We cannot, in the brief compass of an address, state the reasons which have led us to the adoption of the terms and conditions, upon which each class of workpeople may return to their employment. Those terms may be learnt on application at the respective mills.

But one condition we deem indispensable, and compliance with this will alone enable us to hold out the hope that we can relinquish our associated capacity. It is, that no collection be made among our workpeople, for the support of either local or distant turnouts.

We do not intend to exact any promise to that effect from any individual, but we plainly state, that we shall resist such a course by all the means in our power, even to again having recourse to the total stoppage of our mills.

We cannot, without a great change in our prospects, hold out the expectation of working full-time; but so long as a reasonable spirit is manifested by the operatives, we have every wish to do what we can, to prevent distress and to promote their prosperity.

We think every one must see, that nothing is gained by these combinations and counter-combinations, and we hope, that mutual good understanding, and enlightened views, will lead both parties to rely solely on that system of individual arrangement, which is indispensable to long continued prosperity. This we imagine, is the good which may be extracted from the evil, which we have all so much deplored.

It is our intention, if our views are agreed to by a number of workpeople sufficient to carry on each department of employment, to open our mills on the 28th instant.
THE ASSOCIATED SPINNERS AND MASTERS OF BURNLEY.

The masters had in fact decided that the spinners were to retain the ten per cent, but that it was to be withdrawn from the weavers. Both were to work a four-day week. The operatives returned to work on 28 November in abject surrender. The Padiham turnouts ended their dispute on the same day.[77]

For the moment the lock-outs at Bacup and Bury continued, though the Accrington operatives returned to work on 24 November after a two-week strike.[78] There was no prospect of an early settlement at Wigan, where at least peace had been restored to the streets. On 3 November a group of local clergymen and tradespeople called on the masters to open the mills, but their initiative came to nothing.[79] After more than two months, the operatives' Amalgamated Committee was distributing a weekly total of £24 or £26 to more than 3,000 operatives — 1¾d each. As many again received nothing at all. At the end of the month the overlookers came together and asked the masters to address their hands in the mill yards. Even this hesitant and reasonable request was denied, and the strike dragged on.[80]

By early December short-time working was being adopted on an ever-increasing scale. On 28 November 60,000 operatives in the Ashton district, which included Stalybridge, Hyde, Dukinfield and Glossop, were placed on a four-day week. A fortnight later the Stockport masters' association followed suit, working an 8 hour day instead of the usual 10½, though here normal working resumed early in January.[81] On Christmas Eve the Burnley masters agreed to revert to full-time working in the New Year, but not before a two-day week, and even a second total closure of the mills, had been seriously considered.[82] The Preston operatives viewed the extension of short-time working with deep suspicion, interpreting it as a menacing tactical move by the masters to reduce subscriptions to their own cause.[83] Where such solidarity in the ranks of the manufacturers was lacking, the continued deterioration in the state of trade supplied an even stronger motive for the curtailment of production. In Blackburn the masters' association provisionally agreed, on 15 December to withdraw the ten per cent. There was substantial opposition to the decision from some members, who would have preferred short-time working, and the implementation of the reduction was deferred in the hope of an improvement in trade. The association vacillated for another three months before, it was believed, letting the matter drop altogether.[84]

The Bacup lock-out ended on 5 December, a week after the masters' association there had agreed to follow the lead of their colleagues at Burnley and reopen the mills, this time on a three-day week.[85] Around Burnley the manufacturers lost no time in pressing home their advantage. There was victimization at Padiham,[86] while at Burnley itself the weeding out of militants had developed into a fine art. Cowell dramatically held up, one day in the Orchard, five notice papers of the type issued to the Burnley operatives at the start of the lock-out. Each was marked in a special way, allowing the masters to distinguish, when the mills reopened, between different categories of hands. 'Stump orators' were to be blacklisted for life, and, just above them, doubtful characters would have to abase themselves to qualify for re-engagement. A third category would be accepted without too much difficulty; the fourth paper 'belongs to a full-grown man, who never did any wrong in his life'. Finally, there were those operatives 'entirely passive in the hands of the masters'. To employ a few of the victims of the lock-out, a Burnley Co-operative Commercial Association was established. It soon acquired 50 looms, and declared as its ambition the construction of three co-operative mills.[87]

At Bury the lock-out continued, although two small firms had abandoned the struggle and operatives at another had returned to work without the ten per cent. Here, in December, the operatives were being paid 3s per week, financed by generous contributions from other trades in the town (which was less dependent than most on the cotton industry), and also by loans from what were rather dramatically described as 'the various lodges of secret societies'.[88] The Bury masters' association met on Christmas Eve and agreed to end the lock-out, but on harsh terms. Short-time working (four days per week) was to be mandatory, and the reopening was conditional on 'no collection being made among our workpeople for the support of either local or distant turnouts', a demand copied word for word from the ultimatum of the Burnley masters. Unmoved by this offer, the operatives assembled on Boxing Day to reject the conditions.[89] They maintained their resistance for several weeks, despite the privations described by one turnout in January: 'We have for a long time lived upon two meals per day, and have remained in bed till noon in order to escape the necessity for taking breakfast; and we are determined, rather than yield, to be in bed till four o'clock in the afternoon, and to live on one meal per day.'[90] Not until 27 February, after nineteen weeks of increasing sacrifice, did they return to work on the masters' terms.[91]

The Wigan strike proved equally intractable. On 5 December the overlookers' committee met the entire membership of the masters' association, and secured from them a commitment to open the mills on the following three days to receive applications for employment (at the old rates, without the ten per cent), after which the association would reconvene to consider the response. As in Preston, the turnouts held on grimly, their attitude epitomized by a voice from the floor at a meeting of the cardroom hands: 'We'll never go in at th'owd prices, if we're out till next winter.' Applications, though substantial, were insufficient to induce the masters to reopen. But the Wigan strikers were, in effect, competing with Preston for subscriptions, and it was a hopeless task. Despite promises obtained from Ashton and Stockport, and an attempt to enlist the support of the powerful London trades' societies, material assistance was pitifully small, allowing the payment of a mere 2d per hand each week.[92] Not without considerable dissension in their ranks, the masters' association eventually agreed on 19 December to reopen the mills. Two days later the prominent Chartist Ernest Jones arrived in Wigan to promote his Labour Parliament, provoking a magisterial warning against any renewal of the recent disturbances. After four days 1,600 operatives had gone back to work, but three-quarters of the strikers remained adamant.[93] Their return was a protracted and contentious affair. At the beginning of the New Year another thousand operatives had resumed work, but many had done so only on the understanding that they were to be offered at least some advance in pay. Messrs Eckersley, proprietors of one of the largest firms in the town, pressed the masters' association on 6 January for permission to come to their own arrangements with their hands. When this was denied they gave notice of their decision to leave the association, and were promptly threatened with forfeiture of the £500 bond.[94] The masters' obduracy now broke the back of the strike, and by the middle of January only a thousand of the original 5,000 remained idle, along with a further thousand in the neighbouring village of Hindley (the latter somehow continuing to subsist on 3d per week). The stragglers held out into February, but to all intents and purposes the Wigan strike was now at an end.[95]

In Preston the mills had opened on Monday 5 December, not for the resumption of production but only to receive applications for employment. The anonymous author of a placard urged the operatives to take advantage of the offer, noting that the masters had imposed no condition concerning the renunciation of union membership: 'The unions are left untouched, you may resume work and maintain your unions, and can you reasonably require more?'[96] The operatives still required their ten per cent. Large crowds gathered outside the mills on Monday morning, ignoring the police and hooting and jeering at the few applicants who appeared. The delegates defused a potentially explosive situation by calling the turnouts to a meeting in the Orchard, where they were admonished for threatening the peace; but care was taken to leave a representative at each mill to note the names of any applicants.[97] Not surprisingly, the outcome was a disaster for the masters. Potential blacklegs had to weigh the uncertain prospect of eventual re-employment — for there was no guarantee that the mills would open for work in the near future — against the certain loss of their relief payments if they registered with the masters. On the Monday morning a bare hundred did so in the whole of Preston, and by the end of the week that number had only doubled. Of these, Cowell claimed that many were 'firebeaters, mechanics, sweepers and others', whose involvement in the dispute, however distressing to the individuals concerned, was peripheral. Many mills received not a single applicant.[98]

Horrockses accounted for about 100 of those who did register, and reports of an impending mass defection here forced the convening of a hasty 'shop meeting' to scotch the rumours. Outside the borough itself, Bashall's again proved a problem. Still deprived of relief payments, almost a thousand of the Farington operatives registered their willingness to return on the masters' terms, and were bitterly condemned as 'knobsticks'.[99] To prevent weakening elsewhere, the operatives found it necessary to extend payments to individuals who, previously refused support as having only a marginal connection with the dispute, might now be regarded as potential blacklegs. The weavers' committee alone added 466 names to their rolls in the first week of December, and began to subsidize the removal costs of operatives who wished to seek work in other towns.[100] On balance, though, the masters had suffered a humiliating defeat over the opening of the registers, and the turnouts' confidence was greatly enhanced. According to the weavers' delegates the lock-out would end by Christmas, or by January at the latest. 'Should the operatives be defeated in this agitation,' Cowell rather rashly promised, 'my name will be Walker out of Preston.'[101]

He and others had taken the train to London on 5 December to solicit support from another meeting of the metropolitan trades. Cowell promptly returned to the North, but Mathews and Bowman stopped over for another meeting three days later, where they successfully defended (against the claims of the Wigan strikers) Preston's right to the entire proceeds of the London collections.[102] The irrepressible Mortimer Grimshaw travelled to Sheffield, where he was so impressed by the donation of £50 at the first place he visited that he came back confidently predicting a weekly inflow of £200 from the city.[103]

On 14 December a carefully stage-managed 'meeting of the middle classes' took place in the Theatre. Presided over by Councillor Dixon, one of the victors in the recent municipal elections, and attracting a substantial audience of tradespeople and professional men, the meeting was dominated by the operatives, who secured unanimous approval for their cause. Dixon stressed his neutrality but commended the operatives for their peaceful conduct, and George Cowell declared his belief in arbitration. Apart from letters which appeared in the local press, this meeting was the first positive sign of support from the middle class of Preston; it was widely reported.[104] Additional moral support of a welcome (if naive) kind was provided by Sir George Strickland, MP, who in an open letter to his constituents asserted his belief that a compromise could easily be found. 'After all,' he wrote, 'it is only the usual difficulty of striking a bargain. In 99 cases out of 100, the truth and justice are obtained by "splitting the difference".'[105]

Strange rumours began to circulate. The spinner Giles Howarth received considerable publicity for his macabre claim that some Preston families were reduced to consuming animal blood obtained from the slaughter-house.[106] No less exaggerated was William Brown's exciting report that the Earl of Wilton, in person, had promised to rent the operatives land for the construction of co-operative mills, and would lend them £2,000 for that purpose. The rumour, which was at best third-hand, stimulated renewed interest in co-operative production until Wilton's denial was published in the *Times* and placarded on the walls of Preston, Burnley, Blackburn and elsewhere.[107] An incident at one of the mills which had continued to operate was, in its way, equally odd. The proprietor, William Calvert, had given notice of a reduction in wages, claiming that his rates were in excess of those paid in Blackburn. His hands threatened to strike, and sent a deputation to the weavers' committee room for assistance. Here they found Edward Whittle, secretary of the Blackburn weavers' union, who discovered that Calvert's calculations were correct; the committee immediately ordered the operatives to return to work at the reduced rates.[108]

Christmas brought only a momentary lull in the campaign. The weavers met as usual in the Orchard on Christmas Eve. They assembled again on Boxing Day, this time at the request of visitors who were anxious to witness one of their (by now famous) open-air meetings. Cowell took the opportunity to characterize the tyranny at Horrockses as 'worse than Egyptian bondage'. 'Rather than work at that mill,' he exclaimed, 'I would rather be transported beyond the Atlantic tomorrow.'[109] Earlier in the month the weavers had been promised a seasonal treat, the committee having set aside £1,000 for Christmas dinner.[110] In Blackburn, voluntary contributions were collected (in addition to the normal levy) for the purchase of fat cattle for Preston. One was to be a 'prime fat ox' strong enough to carry the £1,000 on its back.[111] There is no account of the actual festivities, possibly because the local journalists had Christmas dinners of their own to attend to. The £1,000 did arrive, as a 'New Year's Gift', permitting an increase in the weavers' relief payments from 4s to 5s 6d. William Brown was entitled to congratulate his townspeople. After all, 'the oldest man or woman in Preston,' as he said amid cheers, 'cannot recollect a Swainson, an Ainsworth, a Horrocks, or a Miller, giving them an 18d extra at Christmas'.[112]

They were to need every last penny. Rumours had circulated on Boxing Day that the Masters' Association would soon reopen the mills with an increase of five per cent.[113] This proved to be thoroughly misleading. The masters, thus far outflanked in the propaganda war by the much greater activity of the operatives, had already begun a barrage of letters to the national and local press detailing the rates paid in their mills and rebutting claims that wages in Preston were abnormally low.[114] On 27 December their Association issued a lengthy statement in the same vein, provoking an indignant reply from the weavers' committee next day.[115] But the really decisive blow to the operatives' hopes came from Manchester. Here manufacturers from throughout the cotton districts gathered on the 27th to discuss the plight of their colleagues in Preston, who were no closer to victory over their operatives than they had been eleven weeks earlier. Two days later the Preston Masters' Association, acknowledging the stalemate, adjourned until 26 January. On the following Monday (2 January) an even larger assembly of millowners agreed in Manchester that the outcome of the Preston lock-out had become 'a question affecting the interests of the whole trade', and resolved to raise a levy of 5% of their wage bill, every week, to subsidize the Preston masters.[116] The latter, whose determination had never been seriously in doubt, now had the financial support they needed; for the operatives, the future began to look very bleak indeed.

The spinners' immediate reaction was to send deputations to every mill. They were received with the greatest courtesy, but achieved nothing. Similarly, attempts by the weavers produced very limited results. William Seed's small factory resumed work early in January at mutually satisfactory rates, but when Richard Almond's hands secured his agreement to pay very close to the Blackburn list their initiative foundered on the refusal of the Masters' Association to permit him to reopen. Rumours of a settlement with Swainson Bros proved premature, although more was to be heard of this firm later on. Negotiations at Gratrix Bros, which (like Seed) did not belong to the association, came close to success before finally breaking down.[117] Edward Hollins failed in his attempt to reopen his mill on 9 January, despite his exaggerated claim — promptly denied by the weavers' committee — to be paying no less than 93% more than he had in 1847. Matters were complicated by his practice of paying a 10% bonus to weavers who earned (on piecework) at least £2 per month; this system was condemned by Cowell as 'a direct robbery from the working classes'. Although he could not secure the approval of the weavers' committee for the prices offered, Hollins's prospects improved steadily. By the end of January his mill was employing more than 100 hands, many of them drawn from the notorious Farington knobsticks.[118]

With this one exception, the operatives never wavered, and there was no foundation to the *Preston Chronicle*'s claim that their solidarity was cracking.[119] Certainly there was a decline in attendances at the Orchard, but this could in large part be explained by the exceptional severity of the winter. November had been unusually harsh, with sharp frosts and showers of sleet. On Christmas Eve the entire country was blanketed in snow, and the weather deteriorated further in the New Year. On 3 January the maximum temperature in Manchester was an icy 16°F (−9°C), and next day violent winds ushered in a terrible snowstorm said to be unparalleled since 1839. With drifts reaching six to eight feet, roads were blocked and the rail network came to an almost complete standstill. 'Such a severe winter as the present,' the *Economist* reported on 14 January, 'has not occurred for many years, and more snow has fallen than has been known in this country for more than twenty years.'[120] By now the Preston operatives must have begun to notice the holes in their boots and the threadbare patches on their fustian jackets. Small wonder that many decided against standing for hours in the Orchard in freezing conditions, ankle-deep in snow.

The full consequences of the failure of the harvest were now apparent, as food prices reached a peak and discontent smouldered everywhere. At Builth, deep in rural Wales, the dreaded 'Rebecca notices' reappeared in mid-January, threatening violent revenge against food hoarders.[121] In Exeter fury at the high price of bread was reflected in the streets when an angry crowd smashed windows in bakers' shops and helped themselves to the loaves. When troops arrived to restore order the rioters moved to the outlying villages, where they turned their attention to the millers. Bread riots spread to Crediton and Taunton, where a large crowd paraded the streets with sticks and staves, forcing stallholders in the market to bring down the prices of staple foodstuffs (butter, previously 1s 5d a pound, was sold under compulsion for 1s). A farmer who refused to reduce the price of his grain stood by helplessly as the crowd opened his sacks and scattered the contents on the cobbles.[122]

There was nothing in Preston to compare with the disturbances in the agricultural south, but adversity did lead to a further hardening of attitudes. A vituperative anonymous placard asked who stood to gain from the masters' £5,000 bond, and answered its own question in remarkably abusive language: 'Who will pocket the £5,000? Will the renowned MILLER, weighed down by his money bags, or the Proprietor of "Penny Hall", who, having on a former occasion taken off the ten per cent, that is one penny per cut, earned for his mansion the aforesaid sobriquet?'[123] Cowell, remembering the victimization of operatives collecting for the Stockport strikers in the previous summer, was equally bitter. 'What is the difference', he asked, 'between the slaveholders of the United States of America and the tyranny of the cotton-lords of this country?'[124] Precious little, or so it seemed to the turnouts. When William Chadwick asked his Orchard audience whether they were tired of the dispute, the response was a deafening 'No!', someone in the crowd exclaiming, to laughter and cheers, 'We should be more tired if we had to get up at six o'clock!'[125]

The weavers began to play the political economists at their own game. Reducing the supply of labour to Preston would not simply diminish the numbers requiring relief: it would also ensure (so they believed) that the manufacturers would face a severe labour shortage once work resumed. As the construction of co-operative mills no longer offered any immediate prospect of 'thinning the market', the weavers' committee intensified its efforts to encourage operatives to move to other towns. Late in January they were subsidizing migrants at the rate of 100 or more each week.[126] Soon their horizons widened. The weavers' delegates resolved to establish 'a fund to emigrate all operatives who are willing to leave a land of oppression for one of freedom'.[127] They were now to promote emigration with all the energy they had once devoted to co-operation.

Locked Out

Outside interest in the lock-out continued to grow. Cowell told the weavers that their cause was receiving widespread publicity in France and Austria. Grimshaw invoked the support of the *Boston Daily Commonwealth*, which had suggested that a ship-load of provisions be sent to 'the white slaves of England'[128] (though they never arrived). James Aspinall Turner, president of the Manchester Commercial Association, used the annual general meeting of that body on 16 January to deliver a long and extremely tedious attack on the Preston operatives. Its great rival, the Manchester Chamber of Commerce, devoted much of its annual meeting two weeks later to the same topic. Henry Ashworth noted the peaceful conduct of the turnouts: 'So far,' he said with his usual irritating condescension, 'we may congratulate ourselves on the progress of intelligence in this class.' Following Ashworth, John Bright poured platitude after truism, carefully avoiding the necessity to take sides.[129] On the evening of Saturday 28 January, Charles Dickens arrived in Preston. Next day, unknown to those present, he attended the weavers' delegate meeting in the Temperance Hall, which was more than usually fractious. Dickens spared all of ten minutes out of what must have been a very busy Monday to pay a fleeting visit to the mass meeting in the Orchard, before returning to London on the 4.50 train to use his 48 hours in Preston as the basis for a long article and the background for his next novel.[130] In London, though, more immediate affairs were being arranged. Here the Society of Arts were busily preparing for a conference on the subject of strikes.

The Society's conference had been proposed by Dr James Booth on 28 December, the day after the cotton lords of Lancashire had gathered in Manchester to pledge their support for the Preston masters. Ostensibly concerned with strikes in general, the conference was, however, clearly a response to the bitter and protracted nature of the Preston dispute.[131] Booth was careful to stress the Society's neutrality, proposing that invitations be sent to representatives of both sides, and to eminent outsiders who had 'studied and mastered the various bearings of the Labour Question'.[132] The conference took place in London on Monday 30 January, with Lord Grosvenor in the chair. All shades of opinion were represented among the 200 or so who attended: political economists and politicians, Chartists and Christian Socialists, lawyers and trade unionists. The octogenarian Robert Owen rubbed shoulders with Thomas Hodgskin, James Caird with Samuel Kydd, the Rev. F.D. Maurice with Viscount Goderich. George Cowell was there, but the manufacturers (fearful of any outside interference) were notably absent. William Ainsworth, secretary of the Preston Masters' Association, was almost their sole representative, and even he claimed to be attending in his personal capacity.

Immediate disorder resulted when the Chartist leader Ernest Jones attempted to read out a resolution of his own defending the rights of labour against capital; denied permission by the chair, he took his hat and 'hastily quit' the room. The meeting turned calmly to a consideration of the legitimacy of combinations. In the absence of the manufacturers, their case was put by such advocates as

Professor Pryme, late professor of political economy at Cambridge, Edwin Hall (Inspector of Postage Stamps), and a Mr Madisson (London master bookmaker). For the operatives, Samuel Kydd, William Newton and George Cowell defended combinations as the only form of protection available to those with nothing but their labour to sell, advocating arbitration or direct negotiation as the best means of preventing strikes. Cowell denied that the Preston operatives had sought to take their masters in detail, and argued that in fact the reverse had happened, the masters' lock-out being designed to take the working classes in detail 'in order to starve them into compliance'. The discussion lasted for seven hours, and the meeting ended.[133]

The conference was denounced by the working-class press for its alleged bias in favour of the masters,[134] and by the middle-class press for 'folly', 'impertinence' and 'Sentimental Socialism'.[135] In fact the operatives had won a moral victory, their willingness to defend their cause in public debate comparing favourably with the millowners' refusal to put in an appearance. The general feeling of the middle-class participants was accordingly one of sympathy towards combinations of operatives and hostility to lock-outs. Cowell and his allies had put the Society's platform to good use, but it was almost inevitable that nothing more concrete would result from the conference. The Society carefully avoided offering its services as mediator, knowing full well that the manufacturers would have nothing to do with any such offer. Its conference marked the effective end of peace initiatives outside Preston.

Various millowners continued to bombard the press with statements of their case, invariably stressing the generosity of their piecework price lists in comparison with earnings in other towns.[136] These assertions were double edged. At one stage the spinners actually called the masters' bluff, sending deputations to Miller and other manufacturers to express their willingness to return to work at the prices which, so the masters claimed in letters to the press, they had been paying before the lock-out began.[137] The weavers, too, would have been delighted to return at the rates specified by the Blackburn list; and, if the Preston masters' claims were true, this would not have ruined them. As 'An Honest Blackburn Manufacturer' put it, 'Now *if* the Preston masters *really* do pay as high, and in some cases *higher* than we do, then why object to take our standard list of prices?'[138] This rather obvious question did not elicit a reply from the Masters' Association, which met once again on 26 January. Acknowledging that insufficient applications had been received to permit an effective resumption of production, the Association simply adjourned for four weeks, while holding out the possibility of reconvening within that period if the situation should alter materially in the meantime.[139]

The masters' resolution had contained a pledge that, when the mills were eventually reopened, 'effective measures' would be taken 'to protect the operatives against any improper interference or molestation'. This implicit allegation of widespread intimidation was never substantiated. The only overt sanction threatened by the operatives was the withdrawal of relief payments, and this proved quite sufficient to deter all but a handful of potential knobsticks. In mid-January one report did reach the Poor Law guardians which appeared to support the masters' charge. On investigation, however, the allegations proved groundless.[140] For their part the delegates believed that the masters, knowing reports of intimidation to be false, would try to provoke disorder to discredit the turnouts. When, at the end of January, three policemen, one dressed as a factory operative, began acting as provocateurs outside Hollins's mill, these suspicions were reinforced.

Behind the scenes, pressure was mounting on the masters to bring matters to a head by reopening the mills. On 28 January the *Preston Chronicle* stated confidently that this course would be adopted within the next week.[141] On 8 February, the Masters' Association met in special session to consider a memorial from the mayor and other principal inhabitants of the town, requesting them to reopen their mills for business. The Association immediately agreed, and on Thursday 9 February the 17-week lock-out officially came to an end.[142]

The response of the strikers was at once defiant and vigilant. As soon as the masters' decision became known, the weavers' committee brought out a manifesto calling for continued resistance. 'Under all circumstances be peaceable', the weavers were urged, 'and obey the law. Do not allow yourselves to be drawn into any violations of the law, by either officials or non-officials.'[143] Next day, to coincide with the reopening of the factories, both spinners and weavers convened 'shop meetings' of hands from individual mills. The weavers concentrated on Horrockses and Swainson and Birley's, the most likely weak spots. A day later the weavers were called to assemble every hour at the Temperance Hall, one mill after another, over a period of eight hours. Those operatives who failed to attend would evidently be regarded as knobsticks, and be denied any future relief payments.[144] Over the next week open-air mass meetings were held each day, despite appalling weather which actually caused the postponement of one meeting (a unique occurrence). The third week in February saw a tremendous snowstorm followed by winds of almost hurricane force, 'beyond all dispute the most inclement of an unusually hard season'.[145] A new spirit of unity was apparent, and was reflected in the presence on the weavers' platform of the cardroom hands' representative, Huntingdon; H.B. Wadman, for the throstle-spinners; and the spinners' secretary, Michael Gallaher, who addressed the weavers twice in the space of four days.[146]

The continued solidarity of the strikers ensured that the ending of the lock-out turned into yet another defeat for the masters. On the first day of reopening very few hands returned to work. Many mills remained completely empty, and even the giant Horrockses recruited a mere 30 operatives.[147] George Cowell thought this predictable. 'It is not likely', he said, 'that they will go to work at a place where they can only earn 8s 9d a week, when they may have 5s a week for playing.' On 14 February Richardson and Whitworth, the Manchester solicitors who were acting as treasurers for the Masters' Defence Fund, found it necessary to issue a public appeal for continued subscriptions to the Preston masters, 'the number of hands who availed themselves of the opportunity to return to work being exceedingly few'.[148] After a week, the *Preston Guardian* estimated that the Association's members were employing a total of 1,500 hands, of whom 500 were said to be working at Horrockses; many were overlookers and others not directly involved in the dispute. But a week later it repudiated these figures as exaggerated. The masters had made little further progress in the second week, 'and disappointment is expressed by many of those employed at their rate of wages'.[149] The *Preston Chronicle*, which invariably gave the employers the benefit of any doubt, reported 500 working at Horrockses and 120 at Swainson and Birley's, while the knobsticks at Bashall's of Farington now numbered 900. At most other firms the response had been negligible, and many remained closed.[150] If the Farington operatives are excluded, no more than one operative in twenty had broken ranks.

Twenty-one mills were now working on terms satisfactory to the strikers. Most of these had stood aloof from the dispute from the beginning, but there were a few significant newcomers to the list, providing further proof that the Masters' Association's decision had back-fired upon them. Messrs Almond finally parted company with the Association, yielded the ten per cent, and resumed production with a full complement of hands.[151] Gratrix Brothers, where abortive negotiations had also taken place in January, followed suit, as did Orrell's mill at Bamber Bridge.[152] Hollins, who had been employing blacklegs for a month, found that a large proportion of his cloth was 'either entirely spoiled or greatly depreciated' due to the incompetence of his new hands. He swallowed his pride and reached agreement with his original hands, who returned to work on 17 February 'amid loud cheering from the crowd which had assembled to witness the gratifying scene'.[153] When Miles Rodgett's mill in Bow Lane reopened on the 9th it provoked the Masters' Association to issue a public statement claiming that he had done so at the approved (1 March 1853) rates.[154] This was immediately denied by the operatives, who (initially at least) viewed Rodgett's reopening as a victory.[155] Their enthusiasm was soon dampened by Rodgett's apparent inclination to 'insult and enslave his operatives'. At the weavers' meeting on 18 February he was included in a vote of thanks to Hollins, Almond and Gratrix Brothers, 'if he will behave himself as he ought to'.[156]

These successes supplied the strikers with grounds for renewed optimism, which was strengthened by their efforts to encourage emigration. Some weavers had left for America. 'Families are leaving the town by wholesale,' Cowell reported, 'and the subscriptions are improving in every town, village and hamlet.'[157] There was a drop of 1,300 in the number requiring relief (which fell to 14,500),[158] and a corresponding increase in those able to contribute to the maintenance of the operatives who remained idle. After the exhaustion of the New Year's Gift, the weavers had been forced to reduce their weekly payments to 4s; it was now possible to add another shilling. In the second week of February a total of £3,454 was paid to the strikers.[159] The loss of poor relief, brought about by the ending of the lock-out, was hardly felt,[160] and confidence grew. One Bacup delegate became so certain of victory at Preston that he invited Cowell to 'pay them another visit' afterwards, only to be rebuked by the chairman for discussing private business in the presence of the press![161] Cowell himself went so far as to hint that they would soon demand *twenty* per cent rather than ten.[162]

In contrast there was now evidence of panic in the Masters' Association. Manufacturers began to evict strikers from their tied cottages, provoking angry comments from the delegates about the operation of an indirect truck system in the cotton industry. Adult operatives were ordered, under threat of dismissal, to send their children to work in the mills, and the weavers triumphantly paraded one repentant knobstick who had left work rather than submit to this demand.[163] Finally the masters were driven to the most desperate measure of all. A correspondent to the local press had already suggested that blackleg labour be brought in from outside.[164] Early in February it was rumoured that some families in the Fylde were preparing to move to Preston as factory operatives.[165] A week later the *Preston Chronicle* reported that 'the manufacturers are about to make arrangements for importing from the agricultural districts of England, from Ireland, and from various parts of the Continent' large numbers of knobsticks.[166] The decision was eventually taken at the masters' meeting on 23 February, and placards were posted all over Britain and Ireland (though not, as far as is known, any further afield) offering 'employment in factories on liberal terms'. 'The present offers a favourable opportunity', the masters declared, 'for large families desirous of removing to the manufacturing districts.'[167]

With one eye on its working-class readers and the other on the poor rates, the *Preston Guardian* took a more jaundiced view of the Association's decision. Negotiate with the strikers now, it urged the manufacturers, 'before it is too late, before all the skilled labour is transported from Preston (and transported it ere long will be), before the turnip-grubbers of Buckinghamshire are spoiling the fine work intended for the home trade, before utter and irretrievable ruin comes upon the town'. The spinners wrote to the Masters' Association asking for an interview, which was brusquely refused.[168] The weavers, for their part, saw the millowners' new policy as a sinister attempt to provoke them into violence. Luke Wood had already, on 21 February, raised the spectre of another 1842, 'when the blood of the people flowed in the streets'.[169] Four days later James Waddington echoed these fears, albeit in rather less colourful language. 'The object of the masters in bringing strangers to Preston', Swinglehurst alleged, 'is not so much to set them to work as for the purpose of getting up a riot. If they can only do that, they will incarcerate the delegates, and then, they think, their object will be gained.'[170] The delegates simply redoubled their efforts to preserve the peace.

6 Council and Bench

> Come working men of England,
>   No longer idle be,
> But rally to our standard,
>   Assist us to be free,
> For our brave leaders are assail'd,
>   By a despot crew,
> Who wish for to imprison them,
>   And labour to subdue.

The ladder of authority in Preston was similar to that in other mid-nineteenth-century corporate boroughs. At the centre of power was the Town Council. According to one contemporary Preston observer it constituted 'the *primum mobile* of local life', and its councillors the 'Solomons of civic existence'.[1] These then elected the mayor and aldermen from their own ranks and generally nominated, largely by political criteria, magistrates for the local bench. Councillors also provided all the lay members of the Watch Committee which controlled and managed the police.[2] Boroughs were exempt from the jurisdiction of the county police and magistrates, although nominations for the local bench had to be ratified by the Home Secretary and the Lord Lieutenant of the County. Occasionally the Home Office would urge a more efficient enforcement of the law, but in the nineteenth century the administration of local business and authority was quintessentially a local affair.[3]

The Town Council in Preston changed its structure with the passing of the 1835 Municipal Corporation Act.[4] Preston had long been a corporate town but in 1835 the 'unrepresentative oligarchy', which consisted of 12 aldermen recruited by co-option and which had dominated the town with diminishing vigour since 1800,[5] was replaced by a new council composed of 12 aldermen and 36 elected councillors. The town was divided into six wards: St John's, St George's, St Peter's, Christ Church, Trinity and Fishwick (the latter being added to the Preston township under the 1835 Act).[6] Each ward returned six councillors, with two retiring yearly in time for the election on 1 November. Of the 12 aldermen six retired every three years and, like the councillors, were eligible for re-election. Aldermen, though generally chosen from the councillors, could also be selected by the burgesses. The mayor was elected annually on 9 November 'so shivery'.[7]

Whilst the structure of local government changed, the composition of the Town Council remained, predictably, much the same. Before the Corporation Act, Tories and manufacturers dominated the council and, in 1826, actively intervened in the Parliamentary election by supporting the Tory candidate.[8] After 1835 the town's largest manufacturers were still dominant, although a significant number of Liberals had made inroads into the Tory majority. In the 1840s this local elite continued to reign[9] with Tory influence being sustained by the purchase of the votes of a large number of old franchise holders qualified to vote as freemen. The property qualification[10] and the holding of council meetings during normal working hours ensured the cotton lords' grip on local affairs. Municipal reform, as one historian recently noted, merely 'provided an institutional framework within which the political influence of social and economic leadership could be legitimized'.[11]

By the beginning of the strike one-half of the councillors were cotton lords, and some of the wards were represented solely by manufacturers and others closely connected with the cotton trade. But in the November election of 1853, described by the *Preston Chronicle* as an 'election attended by more stir and bustle than has attended ward elections for many years past',[12] the cotton lords seeking re-election were unceremoniously ousted. The biggest shock came in St John's ward. Here the two retiring councillors were Richard Threlfall Jr and H. Armstrong. Armstrong, a popular independent first elected to the council in 1850, easily held his seat with 316 votes but Threlfall, who had been returned every time he sought re-election since 1838, came third in the poll with 220 votes, 159 less than James Parker who finished top. Parker, a grocer, had been induced to stand by those who were increasingly opposed to Threlfall and his connection with the lock-out. He stood for economy in local government, as did Armstrong, and managed therefore to capture the middle-class support of the then loosely organized Ratepayers' Association. Polling started early in the morning and the first few hourly counts quickly showed Parker to have a comfortable lead. During the morning Armstrong was doing badly, but once the voters realized that Parker's election was safe they switched their allegiance to Armstrong to ensure that Threlfall got a sound beating. By mid afternoon Threlfall withdrew, a humiliating experience for a man who, a week or so earlier, had been thought promising enough to be mayor.

In the Fishwick ward, which for years had been associated with the Birleys and the Swainsons[13] (Preston's local pocket borough), the strong feeling against the cotton lords continued. The two councillors seeking re-election were Edward Rodgett, first elected in 1847, and Charles Swainson, who became a councillor in 1844. Swainson was not in fact a cotton spinner 'but is so nearly connected with persons in that business'[14] that he finished bottom of the poll with 172 votes. Rodgett, who in September had been appointed as a magistrate in what were considered suspicious circumstances,[15] clearly guessed the way things were to go. He withdrew before the polling began and nominated in his place J. Woodhouse, a butcher from Church Street. In spite of this manoeuvring the two opposition candidates, Thomas Dixon and Robert Salt, were duly elected with 281 and 254 votes respectively. Woodhouse, who was seen as 'an instrument in the hands of the men who have so long misrepresented the ward, because they were sure of suffering a bitter defeat themselves', came third with 182 votes. According to one of Salt's deputies many of Woodhouse's votes were solicited by a mixture of intimidation, corruption, the beer barrel and bribery — the 2s 6d which was offered at the start of the voting apparently increased by degrees to 10s whilst there was still hope of success. That voters were able to resist these blatant (if customary) temptations at a time when a surfeit of beer would have given them a brief escape from the cold and harsh present, and when the extra money would have given them a little food and clothing for the near future, was a clear indication that residents of the Fishwick ward were no longer prepared to tolerate the hegemony of the cotton lords. This feeling of defiant independence was summed up by Thompson, one of Salt's supporters: 'The Municipal Corporation Act was given to the people of this country for the purpose of investing them with the power of self government. That power', he contended, 'had been absolutely and entirely annihilated, by the fact that all classes were not fairly and equitably represented. Out of six councillors for Fishwick ward, five belonged to a particular trade — the cotton trade (hear, hear).'[16]

This zest for self-government was equally evident in St Peter's ward, where the cotton owners were to lose another seat on the council. Here John Goodair and John Hawkins were the two cotton manufacturers seeking re-election. Goodair, who had been on the council since 1847, was easily re-elected with almost 600 votes. This much was expected. He was unwilling to join the Masters' Association and kept his mill running throughout the strike. He was also certainly the most energetic town councillor and, according to Hewitson, the 'shrewdest man in Preston'.[17] None of these things could be said of Hawkins, and with his mill closed since 15 October he stood little chance. When he was opposed by James Hayes, a local solicitor induced to stand by popular petitioning of 700 of the 1,000 electors, Hawkins could manage no more than 62 votes.[18]

In the remaining three wards there was less hustle and bustle, principally because no cotton manufacturers were standing. Christ Church re-elected M. Myres and R.N. Livesey, and St George's J. Carr and J. Raw, without opposition. In Trinity, where R. Yates and T. Heywood sought re-election, some opposition came from Bryning, a tea dealer, and Joseph Gillow, a local manufacturer, who also kept his mill running through the strike and who in December attacked 'the grasping eagerness of employers to extend their business far beyond any reasonable bounds'.[19] Both polled fairly well, with Bryning getting 204 and Gillow 195 votes, but as neither bothered to give an election address their opposition came to nothing. In the event, Yates (with 283 votes) and Heywood (277) were returned comfortably.

The obvious and significant feature of the November elections was the disastrous showing of the cotton lords. With the exception of Goodair, none of the four who stood for re-election was successful. Threlfall, Swainson and Hawkins, the latter with a humiliatingly low vote, were all bottom of the poll. Through beer and bribery Woodhouse managed, vicariously, to salvage some of the cotton interest's pride, but the local electorate had clearly made their point. Of the 12 councillors newly elected, most had occupations normally associated with middle class and working class reformers. Thomas Dixon was a general provisions grocer, a Guardian of the Poor and an active member of the Ratepayers' Association. He chaired an operatives' meeting on 12 December, and in March of the following year became a member of the Mediation Committee.[20] James Parker was another grocer, whilst R. Yates was a draper, Robert Salt and H. Armstrong owned chemist and druggist shops in North Road and Church Street, and James Raw was in the same business in Friargate.[21] In addition to these shopkeepers there were two solicitors (Miles Myres and James Hayes), one machine maker, one gentleman and James Carr the artist. Goodair was the only cotton manufacturer returned.

The formidable support which enabled Goodair and the others to undermine the traditional dominance of the cotton lords can be explained by three factors: an alteration in the municipal franchise, the vigilant electioneering of the operatives, and the rekindling of the Ratepayers' Association. The alteration in the municipal franchise brought about by the 1850 Small Tenements Rating Act was perhaps the most important factor, for without it the demands of the operatives and ratepayers would have been difficult to achieve. When adopted in Preston in 1853, the Act more than doubled the size of the municipal electorate by increasing the number of people rated.[22] Since 1835, local authorities had been given the power to avoid the inconvenience and expense of rating the smaller houses, occupied usually by working people who frequently moved, by compounding the rate and levying it on the owner of the property. This meant that occupiers were not entered on the ratebook and the burgess roll, although they in fact paid rates to the landlord who 'acted as an unpaid rate-collector'.[23] In Preston, occupiers of houses with an annual rental of less than £6 were thus disenfranchised. With the adoption of the Rating Act the compounding occupiers were now permitted to vote. According to the editor of the *Preston Chronicle* this increased the number of voters from 1,892 to 4,489, and enabled 'cottagers of the lowest class' and tenants of cellars paying 6d per week[24] to cast their votes against the manufacturers. This electorate represented about 6½% of the population: more than Birmingham (3% in 1851), though less than Leeds (9% in 1851) which had an exceptionally large electorate.[25] Tenants paying rents between £6 and £10 were curiously still denied the vote, since their compounded rates were governed by an Act of 1819.²⁶ Had they been included, another 1,800 – making it 9% of the population – would have had the right to vote, and since this group included 'some of the most intelligent, respectable and well conducted of the operative class',²⁷ radicalism in Preston may have been even more successful than it was.

The radicalism which did exist was partly due to the efforts and appeals of the operatives. Speaking at the Orchard on Saturday 29 October, Cowell urged his audience (which included an artist from the *Illustrated London News*) to kick out Hawkins, Rodgett and Swainson 'and every other man whose hands are stained with cotton', not to mention William Ainsworth, secretary of the Masters' Association and the 'Louis Napoleon of Preston'.²⁸ He stressed the necessity of a sympathetic council to control the Watch Committee and to ensure the appointment of an independent stipendiary magistrate.²⁹ At the Orchard two days later, Cowell again urged the electors to throw out 'every Cotton Lord from the Council Chamber', apart from the popular Goodair.³⁰ On polling day Cowell repeated these strictures and became effusive about Goodair. He should become councillor, then mayor, then MP. 'It would be a glorious thing', he continued, 'to have the town represented by a manufacturer who had risen from the working classes (Cheers).'³¹

The ratepayers were also to see the light, but for a quite different reason: economy. In a speech which ended a meeting held on 30 November, Michael Satterthwaite, a Poor Law guardian, asserted in suitably religious terms that it was the 'divine dispensation of the Council Chamber to advocate economy and retrenchment'.³² In the 1850s councils throughout the country were continually harangued by anxious ratepayers who saw rates rising to meet the sanitary duties imposed by the adoption of the 1848 Public Health Act. In Leeds and Birmingham municipal parties of 'Economists' were formed and, as in Hull, 'substantial men' were being replaced, principally by shopkeepers and small tradesmen.³³ In Preston, where the Health Act was adopted in 1850,³⁴ there was less concern about water, drains and sewage. The real concern was about the growth and cost of the police force, the erection of new buildings, and the location of the new public cemetery made necessary by Lord Palmerston's Act forbidding burials in churches.

The Ratepayers' Association was first formed in 1848 to oppose the erection of a covered market, but became less active after it had succeeded in delaying building. In late October and November 1853 a more vociferous body reappeared,³⁵ which by March 1854 had become a force to be reckoned with. Its rigid opposition to increases in the number of borough policemen was the vital issue which cemented relations with the working class, and although Cowell and Dixon (a prominent member of the Association) were later to quarrel over the matter, in November they expressed the same fears about the intentions of the Watch Committee. Whilst shopkeepers and small tradesmen were in general more concerned with the increasing costs of local government and the mass of the operatives with the insidious activities of the police, the election brought radicalism and economy together in a powerful (if informal) alliance against the ruling cotton elite. The 'substantial men' were toppled, and the grocer, draper and chemist became the 'new Solomons of civic existence'.

After the election, the number of cotton councillors had been reduced from 18 to 13, that is from 50% to 36%: nine of these were members of the Preston Masters' Association. Had more come up for re-election their control would almost certainly have been further weakened. The cotton lords continued to dominate St Peter's and Fishwick, providing eight of the 13 councillors. Both were outer wards; if other English towns are anything to go by, this is an unexpected result. Outer wards were usually the areas where radicalism first took hold, while large manufacturers were normally concentrated in central zones.[36] In Preston, however, the two central wards, St George's and Trinity, were represented by only three cotton lords, William Humber, Samuel Smith and William Paley, all as it happens coming from St George's in the eastern part of the town, where cotton spinners and weavers (including a large number of handloom weavers) were most heavily concentrated. Wedged between St Peter's and Fishwick on the western side of the town, Trinity was the only ward not to return a councillor connected with the cotton trade. Their representatives were Isaac Gate, a pawnbroker, R. Yates, a draper, and J. Knowles, a corn merchant, plus Thomas Walker (tobacconist), Thomas Heywood (machine maker) and William Threlfall (ironmonger), showing quite clearly that the voters in Trinity had for some time been prepared to support an alternative social elite. So too were the burgesses of Christ Church in the eastern part of the town, although here the councillors were distinctly upper middle class, the three solicitors, the auctioneer and the gentleman aptly reflecting the residential nature of the area. Peter Robinson, a spindle and fly maker, was the outsider, earning his living by producing and selling goods rather than by purveying fee-earning advice.

In St John's, the scene of Threlfall's disaster, John Humber, one-time secretary of the Masters' Association, remained the only councillor connected with the cotton trade. Like St George's, this ward included a large number of cotton operatives and handloom weavers who had evidently sought for some years to overcome the power of the manufacturers. Parker, Armstrong and L. Billington represented, as far as it was possible, the will of the ward, but it was Thomas Walmsley (St John's) who unexpectedly was to become the single most important member of local government. On 9 November he replaced the lawyer Peter Catterall as mayor.

The rumours about Peter Catterall's successor started shortly after the mayor's dinner at the Bull Hotel on 5 October.[37] William Birley was the first to be proposed but he declined to be a candidate, knowing there was a general feeling amongst the councillors and the local press that no one connected with the cotton trade should be elected.[38] An anonymous memorial called for Catterall's reappointment. This was not only almost unprecedented — the reappointment of a *retiring* mayor had not taken place for 150 years – but was likely to cause a serious split in the new council.[39] In late October Richard Threlfall's name was mentioned, but he was too closely associated with the cotton trade (an association which soon lost him his seat). At the council meeting on 9 November, the manufacturer George Smith proposed Alderman Monk, who had been mayor in 1851, but found little support for his suggestion.[40]

The feeling that the civic chair should be occupied by a 'fit and proper person' was summed up by Alderman Birchall who had himself declined the post. 'At all times electing a Mayor was a task of great difficulty and delicacy, but at the present time, it was one of extreme difficulty . . . We needed a mayor with judgement and unusual qualification', one who would have the confidence of the 'higher classes of the town' and 'to whom the labouring classes could look with a degree of confidence and satisfaction. The cotton trade', he concluded, 'were unlikely to provide a candidate with these qualities.'[41] In the event Thomas Walmsley, whose name had been first mentioned in the middle of October, was unanimously elected. Walmsley was a barrister by profession and came from one of the oldest Preston families. He was a Tory in politics and an active member of the Church of England. According to one contemporary he was exceptionally intelligent and affable.[42] He had little experience of local government, having been elected to the council only in February 1853 when Robert Ascroft, legal adviser to the Preston Masters' Association, became Town Clerk.[43] But, most important of all, he was not connected directly with the cotton trade. Of the 18 mayors elected between 1835 and 1853, 12 had been millowners. In 1836, when Preston last experienced a major strike, the mayor, Peter Haydock, was, significantly, a solicitor. The spinners' strike, which began in October that year, gave the council almost a month to choose a mayor least likely to antagonize the operatives. In 1853 the chronology was much the same and after the elections, which achieved almost everything Cowell had hoped for, the council, by choosing Walmsley, took exactly the same appeasing action. In politics, religion and temperament Walmsley seemed to have – or so it was thought – all the personal qualities to handle the problems caused by the industrial unrest.

The election of an 'impartial' mayor did not affect the real distribution of power and authority. The manufacturers continued to maintain their grip on local politics through the election of aldermen and the appointment of magistrates. The control of the aldermen's seats was often crucial,[44] and predictably out of the 12 aldermen elected in November five were directly connected with the cotton trade, two through family ties.[45] The bench, which of all the civic functions wielded the most authority and which rewarded social leadership with a permanence neither councillor nor alderman enjoyed,[46] was again dominated by the manufacturers. By 1847 Preston had 19 magistrates and 11 of these were cotton masters.[47] In September 1853 William Ainsworth, one of the largest millowners, mysteriously contrived to have two more masters appointed.

Nominations for appointments to the bench were normally drawn up by the

Town Council and then ratified by the Chancellor of the Duchy of Lancaster, after consultation with the Home Office. But in September Ainsworth had, through C.P. Grenfell (a former MP for Preston), written direct to Palmerston and by 'backstairs' influence' added Edward Rodgett and Edward Hollins to the council's own nominees, Peter Catterall and Thomas Monk.[48] The council were incensed by this almost unprecedented interference and on 22 September appointed a committee to investigate the affair.[49] Ainsworth was forced to defend his action. He argued 'that the Council is by no means qualified to make the wisest selection of Gentlemen to serve upon the Bench' and that Catterall and Monk had given their approval.[50] Grenfell, the chief accomplice, later publicly reassured everyone that the appointments were 'not actuated by improper motives' and that there was no desire 'to serve any party or political object'.[51] All this was manifestly ingenuous. Both Catterall and Monk denied ever having given approval and, as the press was quick to observe, the nominations were clearly political. 'While accepting the tribute that has been paid to the personal qualifications of the four gentlemen', the *Chronicle* notes, 'we must protest against the unfair monopoly which gentlemen of one class, the manufacturing interest, now have on the bench ... Latterly, only two magistrates unconnected with the cotton trade: of the four recent additions only one [Monk] unconnected with that business'.[52] The *Guardian* was equally careful not to attack individuals, but argued that 'like Caesar's wife, a magistrate ought to be even above suspicion, but this desideratum can never be realized in large manufacturing towns so long as a great proportion of acting magistrates are mill-owners'.[53] When Palmerston notified the council that they could not challenge his official power to appoint 'proper persons for the performance of magisterial duties'[54] the matter was dropped.

The local authorities intervened in the dispute on three occasions. The first began, and ended, in mid-September 1853 and coincided with the masters' resolution to close the mills. The second, when activity was more intense, began and ended in early March 1854. Again it coincided with an initiative by the Masters' Association: in this case, their decision to import knobstick labour to work in the mills, which had been open since 9 February. The third occasion on which they intervened was in mid-March, when conspiracy charges were brought against the leading delegates. Significantly the authorities only intervened when the operatives were *on strike*. Throughout the seventeen-week lock-out they remained remarkably quiet and restrained. Magistrates and councillors clearly recognized the force of public opinion, which at this time was increasingly critical of the practice of closing mills. Equally, they realized the contradictions of laying all the blame on the operatives when the masters were denying them work. Once the mills were reopened, though, the authorities were given more room to manoeuvre, and from March onwards they began to force the pace.

During the summer of 1853 the authorities kept a low profile. They had not been given reason to react, as the operatives were peaceful and their meetings orderly. By the middle of September tension had increased, and the authorities were for the first time forced to contact Lord Palmerston, to justify the action that they had taken. The tone was set by Swinglehurst when, on 1 September, he attacked the magistrates over the twisters and rovers incident. 'Just imagine a manufacturer summoned before a bench of weavers, for not paying sufficient wages.'[55] This irony was not lost on the operatives who burst into rapturous laughter, but the magistrates thought it contemptuous and Dodd, the magistrate's clerk, was ordered to prosecute.[56] Evidently charges were deferred, although the reasons for doing so are not clear. One possible explanation is that by 12 September the authorities had much sounder reasons for intervening. On that day five youths were arrested for causing a disturbance in Friargate where they had hooted and jeered at hands employed by John Hawkins, who had refused to contribute to the union fund. All five were committed under the Combination Repeal Act, three being sentenced to six weeks' imprisonment and the remaining pair to three months.[57] The magistrates were obviously not prepared to tolerate any form of 'intimidation', even if it meant prosecuting children.[58]

The real trouble did not start, however, until 14 September, when the operatives issued a yellow poster informing the power-loom weavers that a 'rumour had got abroad that the manufacturers are about to lock up their mills'.[59] A meeting was called for the following evening and a procession led by two bands was to leave Marsh Lane at 6.15 pm and proceed to the Orchard. On the 15th these rumours were confirmed by the uncompromising notice issued by the Masters' Association, and on the same day Peter Catterall, the Mayor, prohibited all processions. Four days later, and after the operatives had held two large meetings, the magistrates issued another proclamation forbidding all open-air meetings held after sunset.

The reaction of the magistrates was explained by Catterall in a letter to Palmerston on the 16th. It indicates that their actions were certainly planned, and suggests that they were influenced by the Masters' Association, as much as they were by the operatives. The arguments closely resembled those used by the masters in their lock-out notice: 'You may possibly be aware that for some weeks past the operatives in this town and neighbourhood have been in a very excited state ... They profess to act under the direction of a committee but two persons of the names of Cowell and Swinglehurst appear to have them at their command.' Catterall also made much of the incident on the 12th and of the way in which those willing to work at the going wage were annoyed and intimidated. The operatives 'congregate at the entrance to the mills and when the satisfied hands come out they are hooted and shouted at and occasionally assaulted'. The yellow poster issued by the weavers, they considered, must 'in the present state ... have a direct tendency to breach of the peace'.[60] The decision to forbid open-air meetings after dark had already been taken by Catterall, *before* 16

September. Whilst the meeting arranged by the operatives for the evening of the 15th was not stopped, the mayor told Palmerston that 'I intend to prohibit any other meeting proposed to be held in the open air at an hour when it cannot be terminated before the dark', to prevent 'the populace's [being] excited by the harangues of these paid orators'.[61]

The operatives' reaction to these petty restrictions was as expected: bands simply did not start playing until they reached the Orchard[62] and at the Cockpit meeting on the 19th various speakers attacked the magistrates.[63] Later the suppression of the singing of 'ten per cent' ballads inspired a bitter attack from Luke Wood,[64] but generally the authorities' prohibitions were complied with. The disturbance outside Hawkins's mill, however, greatly disappointed the delegates and, although Cowell was quick to let everyone know that the arrested youths were 'mere children', the incident must have been precisely what the magistrates had been waiting for.

From September to February the authorities remained in the background. Constrained by the lock-out and by the peaceful conduct of the operatives, they let events take their own course. With the ending of the lock-out on 9 February and with the arrival on the 27th of knobsticks from Manchester, the atmosphere began to change. As far as the operatives were concerned, the masters were only bringing in these 'strangers' to provoke a riot so that the authorities would then have grounds for arresting the delegates.[65]

The first 56 workpeople arrived in Preston at 10 am, 27 February, under the charge of George Galloway, to work at Messrs Haslam's, cotton spinners. Of these, 47 were persuaded by the delegates to return to Manchester peacefully. According to Richard Walmsley, police sergeant, the town was in a state of great excitement, and Superintendent Gibbon thought the *habit* of congregating at the mill gates had led to a serious breach of the peace. On their own evidence, however, the story appears otherwise. Walmsley, who had been on duty near Horrockses' mill, could only testify that the 200 who had gathered there '*seemed* as if they had congregated there for the purpose of annoying the workpeople'. Later in the day, when outside Messrs Leigh and Messrs Haslam's mill in Parker Street, he again only *believed* that the crowd was there to annoy. PC Thomas Park also could only *believe* that Humber's hands were afraid to go to and from work because of the hooting of a crowd of a thousand. Even the evidence provided by Joseph Haslam gives no indication of a breach of the peace. The knobsticks were followed by a 'crowd of people', he testified, and 'I noticed some of the delegates of the Weavers and Spinners union in this town amongst those trying to persuade them to go back'. He made special mention of Grimshaw, who promised Mary Doyle, a roving frame tenter, 7s (a shilling more than her expected wage) if she went back to Manchester. Doyle herself gave evidence, but again there was no indication that the variously sized crowds had intimidated or threatened her. The evidence, it appears, failed on every count to support the general belief that the peace had been breached. The authorities nevertheless prepared themselves for the arrival of the next batch of 'scabs' as if this had been the case. On 1 March the magistrates cautioned the operatives against assembling in large numbers near the mills and intimidating people going to and from work.

On the evening of 2 March a crowd gathered at the railway station to await the arrival of knobsticks brought in to work for Messrs Leigh. As the hands were ferried down Butler Street towards Friargate, the crowd hooted and shouted. Some stones were thrown, hitting a cab carrying Thomas Birley and three other millowners, breaking two windows at Leigh's mill and one striking the forehead of a child. Birley sent a messenger to the mayor for police assistance 'as we consider it *very probable* that a serious riot would take place'.[66] As the police made their way, a stone hit their cab, and two PCs, Thomas Pool and T. Whittaker, chased and arrested Dennis Woodhead and Patrick Bennett. On reaching Leigh's mill the police found no difficulty in dispersing the crowd of one thousand. Next day a large number of Irish were brought in to work at Birley Bros' mill. A crowd, estimated by the mayor to be between five and ten thousand, again assembled at the station and hissed and hooted at the newcomers. No stones were thrown, nor was there any evidence of violence. At one o'clock the Riot Act was read, Palmerston was requested to send 100 metropolitan police, and the military were placed on alert. The following day, all meetings within the borough were prohibited.[67]

On closer analysis the events of 2 and 3 March suggest that the local authorities overreacted. The throwing of stones on the 2nd was obviously serious: property was damaged and a child hurt. But whether this amounted to a 'very serious riot' as Walmsley and Gibbon, inspector of police, believed, is another matter.[68] Birley, who was an eye witness, considered it only *'very probable'* that a serious riot *would* take place. Nowhere in his evidence before the magistrates does he suggest that a riot *had* taken place. His failure to do so is very significant: he had, after all, more to gain than either Walmsley or Gibbon; he knew how a riot would greatly have weakened the operatives' cause. In fact, very few threw stones and they were mostly young boys and girls. James Lowe, an independent journalist who had been in Preston reporting the dispute since November and who had dashed up from Manchester on learning that the Riot Act had been read, managed to collect testimonies from 'reliable eye witnesses' to show that this was the case.[69] Significantly, the ages of Dennis Woodhead and Patrick Bennett were not specified in the police depositions (they were both youths),[70] and when they were brought before Judge Cresswell at Liverpool assizes on 27 March only one (possibly Bennett) was found guilty.[71] That only eight policemen were needed to disperse the crowd of a thousand outside Leigh's mill also indicates that there had been no riot.

Nevertheless the belief that a riot had taken place conditioned the authorities' responses on the following two days. The reading of the Riot Act on 3 March was based upon what they claimed to have expected to happen, not on what had in fact happened. The explanation which the mayor sent to Palmerston on 15 March was, given the history of the dispute, misleading. 'I considered it impossible', he wrote, 'for the police to disperse the mob and *apprehending* that the workpeople in the station *would* be attacked and a serious breach of the peace, *if not loss of life, would* take place, I read the Riot Act, which I am convinced had the effect not only then, but since, of preserving the peace of the town.'[72] Since the telegram sent to Palmerston on the 3rd was certainly less alarming, it seems the authorities were later anxious to justify the action they had taken.[73] Lowe, perhaps the best impartial reporter of the strike, thought the 'spectacle of the Municipal authorities marching down [to the railway station] at the end of the Constabulary and fire brigade', actually *attracted* a large number of operatives to find out what was happening. He believed the authorities created, to a very large extent, their own reasons for reading the Riot Act.[74] Whilst the town was not 'in a state of the most perfect quiet',[75] as Robert Baxendale later wrote, the operatives were largely peaceful and orderly, as even some manufacturers and policemen — according to Lowe's account — had to agree. In his letter to Palmerston, Lowe concluded with the opinion 'that if the peace be preserved, it will be in spite and not in consequence of the measures adopted by the magistrates'.[76]

The prohibition of meetings within the borough on the 4th merely confirmed the general belief that the magistrates had overreacted. Again the mayor's reasons for doing so were paper thin. At a meeting in the centre of the town ' ... on several occasions the most violent and abusive language was uttered against not only the masters, but the magistrates and the police force. This had been tolerated for some weeks and ... unless checked, was likely to bring the authorities and law into contempt, and to lead to serious disturbances.'[77] None of this was new, as Walmsley and the magistrates were aware. Language had always been the operatives' chief weapon, and so long as they continued to urge peace and order there was little the authorities could legitimately do. In banning meetings in the borough they were simply panicking. Lowe in fact suggested that, if anything, the prohibition was likely to 'put a crowning point on the natural excitement and lead to a *real* and serious outbreak'.[78]

But despite what they considered to be a blatant act of provocation, the operatives became more and more convinced of the virtues of remaining calm and peaceful. On 6 March the spinners' committee issued a pink poster headed *Peace, Law and Order* which called upon the operatives to continue the struggle within the law. 'Give notice', it concluded, 'that persons violating the peace will receive no sympathy or support.'[79] Palmerston, who had already seen a deputation of operatives and received the letter from Lowe,[80] was obviously so impressed by the spinners' notice that he asked the 'magistrates whether they might not in consequence of the Pink Placards suspend their prohibition of public meetings'.[81]

Palmerston's hint that the civil authorities may have acted hastily had already been taken up by the press and by middle-class opinion in Preston. The *Preston*

Guardian attacked the authorities for overreacting,[82] and the ratepayers denounced the partiality of the magistrates.[83] The operatives were far less astonished by the authorities' behaviour, and their suspicion that they and the masters were working hand in hand to entrap their delegates seemed to be confirmed hour by hour. There is no evidence to suggest that this was the case, but Walmsley's two pious letters of 5 and 15 May, justifying to Palmerston the actions taken, strongly suggest that the authorities were themselves aware that they may have acted unnecessarily. Walmsley's argument that 'if such steps had not been taken and properly attended to, much more serious disturbance would have occurred'[84] was precisely the kind of argument he knew would please the Home Office. In the context of the Preston dispute it was patently spurious, and Palmerston's comment on events in Stockport in April provides confirmation of this. When William Rayner, the mayor of Stockport, prepared to ban the procession to, and the meeting at, Springers Field,[85] Palmerston noted that 'it is very unlikely that the turnouts will break the peace; *it has not hitherto been their system to do so*'.[86] This assessment, it must be added, was not the product of a faulty memory.

The final occasion on which the authorities intervened was on 18 March, when the borough magistrates met behind closed doors in the Town Hall to discuss the conspiracy charges to be brought against the delegates. The authorities had already told Palmerston on the 15th that interference with the knobsticks was an indictable offence and that the operatives were organizing meetings out of the town with that object in view. 'But conceiving it to be more a matter for private complaint, than one to be noticed on public grounds', they did not see any reason 'to direct proceedings . . . against the parties so offending'.[87] Walmsley considered banning meetings outside of the borough, but once the masters brought charges and the delegates were arrested there was no reason to do so. Once the decision to prosecute had been taken, the authorities moved with some urgency since the Liverpool spring assizes were to finish by the end of the week. When the eleven accused delegates appeared at Liverpool on 28 March Judge Cresswell postponed the trial until August because he felt the defence had not been given reasonable time to prepare its case. In the event the charges were later dropped but the proceedings which had taken place at Preston were not forgotten. The *Preston Guardian* bitterly attacked the authorities' handling of the hearing,[88] whilst a petition from the inhabitants of Preston to the House of Commons alleged that there had not been *one* breach of the peace despite the activities of the police, who *alone* had made 'many unwarrantable attempts'[89] to do so.

In his evidence before the 1852–3 Select Committee on Police, Captain John Woodford, the Chief Constable of Lancashire, argued that 'no more prejudicial system to the working of a good establishment of police can exist than for the management of the men to be invested in a fluctuating body, such as Watch

Committees or Town Councils'.[90] By March of 1854 the operatives and ratepayers of Preston had come to a similar conclusion, if for quite different reasons. Woodford's main concern was to expose the deficiencies of the Lancashire borough police forces in order to create a wider support for amalgamating them with the County Constabulary. The operatives, for their part, were concerned with the way in which the local authorities were using the police as a tool for inciting civil disorder. For Woodford, the borough police were lax and inefficient; for the operatives they were devious and overzealous; for both, the Watch Committee and the Town Council were the villains of the piece.

The Preston Watch Committee was formed in 1836, a year after the Corporation Act had allowed incorporated towns to set up their own police forces. In 1832, when the new police station was built in Avenham Street, Preston had six full-time policemen,[91] only three more than there had been in 1810.[92] With the setting up of the Watch Committee, which consisted of the mayor, Aldermen Haydock and Monk, and four town councillors, the force was increased to seven.[93] In 1850 the old argument that '[a few] constables can effectually watch and preserve the peace in a concentrated population which was orderly and quiet, not disorderly and easily excited',[94] still dominated the town's thinking. By that year Preston had reduced its force from the 26 employed in 1848 to meet the threat of Chartism, to 15.[95] In August 1853 the number had increased to 31,[96] but this still failed to meet the generally accepted ratio of one policeman to 1,700 inhabitants. At the beginning of the strike the Preston police force, as with most Lancashire towns, remained seriously undermanned; the reason 'false liberalism and mistaken notions of economy', as one Manchester paper trenchantly pointed out.[97]

By the early 1850s the Watch Committee had increased in size. Now there were seven aldermen (including the mayor) and twelve councillors.[98] As the Watch Committee was a committee of the Town Council[99] it had its expected share of cotton lords, and whilst they did not dominate the proceedings they attended most of the meetings. During the dispute the committee was faced with three problems: the size of the police force and its threatened absorption by the county police; how and when the police ought to be used; and ironically, the level of police wages.

The question of police wages was, in 1852 and 1853, a general problem throughout the country. Rising food prices affected the police just as much as the factory operative. Both expected a fairly stable standard of living and both were prepared to withdraw their labour when demands for increased wages were refused. In June 1853 the Manchester police, after two-thirds of the force had resigned en bloc, were granted a wage increase,[100] and in the following month the Hull police adopted the same tactics, with equal success.[101] After these widely publicised victories the Preston police made their own bid, which came before the Watch Committee on 1 August.[102] The size of the demand is not noted in the Minutes but a decision was held over until the authorities in Liverpool, Manchester, Bolton, Blackburn, Oldham, Wigan, Salford and Lancaster had notified the committee of the wages that they were paying. In all probability this was a delaying tactic, but with the growing possibility of a protracted strike in the town itself parsimony gave way to expediency. On 5 September the 31 constables were given an increase of 1s per week. The five grades of constables now earned 16s, 18s, 19s, £1, and £1 2s respectively. Sergeants were paid a weekly wage of £1 4s and the inspector earned £85 per annum.[103] At most the increase was just under 7%.

The increased wages also had the advantage of attracting new recruits, although the first move in this direction had been made as early as July when the committee advertised for a superintendent to replace Mr Samuel Bannister, who had been 'worn out by 17 years service'.[104] By early August 89 applications had been received, which were then narrowed down to a short list of six. On 1 September Joseph Gibbon, the third son of Sir John Gibbon, was appointed, although he did not actually take charge until 9 September.[105] His selection indicates the Watch Committee's thinking and the difficult circumstances they anticipated. Gibbon was only 36 but had already been a superintendent of the Plymouth police force; he had both youth and experience.[106] Moreover, he was opposed to any amalgamation of the borough and county police which, since the 1852-3 Select Committee, had become the major theme of the Home Office's police policy. When Palmerston's intended Bill was discussed in June 1854 the Watch Committee, over which Gibbon now had some influence, condemned it as unconstitutional and 'subversive of independence and right of self government'. The Town Council were desperate to cling onto their power and Gibbon was equally keen to gather around him an independent and efficient police force.

When Gibbon took over from Bannister the force consisted of one inspector, three sergeants and 26 constables, five of whom permanently patrolled the coal yards, New Quay, Avenham Walk and Moor Park. The effective force was therefore only 21, leaving seven for day duty and 14 for night duty.[107] To overcome this lack of numbers the Watch Committee took two steps: it swore in special constables and increased the number of full-time policemen.

A week before the commencement of the lock-out 30 special constables were sworn in.[108] This was a typical and expected precaution.[109] It showed that the local authorities were making preparations and that they were willing to use force if and when it was required. It had the advantage of saving the rates, special constables being paid only when they actually performed duties.[110] They were a reserve force which could be called upon in cases of emergency — real or imagined. But there were a number of drawbacks. One magistrate in Glossop complained bitterly that 'special constables were a vain alternative ... [for] ... we assure you ... [that] ... they must necessarily be selected from tradesmen but these contribute, for fear of becoming marked men, to the strike fund. In Glossop', he continued, 'we have no class other than manufacturers, operatives and tradesmen. We have therefore no one to turn to to keep the laws.'[111] Although the social structure of Preston was less rigid than that in Glossop, the local authorities still had to rely upon the working class for the bulk of their special constables. Of the 39 special constables suspended from duties on 24 March[112] 17 were labourers, three sawyers, two pensioners, two gardeners, two spinners, one weaver, one tape sizer, one flax dresser, one overlooker, one cab driver, one bookbinder, one porter, one ostler, one tinplateworker, one tobacconist, one joiner, one shoemaker, and one clogger.[113] At the very most, only six could be considered part of the tradesman and shopkeeping class, and even fewer could be considered part of the 'labour aristocracy'. Almost half were unskilled men whose lack of police experience was in all probability only compensated by their brute strength. But strength and force of numbers was not always sufficient to put down meetings and processions of a 'riotous and tumultuous character'. In the Wigan riot of October 1853, 25 of the 30 special constables sworn in disappeared as soon as the 1,000-strong crowd began to assail them with stones and large bludgeons.[114] In Kidderminster, where the carpet weavers were on strike, the magistrates found difficulty in recruiting special constables 'unless sustained by the knowledge that an adequate and disciplined police force [was] on the spot to aid and assist them in case of extremities'.[115]

The deficiencies of special constables were well known, as was the need for a supporting and efficient full-time police force. In Preston the Watch Committee had been pressing, since early October, for an increase in the number of borough policemen. At the Town Council's meeting on 6 October, George Smith suggested that the police should be increased to 40 'in order to preserve the peace of the town which now appeared to be threatened'.[116] But Peter Catterall, the mayor, refused to accept the need for an increase, insisting that special constables could be called in whenever required. With one eye on the rates and the other on what the operatives might do if the police were reinforced, Catterall took his usual appeasing stand. In October he had no intention of inciting disorder. The threatened lock-out was still nine days off and a solution, although unlikely, was still possible.

After the commencement of the lock-out the new mayor, Walmsley, continued to follow this conciliatory line, but pressure from other members of the Watch Committee began to increase. The strike could no longer be seen as 'a nine day wonder'[117] and on 14 November, after Gibbon had presented a fairly extensive report on the state of the borough police,[118] the Watch Committee resolved to increase the existing force by ten.[119] A sub-committee which included Catterall, Goodair and Spencer soon met the magistrates and on 2 December ten constables were duly sworn in.[120] The *Preston Chronicle*, in one of its rare editorials on the police, explained that the increase had little to do with the strike. 'We believe the proposals to have been made, considered and adopted purely with reference to the ordinary conditions of our population.' Preston, it alleged, had the second lowest ratio of police to population in Lancashire, and that the 'cry of economy ... [was] a delusive one'.[121] But the *Chronicle*'s facts were woefully wrong, and its justification of the move was little more than a feeble attempt to allay the operatives' fears. In 1852 the ratio of police to population of the nine Lancashire borough police forces was one to 2,300, Lancashire boroughs having a combined total force of 176 policemen.[122] By late 1853 these numbers had, in all probability, decreased. Wigan, with 11 policemen, had a ratio of 1:2910; Blackburn, with 13 police, a ratio of 1:3615;[123] Warrington, with 11 police, a ratio of 1:2010;[124] Bolton, with 20 police, a ratio of 1:3050. Preston, whose 32 police gave a ratio of 1:2188, compared very favourably. When in March 1854 the Home Office carried out an incomplete survey of the police, Preston's *relatively* favourable position becomes even clearer (Lancaster 1:3860, Stockport 1:3588).[125] Only Liverpool and Manchester, both well known for their efficient police, could boast lower ratios (1:466 and 1:681 respectively). If Preston's police strength was deplorably low it was less so than other Lancashire towns, even after these towns had increased their forces to meet the exigencies of the ten per cent campaign.

That Preston increased its police force to cope with the strikers is beyond doubt, and the public statements made by Gibbon, Woodford and the *Chronicle* could not hide that fact.[126] Indeed, by April 1855 the force had been reduced from 42 to 37[127] and in 1856 it was reported that some inhabitants were paying for private protection[128] just as they had done during the Napoleonic wars.[129] Preston, as with other Lancashire towns, was only prepared to incur police expenditure when it was unavoidable.[130] The optimal size of the force for ordinary circumstances was clearly less than that required to help the local authorities in their fight against the operatives. In the 1836 strike it was the Home Office which suggested augmenting the police.[131] In 1853 the Watch Committee needed no prompting.

The public reason for increasing the number of police was so transparent that it did not elicit any response from the operatives. They were determined 'never to give the policemen a job',[132] and throughout the period of the strike there was a sharp decrease in crime 'despite outbreaks of violent crime over the whole country between 1850 and 1853'.[133] Between November 1853 and April 1854 the number of prison committals in Preston totalled 215, which according to the Rev. Clay represented a decrease of 22.7% on the period November 1852 to April 1853 and a 32% decrease on the six months May to October 1853.[134] Prison committals do not of course truly reflect the actual level of crime, but Clay's statistics do reflect the rigid discipline of the turnouts: they knew it was all too easy for the authorities and the police to pounce on the slightest indiscretion. But if the reduction in crime was unexpected so too was the absence of disorder. After the riots at Blackburn and Wigan and threatening behaviour elsewhere the local authorities must have been surprised to find that the Preston men were able to act out their public pronouncements regarding patience, peace and order. Earl Cathcart, military commander for the Northern and Midland districts, told Palmerston in February 1854:

> It is certainly *very remarkable*, notwithstanding the many thousands of factory operatives who have been thrown out of employment, and living in idleness for so long a period, that they should have uniformly conducted themselves in so peaceful and so orderly a manner. Individually they have rarely offended against the law and collectively they have not occasioned any riots or other serious disturbances.[135]

With the reduction in crime and the absence of disorder the police were left to patrol the mills and public houses suspected of breaking licences and harbouring prostitutes.[136] There was little else for them to do. As the special correspondent for the *Daily News* reported, Preston was in a state of suspended animation.

> Men in groups of five or twenty were standing on corners of streets, or in front of shop windows, looking at nothing and apparently unconscious that they were objects of attraction or speculation to the passers-by. They seemed under the action of some mental chloroform voluntarily taken. The only expression, if expression it may be called, visible on their faces, was that of waiting – waiting quite patiently – for something to turn up. Nothing violent, nothing even obstinate, still less vicious, was to be noticed.[137]

This tranquillity was disturbed on 31 January when the police broke ranks. The incident took place outside Hollins's mill at 6.30 pm when three policemen – one in uniform and two in plain clothes – contrived to provoke a disturbance of the peace. Assuming the role of a turnout, one of the plain-clothes policemen began to hurl abusive comments at the knobsticks employed by Hollins. As a crowd began to gather, the two remaining policemen made their arrest and carried the man away to the police station. According to Thomas Carter, a tailor from Park Street, the 'prisoner had his coat collar turned up, and it so covered his face that scarcely any portion of his face could be seen except for his forehead and eyes'.[138] Clearly no-one realised that the arrested man was in fact a plain-clothes policeman, yet for all this the crowd were not willing to intervene. They stood by as the three men made their way to the station. The following day the inquisitive Carter went to the Town Hall, only to find the prisoner had been released and that there was no entry in the police records of the arrest. The matter was then reported to the Watch Committee which expressed its disapproval and fined the three officers concerned 5s, 4s and 3s. As far as the local authorities were concerned the police had indulged in a silly 'lark'. For the operatives it was a much more serious affair. As Robert Baxendale told Palmerston later, 'we see it as provocation' and as an explicit attempt to bring the operatives 'into collision with the Authorities of the Borough'.[139]

The only definite conclusion which can be drawn from this incident is that it failed. Whether the local authorities were actively involved in devious plans to provoke the normally peaceful turnouts is difficult to say. At the time, the operatives reserved judgement, even though they may have privately thought so. In public they accused the authorities of falling down on their duty, but at first never directly accused them of attempting to break the peace. They were content simply to condemn the base actions of the police and to recognize that the three policemen acted on their own misguided initiative. But by 8 February the weavers began to hint at a conspiracy: 'under all circumstances be peaceable and obey the law. Do not allow yourselves to be drawn into any violations of the law by either officials or non-officials.'[140]

That the three policemen probably acted quite independently is supported by the fact that the borough police were widely known to be pathetically indisciplined and greatly inexperienced. An amusing letter published in the *Preston Guardian*, only three days before the debacle, portrayed the Preston police as comically incompetent.[141] Drunkenness, misconduct and neglect of duty were commonplace. The turnover of police was, as a result, rapid.[142] Between 17 November 1853 and 28 September 1854, twenty-four vacancies occurred; two died, three retired because of sickness, two moved to other police forces and three are unaccounted for. Nine were discharged for drunkenness. Of these, two had been in the force for only five weeks, one for seven weeks, one for two months, one for four and a half months, one five months, one six months, one fifteen months and the last for two years and seven months. Five were also discharged for misconduct; one served seven weeks, one nine months, two a year and a half, and one just over three years.[143] In one sense this rapid turnover indicates that Gibbon and the Watch Committee were prepared to set high standards. But the police force was only as good as its recruits, and since the selection procedure was, according to one recent authority, largely based 'on the proverbial thesis of poachers making the best gamekeepers',[144] it seems the local authorities had little option but to enforce dismissal, if only to salvage their own reputations. Drunkenness and misconduct were always publicly obvious; provocation could always be seen as over-exuberance.

In early February the operatives were thus only prepared to hint that the action of the police was part of a premeditated plan. After the reopening of the mills, when the activities of the police became increasingly sinister, they discarded all their caution. Apart from the uniformed police on duty outside the mills and at the station, the number operating under cover of plain clothes increased. With the operatives meeting daily, they were now able to mingle freely in the crowd. The recent eviction of strikers from tied cottages and the rumour that knobsticks were soon to be imported from Ireland and elsewhere all added to the tension. Now careless thought and abusive language were to be the spying policeman's diet, and libellous attacks on the magistrates the civil authorities' hope. Both were to be disappointed. Occasionally Swinglehurst would mount an incautious tirade but the operatives still maintained strict adherence to the principles of patience and peace.

With the arrival of the knobsticks, things began to change. Batches of police were sent to the railway station to escort incoming labour to the mills. Sixty special constables, including some millowners and their managers who freely offered their help, were sworn in.[145] With the support of George Smith, John Humber easily persuaded the mayor and the council to request the Home Office to send a hundred metropolitan police (later refused); similar requests had been made by some towns in the Chartist period.[146] More and more local police were dressed as factory operatives. They went about the crowds and attended committee meetings despite, as the *Preston Guardian* insistently made clear, the 'strong feeling in the town against the practice'. One or two unnamed councillors, aware that this espionage was likely to cause unnecessary trouble, attacked the *plan*[147] of provocation, but they were out-numbered in a council sensing its chance of imposing its increasingly dubious authority under the banner of law and order.

The unconstitutional activities of the police were publicly defended by Robert Ascroft, the Town Clerk, variously known as 'the paid servant of the Preston Masters' Association', 'the Attorney-General of the Masters' and the 'Town Council, Mayor, Magistrate and all'.[148] His defence rested on the similar use of plain-clothes policemen in London. Cowell was quick to point out that 'that was true, but they were not employed for the purpose of entrapping people who wished to obtain an advance of wages'.[149] The operatives claimed, with some justice, that 'scarce a single case of misdemeanour would have occurred had it not been for the system of espionage adopted' (Grimshaw's words). Cowell sought an interview with Gibbon and Walmsley; neither was prepared to withdraw their men, who were successfully carrying out the authorities' wishes. The operatives were now no longer able to restrain their language. In the Orchard on Thursday 2 March Cowell argued forcibly that it was the clear intention 'of the police of this town to create a disturbance in order that the people might be entrapped. The Mayor and the police knobsticks', he concluded 'were in the hands of the masters.' At the same meeting Swinglehurst urged the 'Lilliputian Superintendent to go back where he came from ... they were not to have spies amongst them at every door and at every street; they should not permit it'. Two days later, in a distinctly menacing speech, Swinglehurst continued 'if ever I catch a fellow in plain clothes in my company with a bludgeon in his pocket I'll knock his teeth down his throat. No man shall be a spy on my actions.'[150] At the ratepayers' meeting on 8 March the middle class joined in the attack. Edward Ambler set the tone.

They could not fancy that they were in a land which was generally called 'free England' and 'liberal England' when parties were allowed to go into the mills with their hands and faces daubed; with a check shirt on — they could not fancy that they were in England when such things existed, but rather that they were translated to some of the continental countries where the people suffered from the parental care of some liberal despot.[151]

Others were less committed. Dixon, as a member of the Watch Committee, was asked by Cowell why he had not resisted the application for the metropolitan police. Dixon answered that there had been confusion over the time of the meeting, and that when he went at 3 pm he found the meeting had taken place at noon. Since this was the usual time for the Watch Committee meeting it became obvious that Dixon had deliberately absented himself. His tardy repudiation of the 'abominable spy system' came too late to save him from embarrassment.

Whilst middle-class commitment was beginning to show signs of weakening, the operatives remained defiant and indignant. On 7 March Robert Baxendale and James Whalley sent Palmerston written complaints against the police and the local authorities. The events of 31 January were now, with hindsight, seen as a deliberate act of provocation,[152] and the reading of the Riot Act at a time 'when the town was in a state of tranquillity, could not have been resorted to for the preservation of the peace, but in the hope that this might lead to its violation, no doubt to offer a pretext for the augmentation of the police force, who in various DISGUISES, may assist [our] opponents in their intellectual occupation'.[153]

This view of events is as understandable as it is misleading. The operatives' suspicion that the masters and the authorities were conspiring to entrap and incarcerate the delegates was, in a sense, self-fulfilling. The prohibition of processions and the ban imposed in September on all open-air meetings held after sunset were considered nothing more than petty restrictions, and merely served to strengthen the operatives' resolve to keep the peace. The insidious activities of the police, together with the importation of knobsticks and the consequent reading of the Riot Act, were seen, however, as a more sinister connection and one which led inexorably to the arrests in March. Duncombe's petition, and the *Preston Guardian*'s bitter attack on the authorities, as well as the ratepayers' cry for a free and liberal England, appear to have confirmed the operatives in their belief that the masters, magistrates, town council and police were working hand in hand. The authorities' failure to contradict any of these accusations until after the weavers' defeat suggests that they too were perhaps conscious that this is how it may have seemed. As it turns out, though the authorities' actions always coincided with some action taken by the masters, there is no evidence to support this interpretation of events. In fact, to suggest a conspiracy of this kind is to give the authorities too much credit, and to make the masters out to be more devious than they were. The masters always made their intentions blatantly clear, and, whilst the authorities were equally clear about the preservation of law and order, their behaviour in March suggests that they acted unnecessarily and hastily, rather than with forethought.

7 Guardians of the Poor

> The Pop-shops that's in Preston, is as full has [sic] any crate,
> Shirts and shifts has all gone to pay the Poors' Rate;
> Dickeys, stockings, shawls and caps, all come in a russell,
> And one of the Cotton Lords brought his misses' bussell.

The administration of poor relief provided the local authorities with yet another opportunity for exerting influence. With 18–20,000 operatives out of work in the worst winter since the Napoleonic wars, the Guardians were invested with more power than they could possibly have dreamed of. For the *ex officio* members of the Board, like Miller, Jacson, Paley and Swainson, there by right of being JPs, it must have been seen as part of some wider design within which they could fittingly evangelize on the moral inadequacy of the ignorant operative class and on the virtues of less eligibility, the bastille and the market place. For others, especially those with no cotton connections, the position was less enviable. The strike and the lock-out raised an unprecedented social and moral problem.

The crucial question was whether or not the local Board of Guardians ought to distribute relief and, if so, in what form and to whom? Poor authorities, it is true, were always faced with this issue. Relief policy was a controversial issue at the best of times. But the dispute, which since mid-September had materially hardened into a class war, gave the problem a political as well as an economic twist.[1] A generous relief policy was always likely to bring severe pressure both from ratepayers and from those employers whose hands would be maintained. It would give a boost to the morale of the operatives, generally sustain the cohesion of the movement, and protect the union fund. In effect, the Poor Law authorities would subsidise the working class in their fight against the employers and, in the case of a large manufacturing town, use the masters' own money to do so. This paradox escaped neither the Preston cotton lords nor the *Economist*, which in one of its more bombastic leaders noted that:

the application of the unemployed operatives to be maintained (or relieved) out of these rates is simply a demand that, their own funds being exhausted, they shall be maintained out of the funds of the antagonists; – that, their own ammunition being at an end, they shall be supplied with ammunition from the stores and magazines of the enemy whom they are endeavouring to overpower; – that, when the contest is about to terminate from the exhaustion of one of the belligerents, the law shall step in and enable that belligerent to continue the contest by drawing on the resources of the opposing party – shall, in a word, enable the men to fight the masters with their masters' own money.[2]

In matters of this kind the *Economist* was prone to exaggeration, but there is some merit in the drift of its conclusion, and it reflected the ironic position in which the manufacturers thought themselves to be.

A more parsimonious policy, on the other hand, held certain advantages for the manufacturers. It would increase the number of operatives drawing on the fund; seriously weaken the psychological and material conditions of those operatives unable to make a claim on the union fund; probably increase the number of knobsticks; and certainly reduce the burden on the ratepayers' pocket. Dividing the cohesion of the labour movement and getting the support of the ratepayers were clear gains for the cotton lords. For the guardians, the problem was less simple. They had to weigh the possible gains from precipitating the end of the dispute against their own conscience, and the possibility that withholding relief would fuel the fires of discontent and increase the threat to private property. In short, the local poor authorities were put in an extraordinary position by a combination of extraordinary circumstances.

Only recently the Poor Law Board, through the 1852 Relief Regulation Order, had defined the general conditions under which outdoor relief was to be granted. There were, however, no guidelines concerning strikes and lock-outs. Yet this was a vital question and, as the *Economist* warned, 'involves those very first principles of social justice and expediency which lie at the bottom of a national provision for destitute poor'.[3] As it turns out the debate which this question raised was far more important than the effects it had on the ten per cent campaign. To appreciate the way in which the Preston guardians handled this largely undefined problem, it is necessary to see how other Lancashire guardians responded.

The problem of Poor Law relief during the ten per cent campaign first raised its head in November 1853, when the Burnley Board of Guardians asked the Poor Law Board for guidance.[4] On 1 October the Master Spinners' and Manufacturers' Association, fearing that they would be taken in detail, had resolved to close their mills on 28 October.[5] Almost immediately the magistrates warned the Board of Guardians that there was likely to be an increase in the number applying for relief, and informed the Home Office that they were making arrangements to preserve public order.[6] In turn, the Burnley guardians informed the Poor Law Board of the intended closure and of the growing threat of widening distress.[7] On 20 October H.B. Farnall, Assistant Commissioner for Lancashire, attended a special meeting where he urged the guardians to apply the Labour Test and to give relief as far as possible in kind. He also suggested that relief might be made by way of loans which the operatives would repay once they regained employment. Apparently these suggestions were favourably received, and on 12 November the Poor Law Board wrote telling the guardians that they saw no reason why the 1852 Relief Order should not be observed.[8]

In the event this advice did not go down well. Ever since the issue of the 1852 Order the Burnley Union had resisted its implementation. On 25 October 1852 they sent the Poor Law Board an able, if typical critique, explaining that the various provisions of the Order would inevitably mean treating the undeserving poor and the deserving poor in precisely the same way; and that this would involve many cases of extreme and unnecessary hardship. They objected to three crucial clauses; payment in kind, which by denying the guardians a choice amounted to a violation of their liberty (Article 1); allowances in aid of wages (Article 5); and the Labour Test (Article 6).

On the issue of allowances in aid of wages the Burnley guardians were strident and uncompromising. They accused the Poor Law Board of holding an 'erroneous and fallacious view of the mode in which wages were paid in the manufacturing districts', pointing out that, unlike agricultural labourers, factory operatives were paid by the piece and that their earnings depended upon the number of hours worked. In times of depression, short-time working would, they noted, involve a reduction in earnings and lead to starvation. Without allowances in aid of wages able bodied men would be compelled to 'relinquish all independent labour' in order to obtain poor relief. Insofar as this would increase pauperism during depressed times and 'pervert moral energies and self dependence', the Burnley guardians were convinced that the 1852 Order was self-defeating.[9]

On the issue of the Labour Test the guardians, in 1852 at least, were almost moderate in their criticism. They agreed to accept the principle that an able bodied man should be set to work before he became eligible for relief, but could not accept the Poor Law Board's right to establish an unbending law which was to be enforced in all cases.[10]

In essence it was a question of discretionary powers, and the Burnley guardians felt that they had the experience and the right to determine, in ordinary circumstances at least, whether the test ought to be applied. In November 1853 circumstances were different and, through a special committee which included Sir James Kay-Shuttleworth, the guardians attempted to make the Poor Law Board clarify their position regarding strikes, lock-outs and relief.

In clearly marked cases of indigence in which not only weekly wages have ceased but all other resources arising from the sale of furniture and clothing have been exhausted are we right in conceiving that the Board of Guardians, without reference to the *origins* of indigence are bound to extend relief administered in strict conformity with your general Order? ... In this class of case we conceive that we recognize the operation of the principle which provides security of life without which there can be no security for property ...

On the other hand, if there be any cases short of this degree of indigence caused by the suspension of employment in the cotton mills of this district for the support of which the rateable property of the Union is legally liable you are requested clearly to define them for our guidance ...

While we feel actively the suffering which must gradually extend over this Union if this lamentable dispute be prolonged, and would by any legitimate means mitigate its intensity, we are as deeply impressed with the responsibility we should incur if we were to use our power over the rates for any purpose inconsistent with public welfare. We therefore seek from you a clear and simple definition of the nature and degree of indigence to the support of which the property of this Union is liable under the circumstances described as well as to be informed whether we are strictly to adhere to your general Order in the administration of such relief, and especially to Articles 5, and 6.[11]

The Poor Law Board's reply was predictable:

The principles by which the guardians ought to be guided in treating applications for relief from the poor rates . . . are few and simple. It will be for the guardians to apply them, after a careful enquiry into the circumstances of each particular case.

In each case the question will be whether the case is one of actual destitution. Where the applicant has the pecuniary means of subsistence for himself and his family, from *whatsoever funds* those means may be derived or where he may, if he *pleases* immediately obtain work and so earn the means of subsistence the Board are of the opinion that he ought not to be considered as actually destitute.

If on the other hand he has neither money nor work, and is really without the present means of obtaining either, so that aid from the poor rates is absolutely necessary for the subsistence of himself and his family, the guardians ought to relieve him. Every case . . . ought to be carefully investigated in all circumstances.

With regard to the question as to an adherence to the general relief order . . . especially Art. 5 and 6, the Board must expect the guardians will adhere to it, unless upon a consideration of the special circumstances of any particular case they deem it expedient to depart from the regulations and report to the Poor Law Board in the manner prescribed by Art. 10 of the general order.[12]

In this circumspect reply the Poor Law Board tentatively suggested two guiding principles. Firstly, though the Board was careful not to mention either strikes or lock-outs, it seems that those operatives on strike, and who could get work if they 'pleased', and those receiving relief from the strike fund, whether as a result of a lock-out or strike, were not actually destitute. Secondly, and rather less tentatively, they urged the guardians to observe the 1852 Order. Yet at the same time they provided a number of significant escape clauses. Guardians were permitted to depart from the principle of allowance in aid of wages and the Labour Test, so long as they notified the Board of the particular circumstances of each application (Article 10). Since these applications were generally sanctioned by the Board almost automatically, Articles 5 and 6 were persistently breached in practice.[13] Since the definition of destitution was also left entirely in the hands of the guardians there was nothing to stop them relieving those already receiving some small relief from the strike fund. The clause relating to obtaining work 'if he pleases' created further room for discretion. During the lock-out, mills were unlikely to open if only a small proportion of the work force reapplied for their jobs. Were these then able to apply for relief? The Poor Law Board remained silent. This is probably what the Burnley guardians expected. They knew from experience that the central authorities were unlikely to commit themselves or to force the issue. Having given them the opportunity to do so, the Burnley guardians now felt they could do as they liked — and within the bounds of economy they did.

It is not clear precisely how many operatives locked out by the millowners were given relief, but there is little doubt that the Burnley guardians gave assistance when it was required. John Acombe, a 34-year-old power loom weaver, is a fairly typical case: for the upkeep of a wife and five children under the age of 12 the guardians gave 3s in cash and 3s 6d in kind weekly. This was not significantly different from the relief given James Hargreaves, a weaver (probably a handloom weaver) not directly involved in the lock-out. For a wife and six children under the age of 13 Hargreaves received 4s in cash and 4s in kind weekly.[14] As far as the Burnley guardians were concerned both were deserving poor and needed to be treated in the same way, irrespective of the cause of their destitution.

On 17 November Farnall revisited the Union and once again exhorted the guardians to act within the existing law, and recommended that they should look for a piece of land on which to employ the able bodied.[15] This the guardians agreed to do, but within the short space of a week they wrote telling the Poor Law Board that 'no person could be found within the Union willing to let the Guardians have a piece of land'.[16] As an alternative, they suggested that the labour test might best be provided within the workhouse itself and resolved to set up a committee to discuss the matter on 8 December. On the 9th the guardians reported that the majority of the committee had failed to turn up and asked for more time to consider the issue.[17] By now Farnall guessed what was going on. In a memo to the Poor Law Board he noted 'hope this is not a premeditated attempt to avoid the labour test — procrastination is quite annoying'.[18] A few days later he warned 'it is clear that such a proceeding is not only illegal but impolitic. It is in fact playing into the hands of the turnouts.'[19] On his advice the Poor Law Board threatened to refuse to authorize relief under Article 6, unless the labour test was introduced immediately. All this was to no avail. By 22 December, with the Burnley lock-out over, the guardians became even more resolute. With a final touch of defiance the guardians passed a resolution claiming that they 'do not feel inclined under the present position of the Union to provide an outdoor relief test for the Union, but are disposed to allow such outdoor relief to applicants who are not able wholly to maintain themselves by work as they may think necessary according to the circumstances of each case before them'.[20]

By shrewd delaying tactics, the Burnley guardians defied the Poor Law Board at every turn. Their implacable opposition to the Board's Order continued, despite the collision between the masters and their men. Through the lock-out relief increased, and this was distributed to those directly affected, as well as those who suffered from the subsequent decline of work in the area.

At Haslingden this defiance continued, although here subtlety gave way to open hostility. On 16 December Farnall attended a special meeting arranged and chaired by James Black.[21] Farnall opened the discussion with a brief statistical analysis of the effects of the lock-out. He admitted that the affairs in China and Turkey made the immediate reopening of the mills unlikely, and told the guardians that they could not allow the 'men, women and children of England, to starve as a result'. Where wages were less than subsistence levels those applying for relief were perfectly entitled to receive it. Nor did it matter, he claimed, whether those wanting relief had put themselves 'in a false position by turning out', nor whether they were locked out by masters avoiding the threat of being taken in detail. Whatever the reason, those applying for relief were not to be refused.

Once Farnall insisted that 'able bodied men should not be permitted to dip their hands into the parochial purse without being subject to the [Labour] test', he lost whatever sympathy he may have gained at the beginning of the discussion. His claim that Wigan, Burnley (mistakenly) and Rochdale had all passed resolutions to negotiate the purchase of land so that the test could be applied was no consolation for the Haslingden guardians. Nor was his elevating claim that digging — as opposed to the usual oakum picking, stone breaking, woodcutting and corn grinding — was the 'most facile and best test for any large number of able bodied men'; it merely stiffened opposition. Mr Black stated it was 'morally impossible for the guardians to find a labour test for those who applied for relief under such circumstances as had recently existed'. On a more practical note, Mr Priestly suggested 'it would never do to send a man to work the land for a month and then expect him to transfer back into a warm factory afterwards; it would make him helpless'. In a more typical vein, Mr Aitken argued that, since strikes occurred so infrequently, any land specifically bought for the able bodied would remain unused for most of the time, and that as a result Farnall's wish to reduce costs through imposing conditions for relief was, once again, self-defeating.

In the face of this mounting opposition Farnall was forced into revealing more clearly the brief given him by the Poor Law Board. In a desperate bid to capture the support of the ratepayers he strongly urged them to accept a labour test 'so that it might be known that the guardians did not mean to make the rates a fund for agitation to fall back on'. When this failed to cause the intended embarrassment, Farnall resorted to the sanction of the law, claiming that relief to the able-bodied without a labour test was illegal and those operatives who refused to submit to such a test were likely to be imprisoned. For a Board which had uncharacteristically elected guardians without delay, and which in the recent past could only reduce absenteeism by holding meetings at the Commercial Inn[22] — rather than at the Haslingden National School — Farnall's threats may have been well measured. But in 1853 the Haslingden guardians were made of sterner stuff. Neither deference nor provocation was to alter their stand. After a hectic discussion in which Black 'wished someone would lock-out the Poor Law Commissioners, for they could do better without them',[23] it was resolved that relief policy would remain the same.[24]

In 1852 the Preston guardians were equally opposed to the Poor Law Board's Prohibitory Order and passed a resolution to rescind the clauses relating to relief in kind, allowances in aid of wages and the labour test. Only Addison, Pilkington, Rev. Brickell and Dobson, the editor of the *Preston Chronicle*, voted against; twenty-two were in favour.[25] When the Oldham Board of Guardians organized a protest meeting in Manchester in late October,[26] Ashworth and Calvert were sent as delegates.[27] In 1852 Farnall noted his 'views were always in the minority at Preston'.[28] In 1853 and 1854 this was no longer the case. By then the attitudes of the Preston guardians had significantly changed.[29]

In August and September Board meetings were generally inconsequential and, as usual, few guardians attended.[30] Strikes and lock-outs were not on the agenda. In this period outdoor relief remained steady, at about £108 per week, whilst indoor relief averaged between £75 and £85 per week, and the number in the workhouse between 600 and 620. After the commencement of the lock-out on 15 October the number receiving relief began to increase and on 18 October, the day the guardians were informed of Farnall's intended visit, the total had reached 3,217 (2,479 outdoor and 738 indoor) at a cost of £239 0s 8¼d. Farnall's visit on 25 October,[31] when nearly all the guardians attended, was the first occasion the dispute was discussed.

Farnall opened the meeting with a review of the year's business, observing that there were 428 fewer paupers on the books than in the previous year which, he noted, was one of vast prosperity, and that £993 had been saved as a result. After more faint praise, he moved on to the thorny question of the strike — as he called it.[32] In typical style he urged the guardians 'to meet the crisis with the greatest firmness possible and not to extend to the [strikers] that sort of feeling which was so often extended and which ought to be extended to the legitimate poor who struggled with their fate and were ultimately borne down by adverse circumstances'.[33]

Relief in Preston was to be conditional upon entering the workhouse, thus raising the spectre of the 1834 Act, which Lancashire had generally managed to evade ever since the assistant commissioners first invaded the north in 1837–8.[34] No outdoor relief was to be given until the workhouse, with an estimated capacity of 914, was full. The sick and the disabled were to be lodged out of doors in order to make extra room for the 'strikers' if it meant an increase in costs 'even of 2s 6d a week'. Once the workhouses were full the guardians were told to employ the able bodied on a 20 acre piece of land attached to the workhouse, and if men were not fit other work had to be devised. 'No relief should be given to any one of those families, or all of them, if they could be possibly set to work — use rooms anywhere to employ them — let them grind the corn that was to become the loaf of their support.'[35] They must not starve, he concluded, and the guardians were to teach 'the people that they could not look to the poor rates as a fund to fall back upon when they quarrel ... with their masters. It would be highly injudicious to take any step which might lead to the supposition that the poor rates were always a safe ground for reliance (Applause).'[36]

By 1 November the number of applicants for relief had doubled on the previous week,[37] yet the total number actually relieved only increased by 21. The cost of outdoor relief fell slightly, from £120 to £118, and indoor relief from £144 to £126. In line with Farnall's advice, new and old applicants were being pushed into the workhouse. Heads of families and the able bodied were set to work on the Moor and there was a move to use the empty Woodplumpton workhouse where, in the following week, inmates were obliged to break stones especially imported.[38] Throughout the rest of November the labour test was rigorously used as the workhouses began to brim over with men, women, children, the old and the sick.[39] Most of these were made to take relief in kind.[40] By 29 November the cost of outdoor relief had risen to £186, and an extra 1,037 were working for their relief.

Once the Preston Masters' Association had declared their intentions to reopen the mills, the guardians wrote asking the Poor Law Board for advice[41] and on 6 December received the same reply – and this it is reasonable to suppose they must have expected – that those who could get work 'if they pleased' were not entitled to relief. In fact, they agreed to give only one more week's relief, in anticipation of *some* of the mills resuming work.[42] The 'considerable' reduction in the number of applications following the masters' notice must also have reinforced their over-optimistic view that the opening of *all* the mills was imminent. Little did the guardians know that the decrease in applications was largely caused by the union's funding of those normally dependent upon the rates in order to maintain the unity of their cause.[43]

The guardians met to discuss the Poor Law Board's letter on 13 December. Howitt, Ward and Pilkington (none of whom was a master)[44] wanted a strict adherence to the Board's directive, and urged the withholding of all relief until the operative applying for it could produce a certificate proving that a *bona fide* application for work had been made. The struggle, as Pilkington reminded them, was not about the ten per cent but about mastery.[45] Richard Ashworth, who had resisted joining the Masters' Association, but who had locked-up his Walton Mill on 22 October, championed the opposition's cause. It was useless, he argued, to send people to ask for work when there was no day fixed for re-opening the mills – they had a right to relief whilst the mills were closed. This interpretation of the Poor Law Board's letter was also supported by Dixon, Cartwright and Parr. All four agreed that the case would be different if the mills were actually opened, but since they were not they exhorted the guardians to continue relieving as they had been doing. At this point, T.B. Addison, the chairman, intervened.

Since the introduction of the 1834 Poor Law Amendment Act, Addison had led the pro-Poor Law faction and, whilst chairman, he continued to preach the virtues of abstinence, self-reliance and self-discipline.[46] In 1852 he pleaded with the guardians to give the Prohibitory Order a fair trial.[47] He opposed allowances in aid of wages, and argued that the rates should not be used to finance the Micawber-like handloom weavers when the mills were desperate for hands.[48] Predictably, he saw the labour test as an 'ideal' and the workhouse as an institution of salvation. Up until the Poor Law Board's letter, Addison attended Board meetings irregularly and said very little when he did. He was absent when Farnall visited Preston on 25 October and only began to express his views after the publication of the masters' notice. Like Pilkington he saw the struggle as a question of mastery, and interpreted the Poor Law Board's advice as a clear indication that the laws of supply and demand were not to be diluted by mistaken philanthropy. The guardians, he alleged, had an obligation to protect the ratepayers and an even greater obligation to instil in the operatives the moral code of respectability and self-help.[49] The Board, he argued, acted wisely in demanding the imposition of the certificate system: 'we must not be guided by what the operatives' union might do even if it means a £1 rate'.[50]

It is difficult to assess what influence Addison had on the guardians. He had a strong personality and his position as chairman of the Board and of the magistrates (he was elected to that position in October 1853) made him one of Preston's most powerful politicians. But just when it seems his influence was beginning to tell, the increase in the number of relief applicants began to stretch the administrative capacity of the guardians, and appears to have weakened their determination to carry out the Poor Law Board's advice. There is certainly no evidence to suggest that Addison's wish for a certificate system was ever implemented. Whether this was a deliberate decision is difficult to say, but as applications surged it was probably impossible to enforce. Between 6 December and 17 January an additional 1,864 were put to work, breaking stones and grinding corn, and by 7 February — two days before the opening of the mills — the total number receiving relief peaked at 6,651, with all but 851 receiving some form of assistance out of doors.[51]

The guardians were now under a great deal of strain and were finding it more and more difficult to assess whether those applying for relief were entitled to it. Dixon, who ran the Relief Committee, complained that he had a 'list of six or seven parties who were receiving pay from the operatives' union without acknowledging it', and more were likely to apply if the guardians continued to absent themselves from the committee meetings.[52] Administering the labour test also proved burdensome. On 7 January Addison — who himself never sat on any of the Board's committees — suggested relief by loans.[53] In the following week, S. Parker managed to pass a motion giving the Farington lock-outs not receiving union funds[54] outdoor relief without the labour test, because the bitter weather made the six-mile journey to Preston impossible.[55] On 17 January rumours that the guardians were thinking of easing their problem by providing Hollins with labour to work his mills, soon brought a dusty reply from the ratepayers. 'If any guardians should act as the tools of the manufacturers do with them as we (the ratepayers) did with the masters' candidates in November last — throw them out.'[56]

Whilst the guardians were unable to do anything to ease their own plight, the masters did. On 8 February they agreed to reopen the mills on the following day. Ashworth immediately raised the question of relief for those who opted not to accept the masters' conditions. Unlike the masters' offer made on 1 December, the mills were now definitely going to be opened; the position was different, and Satterthwaite, acting chairman, made this plain. 'We must carry out the law; we have no discretionary power in the matter: when the people have work to go to we cannot give them relief.'[57] On the 14th the guardians began discharging all the factory hands between the ages of 16 and 41 from the workhouse,[58] and by the 21st only 59 factory operatives were in receipt of relief. Within a week these were struck off the books.[59] The hard-liners were now rampant. Mr Abraham could barely restrain himself: 'we cannot compel persons to work but if they did not work they must not have the benefit of the poor rate in carrying out their notions of what was right and wrong. The heads of families having the opportunity to work and who refuse to do so should be taken before the magistrates for neglecting their families.'[60] This was supported by the ever aggressive Pilkington, by Addison and by the Board as a whole.[61] Even Ashworth succumbed; he notified the Board that 19 boys under the age of 13 in the Walton workhouse might earn their living in the spinning mills.

The guardians' now unquestioning acceptance of the Poor Law Board's directive was soon reflected in their actions. Between the official opening of the mills and the quarter ending Lady Day (21 March) the number receiving relief fell drastically from 6,651 to 4,650;[62] 96% of these had been receiving relief out of doors, the cost of which had correspondingly fallen from £276 per week to £162 per week.[63] Yet by the middle of March most of the mills remained closed. This action was quickly condemned. Mortimer Grimshaw called for the defeat of the cotton lords at the next election of the guardians,[64] and at the ratepayers' meeting on 8 March Mr Boyd, in the company of Cowell, Swinglehurst, Dixon and Ambler, preached the abolition of the Poor Law Board.[65] Farnall, of course, held a different view. When he visited Preston on 11 March he told the guardians that 'no Board could have improved the position that they had taken, or acted with a better spirit. They adopted very steady, honest and just measures ... [and] had got very easily through the difficult problem in which they had been placed.'[66] Anticipating that trade was unlikely to revive, Farnall encouraged the guardians to keep up the good work. By 1 June the number receiving relief slowly dropped to 4,189,[67] but by then the strike had ended.

In one very important respect the poor relief issue was much less important than the guardians imagined. Throughout the dispute, few operatives applied for relief. When Dixon complained that he knew of six or seven operatives attempting to claim relief whilst in receipt of union funds, he clearly saw it as the exception rather than the rule. Farnall's praise of the guardians' 'good work' was therefore largely earned by default. Most relief applications, it appears, were made by those who had suffered *indirectly* from the cessation of production and the high price of provisions. Naturally, those operatives without the support of the union fund had to rely upon the Poor Law, but their numbers do not seem to have been significant. This was confirmed by Addison in March when he paid tribute 'to our humbler fellow citizens, for the admirable self reliance and spirit of independence which had led them in so large a proportion to abstain from applying for relief ... [and for keeping] ... their applications within bounds far more moderate than could have been anticipated'.[68]

Two questions now arise. If the guardians knew that most of the factory operatives were not applying for relief, why were they determined to employ the labour test during the lock-out and to withdraw relief during the period of the strike? Why did the delegates not organize a co-ordinated campaign to exact outdoor relief for the turnouts?

There are perhaps three interrelated reasons for the guardians' relatively tough attitude. Preston was, after all, the recognized centre of the ten per cent campaign, and a victory for the operatives there would have meant a serious defeat for the manufacturers throughout the cotton district. Preston was the test case, and the guardians were as much aware of this as were the masters and the operatives. Mastery, not wages, was the issue as they saw it and, on a point of principle, they were unwilling to grant outdoor relief unless it came within the Poor Law Board's Prohibitory Order and their letter of 6 December. During the lock-out they therefore imposed the labour test (despite their criticism of it in 1852) and, during the strike, they withheld all relief for those who could get work 'if they pleased'. In Burnley and Haslingden, where the guardians were only faced with the problems posed by a lock-out not a strike, the pressure to comply with the 1852 order was less severe and, since neither town was crucial to the ten per cent campaign, they could continue to defy the exhortations of the Poor Law Board without having to consider (in a wider sense) the consequences of their actions. In Preston, any departure from the Poor Law Board's advice would have been seen, in all probability, as a sign of weakness. To have given relief unconditionally would, in effect, have meant that the guardians condoned the strike.

Moreover, even though relief policy did not directly affect the strike, it did have an indirect effect by increasing the actual number of claims on the union fund and by making it necessary for the delegates to encourage emigration on a scale greater than they perhaps had wished. Withholding relief once the mills were opened also increased the chance of old mill hands and non factory workers seeking work in the factories – a disguised form of knobstick labour.

Lastly, the guardians had an obligation to protect the ratepayers and to prevent the operatives from using the rates as a means of subsidising their campaign. The best way to achieve this was to anticipate any increase in applications for relief by a show of strength from the very beginning.

As it turned out, the operatives did not apply for poor relief on any scale. In part, this can be explained by their realism; they simply did not believe they would get it. The guardians' use of the labour test and their careful investigation of every application was precisely what the operatives had expected them to do. Compared with the funds which the operatives raised themselves, the amount of relief was at best marginal and at worst trivial. Individual turnouts who applied for relief were, moreover, liable to forfeit − where they were detected − their claim to the larger sums offered by the union fund.

The operatives were not, however, simply guided by their realism. Their struggle was also informed by ideals of independence and self-respect. They genuinely believed in the justice of their cause. To have contemplated organizing a campaign to exact poor relief from an institution which they looked upon with utter contempt, would not only have undermined almost everything they stood for, but also nourished the image which the masters had of the working class as a whole. On the issue of poor relief the operatives shared, if for different reasons, the social philosophy preached by the Board of Guardians' own chairman. Independence and dignity were far more important than the demeaning charity provided by the rates. Ten per cent and no surrender meant what it said.

8 Lord Palmerston

> We will not use a gun or pike,
>   For that's a thing we do dislike,
> But we shall fight and gain the strike,
>   By Moral Agitation.

The government showed very little interest in the ten per cent campaign. The *Economist*'s tub-thumping question, 'Pray is Palmerston aware of these things?',[1] captures the atmosphere of indifference. The Eastern question, Parliamentary reform and the survival of Aberdeen's weak coalition were the important issues which occupied the government's time. Provincial wage disputes were, after all, matters for masters and men to sort out for themselves; and the discipline of the market would ensure that the masters would buy in the cheapest and that labour would sell in the dearest. As far as the government was concerned it had neither the authority nor the will to intervene in this exchange except in so far as it provided the legal framework within which it could freely take place. When Palmerston was summoned to Queen Victoria to give the latest news of the strikes, he replied 'There is no definite news, Madam, but it seems certain that the Turks have crossed the Danube.'[2] Apocryphal but indicative. Indeed, if anything, the Preston operatives were conscious of government rather more than the government was of them.[3]

Lord Aberdeen's coalition government came to power in December 1852 after Lord Derby's minority protectionist government had resigned over Disraeli's budget. The new government, which few expected to last long,[4] was an uneasy alliance of Whigs, Peelites and Radicals. Lord John Russell was given the Foreign Office, before becoming Leader of the House, and Lord Palmerston, having rejected the Admiralty, accepted the Home Office. Palmerston chose the Home Office because Aberdeen refused him the chance of the Foreign Office. In Russell's 1851 government Palmerston had managed to embitter Queen Victoria on almost every issue of foreign policy and was subsequently forced to resign. Aberdeen could not ignore the Queen's determination to keep Palmerston away from foreign affairs but equally he could not afford to have Palmerston counted with the opposition. Palmerston was an influential statesman, respected abroad and admired by liberals and radicals at home. Politically, he was likely to be more dangerous outside than inside the Cabinet.

Palmerston was clearly disappointed not to get the Foreign Office, where he had been Minister between 1830 and 1841 and 1846 and 1851, but as he told his brother, he was happy enough with the Home Office. 'It does not do for a man to pass his whole life in one department, and the H.O. deals with the concerns of the country internally, and brings one in contact with one's fellow-countrymen, besides which it gives one more influence in regard to the militia.'[5] For Palmerston a strong militia was of crucial importance. Not only did the militia question provide him with sweet revenge over Russell in the 1852 'tit for tat', but it also provided an important stabilizing element in his own social philosophy. The militia, he reported to the Commons, was 'a most valuable social element inasmuch as it brought the gentry ... in contact with the lower and working classes ... and cemented the bonds of union, which should always unite them, by common pursuits, common associations, and common objects'.[6] Palmerston's ideal society was organic, paternalistic, rational, ordered, just and clean.[7]

Palmerston soon mastered the routine of the Home Office where, in spite of the growing amount of business, he at first found the burden of correspondence to be much lighter than at the Foreign Office. Although by mid 1854 he was to change his mind, finding it impossible to read the ever-increasing pile of reports, he continued to urge his staff to improve their efficiency. He was pedantic about poor handwriting (even though his own is at times almost unreadable) and allegedly sent his clerks to the Foreign Office to learn how to fold dispatches and papers.[8] Outside, his reforming zeal soon captured the imagination of a society increasingly interested in social reform. In 1854, approximately 40% of the Acts passed originated with the Home Office. Sewers, pollution, prisons, the inspection of mines, factory Acts, betting houses, burial grounds, smoke nuisance, cholera, water purification were the problems with which Palmerston grappled daily: local authorities, ratepayers, manufacturers, operatives and sewer commissioners the people he grappled with. Each in their way were every bit as testing as Mehemet Ali, Louis Philippe and Tsar Nicholas. Despite Palmerston's inexperience in these matters he soon earned the praise of the Press. The *Spectator* referred to his 'brilliant exploits at the Home Office'.[9] The *Morning Post*, Palmerston's political mouthpiece, saw his resignation on 14 December (to which we shall return), 'as a great practical damage to the condition of England question',[10] and even the *Times*, which vehemently opposed Palmerston's foreign policy and political opportunism, ungrudgingly saw him as an efficient administrator of home affairs.[11] The press's reaction to Palmerston's attitude to the ten per cent campaign was less unanimous and certainly less flattering.[12]

Palmerston's attitude towards labour was fairly typical of the governing classes and his views on the strikes soon became evident when he replied to a memorial sent by the Preston operatives. This memorial was adopted at the weavers' delegates' meeting on Sunday 13 November. It was written on the 15th, sent on the 21st and outlined the history of the dispute (rather more objectively than Lowe later suggested).[13] In tone it was conciliatory. The weavers' case rested firstly on the argument that the masters had promised to restore the 1847 wage cuts when economic conditions improved and, secondly, on the argument that economic conditions had improved: 'we see evidence of accumulated wealth in every form ... yet the manufacturers cannot honour their word'.[14] They told Palmerston that 'Preston has been proverbial for paying a low rate of wage' and that if some disinterested party could 'prove by plain facts' that the masters were unable to pay the ten per cent they would 'abandon [their] claim to a more favourable time'. They also told him that up until the present dispute they had no 'thought of Combination or Union' and that it had come into being because of 'sympathy between the men' and because some employers, Birleys in particular, were only prepared to discuss wage settlements with a committee, not with deputations from their own mills. Against this intransigence it was necessary, they argued, 'to assist by pecuniary aid those who have been thrown out of employment for soliciting their just claim'. They also denied that they were dictating to their masters, and noted how their attempts at referring the question to arbitration had been ignored even though the masters had been asked to make their own proposals on this count. They hoped instead that Palmerston would offer to serve in this capacity.

Predictably, things worked out quite differently and Palmerston, who usually replied to incoming letters within a day or two, reserved judgement until 22 December. This delay certainly angered Cowell. Whilst soliciting support in London from the Metropolitan Trades he revealed his disgust to the gathering by scornfully comparing how quickly Palmerston sent troops to Blackburn at the request of the Preston masters. Other delegates were less outspoken, presumably because they realized that Palmerston was likely to choose to do nothing. The *People's Paper* had already warned that this was likely to happen. It condemned the operatives' memorial as useless, humiliating and the wrong way to gain the People's Rights. 'To memorialize Lord Palmerston was as much as to to say "we cannot fight our own battle — will you help us", and it is rather eccentric to ask an avowed enemy of labour to do so . . . How could he help? He could not order the manufacturers to open the mills or pay the ten per cent.' Whig governments, it continued, were mere 'tools and puppets of the cotton lords and in this sense were no different from Tory governments who were the tools and puppets of the Church and the Landed Interest'.[15] Clearly, Ernest Jones was prepared rather to be 'damned with Plato and Bacon than to go to heaven with Paley and Palmerston'.

When the reply came it contained none of the seasonal surprise. Instead, the operatives were given a flattering lecture on political economy; labour was a commodity pure and simple, whilst strikes increased foreign competition and caused the flight of British capital and enterprise to the farflung corners of the earth. A mid-nineteenth century manual of economic etiquette:

I read your memorial with much sympathy and with deep regret. It is impossible that I should not warmly sympathize with the feelings of a large number of the most deserving classes of the community who have been led to think that they are suffering under acts of injustice, and it cannot but excite my deep regret to reflect upon the deprivation which the state of things to which the memorial refers, must have inflicted . . .

I am sorry, however, to say that I have no means of interposing to apply a remedy for these evils. It would be impossible for me without much more detailed information than I possess to form a just opinion as to the merits of the points in dispute and I could not as a member of the government possess any power to interfere in the matter.

Under these circumstances I would only venture to suggest in the most friendly [spirit?] some topics for further consideration of the memorialists. They must be well aware that labour being a commodity like any other, its money value in the market must be regulated by the same general principles which govern the price of other commodities; and that among those governing principles the most influential are the cost of production, and the relative proportions of demand and supply. The cost of production in regard to labour means the price of the necessaries of life and the proportion of demand and supply must depend very much upon the periodical fluctuations of trade . . .

It may be said that in times when according to the general principles which I have advocated to [sic] an increase in the rate of wages would be just, that increase might be too long delayed and the working men be then subjugated to undue privation if the adjustment was left to the gradual operation of forbearance and goodwill.

But may not an appeal be made to the results of recent events to show that even such inconveniences would be less than the evils arising from extensive and general strikes. These evils are many and great. The strike of workmen deprives them of the means of subsistence, on the other hand, the strikers of course stop production and unless markets happen at the moment to be much overstocked, strikes give to the foreign producer a position of advantage from which he may not afterwards be so easily dislodged; and if strikes were to become too frequent or of too long a duration a part of that capital which is now applied to giving employment to labour at home might possibly be transferred to other countries to the disadvantage of British Industry, and that this is not a groundless supposition is proved by the fact that British manufacturing establishments have been formed in Belgium and in Mexico. This too leads to a reflection upon the opinion which seems to have actuated the strikers that the general prosperity of our export trade was in itself a proof that the rate of wages might be increased. I do not pretend to form any judgement in the particular instance to which is referred, but I would wish to remark that our power to supply foreign markets with manufactures depends upon the cheapness at which those manufactures can be sold, that their price must depend mainly upon the cost of production, and that the wages of labour are a material part of that cost. Therefore as our exported manufactures must always be running a hard race with similar manufactures of other countries, an apparently flourishing trade may possibly be checked by an increase of wages which would add to the cost of production and the gains made by the manufacturers may often consist of a very small profit upon each separate article, the aggregate amount of gain depending on the quantity exported and that quantity depending on the cheapness of the commodity, which cheapness again is governed by the cost of production.

In submitting these general reflections to the consideration of the memorialists I do not mean to give any opinion on the immediate subject of dispute, but I would earnestly entreat the working men to lay aside those feelings which are too apt to be engendered by a struggle, and to endeavour if possible to come to some arrangement with their employers.[16]

This reply was reprinted in almost all the national and northern provincial newspapers and soon started a controversy which went beyond the subject of the Preston dispute. *Lloyd's Weekly*, which ironically noted that 'His lordship does not condescend to give any reason for his own strike — but at once proceeds to give the men of Preston his opinion on theirs', attacked Palmerston for using the Preston dispute for his own political ends. It sardonically congratulated Palmerston for his ability to write 'pompous economic platitudes' and for returning to work, but found it difficult to understand why the operatives were 'dressed in kindness and sympathy', unless it was a move to outbid Lord Aberdeen and the old Whigs.[17] *Reynolds' Newspaper* also emphasized the political aspects when it argued that Palmerston merely set out to conciliate the cotton lords so as to prevent the desertion of the Manchester School from an already weak coalition. The vote of the cotton lords was certainly not going to be lost 'by such inferior considerations as truth and justice for the working classes'. As far as *Reynolds'* was concerned, Palmerston's reply was marked by 'ostentatious affectations of sympathy with the suffering and oppressed which when contrasted with his public conduct serves to brand him as the most consummate dissembler and the most disgusting hypocrite of all the statesmen of the present day'.[18] The *Daily News* was equally disgusted, if for quite different reasons. It interpreted the operatives' memorial and their call for mediation as an admission of guilt and it saw Palmerston's 'milk and water dilution of political economy' as a flagrant attack on the middle classes, 'the backbone of the nation', and as part of his plan to squash Russell's reform initiative.[19] The *Manchester Examiner* took a similar line on the question of reform but was more generous in its praise of Palmerston's economics.[20]

This emphasis on national politics is to be expected from a press which relied upon politics and intrigue to maintain circulation. The Victorians were obsessed with politics and politicians,[21] and whenever it was possible — and often when it was not — newsworthy material was woven into the political events of the moment. In December 1853 Russell's Reform Bill and Palmerston's resignation and subsequent reinstatement were the two crucial political events.

With an Eastern war threatening but not imminent, reform became the major political issue. Since the radicals were promised, in 1852, that the matter would not be dropped, the Cabinet renewed discussions in November and a subcommittee, which included Palmerston, was set up. Palmerston's objections to reform were well known.[22] Firstly, he believed that an enlargement of the franchise would upset the existing balance of power within the House of Commons by increasing the 'weight of the manufacturing, commercial working classes' at the expense of the aristocracy and gentry. Since the repeal of the Corn Laws (1846) and the Navigation Acts (1849) the commercial and manufacturing interests, Palmerston thought, were sufficiently represented in Parliament.

Secondly, he was determined to oppose any measure which would 'overpower intelligence and property by ignorance and poverty'. Russell's proposal to reduce the occupational qualification in boroughs to £5 (later £6) was likely to do just this. Working-class voters, Palmerston claimed, were 'comparatively poor, ignorant and dependent. Their ignorance will prevent them from exercising a sound judgement, their poverty will make them victims of intimidation.'[23] Nor were the working class free agents and the Preston strike, Palmerston alleged, was ample proof of this. Trade union leaders, he asserted, repeatedly acted with absolute despotism over those 'low in the scale of intelligence and political knowledge' and such men were 'incapable of taking large views and [look] only to penny and shilling gains and losses'.[24] The working class were, in his view, already well represented by employers and by their borough members.

Palmerston resigned from the government on 14 December after Aberdeen had told him that his objections to reform were too fundamental to allow any 'useful alteration' in Russell's proposed Bill. Aberdeen had anticipated Palmerston's reaction and, with Queen Victoria's advice, made certain that Palmerston was seen to resign on the reform issue in order to ensure that he would lose the backing of the radicals who supported his views on foreign policy. Palmerston was careful to avoid this, and through the *Morning Post* attempted to show that he had resigned over the Eastern question. The news of the massacre of Sinope, widely reported in the press on 11 December, had enraged public opinion and the popular newspapers soon rallied against Aberdeen's policy of appeasement. Palmerston, who had urged that the Navy be sent in to protect the Turkish fleet, now became a more popular hero and his resignation on 14 December was generally construed as a rejection of the government's handling of the Eastern question rather than as rejection of reform. Aberdeen had been out-manoeuvred and Palmerston, who 'was not without hopes that he would be the next Prime Minister',[25] had greatly increased his popularity without losing his radical following. The government, now knowing that it was unlikely to survive, agreed to a reconciliation and on 23 December – the day after the reply to the Preston operatives – Palmerston resumed his position at the Home Office.[26]

The press's reaction to Palmerston's reply to the Preston operatives clearly has to be seen in the context of these political manoeuverings. Whether their political interpretations were correct is another matter. Palmerston was, of course, an astute politician and, in a period when MPs were not constrained by party,[27] he was free to do almost as he liked. That he chose to delay his reply until the day before his reinstatement clearly suggests, though, that he was using the strike for his own political ends. So, too, does the publication of his reply in the press. Palmerston was adept at manipulating public opinion and, during the resignation 'crisis', he needed to reassure the cotton lords to keep their support. He knew the Manchester School was committed to reform and he probably knew that many of them saw the industrial unrest as a symptom of the restricted franchise. Whilst Bright explained the strikes in terms of the operatives' ignorance of the laws of political economy, he also stressed the importance of reform.

> It is an unhappy circumstance that employer and employed in this country are so far apart — are supposed to have opposite interests — and are in fact almost two nations. The ten pound franchise — it has excluded them most effectually, and it has therefore placed them on all occasions of political or other excitement on a lower platform, a platform of their own to which men of higher position have not been admitted. Hence has aggravated the evil of separation between the capitalist class and the workmen. I think a more moderate franchise that would give the vote to the best of the working men would give them self-respect, would identify them more with public order and with the institutions of government of the country and would do much to unite that which is in any degree intelligent and powerful in the working class with those above them in social position. It can never be safe, or statesman-like, in a country professing to have a free constitution, to shut out the great mass of the people whose industry and skill do so much to make the nation what it is.[28]

Since Palmerston thought precisely the opposite it was important for him to let the Manchester men know where he stood on the Preston dispute, if only to strengthen and consolidate his political support.

Palmerston's own explanation for the delay was clearly insincere. He told the operatives that the delay was caused by the 'daily hope that I might hear that an amicable arrangement of difference had been come to'.[29] In early December, he had been told as much by Earl Cathcart, military commander for the Midland and Northern districts. 'There are some indications', he wrote on 4 December, 'that both parties having become weary of the contest, and being desirous of it being brought to a close I have reason to believe that a large proportion of [the operatives] would willingly submit if they were allowed to do so by the delegates.'[30] These impressions may well have been reinforced by the masters' victories at Burnley, Padiham and Bacup, by the introduction of extensive short-time working elsewhere in Lancashire, and by the Preston masters' notice that applications for employment would be received at the mills on and after 5 December. December was a bitterly cold month and, with food prices soaring, the operatives' call for mediation was, in all probability, interpreted as a sign of weakening determination. But, on the other hand, the *Times* and the *Economist* never once suggested in December that a reconciliation between master and men was imminent. Nor was Cathcart's report so one-sided. He saw Preston as the 'chosen field upon which the [ten per cent] battle is to be fought', and noted that the operatives were 'still sticking to the ten-per-cent'. Moreover, there is no reason to believe that Palmerston was influenced in any way by Cathcart's view that the mass of operatives were only prevented from returning to work by the delegates. Throughout the strike he had characterized the operatives as an 'ignorant' mass who had been led and stupefied into submission by the delegates' despotism. If Palmerston hoped for an amicable agreement it was not because he thought the operatives would ever defy the wishes of their delegates.

Palmerston also justified his delay on the grounds that he had insufficient information on which to form an opinion, but there is little reason to believe that he was any better informed by December. The military report for December did not come into the Home Office until early January, nor was the failure of the Preston masters' initiative fully appreciated until that time. The national press published fairly detailed accounts of the causes and progress of the dispute. A few sent their own correspondents to Preston and some reprinted material published in local newspapers. Leonard Horner, the factory inspector and a family friend,[31] must also have kept Palmerston informed on the latest developments. In fact, the Factory Reports belie the idea that Palmerston was not well informed. 'The depression that has now existed for some months, especially in the cotton trade, must be so well known to your lordship, that it is unnecessary for me to enter into any particular ... ' and the 'circumstances of the strike and lock-out have been given so much in detail for *many months* in the ordinary channels of information that it is unnecessary for me to make a special report on the subject'.[32] Admittedly, Horner found the reasons for the 'commencement and continuance of the strike conflicting' but he knew what was at stake, and in contrast to Palmerston's largely unfounded hopes he noted that the feeling of distrust and alienation which existed between masters and men 'will last long after the re-opening of the mills, whether that be brought about by mutual concession, or by the stronger party prevailing'.[33]

It seems, then, that the timing of Palmerston's reply was largely governed by political factors, not by hope and ignorance as he alleged. Of course, the two are not mutually exclusive, but it does indicate Palmerston's lack of interest in the Preston dispute *per se*. He was rather more interested in using the dispute to show that Parliamentary reform was dangerous and to ensure the continued support of the cotton lords on the Eastern question. This expediency is also suggested by the content of the reply itself. Naturally as a piece of mid-nineteenth-century liberal economics it was entirely predictable. That he should lecture the operatives as if he were high priest of the 'Steam Intellectual Society' was rather less so. He could simply have said — as he did — that it was not within the power of the government to intervene. There was very little need to embellish this statement with popular economics, unless he had another reason for doing so. During his stay at the Home Office, Palmerston frequently launched into lectures on law and order, but only once, it appears, did he sally forth into the subject of political economy. If Grimshaw's question 'What did Lord Palmerston sit at London for if not to settle such questions as these?'[34] indicates a degree of naivety, Palmerston's manoeuverings in December did not.

In early January Palmerston curiously changed his tack. On the 6th he wrote to the Board of Trade suggesting that they might send an official to 'communicate confidentially' with both masters and operatives, 'to ascertain the present state of feeling on both sides'. In so far as this suggestion was intended to gather more information, it did not entail any serious departure from the work carried out by government inspectors. Official returns for factories, mines and the Poor Law

Lord Palmerston

frequently included reports on the relationships between employers and employees. But Palmerston's suggestion went much further. He wanted to consider if any 'amicable arrangement could be proposed', and although he was at pains to point out that the official to be sent was not authorized to act as a mediator, he concluded by saying that 'HMG would, if asked to do so by both parties, readily endeavour to effect a reconciliation between them'.[35] Though Palmerston never indicated how this reconciliation might be achieved, his suggestion was clearly heretical. In a carefully worded reply, the Board of Trade officially said as much.

> Their Lordships are very sensible of the great importance of bringing about, if possible, a right understanding between the workmen and their employers ... [but] it appears to them that the sending of a special messenger by this Board might be open to very serious misconstruction in as much as it would appear to indicate an intention of removing the question from the province of [the] police and making it a matter of trade, or in effect to contemplate the possibility of the interposition of the government in arranging the rate of wages.

Whilst the Board of Trade refused to be seen to mediate they were prepared to suggest that Palmerston might achieve his object 'through some of the authorities acquainted with the district or some other person under his Lordship's more immediate direction and not appearing to exercise any special function as being peculiarly connected with the government in respect of trade'.[36] Officially, therefore, the Board of Trade's position was quite clear: wage disputes were to be settled by markets, not by government departments. As it happens, things turned out differently. In a strictly private capacity, Edward Cardwell, the President of the Board of Trade, arranged for William Playfair, who had already planned to attend an education meeting whilst staying with Kay-Shuttleworth at Burnley, to act as reporter. 'He has no knowledge', Cardwell wrote in a private letter, 'that any wish had been expressed by the H.O. as I gave him no intimation that I had any particular object, except to acquire information for myself.'[37]

Playfair left London on 10 January and stayed one night in Manchester, where he met and discussed the manufacturers' policy with a spinning master from Burnley. Next day he arrived at Kay-Shuttleworth's home and, whilst there, met the editors of the *Manchester Guardian*, *Manchester Courier*, *Preston Guardian* and *Preston Chronicle*, and reporters from the *Manchester Examiner*. 'Naturally', he noted *'all* the conversation turned on the strikes and the views of the two classes, both master and workmen.'

As far as the masters' position was concerned, Playfair reported that it was unlikely to change, even though it was generally accepted by the manufacturers themselves that wages in Preston were lower than elsewhere. Two reasons for the masters' stubbornness were given. Firstly, they refused to raise wages under the threat of dictation. This was an expected explanation and one which the middle class and the government felt little need to question. Secondly, Lancashire masters were not anxious to see the mills in Preston reopened, because it 'would produce a sudden and unnecessary rise in the price of cotton', which subsequently would lead to reduced profits and increased competition. This was especially the case with the Blackburn manufacturers who, Playfair claimed, had a 'direct interest' in keeping the strike going: they produced much the same goods as at Preston and sold them in the same overseas markets. Disadvantaged by Preston's lower costs of production, Blackburn masters encouraged their own operatives to continue contributing to the delegates' strike fund in the hope of equalizing wages.

As far as the operatives' position was concerned, all agreed that their financial means of support would not, at least in the immediate future, cause them to lose the fight. But, with the opening of Hollins's mill, there was a growing belief that there was a 'giving way on the part of the workmen'. The offer of work taken up by twenty men was seen as an indication that the operatives were beginning to re-think their position. Playfair also noted that the moral force of the cause 'had suffered much from [the] bad conduct in resisting the employment of hands'. Cowell was alleged to have been more careful in his public statements, and to have lost some of his influence. As a result, all anticipated a 'speedy termination ... The operatives were beginning to show that they ... have been mistaken [and once this] feeling spreads, the *will* to pay the self-imposed tax of 7d will quickly subside when not supported by the enthusiasm of strong conviction.'[38] When Palmerston received Playfair's letter (via Cardwell) on 14 January, he told his officials 'This may rest as it is, the strike is nearly over.'[39]

Why Palmerston should have considered casting the government in the role of mediator is puzzling. Both Blackburn and Wigan were, at this time, quiet, and although magistrates in Glossop warned that the 'state of the working class throughout the district is of a highly menacing character', because the cotton operatives 'are strongly inclined to the mischievous views adopted by the manufacturing population of Preston',[40] there was little else to report. Nor was the revival of Chartism and Ernest Jones's Mass Movement considered threatening The government, naturally, thought that 'Chartist agitation was quite at an end',[41] even though police reports of Chartist revival had been coming into the Home Office since mid 1853. The large 'Reinauguration' meeting held at Blackstone Edge on 19 June was less remarkable for its size (about 1,000) than for its rhetoric. Gammage contrived to lampoon aristocrats and MPs and Jones predicted that the present high wages, caused by emigration thinning the market, were unlikely to last, given the tensions growing in Europe.[42] At Bolton, a small gathering of 150 heard William Hill of Stalybridge claim that he would rather have a dozen converted to the Charter 'in times of good trade than 100 in times of bad trade'.[43] In London, Jones, Gammage and Finlen repeated the theme that Chartism was growing stronger and that 'working men were determined to have their political position changed'.[44] None of this alarmed Palmerston.

The much publicized Labour Parliament, through which Ernest Jones attempted to graft Chartism on to the ten per cent campaign, was treated no more seriously. A superintendent of police present at the preparatory meeting in

November claimed that it was thinly attended and a complete failure. Earl Cathcart told Palmerston that the London newspapers had given it much more importance than it deserved, and that it would 'require something more than Jones' powers of persuasion to collect a second Kennington Common meeting, with a view to coerce the government of the rate of labour in Lancashire'. He realized that monster meetings on the subject of wages might cause some 'mischief', but saw no threat in the cry for 'national industrial action'.[45]

It seems that Chartism and its growing links with the wage movement cannot explain Palmerston's apparent change of mind. Nor can it be explained by the politics of reform, even though everything in January pointed to the Bill's success. On 3 January the Cabinet had given Russell its support, and the prospect of war had not yet pushed reform, as Palmerston had hoped, into the background. Palmerston's repeated strictures concerning the political ignorance of the working class had decreasing impact and, although he may have been looking for new arguments to reinforce his case, it seems unlikely that Playfair's visit was part of this purpose. In fact, when Palmerston wrote to Aberdeen on the eve of the Bill's introduction to Parliament, he inexcusably misused the information Playfair sent.

> The strikers are compelled to refuse to work at a certain Rate of wages on the Pretence that those wages are not enough to support them with the Prices of Things and yet other Men at work at those Rates are compelled to contribute a Portion of those wages towards the support of those who have struck, and are earning nothing. These £6 voters will ... be coerced by their leaders to vote for Chartist or ultra Radical candidates.[46]

That Palmerston knew all this was manifestly untrue indicates his deep opposition to reform. He was prepared to go to any lengths and where the Preston dispute failed to provide him with the right kind of facts he invented them. From mid-February onwards this became unnecessary as Parliamentary pressure and war forced Russell to drop the Bill.[47]

If anything caused Palmerston to think of mediation it was probably the action of the Lancashire manufacturers. Their claim that the Preston dispute was now 'a question affecting the interests of the whole trade', together with the 5% levy, was a blatant reminder that the matter was not likely to be resolved soon. Grimshaw's bitter declaration that the manufacturers had exchanged Free Trade for protectionism was probably a thought which also passed through Palmerston's mind. On the day he wrote to the Board of Trade he received a report from Cathcart confirming that the masters' combination was likely to widen the breach between the Preston employers and their hands.[48] Newspaper reports of the operatives' reactions to the masters' renewed resistance added further weight to the threat of disorder, and it is probably for this reason that Palmerston sought to find a solution of his own. But once he was informed that the strike was almost at an end, he quite naturally dropped the idea.

One last explanation which can be dismissed is that Palmerston may have been sincere in his wish to settle the dispute. Privately, he may have had some sympathy with the justice of the operatives' claim, and this may have been strengthened by the masters' combination, but none of his correspondence suggests that this was the case. During the 1842 general strike he had insisted that the hands would always return to work, because 'in the long run they would prefer labour to death'[49] by starvation. There is nothing to suggest that by 1853 Palmerston had changed his mind on this count, although the harsh winter and high food prices may have tugged at his conscience.

Although circumstances had changed by March, Palmerston was set against mediation. On 10 March a deputation of operatives, which included J. Sergeant, G. Eccles, T. Banks, J. Bowman, E. Whittle from Preston, W. Allen, W. Newton, R. Hooper, T. Winter from London, and Sir G. Strickland presented their complaints against the Preston authorities. Palmerston offered to investigate these complaints, but asked for a written statement,[50] which he received on the 17th. In this, the operatives accused the police of provocation, condemned the magistrates' reading of the Riot Act and reiterated their claim that the dispute could and ought to be settled by reason, not force. In conclusion, they again hoped Palmerston would use his influence with the employers to set up an impartial tribunal.[51] In his reply Palmerston regretted 'that matters have gone too far to admit of his hoping to be able to do any good in terms of mediation', supported the actions of the civil authorities and exhorted those on strike to 'abstain from molesting in any way the Irish or others . . . brought to Preston. It would be a great injustice', he continued, 'towards the mill-owners and towards the Irish and others . . . if the Preston men were to endeavour by any intimidation, violence or molestation to deter from work persons who are willing and ready to work. The persons so brought into Preston', he concluded, 'must come thither because they were unable to earn at home as much as they earned at Preston and it would be unjust and cruel to prevent them from thus bettering their situation.'[62] By resorting to the language of morals, Palmerston skirted around the fact that it was the masters, not the market, who fetched the 'knobsticks' to Preston.

To a certain extent Palmerston's moralizing was understandable. During the early part of the month reports of rioting and intimidation flooded in from the civil authorities. Lengthy police depositions and evidence from injured knobsticks and from manufacturers all pointed to a serious lapse in the operatives' otherwise peaceful conduct. Nor at first was there any reason for Palmerston to doubt the content of these reports. In his view, the authorities were responsible for the preservation of the peace and, being on the spot, they were the best judges of what to do.[53]

As with the operatives, Palmerston's official dealings with the Preston authorities were limited. In September, he was informed that the town was in an excited state, that the operatives were under the command of Cowell and Swinglehurst, and that meetings after dark were prohibited.[54] From then, until the beginning of March, he heard no more. In the meantime, the operatives rigidly kept the peace, except at Wigan and Blackburn where the authorities persistently incurred Palmerston's displeasure. The first duty of any municipal body, Palmerston wrote, was to 'keep and maintain a sufficient body of police to preserve on all ordinary occasions of disturbance the Peace of the town'.[55] In Wigan and in Blackburn the ratios of police to population were amongst the lowest in Lancashire and whenever riots broke out both authorities relied upon the military to restore order.[56] Although Palmerston was warned that it might not be within his 'province to advise [the authorities] as to their protection',[57] he repeatedly urged the authorities in Wigan and Blackburn to strengthen their police and to swear in special constables.[58] Reliance on the military, he believed, was likely to lead to injury and loss of life and, unlike a civil force, could not be used in anticipation of a disturbance; they were almost always called in after it had taken place. Despite these remonstrances, the Wigan and Blackburn authorities continued to economize on their police expenditure and, when riots broke out in October and November, the military were called once again.[59] Cathcart soon expressed his disgust at the 'apathy and supineness of the authorities at Wigan', and at the 'baneful spirit of Party'[60] which existed at Blackburn, and Palmerston took both authorities to task for their inexcusable inability to preserve the peace.[61]

The Preston authorities remained immune from such criticism. Throughout the strike Palmerston approved almost everything they did. The arrest of the four youths in September especially pleased him, as did the increase in the police and the swearing in of special constables. Compared with Wigan and Blackburn, the Preston authorities were seen to be carrying out their duties. Civil disturbances, especially at Blackburn, were expected. At Preston they were not, and it is probably for this reason that Palmerston initially accepted the Preston authorities' interpretation of the events of early March. Although he refused to send the aid of the metropolitan police,[62] he warmly approved the prohibition of meetings and the reading of the Riot Act.

Palmerston's note of approval was sent on 8 March,[63] but by the 13th he was beginning to sense that the Preston authorities had overreacted. On the 9th he received James Lowe's letter[64] substantially supporting the operatives' criticisms of the authorities made on the following day, and on the 13th he asked the magistrates to consider suspending their prohibition of meetings.[65] On the 18th, in a carefully worded letter, he reminded them that whilst they were in the best position to judge how to preserve the peace they 'will on the other hand avoid anything which could create unnecessary irritation on the part of the workpeople out upon strike'.[66]

Palmerston's veiled criticism of the Preston authorities is as understandable as his reaction to the operatives' pleas for mediation. Law and order was an essential element in his organic society and, whilst he was keen to ensure that the civil authorities were sufficiently prepared for any local disturbances, he was not prepared to impose his will upon them. The independence of local government was as sacrosanct as the laws of political economy. Except in emergencies, and in obvious cases of dereliction of duty, municipal bodies had always been left to their own devices.[67] Palmerston would give reassurance and advice, as had other Home Secretaries, but his involvement was limited by custom and tradition. In the case of the operatives, Palmerston's involvement was equally limited, not by custom or tradition, but by the laws of nature and by the scribblings of the new science. Whilst he may never really have understood the views of the working class he knew well enough that wages were determined by markets not by governments. He once wrote:

There are sometimes occasions in public affairs when the opinion and wishes of the great bulk of the 'nation' are strongly directed to some particular object, and on such occasions it may be wise and even necessary for men in public life to surrender their own opinions if contrary to the public wish, and to yield in some degree at least to a current which they are unable to stem.[68]

The Preston strike was not one of these occasions.

9 The Press

> Cowell has a dangerous tongue:
> > He told us we should get more wages;
>
> But Cowell has deceived us long,
> > For still the hopeless contest rages.
>
> Although we starve, it does not matter
> > To delegates at dainty dinner;
>
> For day by day they each get fatter,
> > While we, their dupes, each day get thinner.

The futility of strikes was undoubtedly the central theme of the press's wide coverage of the Preston dispute. Strikes were considered undesirable, injurious and self-defeating. Though each paper varied in tone, editorial opinion had noticeably changed since the engineers' strike. In 1851—2 all middle-class newspapers attacked the union with unbridled hostility.[1] In 1853—4 the operatives' cause was treated, by comparison, more favourably. This reflected a partial recognition of unions and combinations and, perhaps for the first time, a general admission that the masters were partly responsible for their own plight. How much this shift in emphasis can be attributed to the peaceful and sensible conduct of the strikers is unclear, but there is little doubt that the operatives, unlike the masters, realized from the beginning the importance of the relationship between the platform and the press. In part, the effectiveness of the strike depended upon the extent to which the operatives could swing public opinion in its favour;[2] the engineers' strike had taught them that much. Whilst the masters arrogantly persisted in meeting behind closed doors, reporters were freely admitted to the operatives' meetings and these were often concluded with a vote of thanks for those 'attending and faithfully recording their speeches'.[3] Delegates like Grimshaw, who spoke out too violently against the press, were 'gently rebuked' for their intemperate language.[4] Cowell, and in turn Horsfall and Kinder Smith, repeatedly stressed the need to gain the sympathy of the press and, in the early days of the dispute, they optimistically believed it was all possible.[5]

Of the three Preston papers, only the *Preston Guardian* expressed any sympathy for the operatives' cause. Edited by Joseph Livesey,[6] it had, in 1853, a weekly circulation of 4,744, which made it the most influential provincial paper in north Lancashire.[7] It remained consistently fair and impartial throughout the dispute and refused to endorse the one-sided censure of the operatives, because it feared this would 'add the power of the press to the terror of starvation'.[8] In politics it was liberal and radical, though its liberalism was pragmatic and its radicalism romantic. In principle it preferred 'seeing trade disputes arranged between the parties themselves without the intervention of strangers',[9] and persistently urged both sides to abandon their combinations so that wage settlements could be negotiated at each individual mill.[10] This was not an argument against the workers' or masters' right to combine, which was accepted without question, but a reminder to both parties that they had surrendered their 'individual independence'.[11] The union was a symbol of weakness whilst the Masters' Defence Fund, which it described as pernicious, was an expression of the masters' lack of duty.[12] Both indicated that the social system was crumbling. On Christmas Day it appealed to the past.

Two hundred years ago, there was more hospitality and more real charity in England than can be found now ... The Lords of industry are now, in a manner, the successors of the Squires and consequently the lords of the land. They stand in relation to the commons as formerly did the Squire, they are the owners of wealth and should be the dispensers of kindness and bounty; links to bind the mass of men to the aristocracy of the kingdom. Have they, in assuming this position, always weighed the duty of it? We fear not. Where then is our boasted progress? We have invented a steam engine, a thing of brass and iron, but God's own machine, that beautiful social system, whose parts are so cunningly adapted and which ought to work so perfectly for the good of all, is really out of order.[13]

For the *Guardian* both parties were wrong: the operatives, because they rigidly insisted on an unconditional ten per cent and standard lists; the masters because they inexcusably failed to initiate the reconciliation expected of their superior education, station and respectability.[14] Both had irresponsibly given themselves up, one to the agitator and the other to the bond.

The *Guardian*'s impartiality and its faithful reporting of Orchard speeches soon won it the acclaim of the operatives. Its vigorous denunciation of the *Manchester Guardian*'s insinuations concerning the delegates' misappropriation of the union funds,[15] and its equally vigorous attack on the *Preston Pilot*'s support of the masters,[16] turned acclaim into positive support. When Cowell heard rumours that some manufacturers had ceased taking the paper because of the favour it showed the operatives, he urged the strikers to 'club their money together to buy as many *Guardians* as possible'.[17] *Guardians* were bought in public houses, read out at the weekly meetings and their reports frequently compared with those of the hated *Preston Chronicle* and *Pilot*. 'Support those who support you', was Cowell's message, and although the *Guardian* may have been slightly embarrassed by this exaggerated claim it never sought to deny it. By February the operatives' support amounted to 'exclusive dealing'; the *Chronicle* had by then been boycotted and the *Pilot* dismissed.

The boycott of the *Chronicle* owed less to its philosophy of strikes than to its intemperate language, and its vicious attacks on the delegates. In fact in its philosophy of strikes and its reporting, the *Chronicle* was fairly close to the *Guardian*. Lawrence Dobson, the *Chronicle*'s editor, was a reforming liberal and, like many of his kind, realized the futility of the wars between masters and men.[18] He criticized the masters for not advancing wages with the revival of trade and regretted that they now possessed less of the 'chivalric' and more of the commercial spirit.[19] Equally, he criticized the operatives' demand for a universal ten per cent, and considered the idea of wage equalization as 'hapless and chimerical'.[20] In December the paper even advocated wage negotiations on a mill by mill basis.[21] But here the similarity ends, as is strikingly illustrated by another Christmas editorial, in which it was hoped that the Masters' Association would abandon its attempt to dictate the level of wages. 'We hope [the masters] will offer terms to be mutually agreed upon between employer and employed and as favourable as the state of trade will permit ... it will assuredly be the only way of detaching industrious men from the standard of wily demagogues.'[22] The first part of this argument could easily have been found in the *Guardian*, but not the sting in the tail. The *Guardian* warned of the dangers of leaders with 'false and selfish spirits' but argued that this was inevitable and could not be helped.[23] The *Chronicle*, in contrast, turned its hatred of the strike leaders into a crusade and, though it was never the masters' mouthpiece, these bitter attacks created the impression amongst the operatives themselves that it was.[24]

The battle of words which began in early October intensified as each month passed. Cowell, Grimshaw and Swinglehurst all suffered Dobson's vitriolic attacks and they in turn denounced him as their 'bitterest enemy and their deadliest foe'.[25] In December, Dobson had assailed the 'Orchard Orators' for their violent harangues and for their misrepresentation of the *Chronicle*'s position.[26] In the following month he accused the operatives, Cowell in particular, of refusing the chance of mediation. In a leader 'Are the Delegates Anxious for a Settlement of the Wage Dispute?', Dobson noted that he had sent a message to Cowell on 2 January, telling him that a certain influential (but unnamed) gentleman 'practically acquainted but without private interest in the cotton trade', had offered to act as mediator. Cowell, who visited the *Chronicle* office on the 17th, allegedly told Dobson that he had forgotten to mention the mediation initiative to the delegates' committee. 'The strike is continued because Mr Cowell *forgets* what is communicated with a view of putting a stop to the agitation.'[27] Cowell then denied that he promised to inform the delegates' committee, and with even more vehemence defended himself against the accusation that he was 'wishful of lengthening the strike for his own pecuniary reward'. He also made it plain that he felt that Dobson had attempted to lure him into a 'suicidal act', so as to confirm the 'fallacious impression entertained by the manufacturers that the hands were giving way'. Indeed, there is no other evidence to support Dobson's claim that an unnamed gentleman had offered to mediate, and Cowell may well have (rightly) suspected some sort of intrigue to exploit the operatives' genuine belief in mediation.[28] From this point the relationship between the *Chronicle* and the operatives abruptly deteriorated. Cowell, who in January had been reluctant to sanction the appeal of one spinner to burn the *Chronicle* in the presence of the crowd,[29] in February proposed a resolution which called on the strikers to suppress the paper.[30] Dobson was accused of earning vast sums for the reprinting of his articles attacking the operatives – although the reporters were vindicated from any complicity in the curtailment of operatives' speeches[31] – and, whilst he continued to address the delegates as 'parasites' and 'vampires'[32] the operatives were busy boycotting public houses and shops whose proprietors were known to take the paper.[33] In April, Rhodes predicted the paper's downfall[34] and, on May Day, Cowell 'trusted that the working classes of Preston, the working classes of Lancashire, would use their utmost exertions to swamp that Journal'.[35]

With the operatives' defeat, the *Chronicle* gloatingly reflected on its repeated claim that the 'only rational mode of obtaining an advance of wages ... is by each man husbanding his means, that he may have a fund to fall back upon, which may enable him to transfer to some other master who may give him higher wages'.[36] It delighted in reminding the operatives that strikes were futile and the price which was now to be paid for being 'blindly led by unions'.[37] The masters' conspiracy charges were unconditionally supported, and never once did the *Chronicle* express – as the *Guardian* did – any doubts about the masters' victory. It was considered just and inevitable. The masters' victory was, in a sense, the *Chronicle*'s victory too.

The *Preston Pilot*, edited by the Tory Robert Clarke, did not feature nearly as prominently as the *Guardian* or the *Chronicle*. At the beginning of the dispute it showed some sympathy for the operatives' cause, but within the space of four weeks its call for patience and moderation[38] turned into a violent attack on the operatives, who were being misled and grossly deceived by 'agents from other places'. In August, combinations were justified because they protected workers against 'the cupidity of those masters who are not disposed to deal fairly with their workers' but by October they were stridently condemned for dictating to the masters.[39] In February, Clarke announced that 'we do not enter into the question of wages', yet the paper had persistently appealed to the wage fund theory, and repeatedly urged the operatives to recognize the argument that labour depended upon capital; strikes were utterly suicidal and self-defeating. Like the *Chronicle*, the *Pilot* mounted a vicious campaign against the delegates and, in October, attempted to persuade the *Guardian* to take a similar line.[40] The weavers' union, it alleged, was nothing but a 'distasteful alliance' brought about by extensive coercion, especially of the 'younger classes of the operatives in this town'.[41] It noted how the blackmail of shopkeepers served to augment the union fund and, in early February, recommended the reopening of the mills as the delegates were then, it believed, fast losing public confidence.[42] Not once throughout the dispute were the masters' actions criticized and their combination was, predictably, ignored. It is little wonder that Cowell hated the *Pilot* and saw it as a tool of the parsons and aristocrats.[43]

Apart from the *Preston Guardian* Cowell frequently recommended the operatives to read *Reynolds' Newspaper*, edited by George Reynolds, and the *People's Paper*, edited by Ernest Jones.[44] These two leading working-class papers, which had their roots in the Chartist movement, together with the *Glasgow Sentinel*, *Lloyd's Weekly* and William Owen's *Potteries Examiner*, were almost the only sections of the press committed to supporting the trade union movement. But compared with the middle-class press these papers had a small circulation. In the early 1850s the press was still dominated by a capitalist bias. 'With few honourable exceptions', wrote George Reynolds, 'the whole of the English press is devoted to the service of manufacturers and opposed to the working classes'.[45] This bias is understandable. Newspapers were generally created by the wealthy middle class for themselves. The stamp duty and advertisement tax, although reduced in the 1830s and 1840s, had held back the development of a national working-class paper until their repeal in 1853 and 1855. Improvements in printing techniques were also not widely available until the late 1840s and 1850s, and only then did the falling price of paper and print make a working-class newspaper possible, if not always viable.[46] In the 1830s, though, the unstamped press and a few papers like the *Northern Star* and *Northern Liberator* were able to voice the needs of the working class[47] and, in the 1840s, a Sunday press which included the *Dispatch*, *Chronicle*, *News of the World* and *Lloyd's Weekly* began to appear.

The London *Lloyd's Weekly*, edited by Edward Lloyd, first appeared in 1842; by 1853 it had an annual circulation of some 90,000.[48] Although it was essentially aimed at the superior artisan and mechanic it regularly reported on trade union matters and on strikes. In the middle of 1853, after the failure of the Combination of Workmen Bill, it attempted to co-ordinate a national wage movement.[49] It suggested the establishment of a Labour Congress to protect workers and to ensure a fair day's wage. 'Touched by the magic of unity', the working classes could then bombard Parliament with petitions to 'stop the moneyed class violating the law'.[50] This emphasis on peaceful and constitutional co-operation was the paper's main theme throughout the strike, on which it was initially ambivalent. In August it urged caution and moderation: 'Try conciliation and negotiation with your employers. DO NOT STRIKE'.[51] Yet, when the Stockport operatives went on strike, it attacked the masters for failing to fulfil their promise of restoring the wage reductions of 1847–8, and claimed it knew of 'no case in the history of strikes in which the men were more completely justified'.[52]

When the Preston operatives went on strike the paper's tone changed. 'It is only fair to state that in several cases the hands have struck in consequence of a *mere* difference between the concessions made and advances demanded.'[53] A month later it suggested that the 'general feeling seems to be that if some *slight* concessions on *immaterial* points on the part of the masters and men were made ... the lock-out might be speedily terminated'.[54] In December it argued that there was no reason to believe, given the differences in the nature of production, that the masters of Preston could advance the ten per cent that had been advanced at Blackburn.[55] By February it urged the working men to drop the cry of ten per cent and no surrender; 'it is a cry without meaning ... and the attempt to exhort it on the part of the men will peril all that has been gained'.[56] Wages, it consistently asserted, were determined by supply and demand,[57] and after the masters had opened their mills it pleaded with the men to submit: 'We say to the strikers ... prove yourselves reasonable, practicable men; close with the employers who offer the highest terms ... by taking the best offers, the workmen will divide the masters [and] create dissension among them'.[58]

Lloyd's completely misunderstood the issue involved in the dispute, and by March almost admitted as much. 'Few of us have understood from the beginning the strength and character displayed at Preston, or the power of that spontaneous organization of the working classes throughout Lancashire in support of their Preston comrades.'[59] But with the weavers' defeat and with the spinners 'regrettably declaring their intentions to stay out', *Lloyd's* returned to its theme that working men could only achieve their objectives through 'reasonable patience, good temper and steady persistence'.[60] The failure of the strike 'will prove to all those who live by labour, that labour is not yet organized'.[61]

Lloyd's acceptance of the masters' political economy did not prevent it from attacking them on every possible occasion. When the masters refused to advance the ten per cent because trade was no longer prosperous, *Lloyd's* delighted in claiming that 'tyrants [were] never wanting in excuses for their tyranny'.[62] The masters' absence from the Society of Arts' conference – which *Lloyd's* optimistically argued had done more for the artisan than 'ten years of sterile agitation in nooks and crannies'[63] – put them clearly in the wrong, whilst the arrest of the delegates 'irretrievably damaged the masters' cause in the moral judgement of the outside world'.[64]

The Owenite *Glasgow Sentinel*, edited by Robert Buchanan and Alexander McDonald, was less naive than *Lloyd's* but was equally certain that arbitration was the only solution.[65] From the beginning it predicted that the passing of the trade boom inevitably meant defeat for the Preston operatives.[66] It condemned the masters' lock-out, which it asserted was a repetition of the shoddy tactics used by the employers in the engineers' dispute, and used it to show that the 'laissez-faire system, so much vaunted, has so constantly broken down, that its utter worthlessness is obvious'.[67] In November it asked why arbitration was 'good for the Russians and Turks, for the French and English', but not 'for factory owners and factory workers', and urged both Bright and Cobden to do something to resolve this contradiction.[68] The *Sentinel* forcefully defended the rights of unions to benefit from improving trade, but in an editorial on Ernest

Jones's proposed Labour Parliament warned that it was a great mistake to identify trade disputes with political movements: 'They are essentially distinct and separate; so much so that the working man of ability, who may transfer his public exertions from the former to the latter, almost invariably ceases to have any influence in trades questions, however much he may have previously possessed.'[69]

The affiliation of industrial and political activity was, in contrast, the *People's Paper*'s consistent theme, and the Preston strike provided Ernest Jones with an opportunity to unite the increasingly divided Chartist movement with the Trade Union and Short Time movements. Throughout late 1853 Jones actively campaigned for working-class unity, and in September the *Paper* set the scene with a warning of the imminent economic panic. 'A tremendous panic is coming which will be all the more terrible for the enormous amount of capital invested in trade. When that panic arrives millions of men, women and children will be thrown idle and will suffer all the pangs and woes of want.' 'Monopoly', it continued, 'trembles at the approaching crisis of dull trade [and] we stand on the threshold of a social war. The tone and character of that war will depend on the conduct of the employers – but the result of the contest will be the annihilation of monopoly.'[70]

In the following month Jones began touring the country to gather subscriptions for Preston and to raise support for the mass movement. His huge personality and fiery speeches soon won him support throughout Lancashire but embittered other Chartist leaders who saw the mass movement as the ramp by which Jones sought to dominate Chartism itself.[71] When he visited Preston on 4 November he spoke for one and a half hours to some 15,000 operatives, who had gathered on the Marsh. In his speech Jones tempered hope with experience. 'Whatever may be the extent of your union, I don't believe that of the masters will be very firm and lasting. It is based on avarice – yours is based on brotherhood. They have a bond of £5,000, you have a bond of five million hearts.'[72] He then reminded them that there was more at stake than wages, and warned that any attempt to affiliate with middle-class sympathizers was nothing short of betrayal. He launched a vicious attack on Busfield Ferrand's Labour League, which continued to urge arbitration under the banner of protection with some fleeting success.[73] For Jones, Free Trade was an unimpeachable policy 'founded on the soundest principles of political economy'. The fault he claimed 'lies not in competition itself; it lies in the improper application of its principles'.[74]

Jones's repeated claim that the working class had to be self-reliant became more and more strident as the strike continued. In December he condemned the weavers' memorial to Palmerston as another humiliating indication that 'we cannot fight our own battle',[75] and in February condemned Cowell for not defending him at the Society of Arts conference.[76] Throughout, the *Paper* stressed the urgent need for the mass movement and for greater class unity before the operatives were defeated;[77] 'more and more the present machine proves hopelessly defective, even for Preston itself'.[78] In March the *Paper* pointed out the inherent weakness of the ten per cent campaign. 'Either way the [masters] have you. If you resist, you weaken your own fund – if you submit you strengthen the funds of the enemy. They have you on every side.' On these grounds the Stockport operatives were advised not to strike 'until THE COUNTRY IS READY FOR YOU.'[79] Nine days previously the widely canvassed Labour Parliament had met in Manchester. Here Jones managed to get his own way, and a detailed programme for the mass movement was finally worked out. But by this time the Preston strike was struggling to survive, and when the Stockport masters withdrew the ten per cent, as the *Paper* had predicted,[80] defeat became inevitable. 'In future' the *Paper* acidly concluded, 'let no strike take place that is not based on self employment as well as on mere contributions of others.'[81] For the *People's Paper*, the failure of the ten per cent campaign was a bitter disappointment. As far as Jones was concerned, the operatives had largely squandered the chance of unifying political and industrial action without which, he believed, there was little chance of victory. By August the mass movement was itself in ruins.[82]

Whilst the *People's Paper* attempted to rally support throughout Lancashire, *Reynolds' Newspaper*, though very popular in the northern industrial districts, actively organized support in London. Reynolds soon became involved – as he had in the engineers' strike[83] – in helping set up subscription lists so that the London trades could finance the men in Preston.[84] Details of subscribers, subscriptions and reports of the delegates' meetings (held usually in the Bell Inn) were published with unfailing regularity, and these served to encourage Cowell and the other delegates who came to London to widen the base of their cause. Compared with its main rival, *Lloyd's Weekly*, *Reynolds'* was very much closer to the spirit of the men and endorsed their struggle weekly. In November it attacked the Poor Law Board and the government 'for abetting the capitalists in their murderous attempts to reduce the workpeople to the vilest and most degrading servitude', and vehemently claimed that the only remedy was to give the working classes 'political power via the vote'.[85] It returned to this theme in January whilst launching a vicious onslaught on 'that paltry knot of nobodies', the Society of Arts.[86] Strikes, *Reynolds'* believed, were a necessary evil and could only be removed by 'enfranchising the working classes'.[87] Neither conferences nor arbitration, it urged, were ever likely to settle disputes, especially when prompted by the hated Prince Albert. *Reynolds'* distrusted the instinct of 'German despotism' and feared that Prince Albert might persuade Lord Aberdeen's government to reintroduce the combination laws to arrest the progress the working classes had made throughout 1853 'towards their self emancipation' from the 'tyranny of capital'.[88]

The *Reynolds'* attack on Prince Albert was mere indulgence and reflects the paper's republican views rather than any devious interference on the part of the Prince Consort.[89] Its defiant crusade against the 'unscrupulous views' of the daily press was, on the other hand, well measured. As each middle-class paper sought to expose the selfish and dangerously misleading motives of the delegates, *Reynolds'* rushed to their defence. The *Daily News*, it alleged, 'is seconding with its small artillery the great guns of the *Times* who see the Preston operatives as revolters'.[90] And when the *Morning Chronicle* attempted to show that the delegates wished to keep the strike going for their own advantage it 'actually surpassed the *Times* itself in virulent (even reckless) denunciation'.[91] Only the conservative *Morning Herald* went unscathed, while the much despised *Times* remained the villain of the piece.

The *Times* was the most important middle-class national newspaper in the 1850s. Between 1847 and 1855, when its circulation doubled to almost 60,000, it was 'at the peak of its influence'.[92] Throughout the strike it steered a fairly neutral course and, although it consistently supported mediation and compromise,[93] it would occasionally revive all its old scathing bitterness.

The operatives of Lancashire have discovered a new religion [... and] their spiritual zeal carries them beyond the vulgar consideration of comfort or economy. Monster trains convey them to the places where this new-born piety may be refreshed by the exhortations of suitable preachers and the devotional hymns of new worship. Under the cold blue sky they listen with edifying submission to the pious raptures of inspired teachers ... and what is this new gospel which has illumined the darkness of Lancashire, and made it the Galilee of this land? Prepare yourself, gentle reader, for this new and astounding revelation of the Divine wisdom and mercy. The awful truth which has broken through the darkness of ages, which has penetrated every heart and warmed every soul in the industrious north, is the eternal and immutable necessity of Ten per Cent more wages [and] Preston is the favoured city of this new Church.[94]

Nor were the masters spared.

Here is an extract from the resolution of the Masters' Association [which] makes it manifest that they do not understand their true position, as employers of labour, and it proves that what they condemn in their operatives they do not hesitate to put into practice against them ... They consider themselves entitled to fix beforehand, and by combination, what shall be the state of the labour market at some future indefinite time. They even go so far in absurdity as to reserve power to the committee, to make recommendations in particular cases when the mills open again. Can they accuse the operatives of dictation and interference after this.[95]

The recognition that neither side was blameless indicates that the *Times* had changed its attitude towards strikes since the engineers' strike of 1851–2 when it came out strongly against the union. By 1853 the operatives' right to strike was accepted, as was their right to combine to increase wages.[96] How much the *Times'* special correspondent, sent to Preston in November, was responsible for this change in attitudes is difficult to say. But his discovery of an active masters' association prior to the strike itself, may have diminished the *Times'* usual zeal for blaming the despotism of self-seeking delegates. Individual delegates were, of course, still attacked. In October Cowell was condemned for his involvement in the coercion of those wanting to return to work. But the claim that agitators were 'no doubt back at work in the usual way' was expressed with resignation rather than the usual frenzied indignation.[97] In fact the operatives were the ones to express their fury,[98] especially during the early months of the strike. By Christmas, though, they preferred the bite of irony. 'What did the Editor of the *Times* know about the steam loom?' asked John Brocklehurst. 'Why as much as a pig knows of geometry (Laughter and Cheers)'.[99] When the *Times* actually expressed some support for the operatives' cause, as they did in April, Cowell was as quick to praise it for its 'splendid article' as he had been to condemn it when it supported the masters or misrepresented the strikers' intentions.[100]

Like the *Times*, the *Daily News* dispatched its own special correspondent to Preston. In early November the *Daily* had insisted on the 'obvious' advantages of arbitration.[101] It urged the masters to be less secretive and called for a full revelation of the facts. But by the end of the month this conciliatory tone had been abandoned. Mediation was impossible 'now that the sword was drawn and the scabbard thrown away'. Indeed, the *Daily* then alleged that 'the party who calls out for mediation ... is the party who is in the wrong'.[102] 'The conduct of the men at the present time', it continued 'is imitated from that of the sagacious carpenter in Hogarth's picture, who is represented sitting at the extremity of a sign-board, and sawing through the limb which supports him.'[103] In January, it printed a letter which explained Cowell's leadership in terms of Preston's easily led Catholic population 'accustomed to give themselves up to their priests, for them to think and choose for them'.[104] And by the end of the strike it reminded those who had made the 'noble sacrifice' that strikes could never increase wages.[105]

The argument that 'economic laws forbid the strikes to succeed'[106] was a point taken up by the Peelite *Morning Chronicle*. In January it unreservedly supported the masters' combination, fearing that a victory for the operatives would be a 'public calamity, utterly subversive of both employers and employed, and would involve all in communism'.[107] It saw the contest in terms of power not wages, and as an attempt to 'invert the natural order of things and to subject the master, at once and forever, to the capricious tyranny of organized agitation'.[108] This theme was also taken up by the *Economist* – the voice of the Manchester School[109] – in the early stages of the dispute. The operatives, it alleged, were blind to their own interests. 'Ten per cent is a mere rallying cry, like many other cries, which in all ages, from the Crusades to Church and King riots, have been used to lead the multitude into evil.' To demand such an increase, 'without regard to the previous rate, to present circumstances and to those diversities which would make it in some cases too much and in others too little, is a palpable error'.[110] By November the criticism of the delegates, whom the *Economist* asserted were only interested in making political capital out of 'kindling discontent', was also extended to the masters themselves. 'When the masters blame the men, they ought not to forget that many of them hold quarterly and other meetings and agree amongst themselves the price at which they will sell their goods, thus encouraging in others combinations so injurious to all'.[111] In an exasperated New Year leader on the 'alarming national evil' the press, which represented the weight of public opinion, was urged to arbitrate between the 'conflicting parties ... to restore ... the harmony which is equally desirable for the interests of individuals and for the public welfare'.[112] In practical terms this meant the abolition of combinations, the abandonment of mischievous philanthropic legislation and the restoration of the free market so that wages would find their own level.

The northern press was equally vigorous in claiming that strikes could not affect the level of wages, and throughout the dispute the themes of intimidation of the unions and paid agitators were taken up with undisguised zeal. The Tory *Bolton Chronicle* referred to the reign of terror and the extortion involved in gathering funds from unwilling workmen and shopkeepers.[113] The Free Trade bi-weekly *Manchester Examiner* reminded the operatives that 'in allowing themselves to be made the dupes of ignorant and self-seeking agitators the inevitable result must be disappointment and misery'.[114] In November it attempted to blacken Cowell's character: 'we may presume that he is at this moment receiving some sort of remuneration for his services ... [and] he is no doubt well paid, well clothed, whilst turnouts are starving'.[115] The *Manchester Guardian* also embarked on a smear campaign, insinuating that the delegates personally made £25 out of every £100 collected for the operatives' fund. Comparisons were made with O'Connor's Land Plan, and soon these allegations of fraud were 'plastered by the masters all over the walls of Preston'.[116] This prompted an angry Cowell to call on the *Guardian*'s editor to denounce his blatant misrepresentations,[117] and prompted Grimshaw's blasphemous remark: 'the *Manchester Guardian* was the Bible of the manufacturer, the *Examiner and Times* was their testament. Gold was their God, Silver their Jesus Christ and Copper their Holy Ghost.'[118]

The operatives' battle of words with the Manchester press continued throughout the strike[119] and even in May, with the weavers already defeated, the spinners excluded the *Guardian*'s reporters from their delegate meeting, agreeing to send their resolutions only to the *Liverpool Mail*, *People's Paper* and *Reynolds*'.[120] There was, of course, much in the operatives' claim that the Manchester press were the tools of the 'shoddyocracy' and their reporters 'lying and miserable scribes'.[121] Editorials were naturally one-sided, but, in certain respects, the Manchester press did not shrink from condemning the masters' intolerance. The *Examiner*, which professed to 'always take a deep interest in everything connected with the rights and welfare of the working classes' (which meant lecturing them on political economy), did note that the masters were not without blame, especially the young and inexperienced. 'Young men invested with a little power, and with a small amount of experience and knowledge of human nature, are but too apt to be distant, repulsive and unreasonable.' It regretted the masters' unreasonable rejection of conciliation,[122] but supported their combination with more conviction than the operatives', which, it grudgingly conceded, 'might be useful' in advancing its members' interests. Like the *Guardian*, it was anxious to impress the necessity for moderation whilst largely failing to heed its own advice.

Other northern papers were less reticent about the masters' position. The *Bradford Observer* attacked the strike-prone manufacturers as 'lashing captains,' who insisted on the 'serf-like surrender of their workpeople',[123] whilst the *Liverpool Journal* referred to the fact that some masters were contemplating the strike with 'a kind of grim pleasure'.[124] The *Stockport Advertiser* and the *Blackburn Standard* both supported the operatives' claim, and asked why the Preston masters could not pay the ten per cent when the masters at Stockport and Blackburn had already done so. The *Standard* warned that the 'day is most certainly approaching when the combination of the many must most inevitably defeat the combination of the few', whilst the *Advertiser* attacked the misleading promises of the Free Trade League 'who, like Frankenstein, have created a monster'.[125] The *Lancaster Guardian* also called on the masters to state what had prevented them from 'redeeming their pledge'. 'A candid admission of this fact,' it noted, 'if a faithful representation of the condition of the manufacturing trade, we feel confident would have diverted the catastrophe now destined to involve an incalculable amount of suffering . . . But the employers deny the right of the operatives to intrude on such a sacred province as that of profits.'[126] Both Burnley papers added their support to the wage agitation, and the *Advertiser* thought the Burnley lockout 'unwise' and called for a 'more humane plan for settling disputes'.[127] This line of argument was taken up by most of the Lancashire press. The *Liverpool Mercury* savagely attacked the masters for refusing mediation and called for arbitration to avoid future disputes.[128] The *Liverpool Journal* wanted a commission of enquiry, whilst the *Bolton Chronicle*, which had already attacked the 'Lynch Law' and operatives' extortion of subscriptions, suggested that the county MPs should act as arbitrators.[129] Some were more lukewarm in their advocacy, but both Tory and Liberal papers, for reasons of their own,[130] were not prepared to remain silent.

The freedom of labour, as has been said over and over again, must and ought to be vindicated. That is an absolute right. The liberty of the employer to fix his rate of wage is as undeniable. But this is a qualified right, inasmuch as it may be used to the injury of all classes of society and be made subservient to oppression and sordid ambition. No man, and no body of men, can be permitted to trade on the necessities of poverty.[131]

If some of the London and provincial press partially concealed their hatred of the delegates and strikes behind their veiled criticism of the masters and their acceptance of unions, the influential quarterlies were generally hostile. The Whig *Edinburgh Review* relied upon language little removed from the simplistic views propagated by Harriet Martineau and W.R. Greg in the 1830s and 1840s.[132] It saw the relation between labour and capital as the great social problem of the age, and rigidly blamed it on the uneducated operatives who refused to 'bow . . . before those eternal laws of economic science against which all rebellion is childish, futile and suicidal'. The wage fund unerringly determined the level of wages and proved that successful strikes were economically impossible. The *Review* extolled the virtues of thrift and damned the operatives because their demands were 'utterly irrational' and their cause 'hopelessly bad'.[133] The Tory *Quarterly Review*, which Cobbett once described as 'a villainous, an almost infamous publication . . . from its beginning the deadly enemy of the liberties of the people . . . In short . . . the basest, the most execrable tool of power that ever has appeared in England'[134] came to much the same conclusion, despite its earlier professed distrust of political economy. It alleged that strikes could never increase wages in the long run, that they were self-defeating and that unions were little more than restrictive practices. Savings, it had continually urged, 'were the richest most powerful and most natural fund on which the working man can rely'.[135] Even *Blackwood's Magazine*, which normally defended the aristocracy's enlightened right to care for the poor, succumbed to the arguments of political economy. It attacked the tyranny of the 'irresponsible council of the Trades Union' and smooth tongued demagogues, and ridiculed the failure of the masters' attempt to defeat the operatives by meeting combination with combination. Overall, though, it remained lofty in tone and tried to play down the whole affair, by claiming that it was of no more interest to the country 'than a serious railway accident or a fatal coal pit explosion'.[136] The *Westminster Review* thought otherwise — 'there is enough in this Lancashire strike to excite the interest of every Englishman' — but in a rather sympathetic piece, which condemned some sections of the press for making political capital out of the labour question, all the contentious issues were avoided. It marvelled at the operatives' self-inflicted suffering, their loyalty and their peaceful conduct, but found it shameful to admit that 'civilization and culture' could not find an 'easier method by which to teach the laws of political economy to men and women such as these'. It rightly scoffed at the suggestion that the operatives should rely upon savings rather than combinations, but questioned the feasibility of the strike tactic, recommending instead voluntary arbitration as a second best solution.[137]

In his assessment of the strike, Henry Ashworth suggested that the press and its full discussion of the struggle merely served to 'give fixity and force to the quarrel', and undeserved reputations to the leading delegates. 'Men who had suddenly emerged from obscurity to play the part of heroes, were concerned to act worthy of the world-wide reputation which they had now acquired; and vanity conspired with self-interest to dictate the cry of "no surrender".'[138] This carping judgement was clearly a reaction to the press's changed attitude on unions and strikes. Ashworth almost certainly expected the press to condemn the operatives as they had done during the engineers' strike, but, in 1853—4, the press were no longer indiscriminately and unreservedly hostile to peaceful trade unionism. Strikes, they nearly all agreed, were futile, the working-class press largely because the operatives failed to see the advantage of uniting political and industrial action, the middle-class press because strikes were ruinous for men and masters alike. But very few papers were unmoved by the pathos of the operatives' struggle. The special correspondents who visited Preston in the early part of the dispute seem to have set the tone. Their favourable reports of the operatives' conduct were on their own significant enough. When the masters' rigid refusal to accept any sort of compromise became more and more apparent, the press were forced to recognise, some rather grudgingly (and some not at all), that industrial disputes were not always one-sided affairs.

10 Defeat

10 February 1854 – 13 May 1854

There's Thomas Miller, we can tell,
For knobsticks he does ring his bell,
Such Gentlemen will ne'er do well,
 For robbing poor people;
His bells may ring and loudly sing,
 As loud as they can shout, sir,
We'll make these Cotton Lords repent,
The Day they lock'd us out sir.

At the end of February the newly-recruited knobsticks began to arrive. The first of the newcomers were not 'the turnip-grubbers of Buckinghamshire' (though these were soon to appear) but a small number of unemployed cotton hands. George Galloway, a partner in the Preston firm of Sharples and Wilding, maintained a warehouse in Manchester, which he had begun to use as a base for the recruitment of knobsticks. In a vain attempt to preserve secrecy Galloway relied upon the efforts of his warehouseman rather than on the posting of handbills. By Saturday 25 February he had engaged 57 operatives, a dozen for Haslam Brothers and the remainder for his own firm. On the following Monday, the 27th, he accompanied them on the train to Preston, where they arrived at ten o'clock. At the station he ushered them into the guards' room, in the charge of a certain Bright, while he went off to find transport to take them to the mills. This proved to be a fatal mistake. On his return Galloway discovered no less than 45 of his recruits being escorted down Fishergate by the strikers' delegates, bound for the spinners' committee rooms at the Farmers' Arms. He loaded the dozen who were left onto a shandry, only to find a large number of strikers following the vehicle through the centre of Preston. Prominent in the crowd were Mortimer Grimshaw and Luke Wood, who were busy offering the knobsticks 7s each to abandon Galloway and come with them. One, by the name of Kelly, was spirited away, and the wretched Galloway eventually delivered less than a quarter of his original consignment to the mills.

At the Farmers' Arms the knobsticks were given food and drink under the close supervision of the delegates, who even accompanied them whenever they needed to go into the yard. In the afternoon Cowell and Grimshaw took time off to tell their audience in the Orchard of their success in 'rescuing' the knobsticks from the clutches of the masters. At seven o'clock the visitors were escorted to the station, where Grimshaw bought them single tickets back to Manchester. Michael Gallaher was one of several delegates who served as couriers on the journey. The party was met in Manchester by Bright and Kelly, who had evidently been acting for the strikers all along, and by the Blackburn delegate, John Lang, who had kept a watchful eye on Galloway's warehouse on the previous Saturday. After receiving further hospitality from the delegates, the knobsticks dispersed. Some of them returned to the warehouse next morning, only to find pickets placed outside, who once again took them to a nearby tavern. Showing considerable determination, a handful did manage to enter the warehouse unobserved, by a rear entrance, on Wednesday, and eight of the 45 eventually found their way back to Preston. Some had to walk as far as Bolton, for fear of being recognised at the station in Manchester.

Individual knobsticks were not neglected. Patrick Conway, a Preston lad employed as a piecer at Horrocks and Jacson, was taken to the Farmers' Arms by some lads. He was offered a job on a farm near Accrington, and escorted there by Gallaher. When he returned to Preston next day William Parkinson offered him 3s 6d per week if he joined the strike. Conway proved to be incorrigible, and was eventually told to 'go a knobbing'. Christopher Riley, a 19-year-old piecer working for Naylor, went home to Lancaster on the train one Saturday, and found that he had been followed by the delegate John Gardner. Having failed to dissuade him from returning to Preston, Gardner invited himself to Sunday tea and prevailed upon the lad's father to restrain his son. Frightened of prosecution by Naylor for breach of his engagement, Riley finally walked back to Preston with a friend. He soon found himself at the spinners' committee rooms, where Gardner persuaded him to seek work in Bolton. When it was discovered that they had missed the last train to Bolton, it was arranged that he be escorted to Blackburn instead. Here Riley was met and entertained by Parkinson. He looked for work in Blackburn without success, and returned to Naylor's mill in Preston.

Birley Brothers had sent William Abbott, one of their warehousemen, on a recruiting mission to Ireland. He went straight to the Belfast workhouse, where he succeeded in engaging 141 hands. Arriving with them at Fleetwood on the morning of 3 March, Abbott repeated Galloway's error of leaving them unattended at the jetty, while he went off to arrange transport. During his absence the majority of the Irish were attracted into the Victoria Inn by Parkinson, James Waddington and James Dolphin. Here they were given bread, cheese and coffee (later ale), and offered their return passages and small sums of money. Despite the intervention of the county police no less than 101 accepted; they were accompanied back to Belfast by Dolphin, who organized their readmission to the workhouse there. When Abbott finally reached Preston, he required the assistance of the police to usher the remaining 40 knobsticks through the crowds to his employers' mill.

179 Defeat

Other masters had been recruiting in the workhouses of Yorkshire, but with little success. Arkwright and Naylor enlisted the support of the Board of Guardians in Bradford, and engaged two hundred people from the local workhouse. Their plans were thwarted by the irrepressible Mortimer Grimshaw, who covered the walls of the town with placards denying the manufacturers' claims that the Preston dispute had been settled. The guardians now had second thoughts, and allowed Grimshaw to address the potential knobsticks inside the workhouse. This brought immediate results, as Grimshaw informed the weavers in the Orchard on 1 March. He assured them:

The feeling of the people of Bradford is that they will die of hunger before they will come and take your places ... [they] were so indignant at the conduct of Arkwright and Naylor that four fierce-looking fellows came to me and asked me to point them out, and they would keep their eye on them till dark and would give them the d − t hiding that ever they got in their lives.

Wisely, Grimshaw declined the offer. Sporadic recruiting did continue in Bradford under the auspices of an extremely dubious character named Joseph Mitchell, who had assisted Grimshaw in his efforts at the workhouse and somehow managed to take money from both sides.[1]

Precisely what the manufacturers had expected to gain from all this is uncertain. Any hopes that the immigrants would enable production to resume on a significant scale were soon dashed when they proved to be as deficient in quality as they were limited in numbers. The *Preston Guardian*, urging the strikers not to impede the knobsticks, found it 'extremely probable that nothing would sooner impress upon the employers the desirableness of making some arrangement with their old and efficient hands, than the incalculable trouble and expense to which they will be put by employing such unfortunates as have this week been brought among us'. The Belfast contingent, for example, was 'a wretched specimen of what Irish famine has reduced the peasantry of that country to'.[2] Nor was the threat of competition from such a source sufficient to endanger the unity and determination of the turnouts. In fact the only concrete benefit to the millowners came, as the delegates had predicted, from the pretext it provided for further repression.

The delegates, meanwhile, continued to urge the preservation of the peace and, despite the relatively minor incident at the railway station on 2 March, which to everyone's surprise led to the proclamation forbidding all open-air meetings, the great mass of strikers willingly complied. The delegates now missed no opportunity to denounce what Swinglehurst described as 'the greatest despotism in the world'. Grimshaw called for the defence of 'a right which has been handed down to us by our forefathers − the right to assemble in our public meetings and discuss our grievances'.[3] They agreed to send a deputation to Palmerston to protest against the conduct of the authorities, and, at a meeting of the Preston Ratepayers' Association, successive speakers attacked the magistrates for lack of impartiality, the Watch Committee for entrapment and provocation, and the manufacturers for threatening to inflate the Poor Rates with unemployable strangers. Supported by Cowell, Waddington and Parkinson, the ratepayers demanded the prohibition of outside work by council officers; called for the appointment of a stipendiary magistrate; and agreed to petition Palmerston against the recent repressive (and costly!) decisions of the Watch Committee, magistrates and cotton masters.[4] If the first wave of immigrants had polarised public opinion, it had been very much to the advantage of the operatives.

The turnouts were now forced to meet in the countryside, safely outside the borough limits. In a defiant mood Cowell declared his willingness to go to prison in defence of their right to meet in the Orchard, but evidently thought better of the idea.[5] On 4 March a planned meeting at Ashton Marsh was hastily moved to Cottam, three miles away, when notices were encountered threatening the prosecution of trespassers. Next day between 20,000 and 30,000 people assembled at short notice in another field at Cottam, made available by a local farmer (whose address, 'Teetotal Cottage', suggests that Cowell's abstinence from the demon drink was not without public, as well as private, advantages). Further meetings took place on Ribbleton Moor, in Freehold Park and at Fulwood. Saturday 11 March saw the great assembly at Hoghton Tower, an event repeated next day when it attracted a crowd estimated at between 50,000 and 100,000 people. 'Before long', declared Mortimer Grimshaw, recalling the great Chartist demonstrations of earlier days, 'we shall convene a meeting at Blackstone Edge, and summon the labourers of Yorkshire and Derbyshire to the rescue.'[6]

There were other successes to report. Early in March operatives at Hugh Dawson's Old Mill returned to work at mutually satisfactory rates.[7] Dawson, who did not belong to the Masters' Association, was not subject to hindrance from that source. Nor is it clear whether the Association became involved in the case of Edward Edge, who was a member, and whose negotiations with his hands seemed, for a time, very close to success.[8] It certainly had to intervene, rather dramatically, when Swainson Brothers reopened on 13 March. The delegates hailed the return of John Swainson's hands as a major breakthrough, and poured scorn on the Association's claim that the operatives had gone back to work at the rates paid on 1 March 1853. It proved necessary to threaten Swainson with the forfeiture of his £5,000 bond before he could be induced to reduce wages to the approved level, whereupon the operatives immediately resumed their strike. The coercive nature of the millowners' organization had been revealed for all to see.[9]

Swainson's eagerness to settle may well have been prompted by the experience of his colleagues, for the immigrants were proving an unmitigated disaster. Knobsticks were in fact arriving at the rate of 250 or 300 a week, bringing with them many children and old people who were incapable of any sort of work. (At this rate, the *Preston Guardian* calculated, it would take the masters over a year to replace the 15,000 strikers.)[10] The great majority of those who were suitable for work were unskilled labourers. 'A batch which arrived last night', it was reported on 11 March, 'were dressed in smock frocks, as if recently residents of some agricultural district. A few dashing young women from the South, decked in veils and other finery, arrived about the middle of the week.'[11] Three days after the arrival of the country folk, Preston welcomed a party of 35 Irishmen from Manchester. These were 'miserable-looking specimens of humanity, and in a most disgusting filthy condition. Their bedding, etc., swarmed with that species of loathsome vermin so obnoxious to cleanly housewives, and when the articles were removed from the truck on which they were packed, the lively insects dispersed themselves over the platform, much to the alarm of persons present.' (A Mrs Lambert, proprietor of the station bookstall, was seized with fear for the cleanliness of her stock.) 'A copious supply of boiling water was put into requisition, and it was believed that the bulk of the enemy was destroyed.'[12] The new arrivals were no less trouble inside the mills. Birley Brothers sent a batch of hands back to Hull because they were (presumably by accident) damaging the machinery.[13] There were reports of a strike at Horrockses of Irish knobsticks dissatisfied with the food provided for them.[14] Richard Eccles had to dismiss two girls, said to be 'abandoned characters' from Wapping, for their 'wanton conduct in the mill',[15] while the wretched Richard Threlfall was forced by the magistrates to repatriate an Irishwoman sacked when the remainder of his hands refused to work with her.[16]

By the middle of March most of the mills remained closed, and where production had resumed it was on a very limited scale. And if the masters had intended to provoke serious rioting against the knobsticks they had been disappointed, while the prohibition of meetings inside the borough had been circumvented without evident difficulty. All in all, the millowners were little closer to victory than they had been a month earlier.

Yet the suspicion lingered that the manufacturers had a further card to play. On 12 March the weavers' delegates had toyed with the idea of establishing a special fund for the defence of those of their number who might be prosecuted, and the proposal was withdrawn only on the understanding that the general funds were available for this purpose.[17] Next Saturday, the 18th, a crowd gathered outside the Town Hall when it became known that the magistrates were closeted in the Council Chamber, where they were interrogating some of the Irish immigrants. The general belief was that the knobsticks were to be charged with misappropriating furniture supplied by their employers, but this appeared less likely by Monday, when the magistrates resumed their conclave. In the afternoon Cowell told the weavers that he expected conspiracy charges to be brought against himself and other delegates. The accuracy of his prediction was established at nine o'clock that evening when he was arrested at the railway station on his way to Manchester. Grimshaw was soon apprehended in Orchard Street, and the arrests of Waddington and Parkinson soon followed. Next morning Thomas Gregson and John Lang were seized. Gallaher, Dolphin and Gardner surrendered voluntarily, followed on Wednesday by John Brocklehurst and Luke Wood.

The charge was conspiracy: the delegates, it was alleged, did 'unlawfully conspire, combine and confederate together', 'unlawfully molesting and obstructing' certain persons hired by various manufacturers named to work in their trade and business, 'to force and endeavour to force the said persons so hired as aforesaid to depart from their said hiring'. Ascroft, the Town Clerk, led the prosecution when proceedings opened on Tuesday 21 March. In the dock stood Cowell, Grimshaw, Gallaher, Gardner and Lang, who were joined next day by Brocklehurst and Wood. The evidence against them centred on the successful 'rescue' of the Manchester knobsticks on 27 February, coupled with the case of Christopher Riley and the delegates' activities in Bradford.[18] George Galloway and three of his recruits testified in relation to the Manchester affair, their evidence being supported by journalists from the local press (who reported on speeches made by some of the accused at public meetings), and by one Henry Rigby, inspector of weights and measures [sic], who had been present at the station on the day in question. In addition, Ascroft produced copies of the weavers' and spinners' balance sheets, citing cryptic entries apparently relevant to the incident ('Expenses of removing many certain parties from Preston, £4 10s.') The balance sheets, the court learned with interest, had been obtained by a plain-clothes policeman who had paid regular visits to the committee rooms, *incognito* and for undeclared purposes. The case of the seven delegates took up two full days. On Thursday Parkinson, Dolphin and Waddington appeared to answer charges connected with the incident at Fleetwood on 3 March. Here the chief prosecution witness was William Abbott, who had engaged the Irish knobsticks in Belfast, supported by two of his recruits, by a mill manager and a county police superintendent who had witnessed the affair, and by one of the local reporters. In both cases the magistrates found the prosecution case convincing enough to commit the accused for trial at the Liverpool assizes.[19]

The indecent haste with which the proceedings were undertaken was the cause of great bitterness, and provoked unfavourable comment in the press. In other respects the proceedings had been fair enough. None of the five magistrates was himself a millowner (though one was the mayor, two were aldermen, and all could be expected to be both acquainted with and sympathetic to the masters). The delegates were legally represented,[20] and were granted bail both during the hearing and at its close. Though the defence called no witnesses of its own the cross-examination of prosecution witnesses was thorough and incisive, often to the annoyance of the irascible Ascroft. He was, for example, refused permission for one of the journalists (whose notes had been destroyed) to refresh his memory from the newspaper in which his report of a meeting had appeared, and he was forced to abandon another part of the deposition when it transpired that the report in question had been copied from another paper. But such minor rebuffs were a small price to pay for the prospect of an immediate (and successful) assize hearing.[21]

All proved to be in vain. When the accused appeared in court at Liverpool on 28 March, Mr Justice Cresswell decided to defer the full trial until the autumn assizes, so that justice might be seen to be done. Until then, the arrested delegates were free to continue with the agitation.[22] At the time opinion was divided as to whether the case would have succeeded. Ascroft was confident that the accused had indeed entered into a conspiracy for an illegal purpose. 'If the people in Preston will not work,' he told the bench, 'the masters are anxious to obtain parties who will work; and it is not the business of the defendants to interfere with those who are willing to take employment. If parties are willing to hire, it is clearly an indictable offence to prevent their going to work or to get them away from the town.' The defence argument, on the other hand, was that 'in the common construction of those phrases, it must naturally be that to molest and obstruct must mean something that is accompanied by violence'. But there had been no violence, only peaceful (if energetic) persuasion. Cross-examination of prosecution witnesses had confirmed that the delegates had repeatedly gone out of their way to condemn disorder and urge the need for peaceful conduct. If it were legal for individuals to agree among themselves not to work on unacceptable terms, it must also be lawful for them peaceably to persuade others to follow the same course.[23]

These sentiments were echoed by the delegates and their supporters. Asked for his opinion, W.P. Roberts insisted that 'one man has a right to persuade another not to work, and half a dozen might peacefully do the same thing'.[24] As Cowell had put it, back in February: 'These people are in England. We have as good a right to bid a price for them as the masters.'[25] If anyone were guilty of conspiracy, argued William Newton, it was the manufacturers. Thomas Rhodes sardonically suggested that the Masters' Association should be charged with intimidation for their conduct towards John Swainson, who had been threatened with the loss of £5,000.[26] The *Preston Guardian*, darkly hinting at 'a gross and unpardonable malversation of the public resources', echoed these sentiments.[27]

The prosecution case was, however, much stronger than this might suggest. The law of conspiracy in trade disputes was far from clear. If the defence could quote the judgement of Lord Cranworth in the case of *R v Selsby and others* (1847), the Preston magistrates were able to respond by citing the quite different opinions expressed in similar cases by Lord Campbell and Mr Justice Erle.[28] In the 1847 case it had been held that criminal conspiracy under section 3 of the Combination Act of 1825 applied only to acts of violence, threats of bodily injury or injury to property, and intimidation, obstruction or molestation produced by such acts or threats. But, as one legal text put it, 'this view, which is clearly untenable, did not receive any further judicial confirmation'.[29] By 1851, in the important cases of *R v Duffield* and *R v Rowlands*, Justice Erle was imposing 'criminal liability on a combination of workmen which, with a malicious motive against the master, set out by peaceful persuasion or the payment of money to induce his workmen to leave his service, even though no breach of contract were involved'.[30] The law on 'molestation' was but little clarified by an Act of 1859,[31] while the successful common law prosecution of peaceful strikers for conspiracy continued until forbidden by statute in 1875. According to Grimshaw, Ascroft confidently expected 18-month prison sentences to be passed on all the accused.[32] Had a full trial taken place, this was not at all an unlikely outcome.

As it was, the delegates left the assizes in exuberant mood. 'I have just returned from a cheap trip to Liverpool', said Waddington amid laughter. 'We have commenced having cheap excursions pretty early this summer, and I suppose we shall have another one next August.'[33] The arrests had caused only slight disruption to the organization of the strike. The weavers had at once issued a placard making an impassioned call for peaceful behaviour, and appointed marshals to help the police preserve order outside the Town Hall.[34] Apart from a minor incident inside the courtroom, when the public gallery was cleared after an outburst of heckling against Ascroft,[35] Preston remained calm. On their return from Liverpool the delegates resumed the agitation with their accustomed vigour. Almost 10,000 turnouts tramped out to Fulwood on 29 March to greet them, and crowds of 5,000 were still commonplace.[36] Grimshaw's enthusiasm produced rhetoric so fiery that he was publicly rebuked by Kinder Smith for his intemperate language.[37] It had little effect. 'For years I have been denied the right of obtaining employment in any of the mills of Lancashire', he declaimed, 'because of my independence of mind, and I assert here today that, in the eleventh hour of this struggle, I shall not be gagged by any party. I shall never consent to have my mouth padlocked by anyone.'[38] The weavers lapped it all up. The masters might still hope to defeat the strike, but to padlock Mortimer Grimshaw's mouth — that was surely beyond them.

Most independent commentators agreed with the *Manchester Examiner and Times* that the manufacturers had made yet another tactical error: just as the alleged conspiracy was beginning to flag, it seemed, the arrests had given a fresh stimulus to the strikers' morale, and to their finances.[39] A Delegates' Defence Fund was established at the Crown Inn in Church Street, and immediately attracted considerable support from local tradespeople.[40] It was at the Crown that the delegates were treated to dinner on 24 March, at the conclusion of the magistrates' hearings.[41] Three thousand Blackburn operatives had assembled on Blakeley Moor the previous day to agree a special levy of 2d per loom for the defence fund.[42] A collection taken at one weavers' meeting in Preston raised £26 for the fund, 'contributed from their starving bellies, for the defence of their delegates'.[43] The craft unions of Glasgow, Liverpool and London organized meetings to declare their solidarity with the arrested delegates, and in Manchester Alderman Heywood chaired a meeting at which W.P. Roberts attacked the validity of the conspiracy charges.[44] By 28 March the weavers were sufficiently encouraged by the renewed influx of subscriptions that they began to talk of increasing their weekly relief payments to 6s once more.[45]

Public opinion had again rallied to the turnouts. The Preston Ratepayers' Association met to draw up a slate of candidates for the forthcoming elections for Poor Law Guardians, who would run against the millowners and their allies.[46] A petition to Parliament was organized, protesting against the conduct of the police and magistrates; it was presented to the Commons by T.S. Duncombe, MP.[47] On 29 March the boxes of the Theatre were packed with tradespeople, while operatives filled the pit and gallery. It was to be a remarkable demonstration of middle-class resentment against the manufacturers and support for the strikers. Edward Ambler suggested that local tradesmen would benefit from the concession of the ten per cent, as working-class purchasing power would be substantially increased. This theme was echoed by other speakers, who urged the masters to accept arbitration. A mediation committee was established, to which were elected (often *in absentia*), the Vicar of Preston, the MPs for the town and for North Lancashire, the Chairman of the Quarter Sessions, and a dozen less distinguished local worthies.[48] Led by the Vicar, the committee spent much of April in energetic, but ultimately fruitless, correspondence with the Masters' Association.[49]

There was no indication that the millowners were in any way concerned at the public reaction to the arrests. When the Masters' Association met on 21 March they turned down a joint request from the spinners and weavers to meet 'a deputation from the operative spinners and weavers of Preston, being themselves operatives working in the mills where the turn-out and consequent lock-out commenced', and adjourned for three months.[50] They were soon to claim that only 11 or 12,000 vacancies existed in the mills, and that at the end of the strike some 3,000 of the hands relieved by the operatives' committees would be surplus to requirements. Employment had, they reported, increased by a thousand in the last week of March alone.[51]

The manufacturers' obduracy was no doubt encouraged by the first real sign of weakness on the part of the turnouts. Surprisingly, it came from the spinners. On 26 March a meeting of spinners at Blackburn urged their Preston colleagues 'to surrender the ten per cent' in exchange for a district or county average. It is not clear whether this call came from the Blackburn spinners alone, or whether it was the recommendation of the Lancashire spinners' union as a whole.[52] It was certainly a major retreat, for 'ten per cent and no surrender' had been the operatives' rallying cry since the start of the dispute. The Preston spinners now revealed a growing anxiety as to the outcome of the strike. On 8 April they issued a circular 'to the manufacturers of Lancashire and the surrounding districts' formally abandoning the ten per cent, and asking instead for a district average.[53]

While not associating themselves with the spinners' initiative, the weavers gave no sign that they resented it. They, too, were becoming nervous. As early as 1 April, Cowell was asserting that a thousand of the 'weavers' being relieved would never find employment in the mills, and hinted that they might have to be struck from the lists.[54] For the present no action was taken, though Lang returned to the theme ten days later, as financial stringency was increasingly felt.[55] Of more pressing concern was the outbreak of the Crimean War, which was certain to produce further dislocation of markets in a cotton industry still deep in the throes of depression. A defensive, almost pessimistic tone began to infect the speeches of the delegates. Against the *Preston Chronicle*'s insistence that reductions in wages were 'no longer a matter of choice'[56] Robert Baxendale and Kinder Smith urged the masters to introduce short-time working instead.[57] The coming Easter holidays were expected to disrupt the collection of subscriptions in other towns, and the weavers' executive committee was already £50 in debt.[58]

Towering over all these problems, though, was the menacing prospect of renewed conflict at Stockport. The Stockport masters' association had met at the end of March to consider their policy in the face of the continuing deterioration in trade, but agreement had eluded them.[59] When they reconvened on 5 April there was little dissent: short time was rejected, and it was resolved to withdraw the ten per cent from 13 April. This was a decisive blow not merely against the cotton operatives of Stockport, but also against the Preston strikers. The victory at Stockport in August 1853 had been crucial in sustaining the momentum of the ten per cent campaign in Preston, and the weekly £200 or £250 subscribed by the Cheshire town came second only to Blackburn in the strikers' balance sheets. If Stockport now decided to resist the loss of the ten per cent, these subscriptions would obviously cease. But if the reduction were to be accepted, the credibility of the Preston strike would be considerably diminished, both there and in other towns, again seriously affecting the flow of funds to the turnouts.

It was an appalling dilemma, and it accounted for the unprecedented confusion in the operatives' ranks during the second week of April. The spinners, at least, were decisive. Their delegate meeting on the 9th agreed to send a deputation to plead with the Stockport masters to reconsider their decision; if this failed, the spinners were to accept the loss of the ten per cent until the end of the Preston dispute. This position had logic on its side. Victory at Preston would hold out the prospect of securing the return of the ten per cent in Stockport, while the defeat of the Preston strikers would almost certainly render useless any resistance elsewhere. Either way, it was better to wait and see. But could it not equally be argued that a tame surrender at Stockport was a sure guarantee of defeat for Preston? It was probably this view which prevented the weavers from urging caution upon their impetuous colleagues in Stockport. The Stockport operatives resolved, at a large meeting in the Cattle Yard on 6 April, to resist any reduction in wages and to press for short-time working instead. Five days later representatives of the Stockport weavers met delegates from other districts and decided upon a strike if the masters persisted with their plans.[60] The Darwen delegate, John Knowles Fish, later condemned the Stockport operatives as 'hot-headed and impatient',[61] a view which others soon came to share.[62] By then, though, it was too late. Even the spinners' caution could not prevail against the militancy of the weavers. On Good Friday, 14 April, the second Stockport strike began.

This time the omens were far from propitious. Trade was depressed, and the attitude of the local authorities had become malignant rather than benign. On 10 April the mayor of Stockport refused the operatives the use of the hustings and market place for their proposed meeting on Good Friday. Two days later the magistrates, imitating the Preston bench but with even less justification, prohibited all processions and open-air gatherings within the borough. The police were sent to break up a meeting in the Cattle Yard, and large numbers of special constables were sworn in. All these repressive measures received the immediate approval of Palmerston.[63] They forced the strikers to assemble out in the country, where Cowell and Mathews addressed an enthusiastic crowd of 3,000 on Good Friday. At first, all seemed to be going well. Over a third of the town's 16,000 cotton operatives remained at work at the old rates, their employers being quite happy to let those firms which belonged to the masters' association bear the brunt of the conflict.[64] Luke Wood assured the Preston weavers that the Stockport strikers were prepared to hold out for six weeks without financial support.[65]

It soon became evident that the turnouts' enthusiasm was less than in 1853, and that divisions were more obvious. Ironically, it was now the spinners, who had wanted no part of the strike, who were most adamant, while the weavers began to hesitate. When the masters' association reopened the mills on 20 April they at once attracted more than 200 weavers who were prepared to forsake the ten per cent. Four days later the strikers were recommended by their delegates to accept an offer by three firms to pay the going rates in neighbouring Hyde. The cardroom hands, for whom this would have meant a substantial reduction, immediately refused, but the offer involved only a 3% cut in weavers' rates and there was considerable dissension before they, too, rejected the offer. The trickle of weavers back into the mills soon became a flood, and by the beginning of May their resistance had crumbled. Only the spinners persisted in the strike, and by 9 May they had been forced to abandon what was by now a hopeless struggle. Stockport's battle to retain the ten per cent had ended in ignominious defeat.[66]

In Preston the impact of the Stockport strike was immediate and disastrous. 'The Stockport operatives have done more in one day to ensure a victory to the Preston masters', the *Preston Guardian* was quick to observe, 'than all that that very energetic body of gentlemen have done for themselves in six entire months.'

The weavers acknowledged that the renewed conflict at Stockport was 'a calamity', though they still hesitated to apportion blame. 'Of this strike and its effects we will not now speak,' read the preamble to their next balance sheet, 'our opinion will be reserved for a future day.'[67] That opinion would not have been a flattering one. Cowell might claim that the weavers' weekly 5s would be forthcoming 'for five months to come',[68] but the truth of the matter was that the disbursements agreed by the delegate meeting on Easter Sunday had been arranged only with extreme difficulty. There had been no subscription from Stockport, and collections in other areas had suffered as a result of the (unpaid) holiday. An anonymous benefactor had contributed a substantial loan, reflected in the balance sheet by the unusual entry: 'My box is open, take your needs, £500.'[69] But such exceptional generosity, which clearly could not be maintained indefinitely, was not imitated; an attempt to borrow £1,000 or more from a local burial society was quickly rebuffed.[70] Other groups fared even worse, for the Amalgamated Committee was forced to strike off 700 names from its books. As a result several hundred cardroom hands, paid only a shilling, were driven back to the mills.[71] When the *Preston Chronicle* gleefully reported a commotion in Gordon Street, where 'a diminutive fellow, one of the leading "delegates" and a defendant in the recent charge of conspiracy' was surprised by his wife in bed with his mistress, it drew a more serious moral: 'the various committees are nearly as bankrupt in means as they have long been in reputation and character'.[72] As regards finance, at least, this was becoming all too true.

For the moment the turnouts continued to deny any suggestion that their struggle was a hopeless one. On Easter Sunday a crowd of 3,000 was drawn to the old Chartist rallying point at Blackstone Edge, on the moors above Rochdale, to hear Grimshaw, Walton and other delegates. In Preston itself even the news that a collector at Hollins's mill had absconded (allegedly to America) with £14 failed to damage morale. Strikers at Horrockses' and at Swainson and Birley's met to reaffirm their solidarity,[73] and the weavers' mass meeting – now held on the south bank of the Ribble near Walton Bridge – continued to attract thousands of enthusiastic operatives. Fears in Blackburn of an impending collapse were temporarily allayed when a deputation visited Preston, and returned to confirm the claims of the Preston delegates that little more than a thousand knobsticks were at work.[74] The Blackburn operatives themselves were cheered by news of deep divisions within the masters' association in their own town. The association had resolved on 19 April to take off the ten per cent, but only if three-quarters (according to some reports, seven-eighths) of local employers agreed to follow suit. There were rumours of dissatisfaction with 'the vacillating and distrustful course pursued by many of the members', which 'renders it not improbable that the association will ere long be dissolved'.[75]

Nonetheless, the end was now in sight. In their estimate of the number of knobsticks, the strikers were engaging in wishful thinking. By 22 April the masters claimed to be employing *seven* thousand hands, almost one half of their

Defeat

total requirements. They supplied the press with a comprehensive list specifying the situation at each individual firm, in far too much detail for it to have been a complete fabrication.[76] Refusing to make the slightest concession, the association dismissed an abject letter from the Preston spinners.[77] When the weavers' delegates met on the 23rd, they were in sombre mood. Even Kinder Smith, who expected an end to the Stockport strike in a matter of days, spoke grimly of the prospect of defeat. 'If the operatives do not surrender till they are actually compelled,' he said, 'they will have the satisfaction of knowing that they have done their best; and they will have another do with the masters at some future time.' Such talk gave credence to the rumours in other towns that surrender was imminent, which, successive delegates reported, had ravaged subscriptions. A mere £200 had been raised in Blackburn, and this had been made up to £500 only by depleting the reserves. The anonymous benefactor of the previous week was again called upon: 'My box is open still. Weavers they shall have their fill – £400.' By such expedients payments to the weavers were maintained at 5s. The Amalgamated Committee, less fortunately placed, was forced to withdraw all support to the throstle-spinners, and to cut back still further its assistance to the cardroom hands. Attendance at the weavers' meetings now fell below 3,000, and Cowell was reduced to threatening the growing number of knobsticks at Horrockses' with the publication of their names.[78]

On 25 April the Blackburn masters finally summoned up all their courage, and gave 14 days notice of the withdrawal of the ten per cent. With this the last chance of averting defeat at Preston disappeared, though it still required an initiative from outside before the turnouts could be persuaded to bow to the inevitable. The weavers of Padiham, alarmed by press reports of massive defections, had sent a deputation to Preston to investigate for themselves. Somehow the manufacturers learned of their visit and arranged for them a guided tour of Horrockses, Swainson and Birley's and other mills. They returned to Padiham convinced that the millowners' claims were substantially correct: several thousand knobsticks were already at work in the mills of Preston, the great majority of them local operatives rather than immigrants.[79] The implication, however unpalatable, was compelling. At the suggestion of the Padiham weavers, the delegate meeting on Sunday 30 April went into private session. No doubt after a good deal of plain talking, the unavoidable decision was made: the weavers were to surrender.

More than 10,000 operatives assembled at Walton Bridge next morning to ratify the decision. It was May Day, a sad precursor of the future working-class festival. The *Preston Chronicle* described a dejected gathering, 'the "Thunderer", Mr. Grimshaw, especially, who looked as if he had never had a bolt in him'. This, though, is a characteristically uncharitable assessment, and one influenced by Cowell's bitter attack on the *Chronicle* itself. Successive speakers conceded defeat, but, like Robert Baxendale, only 'for the present'. Cowell and Baxendale urged the formation of a permanent weavers' union to secure the ten per cent when trade revived. 'If we have a good fund at our back,' he declared, 'it is my decided conviction that the employers will give the advance rather than risk another turnout.' In the mean-time, 'the next in battle array are the mayor and magistrates of the borough'. Even the 'Thunderer' had a bolt to spare. 'The employers might be laughing and sneering at the Bull now', declared Grimshaw, 'but we shall pay them a visit some fine morning when they least expect it, and unfurl the ten per cent flag in the Orchard again. We are not defeated — we are only retiring to gain fresh forces and ammunition, and to renew our strength again ... Ten per cent still, and no surrender!'[80]

As in Stockport, so in Preston: the spinners were the last to admit defeat. Though it could now be no more than a gesture of defiance, the spinners' delegates resolved to continue the strike, a decision endorsed by the Preston turnouts on 1 May. They, at least, were not short of funds.[81] By the end of the week, though, the masters were claiming that almost 70% of the town's one million spindles were in operation, and made no secret of the fact that they were considering the importation of skilled spinners from Scotland to man the remaining mules.[82] On 8 May the strikers made one final attempt to open negotiations, and were duly rebuffed; the first contingent of Scots (fifty in number) reached Preston four days later.[83] But the spinners were determined to bow out in style. On Sunday 14 May they assembled their supporters in Manchester, ostensibly to consider their position, but in fact to put a brave face on a (by now inevitable) capitulation. Waddington and Lawless spoke for the weavers, Baines and Hooper for the London trades, Richard Harnott for the powerful stonemasons' union: all urged an end to the strike. Ambler, Corless and Rigby, representing the 'Reconciliation Committee' set up at the beginning of the month 'to soften the antagonism' between masters and hands, appealed on behalf of a Preston middle class who were facing a crippling burden of poor rates. Meeting immediately afterwards, the spinners' delegates recommended the Preston spinners to end their strike. When this advice was put to the turnouts that evening, it was presented as a concession to the weavers, many of whom had remained unemployed for want of yarn. Their dignity unimpaired, the spinners returned to work next day.[84]

The Blackburn weavers had succumbed to the loss of the ten per cent on 11 May, though not without considerable dissension within their ranks. Under the circumstances no-one favoured an all-out strike, but there was strong support for the unilateral adoption of short-time working in protest against the cuts. On 10 May a mass meeting of weavers on Blakeley Moor ignored the advice of Whittle and other delegates and voted to operate a four-day week, in effect committing themselves to strike for two days each week. The weavers' committee ignored this decision, called on the operatives to work normally, and, after some hard work by Whittle, secured the peaceful acceptance of the reductions. It was a sensible, if entirely undemocratic, decision.[85]

Defeat

Well into the summer the more prominent of the weavers' delegates remained active, organizing relief payments for those turnouts who remained unemployed, attempting to salvage some organizational gains from the defeat, and promoting the ideas of co-operative production about which so much had been said, and so little done, during the dispute itself. The weavers' parting address had contained, in bold type, the warning: 'Above all, remember that there will be one thousand victims.'[86] This sombre prediction, while well below the Masters' Association's estimate of the number of immigrants employed in the mills, was probably exaggerated. The *Preston Guardian* anticipated that any substantial unemployment among the operatives would evaporate as trade improved: there had been vacancies in the factories back in 1853, many hands had left the district since then, new mills were under construction, and relatively few of the immigrants would remain permanently in Preston.[87] (The truth of the last point was soon to be indicated by a series of prosecutions against the knobsticks for stealing household effects from houses rented to them by their employers.)[88] Even on the most favourable assumptions, though, not all the turnouts could hope for immediate re-employment, and the resources of the weavers' committee were strained to the limit by the continuing need to provide for them. On 2 May 7,000 weavers were paid 2s 6d each, leaving the committee exactly 4s 2¾d in hand. Even at this late date Blackburn voted a threepenny levy,[89] and, with the aid of the Amalgamated Committee, still collecting from the trades, this financed a 1s payment to almost 5,000 weavers on 9 May.[90] A week later 1s 6d was paid to 3,150 people,[91] and now the return of the spinners was beginning to break the back of the problem. By the end of May the weavers' committee was able to report that only 500 *bona fide* weavers were still out of work, though one delegate, speaking at a relief concert organized by the Liverpool Trades' Guardians Association, put the total number of unemployed operatives at over 1,500.[92] The weavers' final balance sheet (the 39th), which appeared at the end of July, showed them to be still £900 in debt. As a final flourish, a note at the bottom informed readers that a few proofs had been printed in gold, for framing.[93]

Between them the various strike committees had handled subscriptions totalling £105,000. While there had been some insignificant defalcations by individual collectors, and in spite of the occasional unsubstantiated innuendo from the more hostile sections of the press, the probity of the delegates and the accuracy of their accounts had never seriously been questioned.[94] Never, that is, until the end of the dispute, when George Cooper exploded a bombshell with a widely publicized allegation of wholesale embezzlement. Cooper, while active in the original Stockport campaign in 1853, had always regarded the Preston strike as a blunder, and had not hesitated to say so. On 6 May, challenged to justify his charges, he took on all-comers — Brocklehurst, Tonge, Wood, Rhodes, and Smith of Stockport, John Mathews of Heywood, and William Chadwick of Oldham — at a stormy meeting at Cheadle Heath. Cooper was sufficiently encouraged by his reception to request the lifting of the magistrates' prohibition of gatherings inside the borough. The authorities, no doubt relishing the prospect, readily agreed, and on 15 May Cowell, Mathews and J.B. Horsfall joined the Stockport delegates in the Lyceum to defend themselves against Cooper's accusations. 'A fight, of course, was got up', reported the *Stockport Advertiser* caustically, 'and the police were obliged to step in to preserve both peace and the personal appearances of the parties concerned. If only a tithe of what the delegates charged [each] other with be true, there can be but one opinion on the subject — that the working classes have been most scandalously imposed upon.'[95] In an atmosphere embittered by defeat and privation, such recriminations were perhaps inevitable. There seems to have been little if any substance in Cooper's charges,[96] to which a fitting sequel was provided four days after the Lyceum meeting when Cooper appeared in the County Court and was ordered to pay for the ham and eggs and other delicacies consumed by a gathering of delegates in a Stockport inn, in happier days.[97]

There were more serious matters to attend to. With the end of the weavers' strike, several of the firms which had continued to operate throughout the dispute, including Napier and Goodair, now gave notice of their intention to take off the ten per cent. Robert Baxendale urged the operatives of the mills concerned to keep their union in existence, and to build up a fund large enough to deter the masters from further incursions.[98] As W.P. Roberts told the Accrington weavers, there were lessons to be learned from the success of the masters' own organization. 'Instead of delegates created for a particular occasion,' he insisted, 'you must have delegates existing at all times, always corresponding together by letter and by mutual meeting with the different societies all over the kingdom.'[99] On 15 May the Preston weavers' committee issued a placard in similar vein: 'Our Union we will never abandon, we will never desert: it is our only safeguard, our only help.' A twopenny subscription was to be collected every week, but (to avoid precipitating a renewed lock-out) at the weavers' homes rather than at the mills.[100] Next day Grimshaw advocated a similar course for the Blackburn weavers, who agreed 'to form a union of the factory operatives for the protection of labour', financed by a levy of one penny per loom.[101] By July the Blackburn union — now paying a £3 funeral benefit — had built up a substantial membership.[102]

In the same month Grimshaw was busily organizing support for 240 weavers at a mill in Sabden, at the foot of Pendle Hill, who were on strike against further wage cuts. Kinder Smith addressed the operatives of Burnley on their behalf,[103] while Grimshaw put out a handbill appealing to weavers throughout North East Lancashire to add their subscriptions to those of the Great Harwood operatives. 'Seeing as I do', he wrote enthusiastically, 'that they have done all that men can do to amicably settle the affair, my advice to the operatives of Sabden is, STRIKE, STRIKE, STRIKE! and to the last penny, to the last crust of bread, resist Oppression and Tyranny.'[104] When the Preston weavers finally met on

31 August to collect subscriptions, the Sabden strikers were already back at work. Grimshaw, Smith and Horsfall reported the successful conclusion of the strike, and Cowell took the opportunity to advise his audience to 'rally round your union, and subscribe your three-halfpence each week, in order that you might be prepared for any emergency'.[105] The reduction in the subscription rate suggests that recruitment was not proving easy.

The delegates were equally energetic in promoting the projected co-operative mill. Early in May, Cowell spoke twice at Walton Bridge, exhorting the weavers to invest their savings in the newly-formed co-operative society, for which a prospectus had now been prepared.[106] He repeated the message at Darwen on 10 May,[107] and later travelled to Burnley and Bacup with Grimshaw, to enlist support there.[108] By 6 June the magistrates' prohibition of gatherings in the Orchard had been lifted, and Cowell was able to inform a large crowd that 70 or 80 shares had already been taken up, and that the rules of the co-operative company would soon be sent to Mr Tidd Pratt, Registrar of Friendly Societies, for formal approval.[109] But the odds were stacked heavily against such a venture, and, so far as is known, nothing concrete came of it.

Quite apart from these activities, the delegates were encouraged to remain in close contact by the imminence of the conspiracy hearings, due to begin at the Liverpool summer assizes in August. On a wet night at the end of June, Cowell made a further appearance in the Orchard to solicit subscriptions to the delegates' defence fund, but he drew only a small audience and met with little success. Early in July it became known that Horrockses had granted an unsolicited advance of 5% in the wages of their weavers. Encouraged by this news of unwonted generosity on the part of the largest manufacturer in Preston, Cowell and Baxendale, accompanied by the spinners Banks and Greenough, visited Thomas Miller to ask that the charges be dropped. Miller agreed to put the proposition to the committee of the Masters' Association. When the deputation returned next day he informed them that the prosecutions would be abandoned, and complimented them on the good feeling which now prevailed between masters and men.[110]

Freed from the attentions of the criminal law, Cowell was soon in deep trouble from another source. By a final, savage irony, it was a civil action for debt by one of his closest associates that led to his incarceration. J.B. Horsfall had printed the weavers' balance sheets at his Royton headquarters, but his bills had not been paid. Late in September, presumably under pressure from his own creditors, Horsfall issued writs against Cowell, Edward Whittle and the treasurer of the Preston weavers, Edwin Whittle, for the recovery of £164 owing to him. Cowell and the Whittles issued public appeals for funds, but Cowell's campaign suffered a setback when a well-attended meeting on the Marsh on 1 October was broken up by the police.[111] Further meetings at Walton Bridge in October, and in the Orchard on 4 November (both uninterrupted), failed to raise more than a few shillings,[112] and by 8 November Cowell was imprisoned as a debtor in

Lancaster Castle,[113] whence he issued another placard begging for subscriptions to secure his release.[114] By February 1855 he was again at liberty, taking an active part in collections for striking mechanics in Blackburn.[115] This unpleasant incident marks the end of the ten per cent campaign.

11 Posterity

> Before the masters' tyranny
>   Shall rule our rights and laws
> We'll have another strike, my boys
>   If ever we have cause.

In April Cowell made a speech in which he claimed that the Preston strike would be remembered by posterity.[1] The future, as things turned out, was almost as cruel as the present. The Preston strike was no Rebecca, no Peterloo, no Tolpuddle; there were no riots, no deaths, no martyrs. No matter how much masters and men saw the dispute in terms of class war, it has rarely been celebrated as such. In the end it has been seen as little more than a wage dispute where the monolithic appeal of 'ten per cent and no surrender' eclipsed the alternative visions promised by Chartism and Co-operation.

Though the memory of the Preston struggle faded fairly rapidly, it was not completely forgotten. During the six years following the strike, two full accounts were published. Henry Ashworth's version was published in 1854 and that of James Lowe in 1860. Ashworth's account was based, in addition to his obvious contacts with other manufacturers, largely on local and national newspapers. He had done much the same for the 1836–7 strike, when he wrote up a factual version for the Statistical section of the British Association. His 1854 account, also read before the Association, was more exhaustive and certainly more opinionated. Throughout, Richard Cobden gave him support and advice. In November 1853 Cobden suggested that – in contrast to the 1836 account – a simple record 'of facts or statistics' would not be sufficient. He added:

> It is equally important to preserve extracts from the speeches of the orators and leaders of the turnout to show the kind of doctrine prevalent amongst them. I hope you will therefore watch the reports of the addresses of the speakers – take note of their abuse of capital – their denunciation of employers – their leaning to violence and strong will as the means of influencing the rate of wages – their arbitrary and intolerant conduct towards all who differ from them whether master or man ... If their opinions and doctrines be kept on record alongside of the facts of the case; and if moreover the fine promises and confident predictions with which the leaders delude their followers into the belief in certain success be kept for the calm introspection of the dupes when the disastrous result of their strike shall have been realized, I have no doubt a valuable *lesson* will be learnt by the diligent collection of such facts.[2]

Once the strike was over, Cobden recommended a more cautious line. He reminded Ashworth that being a master millowner had its drawbacks, since 'no attempt will be wanting in certain quarters, *where you wish the truth to be known*, to represent your statement as one-sided'. He consequently advised Ashworth to 'deal guardedly with the labourers' side of the question. In exposing the misdoings even of the leaders,' he concluded, 'do it in a kindly spirit, more in sorrow than in anger and don't attribute bad motives even to the worst of them.'[3] After reading the proofs, Cobden became even more cautious. He altered, in one or two places, the 'too hostile tone towards the turnouts', suggested that Ashworth might consider publishing the work under a pseudonym, and complained that the paper was too long and relied – in contrast to his earlier advice – 'too much on argument and principles instead of narration of facts'.[4]

Ashworth's bitter hatred of trades' unions was the central theme of his pamphlet. For him the struggle was not a question of wages, nor of capital versus labour, but of 'property against communism'.[5] Unions, he believed, threatened the whole fabric of the capitalist system. Their delegates, he insisted, were concerned only with their own vanity and reputation, selfish demagogues who misled the uneducated and ignorant masses. In Grimshaw's speeches he found 'the perfection of mob oratory'.[6] Only Cowell, and then grudgingly, was spared from criticism: 'a man who would do honour to a juster cause'.[7]

On the tactics and management of the strike Ashworth was more complimentary, acknowledging the value of the slogan 'ten per cent and no surrender' and the very business-like handling of the funds.[8] He also found it 'consolatory ... that "strikes" are less violent and conducted with less brutality, than in former times; there is more of an appeal to reason, to justice, and to public opinion, and less of reliance on brute force'.[9] This he attributed to the growing intelligence of the workers which he believed would eventually 'suppress "strikes" altogether'. Nevertheless he persisted in repeating the need for the freedom of industry from the 'mischievous interference and terrorism of Trades' Unions'.[10]

When Ashworth discussed the masters, his understandable bias turned into blatant prejudice. Unlike the masters themselves, he accepted that some must have promised to restore the wage reductions made in 1847 but then dismissed it as 'nugatory' and 'absurd', on the grounds that markets not masters fixed wages.[11] He argued that substantial wage increases had been voluntarily conceded since 1847 and that the masters were willing to meet most, if not all, of the claims made in 1853 until 'the demands of the workpeople became unreasonable, and grew into a spirit of dictation'.[12] Naturally, Ashworth made no attempt to question the morality of breaking the original pledge. Nor did he question the masters' combination or their Defence Fund which was justified rather more uneasily but for the same reason: 'it was purely an act of self defence'.[13] Capitulation of the strikers was, he concluded, the only solution: 'the world united cannot over-ride a law of nature'.[14]

Posterity

James Lowe's account of the strike was by comparison historical, chronological, factual and objective. It was published as part of a collection of papers read at Glasgow in 1860, at a conference on 'Trade Societies and Strikes' organized by the National Association for the Promotion of Social Science. The purpose was to promote a greater understanding of the role of trades' societies, their effect on the 'laws of production' and the relationship between labour and capital at a time when competition from the United States and Europe was beginning to make some impression on Britain's industrial leadership. To a large extent the conference symbolized the acceptance and recognition of trade unions as an essential element in mid-Victorian society;[15] and a retrospective study was considered helpful in promoting the future untroubled prosperity of British industry.

Though Lowe's account was based on a reflection of his first-hand experience of the strike, the intervening years did not alter his initial judgement that both parties were lamentably wrong. Like Ashworth — although without the same insistent emphasis — he pointed to the power of the delegates over the minds of the uncultivated,[16] and to the way in which the leaders strained 'every nerve to inflame and support the agitation' when hands began to resume work.[17] But 'agitators', he reminded his readers, 'arose from the agitation and not the agitation from the agitators'.[18] He also noted how the 'crude speeches' made early in the strike encouraged the masters' inflexibility, but thought the masters greatly mistaken in taking these speeches as the 'real sentiments of the operatives'. By doing so, the operatives, inexperienced in the 'task of haranguing', were forced to act out their words.[19] The masters' easy victory in 1836 and their failure to understand how the development of the railways, the penny post and the press had enhanced the operatives' ability to organize also explained their intransigence.[20] In contrast to Ashworth, Lowe argued that the establishment of the Masters' Association was not a consequence of the operatives' combination, since it had been organized on a new basis in late March 1853, three months before the Weavers' Committee was set up.[21] Lowe doubted the legality of the Defence Fund and the £5,000 bond, which he claimed was 'plainly subversive of the best interests of trade'; it also indicated the lack of confidence the masters had in each others' 'honour and mutual good faith'.[22] The local authorities, ignored by Ashworth, were treated no more sympathetically. The arrests for conspiracy were, he alleged, completed with too much secrecy and haste,[23] whilst the reading of the Riot Act 'was a most dangerous and unjustifiable proceeding'.[24]

These judgements, which are thinly spread throughout an otherwise detailed and factual account, perhaps amount to the fairest assessment of the strike. There are no caricatures. Lowe was concerned with the story as a whole rather than with individuals. Though he understood the sad dignity of the operatives and the rigid attitude of the masters, he hoped that bitter experience would provide the lessons for the future.

Caricatures of the masters and men can be found in Charles Dickens's *Hard Times* (1854) and, to a much lesser extent, in Elizabeth Gaskell's *North and South* (1855).[25] Both books were, in different ways, based on the strike, and perhaps Preston was unique in this respect, since no other strike has ever attracted the pens of *two* such powerful and popular writers. Each novel was first serialized in *Household Words*, to revive its falling circulation, *Hard Times* between April and August 1854 and *North and South* between September 1854 and January 1855.[26] Unlike Mrs Gaskell, Dickens actually visited Preston in search of copy. He arrived on the evening of Saturday 28 January 1854 and attended a delegate meeting on the following day. None of the operatives was aware of his presence[27] and he left after a short time rather disappointed, so it seems, that the town was not in an excited state of disorder:[28] 'I am afraid I shall not be able to get much here.'[29] His account of the delegates' meeting was published two weeks later in *Household Words*.[30]

Dickens had formed his views on strikes before he visited Preston and, although his article 'On Strikes' showed that he was impressed by the operatives' peaceful conduct and by the efficient management of their affairs, he continued to believe that strikes were wasteful and a 'deplorable calamity'.[31] Yet in the novel, which is concerned with the tyranny of fact over imagination and experience, no strike is discussed.[32] Dickens instead attempts to show that the operatives were too easily influenced by their delegates and the masters by their extreme 'stuttering'[33] versions of political economy.[34] Slackbridge, whom Dickens depicts as the union leader, is almost certainly based on Mortimer Grimshaw. The 'Thunderer of Lancashire', or Gruffshaw as Dickens calls him in 'On Strike', is characterized in the novel as a brash, insensitive mob orator inspired by animal cunning; a gnashing and tearing demagogue. This picture is in effect drawn from the incidents Dickens witnessed at the delegates' meeting on Sunday. There, Grimshaw savagely attacked the Warrington committee for denying him the right to speak; two Burnley delegates fell into dispute as one accused the other of being a tool of the Burnley masters; and three Manchester men, who had come to rally support for the Labour Parliament, were refused a platform.[35] Out of this unusually charged meeting Slackbridge was conceived, a man 'above the mass in very little but the stage on which he stood'. This image, however, and the divisive contrast with the men is very misleading, both as a description of Grimshaw and because Dickens failed to recognize the importance of Cowell who, as everyone acknowledged, typified the moderate yet determined aspirations of the union *and* the men. Slackbridge is at best a snapshot of the past and at worst a symbolic confirmation of middle-class prejudice.[36]

When Dickens deals with the operatives themselves he again resorts to symbolic representations. The submissive 'stooping' Stephen Blackpool is Slackbridge's counterpart. Stephen, though full of integrity, is 'awles muddled' and bewilderingly weighed down by his own unfortunate circumstances. He is a victim not only of the union but of a society mechanically activated by self-interest. Death seems the only solution. Only when interrogated by Bounderby on the union does Stephen show any defiance, and then he remains resigned to his fate. ' 'Tis not by *them* the trouble's made, sir. 'Tis not wi' *them* 't commences. I ha' no favour for 'em – I ha' no reason to favour 'em – but 'tis hopeless an useless to dream o' takin' them fro their trade, 'stead o' takin' their trade fro them!'

Though the unions are generally treated as the 'working class equivalent of Gradgrindian inhumanity',[37] Stephen's comments show that Dickens also blames the masters for the ill-feeling which existed between them and their men. In Bounderby, Dickens creates a biting satire of the clinically calculating master. Bounderby is the Bully of Humility, a man without imagination, grace or feeling, whose love for Louisa even 'took on a manufacturing aspect'. 'I am Josiah Bounderby of Coketown. I know the bricks of this town, and I know the works of this town ... I know the smoke of this town, and I know the hands of this town. I know 'em all pretty well. They're real. When a man tells me anything about imaginative qualities, I always tell that man, whoever he is, that I know what he means. He means turtle-soup and venison, with a gold spoon ... ' This knowing, though, is passionless and shallow and represents all that is bad in Coketown. It is a gross caricature of the masters' mindlessness and their inhumane interpretation of the laws of political economy.[38] It is equally a gross caricature of the operatives' aspirations. Turtle soup and golden spoons were nowhere as precious as independence and dignity.

These stereotyped images make *Hard Times* a forceful piece of fiction but a poor historical source. The characters are brilliantly one sided but, with the exception of Sissy Jupe and Sleary, mostly without hope. In *North and South* there is much more hope and the three central characters, Miss Hale, Thornton and Higgins are allowed to develop to show how capitalism could be civilized by and through self-awareness. Mrs Gaskell understands, where Dickens does not, that 'working people could be both radical and responsible',[39] and their masters authoritarian and fair. In this sense *North and South* is more realistic than *Hard Times*. It has also more to say about strikes and certainly draws on newspaper accounts of the events in Preston.

Though the strike in *North and South* seems to take place in Manchester, and ends in October rather than May, the atmosphere of conflict is real enough. The operatives' demand for a five per cent wage increase (ten per cent would have been perhaps too obvious) comes at a time of languishing trade and high food prices. Most of the masters, moreover, are willing to meet the operatives' demands. Only five or six, as in Preston, hold out. Mrs Gaskell also suggests, as had the operatives, that some of the masters 'rather wanted a strike' whilst the market was down. The strike itself is 'simultaneous' and, as in Preston, the operatives are obliged to work their notice. The tactics of the union are remarkably similar to those employed in Preston, although the victimization of Higgins and Hamper's refusal to take on hands unless they signed the document

seem to have been drawn from the 1851—2 engineers' strike. The moderation
and solidarity of the operatives is drawn with precision.

committee-men laid their plans. They were to hou'd together through thick and thin ...
above all there was to be no going again the law of the land. Folk would go with them if they
saw them striving and starving wi' dumb patience; but if there was once any noise o' fighting
and struggling — even wi' knobsticks — all was up, as they knew by th' experience of many
and many a time before ... but whatever came, Committee charged all members o' th'
Union to lie down and die if need were, without striking a blow ... besides Committee
knew they were right in their demand and they didn't want to have right all mixed up wi'
wrong.

The violent riot caused by the employment of bungling Irish knobsticks is an
embellishment, for the purpose of the plot,[40] yet it comes very close to the
views of the Preston masters and local authorities. Significantly, though,
Thornton has the conspiracy charges against Boucher dropped.

The structure of the strike is, then, clearly based on the events in Preston.
Compared with Dickens, the characters are far more real. Higgins is closer to
Cowell than Slackbridge is to Grimshaw. He is honest, proud, defiant and moderate, 'a deep chap and true to th' back bone'.[41] Unlike Blackpool, Higgins is
reluctant to accept charity or the intrusion of ignorant, if well meaning, outsiders; masters and men fight their own battles. Here the union is the only means
by which the working class could protect themselves. Experience had proved
that: 'it's th' masters as has made us sin if 'th'Union is a sin. Not this generation
maybe but their fathers. Their fathers ground our fathers to the very dust;
ground us to powder'. But when Boucher breaks ranks Higgins is filled with
remorse, knowing how acts of violence undermined everything the union and
the strikers stood for. Work not death is his own solution. 'Asking for work, I
reckon them's almost the best words a man can say. "Gi' me work" means "and
I'll do it like a man." Them's good words.'

If Higgins seems too good to be true Thornton is even more so. In the early
part of the novel he displays all the puffing arrogance of the entrepreneurial
class. Plato's Republic is his ideal. Here the despotic masters would wield absolute
power and make wise laws which, as Thornton explains, 'work for my good in
the first instance — for theirs (operatives) in the second'. Like Bounderby,
although with much better cause, he extols the virtues of a social system which
rewards hard work and self denial and which allows the lowly to attain positions
of power. But as the novel proceeds, Thornton, who is the first to bring in the
knobsticks, begins to mellow. He takes on the victimized Higgins, builds a dining
room for his hands and refuses to speculate with his creditors' money to save
himself from impending bankruptcy. In the end his only wish is to have the
opportunity to cultivate 'some intercourse with the hands beyond the mere cash
nexus', and though he recognizes that this would not do away with strikes,
personal contact is to become the 'breath of life'. This gradual transformation
of Thornton and his reconciliation with Higgins, worked through Margaret

Posterity

Hale, is the book's central theme. Both classes are dependent upon each other, and Mrs Gaskell uses the strike to show the futility of thinking otherwise.

In Parliament, where such sentiments would have commanded general approval, little was said about the strike. Whenever strikes were introduced into debate, MPs predictably sought easy refuge in their laissez-faire creed and in the morally elevating effects of education. On Preston *Hansard* is almost silent. There are a few vague references to the troubles in the distant 'northern districts', but if MPs had any thoughts about the affair most kept them to themselves. Sir George Strickland, Preston's MP, spoke only once throughout the whole period, and then without mention of the strike. In the debate on the Payment of Wages (Hosiery) Bill to outlaw the Truck system, he urged a typically Benthamite line in suggesting that the government ought to intervene on behalf of helpless women and children unable to make 'a contract upon equal terms with their masters', but not for adults who 'perfectly understood their own interests ... and were quite capable of protecting themselves against the masters'.[42] Joseph Hume, who like Strickland had urged settling differences by mediation,[43] was less reticent, although he referred only to the Hoghton meeting and then in typically disparaging terms: 'No one who read the proceedings of the monster meeting held in Lancashire the day before yesterday, could but regret the absurd opinions expressed there upon the part of the operatives with relation to their real position, and yet', he continued, 'the ignorance prevailing in [the] House was nearly as great as that which existed out of doors.'[44]

John Bright, who through Cobden and Ashworth knew more about the strike than most MPs, studiously avoided direct reference to Preston. In the debate on the Payment of Wages Bill, where he denied that the Truck system existed in the cotton districts of Lancashire,[45] Bright spoke as if the Staffordshire iron and coal districts were the only areas experiencing strikes. Not until H. Drummond's probing and fiery speech supporting labour's claim that the Truck system was a blatant fraud, did Bright indicate that strikes were in progress elsewhere. Drummond, the Tory MP for Surrey West and the only member to mention the Preston troubles directly, blamed the manufacturing interest for exciting the rebellious state of the men.

I find the honourable member for Manchester saying that it is the industrial people 'who carry the aristocracy on their backs'. Sir, that is all very well in a Manchester committee room, but how is it translated at Preston? The men say there that they have had to carry the manufacturers upon their backs, and that they will carry them no longer. The men apply the doctrine to their own purposes, and the honourable Members of the Manchester School have no right to blame them for doing so.[46]

Forced into a defence of the manufacturers' position, Bright admitted that a 'war' in Lancashire was in progress but claimed that it was unduly magnified by the London press. He congratulated the operatives for keeping the peace, although he believed their aims were mistaken, and warned the House that the 'working population of the country were, in comparison with their employers, more powerful and better organized than they had ever been before'.[47] In the event all this was harmless sparring. Parliament was simply not interested in the bread and butter question of wages or in the relation between labour and capital.[48] The Preston dispute was local not national, peaceful not violent, and was unlikely to be settled by any amount of Parliamentary rhetoric. 'There is not at present', so Henry Ashworth told Cobden, 'any immediate urgency of a social or political character which can be at once responded to by any immediate political or parliamentary proceeding.'[49] And so it was to remain.

Matters had not changed much by 1856, when a select committee was set up to examine more peaceful ways of settling disputes. It has been suggested that Preston's prolonged strike was one of the more important reasons why the government was moved to set up the committee.[50] Even if this were so, Preston was still given poor coverage. Thomas Winter, the Corresponding Secretary of the National Association of United Trades for the Protection of Labour, and one of its members, Edward Humphries, were the only two witnesses to give evidence on the strike itself.[51] Winter, who was part of the delegation which had met Palmerston on 10 March 1854,[52] provided the committee with many facts and figures but it seems strange that neither Cowell nor any of the other leaders of the strike were invited to give evidence, especially since they had persistently argued for arbitration, the very subject the committee was considering. Lancashire and the cotton industry were, in fact, barely considered, most of the evidence dealing with the hosiery, pottery and silk trades: an indication that in 1856 the government were prepared to listen to advantages of the Councils of the Prud'Hommes and courts of conciliation and arbitration (while doing nothing about them). In 1860, when a further committee investigated the subject, Preston was no longer cited as a case where arbitration might have reduced the human misery and the wastage of capital always associated with strikes.[53] Six years after the event Preston appears to have had no historical sponsors, in government circles at least.

The rash of trades' union literature in the 1850s and 1860s continued to defy Preston's bid for posterity. In his new edition of the popular *Knowledge is Power*, published in 1854, Charles Knight briefly mentioned the strike, but then showed how useless union power was against the economic laws which sustained and sanctified private property.[54] Dunning's classic *Trades' Unions and Strikes* at least devotes two paragraphs to the dispute but derides the operatives for failing to realize that the masters' only option was to organize a general lock-out. Cowell is mentioned, but only when explaining to a meeting at Bradford the causes of the strikers' defeat.[55] This is hardly how Cowell would have imagined his place in history. Adam Black's lecture to the Edinburgh operatives in 1859 came a little nearer to what Cowell had in mind. Black asserted that the 'town of Preston is celebrated in the annals of strikes', but then devoted more space to the 1836 affair, presumably because the 'three ... persons known to have perished' gave added edge to his central theme, that strikes were always disastrous to masters, men and country.[56] John Plummer's pamphlet on strikes indicated that the Preston dispute had not become part of the working-class folklore of Northamptonshire and Staffordshire,[57] whilst Sir Rupert Kettle made no mention in his *Strikes and Arbitration* (1866) of the arbitration schemes put forward during the Preston dispute.

In 1902 George Howell, himself once a trade union official, gave a brief and dispassionate narrative of the strike in his *Labour Legislation, Labour Movements, Labour Leaders.*[58] Surprisingly, the Webbs's seminal *History* barely mentions Preston. 'The five or six years following the collapse of the great [engineering] lock-out of 1852', they wrote, 'though constituting a period of quiet progress in particular societies, are, for the historian of the general Trade Union Movement, almost a blank.'[59] This assessment, if a little harsh, is correct in its indication that the Preston strike was not of outstanding importance. Neither for Preston nor for the cotton industry as a whole does the dispute mark a crucial turning-point (though local folklore has it that the town's reputation as a storm-centre of industrial conflict stunted the growth of the industry in subsequent decades).[60] The Preston weavers' union, reconstituted in 1855 and enjoying a continuous existence thereafter, remained relatively weak, boasting a mere 1,600 members as late as 1883.[61] Employer hostility to its activities gradually diminished, though in 1857 a strike at Hollins's mill failed because 'other manufacturers had announced that if any of the persons in their employ were detected in giving them support they would be immediately discharged, and tacklers and others were posted at the gates to prevent the hands from subscribing'.[62] Even the spinners, with their superior organization, proved unable to secure a standard list of prices until 1859, and a fully satisfactory list was negotiated only in 1866.[63]

If the masters found it increasingly difficult to oppose the existence of unions, this did not produce industrial peace. Preston itself was relatively calm for many years after the defeat of the ten per cent campaign, the next major strike there being the bitter struggle against wage reductions in 1869.[64] But the Padiham weavers' strike ten years earlier was a remarkable facsimile of Preston in 1853 (if on a reduced scale), complete with delegates, a Masters' Defence Association, allegations of a bond, accusations of 'tyranny' and 'domination' and exclusive dealing by the operatives.[65] The great strike of 1878, which closed the entire industry in another dispute over ten per cent, echoed 1853–4 in ironic fashion. This time the Preston operatives were locked out by their employers to prevent their subscribing to the striking factory hands of Blackburn. Preston saw more violence than ever occurred in the ten per cent campaign, while in Blackburn a leading employer had his house blown up and the army was sent for.[66]

Samuel Andrew, an Oldham millowner, saw a disquieting continuity in the history of cotton strikes between 1842 and 1887: 'In most of these strikes

there has, I regret to say, been a disposition on the part of labour to overbear capital ... It would seem as if labour had mistaken its vocation — as if it would govern capital, and not obey it; as if it would be master, and not servant ... '
These had been precisely the complaints of the Preston masters in 1853. Even the reasoning behind the operatives' militancy had changed but little.

> The old fad of English over-production still clings to the operatives' leaders like a nightmare, and only a miracle can open their eyes to the dangers which are now besetting our trade ... the old question of over-production, which has now been in use for nearly a century, still stands with them in some stead in waging a war with employers. The old enmity between capital and labour still exists, and in the hands of clever leaders of trades unions becomes intensified.[67]

One Blackburn manufacturer went even further. Eccles Shorrock, whose memories of the Preston strike were as vivid as they were unreliable, looked back to the early 1850s with real nostalgia. 'But all this time [1853–4]', he recalled with pleasure, 'the Secretary of the Operatives' Association was paid to calculate the various sorts. If there was any complaint at any mill, he was sent for and the price was soon arranged ... [Unlike the troublesome weavers' officials in 1880] in those days he was always a quiet, unassuming peacemaker, attending to the duties for which he was paid'.[68]

Two final witnesses may be produced to suggest that those actually engaged in the cotton industry found it difficult to forget entirely the Preston strike. Both are operatives, both old men, and both are testifying in the early 1890s. One was at dinner at a lodging house in Blackpool, seated — as luck would have it — next to a visiting German economist, who listened avidly to his recollections.

> The youths of his time [he recalled] had been red-hot Chartists, he himself one of the most eager ... To my question — What, then, had been the meaning of Chartism? — the aged man answered: A Labour Party in Parliament, State rule by the general vote, in order to evolve from the law against the poor a law for the poor. With Chartism, and after this had stepped above its height as a political movement, there came a time of larger and distressing strikes. He remembered especially the Christmas month of 1842, and the great strike at Preston in 1853, which had lasted 40 weeks, and for which, from Blackburn alone, £700 per week had been contributed. The strikes had brought in their train formidable distress and great bitterness.[69]

This old man, 'like many of his class, described himself as a Socialist, and attacked the trade unions as conservative institutions'. Our second witness is the secretary of the Preston spinners' union, and is writing their history. 'We are in possession of the records', warned Thomas Banks in 1894, 'of every man who r[a]n the blockade, and earned himself the name of knobstick'.[70] Forty years on, life could still be uncomfortable for the blacklegs of 1854.

Epilogue

Never again were the principal actors to participate in anything quite so dramatic. Robert Ascroft continued as Town Clerk for many years. Ill-health finally forced his resignation in 1875, and he died a year later at the age of 71, having 'played a conspicuous, a faithful, and a most useful and worthy part in the public affairs of Preston for nearly half a century'.[1] Cowell's old employer John Goodair continued to play an active role in local politics. He became an alderman in 1859, served as mayor in 1860–1, and was a member of the Central Relief Committee in Manchester during the Cotton Famine. Goodair died in 1873 after being run over in the street in Manchester.[2] William Ainsworth, secretary of the masters' association in 1853–4, dropped out of public life and carried on his business quietly until he died in 1862, in his mid-fifties.[3]

His close friend Thomas Miller died of a liver complaint in 1865, at the age of 54. 'Preston has lost her foremost son,' wrote the *Preston Guardian* rapturously, 'the owner of wealth almost fabulous in its amount, the master of nearly 4,000 operatives, himself one of the greatest powers in the greatest of England's industries'. Ernest Jones had been cynical as to Miller's real intentions in granting the five per cent increase in June 1854. 'Some people want to be Mayors, and Members of Parliament,' he told a Chartist meeting near Bacup, 'and, notwithstanding the Bribery Act, they can bribe with a five per cent'. In fact, Miller had no ambitions in either direction, rejecting an offer of the mayoralty in November 1854. He was still chairman of the Masters' Association in 1859, and remained an alderman until his death. For the funeral, at Lytham, flags flew at half-mast on many Preston mills, and the cortege was accompanied to the borough boundaries by the mayor and corporation, together with 3,000 of his operatives who had been given the day off on full pay. Equally prominent were 'the well-dressed spectators who, in Winckley-Square, Fishergate and Lune Street, stood in some places six or seven deep behind the operatives, and crowded the windows and doorways'. Among his hands, memories of Miller's role in the lock-out were forgotten, or at least suppressed. 'Every one of the operatives had a very neat and respectable appearance, and each evidently felt the solemnity of the occasion . . . Many were shedding tears.'[4]

Among the operatives, Thomas Banks returned to his mules, and served as secretary of the Preston spinners' union for several decades, surviving to write its history in 1894.⁵ Robert Baxendale continued his involvement in local politics, speaking in support of John Bright's Lancashire Reform Union during the election campaign of 1859, by which time he had become sufficiently respectable to serve on C.P. Grenfell's committee.⁶ John Brocklehurst joined the Stockport Chartists, and in 1858 was found supporting an alliance between the rump of the Chartist movement and middle-class reformers.⁷ William Brown was prominent in the Blackburn weavers' union, rallying it to the Liberal cause (against the Hornbyite Tories) in the general election of 1857.⁸ Henry Fellowes, still a weaver, helped to organise the collection of subscriptions for the Padiham strikers in 1859.⁹ John Gregson, Robert Richardson and John Sergeant campaigned for Sir George Strickland in the 1857 election, and spoke on behalf of the Liberals two years later.¹⁰ Edward Whittle was secretary of the Blackburn weavers' union for some years, and later became a schoolmaster and a mill manager. An active supporter of the Tory manufacturer Hornby, Whittle died in 1871 at the age of 48.¹¹

George Cowell became a tea and coffee dealer, with a small shop off Ribbleton Lane.¹² His political activities continued unabated. In the 1857 election he interrogated the Tory candidate, calling for universal suffrage, the abolition of the law of primogeniture, and for 'the employment of the surplus population on the lands not now cultivated'; this drew cries from the crowd of 'Thee go off to bed', and 'Did thy friend Goodair send thee?'¹³ Two years later Cowell led the Preston supporters of Bright's Lancashire Reform Union, and grilled the Tory candidates on matters of foreign policy. Banned from the platform of a public election meeting, he proposed from the floor a vote of thanks to the mayor, who had been responsible for the prohibition.¹⁴ The last record of Cowell comes two years later when, along with three old comrades from the ten per cent campaign he made an abortive intervention in a weavers' strike at Clitheroe. One of the Clitheroe strikers, John Ward, provided a graphic description of the incident. He wrote in his diary on 22 March 1861:

I was in the committee room all forenoon, and just as we were separating for dinner we heard the bellman calling a public meeting of the weavers to be held in the market place, to be addressed by George Cowell of Preston, Mortimer Grimshaw of Blackburn, Matthews of Rochdale and Rhodes of Stockport. Now this was a surprise to us, and as we knew them to be a gang of notorious scoundrels we were determined to know the reason of their coming here, and who sent them . . . We had a long and stormy discussion. They told us they came to see if the dispute could not be settled by arbitration, but they would not tell us who sent them nor who paid them. Mr Redmayne [a local spirit merchant] was among them. He told us afterwards that they sent for him . . . [a discussion ensued concerning the postponement of the public meeting] . . . There was great uproar and confusion. We then went to the committee room and had a very difficult job to get them there. The crowd followed us, throwing stones, pushing them and kicking them, shouting and bawling, telling them they sold the Preston strike and must not come here to sell them. With great difficulty we got them into the committee room and it was two hours before the crowd dispersed, when a cab was sent for and took them to Whalley because they durst not go to the station as some of them might be killed, the crowd was so exasperated.¹⁵

Epilogue

One of this 'gang of notorious scoundrels', Mortimer Grimshaw, had returned to Preston in October 1854 to deliver two public lectures, on political economy and 'the principles and objects of the "Labour League" '.[16] In the same month he wrote a vitriolic letter to Henry Ashworth, the author of a hostile account of the Preston strike, assailing Ashworth's 'remarkable ignorance' and 'willfull and whicked falsehoods' [sic].[17] Ashworth must have been surprised, two years later, to receive a visiting card with the following message:

Messrs. Mortimer Grimshaw and John B. Horsfall present their compliments to Mr. Ashworth and beg to inform him that Messrs. Thos. Cooke, of the Oxford Road Twist Company and Geo. Garnett of the *Manchester Guardian* have recommended them to call upon him and should the present time be favourable for a short interview they will have much pleasure in making known to him the object of their visit.

Grimshaw and Horsfall were, in fact, soliciting subscriptions to enable them to emigrate. At first Ashworth gave them neither money nor encouragement, but when they made a second visit with their subscription list he weakened sufficiently to give them £5.[18]

The last record of Horsfall is as a short-time agitator in Stockport, in 1856.[19] Together with John Mathews, Grimshaw resurfaced in the early 1860s as a campaigner for the Confederacy in the American Civil War. Both achieved some success at Ashton, where the Southern sympathisers were organised by another of the delegates of 1853, William Aitken.[20] But 'when Mortimer Grimshaw tried to get the workers of Blackburn to support British mediation in America, his platform was taken by the Secretary of the local Weavers' Association. Grimshaw lost in a vote which was estimated at 4 to 5,000 against 12. The meeting went on to carry a vote of no confidence in Grimshaw and declared itself in favour of the policies of Abraham Lincoln'.[21]

Grimshaw had, in fact, become an unsuccessful political adventurer, scraping a living by placing his talents at the service of anyone who would pay for them, including that staunch supporter of the Northern cause, John Bright. The last known record of Grimshaw is in Manchester in 1864, when he wrote an abject begging letter to one of Bright's associates, shedding some light on the mysterious Clitheroe incident three years earlier. He wrote to George Wilson, a veteran of the Anti-Corn Law League:

I am not aware that I am known personally to you, but no dought I am by name, and no dought you will remember seeing me with Mr. Bright M.P. at his lodgings in London Lane three years ago. I have taken an active part in various movements, but more particularly during the last five years against *'Strikes Delegates and Trades Unions'*, and I have suffered much of late from the persecution of these engines of tyranny and dictation. I have also made great exertions to obtain from Sir Charles Wood the total abolition of the 'Indian Tariff'. A few gentlemen seeing the importance of my labour have *repeatedly given me their mites* including some of the principle merchants, Cotton Spinners, Manufacturers, Iron Masters etc. – Including *the Proprietors of the 'Manchester Examiner and Times'* and *'the Manchester Guardian'*, but I have suffered very much of late through the want of fair support. It has been suggested to me that you as Chairman of the Lancashire and Yorkshire Railway Company would have no objection to use your influence to obtain me a permanent situation of some sort under the Company, and if you will do so I will be truly thankful, and you will confer upon me a *lasting obligation*. I shall be glad to answer any questions, and give the most unquestionable references. Meanwhile, I am very *destitute – pennyless*, and I shall be very thankful for some little assistance to meet my immediate wants. *My subscription list and letters including one from Mr. Bright M.P.* is at your service for perusal.[22]

Poacher turned (ill-paid) gamekeeper: such was the sad fate of the Thunderer of Lancashire.

Notes

Where no place of publication is given the book was published in London. The following abbreviations are used in the notes and bibliography:

Newspapers

BA	*Burnley Advertiser*
BC	*Bolton Chronicle*
BM	*Burnley Mentor*
BO	*Bradford Observer*
BS	*Blackburn Standard*
DN	*Daily News*
GS	*Glasgow Sentinel*
ILN	*Illustrated London News*
LGa	*Lancaster Gazette*
LGu	*Lancaster Guardian*
LJ	*Liverpool Journal*
LM	*Liverpool Mercury*
LWN	*Lloyd's Weekly Newspaper*
MET	*Manchester Examiner and Times*
MC	*Morning Chronicle*
MG	*Manchester Guardian*
NDT	*Northern Daily Times*
NS	*Northern Star*
PC	*Preston Chronicle*
PG	*Preston Guardian*
PPa	*People's Paper*
PPi	*Preston Pilot*
RN	*Reynolds' Newspaper*
SA	*Stockport Advertiser*
WD	*Weekly Dispatch*
WE	*Wigan Examiner*
WG	*Warrington Guardian*
WO	*Wigan Observer*

Journals

Camb. Hist. J.	*Cambridge Historical Journal.*
Ec.H.R.	*Economic History Review.*
Hist. J.	*Historical Journal.*

Notes to pages 5–8

I.R.S.H.	International Review of Social History.
J. Mod. Hist.	Journal of Modern History.
J.P.E.	Journal of Political Economy.
Trans. Hist. Soc. of Lancs. and Chesh.	Transactions of the Historical Society of Lancashire and Cheshire.
Trans. Lancs. and Chesh. Antiq. Soc.	Transactions of the Lancashire and Cheshire Antiquarian Society.
J. Stat. Soc. of London	Journal of the Statistical Society of London.

Miscellaneous

Add. MSS.	British Museum Additional Manuscripts
H.O.	Home Office Papers
L.C.R.O.	Lancashire County Records Office
M.H.	Ministry of Health Papers
P.R.O.	Public Records Office
R.S.A.	Royal Society of Arts

Prologue

1 *PC, PG* 18.3.1854.

Chapter 1 Industry and Unions

1 D. Defoe, *A Tour Through the Whole Island of Great Britain* (Harmondsworth, 1971), p. 548.
2 Rev. W. MacRitchie, *Diary of a Tour Through Great Britain in 1795* (1897), p. 38.
3 M.W. Flinn (Ed.), *Svedenstierna's Tour of Great Britain, 1802–3* (Newton Abbot, 1973), p. 169.
4 M. Tulket, *A Topographical, Statistical and Historical Account of the Borough of Preston* (Preston, 1821), p. 105.
5 C. Hardwick, *A History of the Borough of Preston and its Environs* (Preston, 1857), p. 340.
6 W. Cobbett, *Rural Rides* (1885 Edn.), Vol. II, p. 98.
7 Rev. G.N. Knight, *Lancashire* (1842), p. 51.
8 M. Anderson, *Family Structure in Nineteenth Century Lancashire* (Cambridge, 1971), pp. 24, 202.
9 F. Engels, *The Condition of the Working Class in England* (Panther Edn., Introduction by E. Hobsbawm, 1969), p. 76.
10 Anderson, p. 34. In 1844–5 the Commission on the State of Large Towns selected Preston for a special study. See *Parl. Papers*, 1844, Vol. XVII; *Parl. Papers*, 1845, Vol. XVIII.
11 For a discussion of the growth of the early cotton industry see A.P. Wadsworth and J. de L. Mann, *The Cotton Trade and Industrial Lancashire, 1660–1780* (Manchester, 1931); S.D. Chapman, *The Cotton Industry in the Industrial Revolution* (1972); D. Landes, *The Unbound Prometheus* (Cambridge, 1970); D.A. Farnie, *The English Cotton Industry and the World Market, 1815–1896* (Oxford, 1979).
12 P. Deane and W.A. Cole, *British Economic Growth, 1688–1959* (Cambridge, 1964); A.E. Musson, *The Growth of British Industry* (Manchester, 1978), p. 83.
13 Handloom weavers generally owned their own looms.
14 S.D. Chapman (1972), p. 29.

Notes to pages 8–11

15 A.E. Musson, 'Industrial Motive Power in the United Kingdom, 1800–1870', *Ec.H.R.* (Vol. 29) 1976, pp. 415–39.
16 S.D. Chapman (1972), p. 18.
17 A.J. Taylor, 'Concentration and Specialization in the Lancashire Cotton Industry, 1825–1850', *Ec.H.R.* (Vol. 2) 1949, pp. 114–22.
18 D. Bythell, *The Handloom Weavers* (Cambridge, 1969), p. 29.
19 R.S. Fitton and A.P. Wadsworth, *The Strutts and the Arkwrights* (Manchester, 1958), p. 195.
20 Bythell, p. 33.
21 *Ibid.* p. 90.
22 A.J. Taylor, p. 116.
23 Bythell, p. 116.
24 R.C.O. Matthews, *A Study in Trade Cycle History: economic fluctuations in Great Britain, 1837–1842* (Cambridge, 1954), p. 132. J. Foster, *Class Struggle and the Industrial Revolution: early industrial capitalism in three English towns* (1974), pp. 21, 82–4 for implications of the falling rate of profit.
25 J. Jewkes, 'The Localization of the Cotton Industry', *Economic History* (Vol. 2) 1930, pp. 91–106.
26 V.A.C. Gatrell, 'Labour, Power and the Size of Firms in Lancashire Cotton in the Second Quarter of the Nineteenth Century', *Ec.H.R.* (Vol. 30) 1977, p. 122.
27 D.A. Farnie, *The English Cotton Industry, 1850–1896* (M.A. Manchester University, 1953, not published).
28 M. Blaug, 'The Productivity of Capital in the Lancashire Cotton Industry during the Nineteenth Century', *Ec.H.R.* (Vol. 14) 1961, pp. 91–106.
29 S.D. Chapman (1972), p. 28.
30 See R. Lloyd-Jones and A.A. LeRoux, 'The Size of Firms in the Cotton Industry: Manchester 1815–41', *Ec.H.R.* (Vol. 33) 1980, pp. 72–82.
31 Gatrell, p. 96.
32 S.D. Chapman, 'Financial Restraints on the Growth of Firms in the Cotton Industry, 1790–1850', *Ec.H.R.* (Vol. 32) 1979, p. 122.
33 Farnie (1953), pp. 194, 197–8.
34 Anderson, p. 25.
35 Hardwick, p. 366.
36 M.E. Edwards, *The Growth of British Cotton Trade, 1780–1815* (Manchester, 1967), pp. 33–4.
37 J. Aikin, *A Description of the Country from 30 to 40 miles round Manchester* (1795), p. 286.
38 Farnie (1953), p. 205.
39 Bythell, p. 29. The great bulk were country handloom weavers.
40 J. Lowe, 'Account of the Strike and Lock-Out in the Cotton Trade at Preston in 1853' in *Trades' Societies and Strikes* (London: National Association for the Promotion of Social Science, 1860), p. 207.
41 E.L. Jones, *The Development of English Agriculture, 1815–73* (1968).
42 Anderson, pp. 34–6. Only 50% of the population of Manchester, Stockport and Bolton came from outside the boundaries.
43 *PG* 1.7.1865 (obituary).
44 Tulket, pp. 105–15.
45 Farnie (1953), p. 211.
46 When investment took place in the 1825 boom, power supplies tended to exceed the immediate needs of the firm. Although existing machinery was not idle the excess floor space of the new mills meant that some firms were subject to 'semi-reserve capacity'.

Notes to pages 11–13

With subsequent increases in output, firms merely used up floor space and excess power supplies and did so with almost no increase in investment.
47 This section is based on R.C.O. Matthews, pp. 127–51.
48 *Parl. Papers* 1842 Vol. XXI. It is important to note that it is not always possible to estimate the number of mills in Preston. The fine spinning category in Horner's report also included mills in Leyland. Those weaving by power loom only included Eccles, Leigh, Winwick, Chorley, Wigan, Kirkham and Lancaster. Those doubling yarn only included Blackburn, and the category of mills not working included Wigan. For fine spinning, four of the six mills were assumed to be in Preston. For weaving by power loom, three of the ten were assumed to be in Preston and for mills not running four of the six. Five of the nine doubling yarn were assumed to be in Preston.
49 Gatrell, p. 118 where the employer is not named. Horrockses also owned other sites.
50 These figures are estimates. In 1836 the percentage of the labour force in separate occupations was: spinners 7.8%, piecers 16%, weavers and cardroom hands and reelers etc. 71.2%, overlookers, packers and engineers 5%. For 1841 the same proportions were used except that spinners were reduced by 1% and piecers increased by the same amount. This was done to take into account the introduction of the self actor after the 1836 strike. A total of 10,450 hands were employed in the 30 mills.
51 John Goodair, a self-made man who came to Preston in 1830 as a manager of a silk and gingham factory, set up on his own account in 1836. J. Paley also built a new factory in 1835. *PG* 18.10.1873, *PG* 2.2.1855 (obituaries).
52 Farnie (1953), p. 209.
53 Gatrell, p. 96.
54 *PG* 29.3.1862, *PG* 18.7.1857 (obituaries).
55 A.D. Gayer, W.W. Rostow, A.J. Schwartz, *The Growth and Fluctuation of the British Economy, 1790–1850*, Vol. I (Oxford, 1953), p. 325.
56 *PG* 8.5.1847. Horrockses & Miller employed 335hp and 2,000 hands. Swainson & Birley & Co. 300hp and 1,400 hands. Ainsworth & Paley Jr & Co. was the third largest firm.
57 J.R.T. Hughes, *Fluctuations in Trade, Industry and Finance: a study of British economic development, 1850–1860* (Oxford, 1960), p. 76.
58 R.A. Church, *The Great Victorian Boom, 1850–1873* (1975).
59 *Parl. Papers*, 1852, Vol. XXI, p. 361. 22 new mills were built in Preston, Blackburn, Accrington, Clitheroe, Chorley, Lancaster and West Cumbria. See also *Parl. Papers*, 1852–3, Vol. XL, p. 524.
60 *Parl. Papers*, 1854, Vol. XIX, p. 270.
61 *Parl Papers*, 1852–3, Vol. XL, p. 551; Anderson, p. 24.
62 There are problems over the precise number of mills. Horner's 1854 report quotes a widely distributed trade circular by C.F. Maudley, which puts the number of *mills* in 'Preston and the immediate district' at 64. In Lowe's account he refers to 64 *firms* and since some firms had more than one mill it is likely that Horner's is an underestimate. Lowe, who reported the 1853–4 strike, relied upon the local press for his information but since some of the 64 firms were flax manufacturers and since some were located outside of the immediate district it is difficult to estimate how many firms there were.
63 *Parl. Papers*, 1854, Vol. XIX, p. 272.
64 Gayer, Rostow and Schwartz, p. 314.
65 T. Ellison, *The Cotton Trade of Great Britain* (1886), p. 64.
66 L.G. Sandberg, *Lancashire in Decline* (Ohio, 1974), p. 168. By 1859 trade with China had increased to 194m yards.
67 Farnie (1953), p. 142. W. Pilkington, a piecer during the strike, suggested that when the strike commenced Preston was noted for fine spinning 'but during the strike it

Notes to pages 13–17

went to Bolton'. See his *Then and Now: Preston's progress for seventy years, 1841–1911* (Preston, 1912), pp. 29–30. Most of this appears to have been derived from T. Banks, *A Short Sketch of the Cotton Trade of Preston for the Last 67 Years* (Preston, 1894), pp. 5–8.
68 Sandberg, p. 260; Farnie (1979), p. 121.
69 This account is based on *The New Cambridge Modern History: zenith of European power, 1830–70* Vol. X (Cambridge, 1967), pp. 685–713.
70 B.R. Mitchell, *Abstract of British Historical Statistics* (Cambridge, 1962), p. 187.
71 Deane and Cole, pp. 191–2; K. Burgess, *The Origins of British Industrial Relations* (1975), p. 232.
72 A.E. Musson (1978), p. 83.
73 N.J. Smelser, *Social Change in the Industrial Revolution: an application of theory to the Lancashire cotton industry, 1770–1840* (1959), p. 188.
74 S. Pollard, *The Genesis of Modern Management* (Harmondsworth, 1969), p. 218.
75 Smelser, p. 202.
76 Anderson, pp. 27–8.
77 Women did in fact work on some of the smaller mules.
78 W. Lazonick, 'Industrial Relations and technical change: the case of the self-acting mule', *Cambridge Journal of Economics* (Vol. 3) 1979, p. 238.
79 R. Burr Litchfield, 'The Family and the Mill: cotton mill work, family work patterns and fertility in mid Victorian Stockport' in A.S. Wohl (Ed.), *The Victorian Family: structure and stresses* (1978), p. 185. Burr Litchfield suggests that women were also regaining some control over the spinning process. In 1841 31% of the spinners in Stockport were women, and by 1850 this had increased to 50%. These figures appear, however, to include throstle spinning.
80 J.R. Cuca, 'Industrial Change and Progress of Labour in the English Cotton Industry', *I.R.S.H.* (Vol. 22) 1977, pp. 241–55.
81 See for example A. Ure, *The Philosophy of Manufactures* (1835).
82 H.A. Turner, *Trade Union Growth, Structure and Policy: a comparative study of the cotton unions* (1962), p. 141.
83 As yet, there is no history of cotton unions in the first half of the nineteenth century. Turner's challenging classic, Smelser, Bythell, and Kirby and Musson's recent detailed life of John Doherty remain the major sources. But, despite these scholarly contributions, the subject remains under-researched and in need of revision, especially for the 1830s and 1840s.
84 Turner, p. 59; Wadsworth and Mann, Book IV.
85 Bythell, p. 183.
86 Turner, p. 86.
87 Foster (1974), p. 44.
88 S. and B. Webb, *History of Trade Unionism* (1920 Edn.), p. 39.
89 Turner, pp. 59–60.
90 E.P. Thompson, *The Making of the English Working Class* (Harmondsworth, 1970 Edn.), pp. 306–7.
91 Turner, p. 62; Bythell, p. 187.
92 Bythell, p. 187.
93 Turner, p. 71.
94 Thompson (1970), p. 328.
95 P. Richards, 'The State and Early Industrial Capitalism: the case of the handloom weavers', *Past and Present* (No. 83) 1979, pp. 90–115.
96 Turner, p. 106; S. and B. Webb, pp. 26–7, 41; S.J. Chapman, *The Lancashire Cotton*

Notes to pages 17–21

    Industry (Manchester, 1904), p. 193; A.E. Musson, *British Trade Unions, 1800–1875* (1972), p. 15.
97 Smelser, p. 321.
98 A. Aspinall, *The Early English Trade Unions* (1949), p. 214.
99 Turner, p. 87.
100 R.G. Kirby & A.E. Musson, *The Voice of the People: John Doherty, 1798–1854, Trade Unionist, Radical and Factory Reformer* (Manchester, 1975), pp. 14–15.
101 Smelser, p. 199; Turner, pp. 88, 95, 126.
102 Smelser, pp. 236–7.
103 For wages see G.H. Wood, *The History of Wages in the Cotton Trade during the Past Hundred Years* (1910); F. Merttens, 'The Hours and Cost of Labour in the Cotton Industry at Home and Abroad' (*Trans. Manchester Statistical Soc.* 1893–4).
104 Turner, pp. 72, 76–7.
105 For details see J.L. and B. Hammond, *The Town Labourer* (1917); Kirby and Musson, Ch. 2; Turner; Cuca.
106 Kirby and Musson, p. 24.
107 Smelser, p. 329; Lazonick, p. 246.
108 Turner, pp. 100–1; Kirby and Musson, Chs. 4–7; G.D.H. Cole, *Attempts at General Union 1818–1834* (1953).
109 See F.C. Mather, 'The General Strike of 1842' in J. Stevenson and R. Quinault (Eds.), *Popular Protest and Public Order* (1974), pp. 115–40. See also T.D.W. Reid and N. Reid 'The 1842 "Plug Plot" in Stockport', *I.R.S.H.* (Vol. 24) 1979, pp. 55–79.
110 *NS* 2.4.1842, 13.8.1842.
111 Because the minders posed an increasing threat to the mule spinners.
112 Smelser, pp. 336–7.
113 *Ibid.* p. 201.
114 Turner, pp. 116–17, 150; Smelser, p. 337.
115 Turner, pp. 127–8; Burgess (1975), p. 237.
116 W.H. Fraser, *Trade Unions and Society: the struggle for acceptance, 1850–1880* (1974), pp. 103–4; Turner, pp. 129–31.
117 S.J. Chapman (1904), p. 264.
118 E. Hopwood, *A History of the Lancashire Cotton Industry and the Amalgamated Weavers' Association* (Manchester, 1969), pp. 193–4.
119 S.J. Chapman, 'The Regulation of Wages by List in the Spinning Industry', *Economic Journal* (Vol. 9) 1899, pp. 592–99; 'Some Policies of the Cotton Spinners' Trade Unions', *Economic Journal* (Vol. 10) 1900, pp. 467–73.
120 A forerunner of the Blackburn list was operating in 1848: see *MG* 2.7.1853, 9.7.1853 and 13.7.1853.
121 Turner, p. 132.
122 Fraser, p. 103; Turner, p. 372; S.J. Chapman (1904), p. 239.
123 Turner, p. 63.
124 Thus in Preston, Joseph Gillow's manager gave evidence to the Royal Commission of 1838 in support of restrictions on the use of power looms: *PC* 2.6.1838.
125 Turner, p. 99. Earlier in the century such jealousies could lead some small masters into tacit support for machine-breaking: see E.J. Hobsbawm, 'The Machine Breakers' *Past and Present* (Vol. 1) 1952, pp. 57–70.
126 On Preston, see above, pp. 86–7; on Stockport *SA* 17.6.1853.
127 See also Turner, Appendix I, pp. 370–3; S.J. Chapman (1904), Ch. X; Fraser, Ch. 4.
128 *The Trials of Feargus O'Connor and 58 other Chartists on a charge of seditious conspiracy . . .* (Manchester, 1843), p. 78: evidence of Samuel Bannister, Chief Constable of Preston.

Notes to pages 21–4

129 Lowe, p. 208.
130 C. Hardwick, pp. 375, 415.
131 Cheryl R. Tabor, *The Preston Cotton Unions: an account of their organization and activities, c. 1830–1850* (unpublished B.A. dissertation, University of Manchester, 1972), pp. 18–19, citing Turner, p. 67 and A. Hewitson, *A History of Preston in the County of Lancashire* (Preston, 1883), p. 353.
132 Kirby and Musson, pp. 87, 113, 164–8, 218, 282–3.
133 Tabor, p. 77, citing Turner, p. 75.
134 Tabor, pp. 18–19.
135 H. Ashworth, *An Inquiry into the Origin, Progress and Results of the Strike of the Operative Cotton Spinners of Preston, from October 1836, to February 1837* (Manchester, 1838), reprinted in *Rebirth of the Trade Union Movement: five pamphlets 1838–1847* (New York, 1972). See also Tabor, pp. 21–2; M.F. Boyle, *Preston Working Class Radicalism in the 1830s* (unpublished B.A. dissertation, University of Lancaster, 1977), Ch. III. The 'document' was in common use by employers in the 1830s.
136 Hewitson (1883), p. 353, cited Tabor, p. 88, n. 9; T. Banks, pp. 4–5.
137 *PC* 13.7.1839, 27.7.1839.
138 *PC* and *PPi*, all issues, August–September 1842; A.G. Rose, 'The Plug Riots of 1842 in Lancashire and Cheshire', *Trans. Lancs. and Chesh. Antiq. Soc.* (Vol. 67) 1957, pp. 75–112; Tabor, pp. 42–4; Mather (1974), p. 131.
139 *PG* 7–28.9.1844, 5.10.1844, 26.10.1844.
140 *PC* 11.5.1844 (the spinners seem not to have been involved in this campaign).
141 *PC* 21.6.1845, 19.7.1845.
142 *PC* 29.11.1845. The affair remains mysterious. Similar tea parties had earlier been held in Bolton and Oldham (*PG* 9.8.1845, 4.10.1845), which suggests that Paley's charge was not without substance. Tabor, pp. 50–2 interprets the party as an attempt by the spinners to secure the manufacturers' support for the repeal of the Corn Laws. Certainly William Ainsworth, an ardent repealer, defended the motives of the organisers; and the spinners did hold a public meeting for Free Trade only a week after the tea party (*PC* 6.12.1845).
143 Two meetings of Preston weavers were held early in 1846, for example, to support striking weavers in Chorley (*PG* 28.2.1846, 19.3.1846).
144 M.F. Boyle, *Preston Working Class Radicalism in the 1830s* (B.A. Lancaster, 1977, not published), Ch. II; Tabor, p. 35.
145 See D. Morier Evans, *The Commercial Crisis 1847–1848* (1848, 1849; reprinted New York, 1969); C.N. Ward-Perkins, 'The Commercial Crisis of 1847', *Oxford Economic Papers* (Vol. 2) 1950, pp. 75–94.
146 The Preston masters rejected the proposal (*PG* 15.8.1846, 29.8.1846). In Blackburn the association agreed on short-time working in August, abandoned it in September, and reintroduced it in October, eventually dissolving itself when several members reverted to full-time operation against the association's instructions! (*PG* 8.8.1846, 5.9.1846, 24.10.1846, 13.2.1847).
147 *PG* 31.10.1846.
148 13,661 as against 7,298 (*PG* 15.5.1847).
149 *PG* 29.5.1847.
150 *PG* 8.5.1847.
151 *PG* 6.11.1847.
152 *PG* 20.11.1847.
153 *PG* 30.10.1847, 20.11.1847.
154 *PG* 6.11.1847.
155 *PG* 14.1.1846, 23.1.1847, 29.5.1847.

156 *PC* 24.12.1846, 2.1.1847.
157 He was quite right:

Wages in Stockport and Preston 1852

	(1)	(2)	(3)	(4)
Spinning (Mule)	30/4	30/4	n.a.	27/–
Spinning (Throstle)	7/6	7/6	8/9	7/6
Self-Acting Minders	15/3	15/3	15/9	12/6
Sizers (male)	34/6	34/6	33/–	30/–
Warpers	24/–	24/–	n.a.	10/6(?)
Knitters	8/9	8/9	n.a.	8/6
Drawers (female)	14/–	14/–	12/5	10/–
Weaving	9/8	9/8	11/4	9/–
Winders	8/–	8/–	9/11	9/–
Mechanics	24/–	24/–	26/–	22/–

Col. (1) Average weekly wages to operatives engaged in the cotton trade.
Col. (2) The Stockport firm, Robert McClure.
Col. (3) The Stockport firm, Messrs Kershaw & Co.
Col. (4) The Preston firm, Lawson & Birley & Co.

These data are based on a survey which H.B. Farnall conducted between November 1851 and January 1852, shortly after taking up his appointment as Assistant Poor Law Commissioner for the Lancashire district (he was appointed 25 March 1851). For his evidence he relied upon government returns, information provided by large employers, and well informed persons. He typically had a great deal of trouble persuading masters to release wage data, but 'I believe', he noted, 'you may safely trust the enclosed return [for Stockport] as it has carefully been gone over by Mr. McClure . . . a personal friend of mine'. Unfortunately, only three firms furnished the information which he sought for the cotton industry. Horrockses and Miller refused to reply. See Thomas Thackery to Farnall 3.11.1851; Stockport Union to Farnall 28.11.1851; Farnall to Poor Law Board 3.1.1851 (MH/32/22).

158 *PG* 10.7.1847. Similar arguments were expressed in 1853–4: see above, pp. 56–7.
159 *PG* 15.5.1847.
160 *PG* 15.5.1847, 22.5.1847, 29.5.1847, 12.6.1847.
161 *PG* 19.6.1847, 26.6.1847, 3.7.1847.
162 *PC* 4.9.1847. Despite the support of the *Manchester Guardian* this proposal was not implemented. Further delegate meetings on 10 and 17 October called for a general stoppage to begin on the 21st in support of striking spinners at Ashton and Mossley. In the event only Ashton struck. The Mossley operatives accepted the reductions, and the other towns did not respond (*PG* 16.10.1847, 23.10.1847, 23.11.1847).
163 *PC* 18.9.1847.
164 *PG* 30.10.1847.
165 *PG* 25.9.1847.
166 *PPi* 20.3.1847.
167 The meeting is reported in all three Preston papers, 15.1.1848. For the subsequent debate, and Goodair's (less than entirely convincing) answer to Marsden's charges, see their issues for 22.1.1848 and 29.1.1848.
168 *PG* 29.1.1848 (Naylor's admission).

Notes to pages 25–30

169 *PG* 22.1.1848, 29.1.1848, 26.2.1848.
170 Wood's wages indices for 1845 and 1850 suggest that the reduction was rather less than this, except perhaps in Manchester, and indicate no reduction at all in Blackburn between 1845 and 1850. G.H. Wood, pp. 115–16. Unfortunately no data are available for the crucial years 1846–8.
171 *PG* 22.1.1848. It is significant that Bowman, a spinner, was speaking at a meeting of weavers.
172 *PG* 29.1.1848.
173 *PG* 22.1.1848.
174 *PG* 26.2.1848.
175 See above, p. 24; a firm promise was apparently made by Smethurst's of Chorley (*PC* 29.1.1848).
176 *SA* 17.6.1853.
177 *PC* 17.2.1849 (Gardner and Naylor); 27.2.1849, 17.3.1849 (Gardner); 17.3.1849 (Napier and Goodair); 24.3.1849 (Bashall and Boardman, of Farington); 31.3.1849 (Hollins).
178 *PC* 3.3.1849, 31.3.1849.
179 *PC* 18.8.1849.
180 *MET* 17.12.1853.
181 *PC* 29.3.1851, 17.5.1851, 24.5.1851, 31.5.1851 (Stanley St mill); *PG* 13.3.1853 (Rodgett); *PG* 17.4.1852 (Ainsworth).
182 *PG* 8.5.1852.

Chapter 2 Ten Per Cent (5 June–14 October 1853)

1 *PG* 9.10.1852, 16.10.1852, 27.11.1852, 18.12.1852.
2 H. Ashworth, *The Preston Strike: an enquiry into its causes and consequences* (Manchester, 1854), pp. 4–5.
3 *PG* 9.10.1852.
4 See Rhodes Boyson, *The Ashworth Cotton Enterprise: the rise and fall of a family firm, 1818–1880* (Oxford, 1970), p. 191.
5 *BS* 26.1.1853; *BS* 9.2.1853; *PG* 12.2.1853; *PG* 26.3.1853; *SA* 1.4.1853; *PG* 2.4.1853, 9.4.1853; *BS* 20.4.1853; *PG* 23.4.1853, 30.4.1853; *WO* 23.4.1853.
6 *BM* 21.5.1853.
7 *BC* 29.1.1853, 5.2.1853; *BS* 2.2.1853; *PG* 5.2.1853.
8 *PG* 19.2.1853; *BS* 19.2.1853.
9 *PG* 19.2.1853.
10 *SA* 18.3.1853.
11 *PG* 12.11.1853, citing an early piece of investigative journalism by the *Times*, 8.11.1853.
12 *PG* 9.4.1853.
13 *SA* 8.4.1853.
14 *SA* 29.4.1853.
15 C.A.N. Reid, *The Chartist Movement in Stockport* (Hull University M.A. dissertation, 1974), p. 378, citing *SA* 13.5.1853.
16 *PG* 23.4.1853.
17 *BS* 27.4.1853, 5.5.1853.
18 *BS* 25.5.1853.
19 See A.G. Rose, pp. 75–112; F.C. Mather (1974), pp. 115–40.
20 *SA* 3.6.1853.
21 C.A.N. Reid (1974), p. 378.

218 *Notes to pages 30–7*

22 *SA* 17.6.1853.
23 *BS* 22.6.1853; *BC* 25.6.1853. In Bolton the weavers' ten per cent campaign proceeded slowly throughout the summer. By October most firms had agreed to pay the full advance (*BC*, various issues, July–October 1853).
24 *SA* 17.6.1853.
25 *PG* 11 and 18.6.1853; *BS* 15.6.1853.
26 *BS* 8.6.1853; *PG* 25.6.1853; *BM* 18.6.1853.
27 *BS* 22.6.1853; *PG* 18 and 25.6.1853.
28 True to his word, Ainsworth played no further part in the movement.
29 *PG*, *PPi* 11.6.1853.
30 *PG* 18.6.1853.
31 *SA* 24.6.1853.
32 *BS* 22.6.1853; *PG* 25.6.1853.
33 *BS* 29.6.1853; *PG* 25.6.1853, 2.7.1853.
34 *SA* 24.6.1853.
35 *PG* 25.6.1853, 2.7.1853.
36 *BS* 29.6.1853; *PG* 2.7.1853.
37 *PG* 25.6.1853, 2.7.1853; *BS* 29.6.1853.
38 *SA* 1.7.1853; *PG* 2.7.1853.
39 *PG* 7.5.1853, 4.6.1853; *SA* 24.6.1853, 29.7.1853; *PG* 30.7.1853; *PPa* 16.7.1853, 30.7.1853.
40 *BS* 18.5.1853, 6.7.1853; *PG* 2.7.1853; *MG* 2.7.1853, 20.7.1853, 23.7.1853.
41 *PG* 9.7.1853, 16.7.1853, 23.7.1853.
42 *MG* 2.7.1853.
43 *MG* 13.7.1853; *SA* 15.7.1853; *PG* 16.7.1853.
44 *SA* 8 and 15.7.1853.
45 *PG* 9 and 16.7.1853. Slightly different sums are cited in *SA* issues for July 1853; see below, p. 223, n. 110.
46 *BS* 13.7.1853.
47 'A Prestonian' [Charles Hardwick], 'Lancashire Stump Oratory and Reminiscences of the Labour Battle: Chapter I, The Orchard', *Eliza Cook's Journal* Vol. XI, 1854, pp. 247–8.
48 *PG* 16.7.1853.
49 *SA* 22.7.1853.
50 Famous in working-class circles as 'the miners' Attorney-General', Roberts was a close friend of the former Chartist leader Feargus O'Connor. He was no stranger in Lancashire, where he spent much of the 1840s defending members of the Miners' Association who brushed with the law. In 1847 he stood unsuccessfully as Radical candidate for Blackburn. Details of his work for the miners are given by R. Challinor and B. Ripley, *The Miners' Association: a trade union in the age of the Chartists* (1968).
51 *SA* 29.7.1853.
52 *PG* 30.7.1853; *SA* 5 and 12.8.1853.
53 *SA* 12 and 19.8.1853, 2.9.1853.
54 *SA* 12 and 19.8.1853, 2.9.1853.
55 *BS* 27.7.1853.
56 *BS* 3.8.1853.
57 *BS* 17 and 24.8.1853; *PG* 20.8.1853.
58 *PG* 3.9.1853.
59 *BA* August 1853.
60 *BA* September 1853; *BS* 31.8.1853.

Notes to pages 37–44

61 *MG* 27.7.1853; *PPi* 6.8.1853. Two dyers were subsequently transported for their role in the assault.
62 *LGa* 3.9.1853.
63 *BS* 7.9.1853.
64 *PPa* 27.8.1853.
65 *PPi* 13.8.1853. See also H.I. Dutton and J.E. King 'The Limits of Paternalism: the cotton tyrants of North Lancashire, 1836–1854' (mimeo, 1979).
66 *PG* 23.7.1853.
67 *PG* 13.8.1853, 3.9.1853; *PPi* 20.8.1853.
68 Lowe, p. 212; *PG* 27.8.1853.
69 *PPi* 20.8.1853.
70 *PG* 20.8.1853.
71 *PG* 27.8.1853.
72 *PG* 27.8.1853.
73 *PPi* 7.1.1854.
74 *PPi* 27.8.1853. Breach of contract by masters counted as only a civil offence. See Daphne Simon, 'Master and Servant' in John Saville (Ed.), *Democracy and the Labour Movement* (1954).
75 *PG* 27.8.1853.
76 *PG* 3.9.1853.
77 *PG* 17.9.1853.
78 It is unclear whether this applied *before* 15 September.
79 *PG* 17.9.1853.
80 Not 37, as Lowe, p. 215, states.
81 DDPr 138/87b (L.C.R.O.).
82 *PPi* 17.9.1853.
83 *PG* 17.9.1853; Lowe, p. 215.
84 *PG* 17.9.1853.
85 This is the most common variant of his name, which is also spelled in some reports as Matthew and Matthews.
86 *PG* 24.9.1853; *LGa* 24.9.1853.
87 *PG* 24.9.1853, 1.10.1853. The Christian Socialists had just held a successful Cooperative conference in Manchester, and were proselytizing in the North. See C.E. Raven, *Christian Socialism 1848–1854* (1920), pp. 314–15; Torben Christensen, *Origin and History of Christian Socialism* (Aarhus, 1962), pp. 334, 353, n. 7.
88 *PG* 24.9.1853, 1.10.1853; *PPi* 1.10.1853.
89 *WO* 10.9.1853, 8.10.1853.
90 *PG* 10.9.1853; *BS* 21.9.1853.
91 *PG* 17.9.1853.
92 *BS* 21.9.1853, 28.9.1853; *BM* 15.10.1853.
93 *BS* 5.10.1853, 12.10.1853; *PG* 8.10.1853; *PC* 8.10.1853.
94 *BA* October 1853.
95 *BM* 15.10.1853.
96 *PG* 13.8.1853.
97 *LGa* 8.10.1853, 15.10.1853.
98 *PG* 8.10.1853.
99 *PG* 8.10.1853.
100 DDPr 138/87b (L.C.R.O.).
101 Known as 'the Working Man's Philanthropist', John Catterall (1803–68) was a native of Blackburn, who was employed by Horrockses as a dresser from the 1840s, and 'for

many years ... engaged heartily in every movement of a charitable and benevolent character'. (T. Walmsley, *Reminiscences of the Preston Cockpit and the Old Teetotallers*, Preston, 1892, pp. 41–3).
102 *PC* 15.10.1853; *PPi* 15.10.1853.
103 An associate of John Catterall, Clay was a man of remarkable energy, who combined his official duties with support for the moderate wing of the temperance movement and a passionate interest in public health and the causes of crime. He gave evidence before a number of Parliamentary committees, and his annual reports give detailed accounts of social conditions in Preston. See Walter Lowe Clay, *The Prison Chaplain: a memoir of The Rev. John Clay B.D.* (Cambridge, 1861).
104 *PC* 15.10.1853.
105 *PPi* 15.10.1853.
106 *PC* 15.10.1853. Emigration on a grander scale was not yet deemed worthy of consideration. When an anonymous correspondent to the local press urged the virtues of employing their funds to finance emigration to Australia, Swinglehurst – echoing the response of an earlier generation of radicals – denied that it was necessary to 'transport the people to a strange land' (*PG* 1.10.1853, 8.10.1853).
107 *PC* 15.10.1853.
108 *PG* 15.10.1853.

Chapter 3 The Operatives

1 *Eliza Cook's Journal* No. 227, 19.8.1854, p. 259.
2 *SA* 18.3.1853, above, p. 28.
3 Foster (1974), p. 170; private correspondence with Dr Foster; *PPa* 9.10.1852, 26.2.1853. On the Radical traditions of Royton, see J.B. Horsfall, *Royton and Chadderton: their associations for mental improvement* (Royton, 1854).
4 *PG* 8.4.1854.
5 *Eliza Cook's Journal*, p. 258.
6 *PG* 22.10.1853; *LGa* 11.2.1854; *PC* 25.2.1854; *PG* 1.4.1854. For a lively portrait of teetotallism in Preston, see T. Walmsley (1892).
7 *PG* 15.10.1853.
8 *LGa* 11.2.1854.
9 *PC* 22.4.1848; Cowell may have been living in Blackburn at this time.
10 *PC* 20.10.1849.
11 *PC* 4.8.1849, 25.8.1849, 16.3.1850, 1.6.1850.
12 *PC* 20.9.1851.
13 *PG* 8.5.1852, 12.6.1852, 19.6.1852.
14 See above, pp. 59–61.
15 A Smith, ' "Hard Times" and the "Times" Newspaper', *Dickensian* Vol. 69, 1973, p. 159. A similar assessment is made by K. Fielding, 'The Battle for Preston', *Dickensian* Vol. 50, 1954, p. 161.
16 *PG* 3.12.1853.
17 *PC* 31.12.1853, 7.1.1854; *MG* 4.1.1854.
18 *Eliza Cook's Journal*, pp. 258–9.
19 *PG* 4.3.1854.
20 *PC* 7.1.1854.
21 *Household Words* No. 194, 10.12.1853, p. 346.
22 *PG* 8.10.1853; Ashworth (1854), p. 28.
23 *PC* 3.11.1853, 17.12.1853.
24 Joseph Livesey, *The Life and Teachings of Joseph Livesey* (1885), p. 106.

25 *NS* 9.5.1840, 21.8.1841, 4.9.1841, 13.4.1844; *PC* 17.1.1846, 15.4.1848.
26 *PG* 29.1.1853.
27 *PC* 28.4.1849, 30.6.1849, 20.10.1849, 23.2.1850, 1.6.1850, 21.6.1851, 28.6.1851, 5.7.1851, 20.9.1851, 1.11.1851.
28 *PC* 4.8.1849, 1.6.1850; *PG* 8.5.1852.
29 *PC* 24.12.1847; *PG* 1.5.1852.
30 *NDT* 14.12.1853; *PG* 1.4.1851. For his involvement in strikes at Chorley, see *PG* 28.2.1846.
31 *PC* 22.1.1848, 26.2.1848, 3.2.1849, 17.2.1849, 4.8.1849, 16.3.1850, 4.5.1850, 1.6.1850; *PG* 22.1.1848; *RN* 25.12.1853, 12.2.1854, 30.4.1854, 7.5.1854, 28.5.1854.
32 *PC* 7.2.1846, 23.2.1849; *PG* 12.6.1852.
33 *PC* 20.4.1844, 7.2.1846, 7.3.1846, 3.2.1849; *RN* 18.12.1853, 25.12.1853, 29.5.1854.
34 *PG* 12.11.1853, 12.8.1854.
35 *PC* 3.2.1849, 4.8.1849, 16.3.1850, 1.6.1850, 20.5.1854.
36 *PC* 22.3.1851; *PG* 1.4.1854.
37 *Eliza Cook's Journal*, p. 258. By August 1854 Waddington was described as a draper: *PG* 12.8.1854.
38 Henry Fellowes was probably the Lancaster man who served one week in jail for breach of contract during the strikes of 1842, of which he was a local leader (*LGu* 3.9.1842).
39 *MET* 17.12.1853.
40 *PC* 4.3.1854; *BS* 12.4.1854. See also S. Lewenhak, *Women and Trade Unions* (1977), pp. 49–51.
41 *Ten Hours' Advocate* 24.10.1846, cited Smelser, p. 301.
42 *PG* 12.11.1853; see also *PG* 3.12.1853; *LGa* 26.11.1853.
43 *BC* 10.12.1853.
44 C.A.N. Reid (1974), pp. 475–6.
45 *Ibid.*, p. 494.
46 *Ibid.*, p. 430; *PG* 12.11.1853; R.G. Gammage, *A History of the Chartist Movement* (1854, reprinted 1969, pp. 342–3); HO 45/2410A Mayor of Manchester to Home Office, 22.8.1848. Chadwick survived into the present century, well known as a stalwart of Manchester liberalism: see T.P. Newbould, *W.H. Chadwick, the last of the Manchester Chartists* (Manchester, 1910).
47 C.A.N. Reid (1974), pp. 480–1; *SA* 28.10.1853. On the Labour League, see above, p. 57.
48 *PG* 26.3.1853.
49 *PC* 20.9.1851. Harbury, who suffered more than most from the vagaries of journalistic spelling, may well have been the 'John Aubrey' who took part in the campaign for the Combination of Workmen Bill in Blackburn in 1853 (*PG* 28.5.1853).
50 *Eliza Cook's Journal*, p. 259.
51 Foster (1974), p. 155; Gammage, p. 342; *PG* 2.11.1853; AJD 1/217 (L.C.R.O.); HO/45/2410 A Clerk to Oldham magistrates to Home Office, 28.6.1848; *PPa* 9.10.1852.
52 Foster (1974), p. 157; *MET* 10.3.1846, 19.12.1846, 16.1.1847; *PC* 14.3.1846. It is not known whether he was related to the better-known James Mills, also of Oldham.
53 Foster (1974), p. 155; Gammage, p. 342; *PG* 2.11.1853; QJD 1/217 (L.C.R.O.); HO/45/2410A Clerk to Oldham magistrates to Home Office, 28.6.1848; *PPa* 9.10.1852.
54 *Factory Operatives' Guide*, Vol. 1, part 6, 5.11.1853; J.T. Ward, *The Factory Movement, 1830–1855* (1962), pp. 398–9; Reid (1974), pp. 376–7; *PPa* 2.7.1853, 8.10.1853, 9.10.1852, 26.2.1853.
55 Gammage, *op. cit.*, p. 324; *PPa* 9.7.1853; *MG* 20.7.1853, 20.5.1854; *PG* 1.11.1853; *BS* 24.8.1853; *RN* 11.12.1853, 27.11.1853, 5.2.1854.

56 S. and B. Webb, Chs. 3–4.
57 T.R. Tholfsen, *Working Class Radicalism in Mid-Victorian England* (1976), p. 308, p. 10. Harold Perkin's notion of the emergence in these years of a 'viable class society', no longer seriously threatened from below, is essentially similar: H.J. Perkin, *The Origins of Modern English Society 1760–1880* (1969). See also F. Hearn, *Domination, Legitimation and Resistance: the incorporation of the nineteenth century English working class* (Westport, Connecticut, 1978), especially Ch. 6.
58 A concise guide to the controversy, heavily critical of the Webbs, is given by A.E. Musson (1972), especially Ch. 6. See also the discussion between Musson and John Foster in *Social History* (Vol. 6) 1976, pp. 335–66.
59 A.G. Rose (1957).
60 F.C. Mather (1974), pp. 115–40.
61 Tholfsen, p. 120.
62 Cited *ibid.*, p. 96.
63 *PC* 31.12.1853.
64 *PPa* 19.11.1853.
65 Early in 1853 R.G. Gammage reported the existence of 58 Chartist localities, together with other areas where Chartist sympathisers might be found. In North Lancashire only Padiham and Bacup featured in either list (*PPa* 26.3.1853). In Preston the last Chartist meeting reported by the local press was in 1849 (*PC* 20.10.1849). The involvement of Chartists (or ex-Chartists) in strike movements in 1853 may well have been common; it is noted for Merthyr by D.J.V. Jones, 'Chartism in Welsh Communities', *Welsh History Review* (Vol. 6), 1972–3, p. 252.
66 *PPa* 10.12.1853.
67 See Marx's famous claim to this effect in the 'Afterword' to the first German edition of Volume I of *Capital*; also T.W. Hutchison, *The Cambridge Version of the History of Economics* (mimeo, Birmingham, 1974), and J.E. King, 'Marx as a Historian of Economic Thought', *History of Political Economy* (Vol. 11), Fall 1979, pp. 382–94.
68 *PG* 14.1.1854.
69 *PG* 28.1.1854.
70 *PG* 17.12.1853.
71 *PC* 14.1.1854.
72 *MET* 17.12.1853.
73 On trade union emigration funds in general, see C. Erickson, 'The Encouragement of Emigration by British Trade Unions, 1850–1900', *Population Studies* (Vol. 3) 1949, pp. 248–73; and R.V. Clements, 'Trade Unions and Emigration, 1840–80', *Population Studies* (Vol. 9) 1955, pp. 167–80.
74 J. Saville, *Ernest Jones, Chartist* (1952). During 1853 and 1854 Marx wrote brief notes on the Preston strike in his articles for the influential American paper, *New York Daily Tribune*. In one article he claimed that 'the eyes of the working classes are now fully opened: they begin to cry "Our St. Petersburg is at Preston!" '. 1.8.1854. See also 4.10.1853, 21.2.1854, 2.6.1854; D. McLellan, *Karl Marx: his life and thought* (1973), pp. 260–1, 264–5, 284–6; W.O. Henderson, *The Life of Friedrich Engels* (1976), Vol. I, p. 206.
75 *PC* and *PG*, 15.4.1854.
76 *PG* 22.4.1854.
77 G.D.H. Cole, *The Life of William Cobbett* (1924), pp. 143–4; A. Gray, *The Socialist Tradition* (1946), p. 209 (Owen), p. 267 (Charles Hall); E. Lowenthal, *The Ricardian Socialists* (New York, 1911; reprinted 1972), p. 55 (John Gray), pp. 93–5 (John Francis Bray); M. Beer, *A History of British Socialism*, Vol. I (1920), p. 228 (William Thompson). J.E. King, 'Perish Commerce! Free Trade and Underconsumption in early

Notes to pages 57–62

British radical economics' (*Australian Economic Papers*, forthcoming). For a surprising echo of these arguments by a Preston employer, see above, pp. 85–6.
78 For Kydd, see Gammage, pp. 286–7, 341.
79 *PPa* 15.1.1853 has the League's platform in full.
80 For Ferrand see Ward (1962).
81 *PPa* 15.10.1853.
82 *PG* 4.2.1854.
83 Ward (1962), pp. 398–9. Foster has noted the emergence of a Tory-working-class radical alliance in Oldham from the mid-1840s, in which Kinder Smith was actively involved (Foster (1974), pp. 208–9).
84 *PC* 6.5.1854.
85 *PC* 20.5.1854.
86 *PG* 8.4.1854.
87 *PC, PPi* 31.12.1853.
88 John Saville, 'The Christian Socialists of 1848', in Saville (Ed.), *Democracy and the Labour Movement* (1954), pp. 138–9. Saville's interpretation, while valid for Maurice and Kingsley, does not apply to Ludlow: see Christensen, p. 161, n. 52. For the influence of the Christian Socialists in the Preston strike, see *ibid.* pp. 353–5, and above p. 219, n. 87.
89 *MG* 31.5.1854.
90 Saville (1952), p. 42.
91 *PPa* 15.10.1853, 29.10.1853, 5.11.1853, 12.11.1853, 19.11.1853; *Warrington Guardian* 5.12.1853; *PPi* 12.11.1853.
92 *PPa* 12.11.1853, reprinted in Saville (1952), pp. 197–204; original stress removed.
93 *PG* 3.12.1853.
94 *SA* 11.12.1853.
95 *RN* 11.12.1853.
96 *MG* 1.2.1854. Charles Dickens attended this meeting; his account is in *Household Words* 11.2.1854.
97 *PC* 25.2.1854.
98 *PPa* 7.1.1854, reprinted in Saville (1952), pp. 264–73.
99 Saville (1952), p. 54.
100 Final Report of the Amalgamated Committee, DDPr 138/86 (L.C.R.O.).
101 John Teer (1809?–1883?), warehouseman and poet, was secretary of the Manchester dyers' union from 1842 (when he was jailed for conspiracy to riot) until early 1854. (See J. Saville and J. Bellamy (Eds.), *Dictionary of Labour Biography* (Vol. 4), pp. 175–7.) John MacLean, secretary of the Preston Amalgamated Committee of trades, was a local craftsman with a Chartist past (*PC, PG* 24.1.1846).
102 *PG* 18.3.1854.
103 *PG* 18.3.1854.
104 *MET* 21.3.1854.
105 *PG* 25.3.1854.
106 F.E. Gillespie, *Labor and Politics in England 1850–1867* (Durham, N.C., 1927), p. 3.
107 Horsfall, speaking at Warrington: *Warrington Guardian* 5.12.1853.
108 *PPa* 3.9.1853, 10.9.1853; *MET* 17.9.1853.
109 *PC* 25.2.1854.
110 No balance sheet of the Stockport strike has survived, and press coverage was less thorough than at Preston. In four successive weeks at the beginning of the strike payments were: to weavers, 1s 10½d, 1s 5½d, 2s and 2s 6d; to tenters, 11d, (?), 9d, 1s and 1s 3d; to spinners, 1s 7d, 1s 2d, (?), and 2s; and to card-room hands (?), 5d, 5d and 9d (*SA* 1, 8, 15 & 22.7.1853). The final week's tally of £1,541 went overwhelmingly to

Notes to pages 62–6

the weavers (£1,235), with the spinners (£243) and card-room hands (£63) well in the rear (*SA* 12.8.1853). Applying these proportions to the £6,284 raised in the entire period, about £5,000 must have accrued to the weavers. Just over 5,000 weavers, and a similar number of tenters, were receiving relief (*PG* 16.7.1853). As the former seem invariably to have received twice as much as the latter, this suggests a total payment of 13s 4d to the weavers and 6s 8d to the tenters (or rather less than 2s and 1s weekly). These figures can be compared with average weekly earnings in 1851–2; see above p. 216, n. 157.

111 *BC* 3.9.1853.
112 There were several minor committees, none of them prominent in the dispute itself. The tape-machine sizers were evidently the true aristocrats of the industry. Possessing a large fund beforehand, they paid out generally more than 10s weekly (to all of 40–50 men). The overlookers declared their neutrality, and financed payments ranging from 6s 3d to 10s for over 100 men (a total of just under £2,000, not £19,624, as reported by Lowe, pp. 256–7!). A handful of 'non-member mill warpers' formed a separate committee, as did the (neutral) 'cloth-lookers, book keepers and warehousemen'. See the various balance sheets in DDPr 138/87b (L.C.R.O.); also Lowe, pp. 256–8.
113 See above, p. 185.
114 There are two surviving balance sheets for the card-room hands, both in DDPr 138/87b (L.C.R.O.) (17th report, 18th week, 31.12.1853; 33rd report, 34th week, 23.4.1854). In addition press reports give some details: see for example *PG* 19.11.1853; *PC* 22.4.1854; also Lowe, pp. 255–6.
115 *PG* 19.11.1853, 24.12.1853; *PC* 22.4.1854; Lowe, p. 256. None of the throstle-spinners' balance sheets appears to have survived.
116 A comparable figure for 1980, when the average manual worker earned perhaps £75, would be in the order of £300,000 *every week*.
117 Weavers' balance sheets Nos. 13, 14, 21, 23 and 29 (some fragmentary) are in DDPr 138/87b (L.C.R.O.). Details of the 39th and last balance sheet are given in *SA* 11.8.1854.
118 For Roberts's candidature, see Challinor & Ripley, pp. 222–7.
119 Only one of the spinners' balance sheets has survived (that for the last week of the strike, week ending 14 May 1854, in DDPr 138/87a (L.C.R.O.) p. 281 and pp. 284–5). Some details were given each week in the press (e.g. *PG* 19.11.1853, 24.12.1853; *PC* 22.4.1854; also Lowe, pp. 254–5). 'The Amalgamation', which can only be the spinners' 'Central Association', also helped finance the Stockport strikers (*PG* 2.7.1853).
120 17th report and balance sheet of the card-room hands, 18th week of the dispute, late December 1853, in DDPr 138/87b (L.C.R.O.).
121 *BS* 25.1.1854.
122 Weavers' 23rd balance sheet and report, 24th week of the dispute, 2.2.1854 in DDPr 138/87b (L.C.R.O.).
123 *PPi* 16.7.1853.
124 Placard dated 14.11.1853 in DDPr 138/87b (L.C.R.O.): 'Let your cry be, "Crook for ever and ten per cent".'
125 Balance sheets of the Amalgamated Committee, weeks ending 1.1.1854 and 16.4.1854 in DDPr 138/87b (L.C.R.O.).
126 *MET* 17.12.1853. The boycott, otherwise known as exclusive dealing, was a traditional political weapon.
127 *RN* 12.11.1853.
128 *GS* 26.11.1853; *PPa* 26.11.1853; *RN* 27.11.1853; *PG* 1.4.1854; *PC* 1.4.1854; Amalgamated Committee balance sheet, week ending 16.4.1854 in DDPr 138/87b (L.C.R.O.).

Notes to pages 66–71

129 The Liverpool Trades' Guardians Association, established in 1848, has a strong claim to be regarded as the earliest of all Trades' Councils, and had already assisted a number of unions in other towns: S. and B. Webb, p. 225, n. 1.
130 *LM* 20.5.1853, 3.6.1853, 13.9.1853, 23.5.1854; *PPa* 18.2.1854; *PG* 1.4.1854.
131 *RN* 12.2.1854; Amalgamated Committee balance sheet, week ending 16.4.1854, in DDPr 138/87b (L.C.R.O.).
132 Amalgamated Committee balance sheet, week ending 1.1.1854, in DDPr 138/87b (L.C.R.O.).
133 *RN* 4.12.1853. 20.11.1853; *PPa* 19.11.1853; *RN* 15.1.1854; *PPa* 17.12.1853; *RN* 5.2.1854.
134 *PG* 29.4.1854.
135 *RN* 11.12.1853; *Brighton Gazette* 2.2.1854; *Sussex Herald* 4.2.1854. Conningham was later MP for Brighton.
136 Amalgamated Committee balance sheet, weeks ending 1.1.1854 and 16.4.1854.
137 *GS* 31.12.1853; *RN* 22.1.1854.
138 *GS*, various issues, July 1853 to June 1854.
139 *RN* 7.5.1854.
140 A. Plummer, *Bronterre: a political biography of Bronterre O'Brien, 1804–1864* (1971), pp. 225–8; A.R. Schoyen, *The Chartist Challenge: a portrait of George Julian Harney* (1958); S. Shipley, *Club Life and Socialism in Mid-Victorian London* (Oxford, 1971).
141 S. and B. Webb, pp. 168–77; Gillespie, pp. 41–3, 48–9; above pp. 24–6; and M.A. Shepherd, 'The Origins and Incidence of the Term "Labour Aristocracy" ', *Bulletin of the Society for the Study of Labour History* (Vol. 37) 1978, pp. 51–67.
142 G.D.H. Cole and D. Filson (Eds.), *British Working Class Movements: select documents 1789–1875* (1967), p. 464.
143 Gillespie, pp. 38–45, 100–2; *PPa* 15.5.1852; for William Newton, see *Dictionary of Labour Biography* II, pp. 270–6.
144 See J.B. Jefferys, *The Story of the Engineers, 1800–1945* (1970 Edn.); T. Hughes, 'Account of the Lock-Out of Engineers, 1851–2', in *Trades' Societies and Strikes* (1860); K. Burgess, 'Trade Union Policy and the 1852 Lock-Out in the British Engineering Industry', *I.R.S.H.* (Vol. 17) 1972.
145 *RN* 1.2.1852, 7.3.1852, 28.3.1852, 4.4.1852; T. Hughes, p. 183.
146 *RN* 25.4.1852.
147 *RN* 30.10.1853, 6.11.1853.
148 *RN* 27.11.1853.
149 He did not speak in Preston between 19 November and 2 December.
150 *PPa* 3.12.1853; *RN* 4.12.1853 (which makes no mention of Jones's presence, possibly because of George Reynolds's bitter hatred of him!).
151 *PPa* 10.12.1853; *RN* 11.12.1853.
152 *Weekly Dispatch* 11.12.1853.
153 *RN* 18.12.1853.
154 *RN* 25.12.1853.
155 *RN* weekly reports, January to June 1854.
156 *RN* 15.1.1854.
157 *RN* 5.2.1854.
158 *RN* 23.4.1854.
159 *Financial Report of the Income and Expenditure of the Amalgamated Committee of Trades and Factory Operatives, during the Preston Lockout, Commencing August 12, 1853, and Terminating May 15, 1854* (DDPr 138/86 (L.C.R.O.)); Lowe, pp. 254–6. (The Amalgamated Committee provided one-twentieth of the weavers' income, and one-ninth of the spinners'.)

Chapter 4 The Masters

1 Clay; Livesey.
2 *PC* 13.2.1847; *PG* 12.6.1852; 1852 Pollbook in L.C.R.O.; *PG* 13.8.1853; *PC* 15.10.1853; *PG* 1.7.1865 (obituary); *Preston Herald* supplement, 28.6.1865 (obituary) in DDX 140/19 (L.C.R.O.).
3 *PC* 29.2.1840, 11.6.1841, 24.7.1841, 12.10.1844; *PG* 31.7.1847; *PC* 17.6.1848; *PG* 17.4.1852, 11.9.1852; 1852 Pollbook (L.C.R.O.); *PG* 29.3.1862 (obituary). For the Rodgett–Hollins affair, see above p. 123.
4 *PG* 28.4.1866 (obituary of Charles Swainson); W.A. Abram, *A History of Blackburn* (Blackburn, 1877), pp. 389–90.
5 *PG* 10.2.1855 (obituary of John Paley Senior); *PG* 18.7.1857 (obituary of John Paley Junior).
6 *PPi* 31.12.1853; *MG* 1.2.1854; A. Hewitson, *Preston Town Council, or portraits of local legislators* (Preston, 1870), pp. 21–4.
7 *PC* 29.2.1840, 25.6.1841, 17.6.1848; *MG* 1.2.1854.
8 *PC* 29.2.1840, 16.10.1841, 17.6.1848, 16.3.1850; 1852 Pollbook; *PG* 21.11.1868 (obituary).
9 Hewitson (1870), pp. 49–53.
10 See the Open Letter 'To Joseph Gillow, Esq.', by 'Consistency', offprint from *PC* 4.2.1865, DDPr 131/34 (L.C.R.O.).
11 See *PC* 27.4.1844, 7.2.1846.
12 *PG* 5.11.1853; Hewitson (1870), pp. 27–31; *PG* 18.10.1873 (obituary). The minutes of a directors' meeting of the Preston Banking Company, 24.11.1853 (now in the archives of the Midland Bank in London) record a loan of £1,000 to Richard Goodair, guaranteed by his father John.
13 J. Vincent (Ed.), *Disraeli, Derby and the Conservative Party: journals and memoirs of Edward Henry, Lord Stanley, 1849–1869* (Brighton, 1978), p. 112. The importance of their supposed moral superiority in the formation of employers' attitude towards trades unionists is emphasised by M.I. Thomis, *Responses to Industrialisation: the British experience 1780–1850* (Newton Abbot, 1976), pp. 78–81.
14 *Final Report* of the Masters' Defence Fund cited from *MG* 24.6.1854. All our attempts to track down an original copy of the *Report* proved fruitless. The £165,000 referred to as the cost of the dispute to the Preston masters is not to be taken as indicative of the amount subscribed by employers elsewhere, for which – alas – no evidence survives.
15 Placard issued by Preston Masters' Association 1.11.1853 in DDPr 138/87b (L.C.R.O.).
16 See more generally E.P. Thompson, 'Rough Music: le charivari anglais' *Annales E.S.C.*, 27e Annee II (1972), pp. 285–312.
17 Masters' Defence Fund Statement, 31.1.1854, cited *MG* 1.2.1854.
18 H. Ashworth, *The Preston Strike: an enquiry into its causes and consequences* (Manchester, 1854), pp. 15–16.
19 And indeed later: see W.H. Fraser, pp. 98–9.
20 Richard Cobden to F.W. Cobden 16.8.1842, cited J. Morley, *The Life of Richard Cobden* (1903), p. 299.
21 W. Cooke Taylor, *Notes of a Tour in the Manufacturing Districts of Lancashire* (1842; reprinted 1969), p. 99.
22 For Cobden's Barnsley speech, see *PC* 5.11.1853. Bright's address to the Manchester Chamber of Commerce is in *PG* 4.2.1854. Both should be compared with James Aspinall Turner's lengthy attack on the strikers at the Manchester Commercial Association (*PG* 4.2.1854).

Notes to pages 82–7

23. Add. MSS. 43,653 and 43,654: Richard Cobden to Henry Ashworth 29.11.1853. See also Cobden's letter to Ashworth 17.6.1854 urging him to moderate the tone of his pamphlet.
24. Samuel Robinson, *Friendly Letters on the Recent Strikes from a Manufacturer to his own Workpeople* (1854), p. 21.
25. Ashworth (1854), p. 98.
26. Anon. [Charles Dickens] 'On Strike' *Household Words*, 8, 11.2.1854, p. 558.
27. Add. MSS. 43,383: Bright to Cobden 5.11.1853.
28. *BM* 15.10.1853.
29. *PG* 21.1.1854.
30. *Morning Herald* 1.11.1853.
31. See A.P. Donajgrodzki, ' "Social Police" and the Bureaucratic Elite: a vision of order in the age of reform', in Donajgrodzki (Ed.), *Social Control in Nineteenth Century Britain* (1977), pp. 51–76.
32. *MET* 14.1.1854. See also R. Johnson, 'Educational Policy and Social Control in Early Victorian England', *Past and Present* (No. 49) 1970, pp. 96–119.
33. *PG* 1.7.1865 (obituary of Thomas Miller).
34. Clay, pp. 520–1; *PC* 9.3.1850. The chapel was soon opened to the public owing to the poor attendance of the factory hands.
35. Catterall's provisions for his operatives dated from 1844. In the following two years Horrockses, Gardner, John Paley and William Taylor all provided mill baths, and Taylor opened a library. William Calvert established a reading room at his mill in 1852. (*PG* 11.5.1844, 23.9.1844, 6.9.1845, 25.4.1846, 30.5.1846, 27.6.1846, 1.1.1853.) Dutton and King (1979b).
36. *PC, PG, PPi* 15.1.1848, 22.1.1848, 29.1.1848. 'If the very Devil were to appear in human shape', said Richard Marsden, 'and take the character of a millowner in Preston, he could not outbeat [sic] Mr. Goodair'. (*PG* 15.1.1848.) It was not until 1851 – two years after the Ten Hours Act had come into force – that Goodair abandoned the twelve-hour day at his mill (*PC* 29.3.1851).
37. 'A Preston Manufacturer', *Strikes Prevented* (London and Manchester, 1854). (A copy is contained in DDPr 138/87b (L.C.R.O.)). 'Coming from a district where a good feeling between the employer and the employed' prevails, the anonymous author has 25 years' experience as a cotton master, and is 'totally unconnected with the movements of the Preston Masters' Association'. He is, without doubt, John Goodair.
38. *PC* 10.12.1853 and 17.12.1853. Gillow supported Sir George Strickland's call for a compromise settlement to the strike (*PC* 24.12.1853).
39. *PG* 30.10.1847.
40. *MG* 2.7.1853, 9.7.1853, 13.7.1853.
41. *BS* 21.9.1853.
42. *Times* 8.11.1853 (cited *PG* 12.11.1853); Lowe, pp. 214–15. The discharge note was frequently employed by anti-union employers to blacklist potential troublemakers and check excessive labour turnover.
43. For example, it reports that Ainsworth circulated members in 1844 concerning a proposed levy, and names three firms (Threlfall, Eccles and Naylor) which benefited from his mediation two years later. Documentary corroboration for these events, at least, must have been available.
44. *PC* 13.8.1842, 15.5.1847, 18.9.1847.
45. See *PG* and *PC*, all issues for February and March 1849.
46. *PG* 22.10.1853; Adam Smith, *The Wealth of Nations*, (1961, Methuen Edn.) Vol. I, p. 75.
47. 1852 Pollbook; Mannex and Co., *History, Topography and Directory of Mid-Lancashire*,

with *An Essay on Geology* (Preston, 1854). Probably in the same area were Wellington Terrace (J. Haslam, J. Hawkins) and Stephenson Terrace (William Lancaster, Henry Seed, R. Slater), which no longer exist.
48 Hardwick, p. 434.
49 *Ibid.*, p. 434, p. 453.
50 See above, chapter 9.
51 Unattributed cutting in DDPr 138/87b (L.C.R.O.), containing a list of partners dated 28.1.1854.
52 See for example *BA* 1.7.1852, 1.10.1852.
53 *PC* 13.2.1847. In Preston, John Cooper and Robert Gardner were prominent supporters of the Ten Hours Bill.
54 *PC* 17.1.1852.
55 See the letter from 'A Manufacturer' in *MG* 2.7.1853, and the editorial in the pro-union *GS* 26.11.1853.
56 Boyson (1970), p. 63.
57 Challinor and Ripley, p. 171, n. 1.
58 *BS* 21.9.1853; *MG* 5.10.1853.
59 Unattributed press cutting 23.8.1855 in *DDPr* 138/87b (*L.C.R.O.*) (Case of Wilson versus Eckersley).
60 See above, p. 180.
61 Four signatories of the association's lock-out notice were reported by *PG* 18.2.1854 as running on terms satisfactory to the operatives: these were Gardner and Walsh, Thomas Blackhurst, R. Almond and Miles Rodgett Junior. The association issued public statements asserting that the latter two concerns were complying with its instructions, but it is far from clear that this was so. (*PC* 24.12.1853, 11.2.1854).
62 Information on the behaviour of individual firms is patchy, and our inferences should be treated with caution. Basic sources are the list of signatories to the Preston Masters' Association's proclamation of 15 September, DDPr 138/87b (L.C.R.O.); two lists of firms 'locked-up' in October (*PC* 15.10.1853; *PG* 22.10.1853); and two lists of mills working and of the numbers employed at various firms in February and April 1854 (*PG* 18.2.1854; *PC* 22.4.1854). For Bashall and Boardman, see also *PC* 29.10.1953; *PPi* 10.12.1853, 31.12.1853; and *BC* 10.12.1853.
63 *PC* 29.10.1853; *BS* 11.1.1854; *PC* 18.2.1854; *PG* 4.3.1854.
64 *PC* 21.1.1854; *PG* 18.2.1854.
65 *BS* 11.1.1854, *PG* and *PC* 14.1.1854; *PG* 18.2.1854.
66 *PG* 7.1.1854; *PC* 14.1.1854.
67 The cases of Messrs Ashworth (Walton), R. Orrell (Lostock), Rodgett Bros (Walton) and R. Worden, are deeply obscure.
68 See Ward (1962); *PC* 27.8.1853.
69 *PC* 15.3.1845.
70 Hewitson (1870), pp. 32–4; *PG* 22.10.1854; *PC* 22.10.1853.
71 *PG* 18.12.1852; 1852 Pollbook (plumps for the Tory, R.T. Parker).
72 See the speeches by the Blackburn delegates William Walton (*PC* 15.10.1853) and John Lang (*PG* 3.12.1853).
73 *PC* 11.6.1841.
74 Abram, pp. 372–3, 389–90, 621; *BS* 23.2.1853, 30.3.1853; *Times* 31.3.1853.
75 *BS* 16.11.1853, 23.11.1853.
76 *PC* 16.3.1850, 23.3.1850.
77 See above, p. 36.
78 See also P. Joyce, 'The Factory Politics of Lancashire in the Later Nineteenth Century', *Hist. J.* (Vol. 18) 1975, pp. 525–53.

79 *BS* 14.9.1853. Now MP for the borough, Feilden's offence was that he had voted against T.S. Duncombe's Combination of Workmen Bill.

Chapter 5 Locked Out (15 October 1853–9 February 1854)
1. *PC* 15.10.1853; *PG* 22.10.1853.
2. *PG* 22.10.1853.
3. *PG* 19.11.1853.
4. Bashall's of Farington.
5. *PG* 22.10.1853.
6. Ashworth (1854), p. 25.
7. *PC* 7.10.1854: Males — 620 boys under 13; 1,530 youths between 13 and 17; 4,050 men 18 and over. Females — 650 girls under 13; 4,400 girls between 13 and 17; 6,750 women 18 and over. Lowe, p. 217, accepts this estimate, and reports that the locked-out firms operated 3,000 horse-power, while 3,000 hands remained at work.
8. Gayer, Rostow and Schwartz, I, p. 456.
9. The range of market discount rates was 2–2½% in the second quarter of 1853, and 4½–5½% in the fourth quarter: see J.R.T. Hughes, *Fluctuations in Trade, Industry and Finance: a study of British economic development 1850–1860* (Oxford, 1960), p. 265, table 98.
10. Hughes, *ibid.*, p. 79, p. 86.
11. Boyson (1970), p. 30, table 8.
12. On the harvest, see *Economist* 3.9.1853 and 15.10.1853. On 28 May 1853 a quarter of wheat sold for 43s 9d, much the same as a year previously. By 15 October it fetched 68s 4d; the price peaked at 83s 3d on 28 January 1854, an increase of 90% over eight months (*Economist*, those dates).
13. *PC* 8.10.1853.
14. *PG* 15.10.1853.
15. *PC* 15.10.1853.
16. *BS* 26.10.1853.
17. *LJ* 5.11.1853.
18. *PG, PC, LGa*, all 22.10.1853.
19. *MG* 26.10.1853; *PG* 29.10.1853.
20. Hume to Walton, 26.10.1853, cited *PG* 29.10.1853.
21. *PG* 29.10.1853.
22. *PG* 29.10.1853; *PC* 29.10.1853.
23. It is only fair to add that another issue influenced the outcome in at least one ward, the authorities having incurred deep hostility through their recent suppression of pig-keeping within the borough.
24. *BS* 19.10.1853.
25. *BS* 26.10.1853; *SA* 28.10.1853.
26. *PC* 29.10.1853.
27. *PG* 5.11.1853.
28. *PG* 22.10.1853.
29. *PG, PC, PP*, all 29.10.1853; *SA* 28.10.1853. Fraser, p. 163 treats this story as well-founded, but names the donor as Sir John Pakington. We have found no confirmation of this.
30. *PG* 29.10.1853.
31. *LGa* 12.11.1853.
32. Master Spinners' Association, dated 1 November 1853, in DDPr 138/87b (L.C.R.O.). See also letter by Birley Bros, *Times*, 3.11.1853.

Notes to pages 97–103

33 *PG* 5.11.1853.
34 *PG* 5.11.1853; Lowe, pp. 217–18.
35 *BA* November 1853.
36 According to Luke Wood, speaking in Preston on 29 October: see *PG* 5.11.1853.
37 *LGa* 5.11.1853.
38 *BS* 12.10.1853; *BM* 15.10.1853; *Factory Operative's Guide* 5.11.1853.
39 The *Morning Herald*'s estimate (29.10.53) of 60–70,000 appears to be exaggerated (it includes the spurious figure of 25,000 at Preston, and the 20,000 for Burnley and Padiham is almost certainly too high).
40 *PG* 5.11.1853; *BC* 10.12.1853.
41 *SA* 11.11.1853.
42 *BS* 9.11.1853.
43 *LGa* 5.11.1853; *PC* 31.12.1853.
44 *WO* 5.11.1853.
45 *WO* 5.11.1853; *ILN* 5.11.1853; HO/45/5128: Postmaster (Wigan) to Palmerston 28.10.1853; N. Eckersley (Mayor) to Palmerston, 31.10.1853.
46 *ILN* 5.11.1853; HO/45/5128: Eckersley to Palmerston (telegram) 31.10.1853. See also Eckersley to Palmerston, 1.11.1853, 4.11.1853.
47 *Economist* 5.11.1853.
48 *PG* 12.11.1853.
49 *PC* 22.10.1853, 26.11.1853.
50 Clay to Henry Ashworth 21.7.1854, in the unpaginated section of DDPr 138/87a (L.C.R.O.).
51 *LJ* 5.11.1853.
52 Clay to Miss Carpenter, 10.1.1854, in W.L. Clay, p. 619.
53 *Ibid.*, p. 553, n. 1. See also M. Hewitt, *Wives and Mothers in Victorian Industry* (1958), on the adverse effects of working mothers. For a different view, see Anderson, p. 74.
54 Ballad, 'Uncle Ned; or, the Preston strike' in DDPr 138/87b (L.C.R.O.).
55 *Household Words* No. 194, 10.12.1853, pp. 345–6.
56 Clay to Henry Ashworth, 21.7.1854, DDPr 138/87a (L.C.R.O.).
57 *PC* 29.10.1853; *PG* 19.11.1853.
58 *MG* 30.11.1853.
59 *PG* 3.12.1853.
60 *PG* 19.11.1853.
61 *PG* 26.11.1853.
62 *LGa* 19.11.1853.
63 *BS* 23.11.1853; *Economist* 26.11.1853.
64 *PG* 31.12.1853.
65 *PG* 29.10.1853.
66 *LGa* 26.11.1853; Lowe, p. 219.
67 *BS* 30.11.1853; Lowe, p. 219; HO/45/5128: Preston manufacturers to Palmerston, 21.11.1853.
68 *BS* 30.3.1853; *Times* 31.3.1853 (on the election riots of March 1853); *PC* 26.11.1853.
69 *PG* 26.11.1853.
70 For background see HO/45/5128: Chief Constable of Lancashire to Palmerston, 18.11.1853; Thomas Dugdale (Mayor) to Palmerston 19.11.1853 and 30.11.1853.
71 *PG* 19.11.1853; see above, chapter 9.
72 *PG* 26.11.1853.
73 *PG* 3.12.1853.
74 Lowe, pp. 220–1.
75 *BS* 30.11.1853; *BA* December 1853.

Notes to pages 103–9

76 *BS* 16.11.1853.
77 *BA* November 1853, December 1853 (text of resolution); *BS* 30.11.1853; *PG* 3.12.1853.
78 *BS* 30.11.1853.
79 *WO* 5.11.1853.
80 *WE* 25.11.1853, 2.12.1853.
81 *BO* 1.12.1853; *SA* 2.12.1853, 16.12.1853.
82 *SA* 30.12.1853.
83 *PG* 17.12.1853.
84 *BS* 21.12.1853, 28.12.1853; *PG* 18.2.1854; *PC* 4.3.1854.
85 *PG* 3.12.1853; *SA* 9.12.1853; *BC* 10.12.1853.
86 *PG* 3.12.1853.
87 *BS* 7.12.1853, 14.12.1853; *NDT* 19.12.1853.
88 *SA* 9.12.1853; *BC* 10.12.1853.
89 *WE* 30.12.1853; *PC* 31.12.1853.
90 *Liverpool Albion* 16.1.1854.
91 *SA* 3.3.1854.
92 *WE* 9 & 16.12.1853; *SA* 9 & 16.12.1853; *Weekly Dispatch* 11.12.1853.
93 *WE* 23.12.1853.
94 The bond was eventually found to be void in law.
95 *WE* 6 & 13.1.1854, 3.2.1854.
96 Placard, 'The Mills Reopened to the Factory Operatives of Preston', by 'An Observer', 3.12.1853. DDPr 138/87b (L.C.R.O.).
97 *BC* 10.12.1853.
98 *PC*, *PP*, *PG*, all 10.12.1853; *PG* 17.12.1853.
99 *BC* 10.12.1853; *PG* 10.12.1853, 31.12.1853. According to a local legend this term originated during a dispute at nearby Catterall, when an old man said of a group of blacklegs, 'They are no better than my knobstick, and I can make as good men as them out of it.' (*PC* 5.11.1853). See also Lowe, pp. 229–30.
100 *PG* 10.12.1853.
101 *PG* 17.12.1853.
102 *BC* 10.12.1853; *Weekly Dispatch* 11.12.1853; *WE* 16.12.1853.
103 *PG* 17.12.1853.
104 *NDT* 14.12.1853; *PG* 17.12.1853; *MET* 17.12.1853.
105 *PG* 17.12.1853.
106 *LGa* 24.12.1853.
107 *NDT* 19.12.1853; *PC* 7.1.1854.
108 *BS* 28.12.1853.
109 *PC* & *PG* 31.12.1853.
110 *PG* 12.12.1853.
111 *BS* 21.12.1853.
112 *PPi* 31.12.1853; *PC* 7.1.1854.
113 *PC*, *PG* 31.12.1853.
114 *PG*, *PC*, *PPi* 24.12.1853.
115 Lowe, pp. 222–6.
116 *MET* 28.12.1853; *PG* 31.12.1853; *PC* 7.1.1854; Lowe, pp. 226–7.
117 *PG* 7, 21, 28.1.1854; *PC* 14 & 28.1.1854.
118 *PG* 14.1.1854, 28.1.1854, 4.2.1854; *PC* 14.1.1854.
119 *PC* 4.2.1854.
120 *SA* 30.11.1853, 6.1.1854; *BS* 30.11.1853; *Economist* 24.12.1853, p. 1439, 14.1.1854, p. 35; *MG* 4.1.1854.

121 *SA* 10.2.1854.
122 *Plymouth, Devonport & Stonehouse Herald* 14 & 21.1.1854; HO/45/5244E 13.1.1854: Montague B. Bere to Palmerston (Mayor to Palmerston 13.1.1854); Henry Cartwright to Palmerston 14.1.1854; Magistrates to Palmerston 16.1.1854; Mayor to Palmerston 20.1.1854.
123 Placard, 'The £5,000 bond. Where is the money to go?' by 'Onesimus, a Servant', 28 December 1853 DDPr 138/87b (L.C.R.O.).
124 *PC* 14.1.1854.
125 *MG* 11.1.1854.
126 *PG* 28.1.1854.
127 Text of resolution passed 29.1.1854 in Lowe, p. 232.
128 *MG* 11.1.1854.
129 *PG* 4.2.1854.
130 *MG* 1.2.1854; Anon. [Charles Dickens] 'On Strike', *Household Words*, 8, 11.2.1854, pp. 533–9.
131 H.I. Dutton and J.E. King, 'The Society of Arts and the Preston Strike, 1853–54', *Journal of the Royal Society of Arts* (July, August, September) 1979.
132 R.S.A. Council Minutes 4.1.1854, p. 80.
133 *Journal of the Society of Arts* (Supplement) Vol. II, pp. 189–207.
134 *RN* 15.1.1854, 22.1.1854, 29.1.1854 (but note the more favourable reaction of *LWN* 5.2.1854, 19.2.1854). Jones's *People's Paper* ignored it totally.
135 *Examiner* 28.1.1854, 4.2.1854; see also *Economist* 4.2.1854; *Morning Chronicle* 7.1.1854.
136 *PG* 21.1.1854; *PC* 28.1.1854. See also the statement of the Masters' Defence Fund, 31 January 1854 (*MG* 1.2.1854).
137 *MG* 11.2.1854.
138 *PG* 11.2.1854.
139 Lowe, pp. 231–2.
140 *PG* 21.1.1854, 11.2.1854 (case of girls from Farington employed at Hollins's Preston mill).
141 *PC* 28.1.1854.
142 *PC* 11.2.1854; *PG* 11.2.1854; Lowe, *op. cit.* pp. 232–3.
143 *PC* 11.2.1854.
144 *PG* 11.2.1854.
145 *SA* 24.2.1854.
146 *PG* 11.2.1854; *PC* 18.2.1854.
147 *PG* 11.2.1854.
148 *PG* 18.2.1854.
149 *PG* 11 & 18.2.1854.
150 *PG* 18.2.1854.
151 *PG* 11.2.1854.
152 *PC* 18.2.1854.
153 *PG* 18.2.1854. Lowe, pp. 229–30.
154 *PC* 11.2.1854.
155 *PC* 18.2.1854.
156 *PC* 25.2.1854.
157 *PC* 18.2.1854.
158 *PG* 18 & 25.2.1854; *PC* 18.2.1854.
159 *PG* 18.2.1854.
160 See below, pp. 146–8.
161 *PG* 25.2.1854.

162 *PC* 18.2.1854.
163 *PC* 28 & 25.2.1854.
164 *PC* 4.2.1854.
165 *PG* 11.2.1854.
166 *PC* 18.2.1854.
167 Lowe, p. 234.
168 *PG* 25.2.1854.
169 *PC* 25.2.1854.
170 *PG* 4.3.1854.

Chapter 6 Council and Bench

1. A. Hewitson, *Preston Town Council* (Preston, 1870), p. 5.
2. The Preston Watch Committee also included the police superintendent.
3. For a general discussion of the ladder of authority see F.C. Mather, *Public Order in the Age of the Chartists* (London, 1959), Ch. 2.
4. 1835 Municipal Corporation Act, 5 & 6 W IV c 76.
5. H.W. Clemesha, *A History of Preston in Amounderness* (Manchester, 1912), pp. 231–9.
6. Fishwick, a separate township, had been included in the borough for the purposes of parliamentary elections since the Boundaries Act of 1832. The Corporation Act simply adopted these boundaries for municipal elections.
7. Many complained that November was too inclement for the pomp and ceremony of elections. See Thomas Hood's ironic 'Ode for the Ninth of November':
   > But still if one must have a Mayor,
   >> To fill the Civic Chair
   >> O Lud, I say
   >> Was there no better day
   > To fix on than November Ninth so shivery
   > And dull for showing off the Livery's livery.
8. A.J. Berry, *Proud Preston's Story* (Preston, 1928), p. 280.
9. W. Dobson, *The Preston Municipal Elections, 1835–1862* (Preston, 1862).
10. A candidate for election to the council had to own real or personal property to the value of £1,000 or occupy property worth £30.
11. D. Fraser, *Urban Politics in Victorian England* (1976), p. 118.
12. *PC* 5.11.1853.
13. Hewitson (1870), p. 44; *PG* 5.11.1853.
14. *PC* 5.11.1853.
15. See above p. 123.
16. *PC* 5.11.1853.
17. Hewitson (1870), p. 30.
18. *PG* 5.11.1853.
19. *PG* 10.12.1853; *PC* 17.12.1853. Gillow also supported legislation against employers' associations.
20. See above p. 185.
21. *PG* 5.11.1853.
22. *PPi* 5.11.1853.
23. E.P. Hennock, *Fit and Proper Persons: ideal and reality in nineteenth-century urban government* (1973), p. 11.
24. *PC* 1.10.1853. See *Select Committee on Assessing and Collecting the Poor Rates, Highway Rates in respect of Small Tenements* (Parl. Papers, 1859) Vol. VII, p. 460. By 1858 the number of voters had increased to 5,738.

Notes to pages 119–24

25 Hennock (1973), pp. 11–12. Information on the Rating Act is largely drawn from Hennock's work.
26 59 G III c 12.
27 *PC* 1.10.1853.
28 Louis Napoleon had seized power in France two years earlier. His dictatorial regime, and alleged determination to invade England, made him universally loathed.
29 *PG* 5.11.1853.
30 *NDT* 1.11.1853.
31 *PG* 5.11.1853. The *Preston Pilot* also noted that one John Hampson impressively presided over a meeting shortly before the Fishwick election where he attacked the manufacturers' monopoly of the town and bench: *PPi* 5.11.1853.
32 *PC* 3.12.1853.
33 E.P. Hennock, 'Finance and Politics in Urban Local Government, 1835–1900', *Hist. J.* (Vol. 6) 1963, pp. 212–25; Hennock (1973), p. 325; Fraser (1976), pp. 152–3.
34 Hardwick, p. 313.
35 *PG* 29.10.1853.
36 Hennock (1973), p. 22.
37 *PC* 24.10.1853.
38 *PC* 24.10.1853.
39 *PC* 29.10.1853. John Paley Jnr was re-elected as mayor in 1847, after having served in this capacity between 1845 and 1846. In 1847 Thomas German was the retiring mayor.
40 An anonymous letter supporting Monk 'because he was not mixed up in our unfortunate disputes' had been published in *PC* 29.10.1853.
41 *PC* 12.11.1853; *PG* 12.11.1853.
42 Hewitson (1870), p. 37.
43 *PC* 29.10.1853. Walmsley had in fact attended only 14 council meetings since his election.
44 Fraser (1976), p. 149.
45 Thomas Miller, William Shawe, John Paley Snr, John Paley Jnr, William Humber, Richard Horrocks. The others elected were Peter Catterall (solicitor), John Catterall, Robert Birchall (tobacconist), Robert Brown (surgeon) and Thomas Monk (solicitor).
46 Fraser (1976), pp. 131, 150–1.
47 Thomas Miller (cotton), Daniel Arkwright (cotton), John Bairstow (Gent.), William Clayton (butcher), John Cardwell (Gent.), George Jacson (cotton), Thomas German (flax spinner), James Mounsey (roper) all appointed 1839. John Paley Snr (cotton) appointed in 1840. William Taylor (cotton) appointed 1841. George Cardwell (corn dealer), Richard Pedder (tobacco), John Addison (barrister), Richard Ainsworth (cotton) appointed 1846. Robert Lowe (silversmith), John Paley Jnr (cotton), William Birley (cotton), Paul Catterall (cotton) appointed in 1847.
48 HO/43/83 H. Waddington to Catterall 2.9.1853; H. Waddington to Duchy of Lancaster 2.9.1853.
49 Ironically Ainsworth's own appointment to the bench in 1846 was the only other occasion the council had been by-passed in this way. The committee included Alderman Brown and Councillors Parker, Spencer, Humber (J.), Goodair and Myres. HO 45/4582 Robert Ascroft to Palmerston 26.10.1853.
50 HO/45/4582, *ibid.*
51 *PC* 7.1.1854.
52 *PC* 1.10.1853.
53 *PG* 10.9.1853, 8.10.1853.
54 HO/45/4582.
55 *PPi* 3.9.1853.

Notes to pages 124–9

56 *PG* 10.9.1853.
57 *PG* 17.9.1853.
58 The five arrested were aged 13 to 17 years.
59 HO/45/5128.
60 HO/45/5128 Catterall to Palmerston 10.9.1853.
61 HO/45/5128 Catterall to Palmerston 16.9.1853.
62 *PG* 17.9.1853.
63 *PG* 24.9.1853.
64 *PG* 1.10.1853.
65 *PG* 4.3.1854.
66 HO/45/5244^B Mayor to Palmerston 3.3.1854 (our emphasis throughout).
67 HO/45/5244^B Mayor to Palmerston 7.3.1854.
68 HO/45/5244^B Mayor to Palmerston 7.3.1854, 15.3.1854. Compared to the riots in Blackburn and Wigan in the previous year, these were hardly dramatic incidents.
69 HO/45/5244^B Lowe to Palmerston 7.3.1854.
70 *PG* 4.3.1854.
71 HO/45/5244^B Mayor to Palmerston 5.5.1854.
72 HO/45/5244^B Mayor to Palmerston 15.3.1854.
73 HO/45/5244^B Mayor to Palmerston 3.3.1854.
74 HO/45/5244^B Lowe to Palmerston 7.3.1854.
75 HO/45/5244^B Baxendale and Whalley to Palmerston 7.3.1854.
76 HO/45/5244^B.
77 HO/45/5244^B Mayor to Palmerston 15.3.1854.
78 HO/45/5244^B.
79 HO/45/5244^B Mayor to Palmerston 7.3.1854.
80 HO/45/5244^B.
81 HO/45/5244^B note dated 13.3.1854.
82 *PG* 4.3.1854.
83 *PG* 11.3.1854.
84 HO/45/5244^B Mayor to Palmerston 5.5.1854.
85 See above p. 187.
86 HO/45/5244^B Rayner to Palmerston 13.4.1854.
87 HO/45/5244^B Mayor to Palmerston 15.3.1854.
88 *PG* 1.4.1854.
89 HO/45/5244^B Walmsley to Palmerston 5.5.1854; see enclosed *Public Petitions: Appendix to 23rd Report*: App. 565, pp. 245–6.
90 *Select Committee on the Police* (Parl. Papers, 1852–3) Vol. XXXVI, p. 97.
91 T.A. Critchley, *A History of Police in England and Wales 900–1966* (1967). This increase was probably due to Reform Bill riots in 1831 (p. 60).
92 Hewitson (1870), p. 332.
93 E. Midwinter, *Social Administration in Lancashire, 1830–1860: Poor Law, public health and the police* (Manchester, 1969), p. 148.
94 Midwinter *ibid.*, p. 143.
95 Mather (1959), p. 241; Critchley, p. 103; Hewitson (1870), p. 333.
96 Preston Watch Committee (hereafter PWC) Nov. 1844 to Oct. 1851. This volume is wrongly titled, as it does in fact contain records of meetings through to Nov. 1853. The error seems to have arisen out of faulty pagination. The records of the PWC can be found in the Preston Town Hall Muniment Room.
97 *MET* 7.1.1854.
98 Walmsley (Mayor), J. Catterall, J. Paley Jnr, R. Pedder, P. Catterall, Shawe, Monk

(Aldermen), J. Humber, H. Armstrong, R. Threlfall, I. Gate, T. Dixon, Spencer, M. Myres, Watson, H. Armstrong, J. Raw, J. Goodair, G. Smith (Councillors).
99 For a more general discussion see J. Hart, *The British Police* (1951).
100 *MG* 6.7.1853. HO/45/5128 Earl Cathcart to Lord Palmerston 4.7.1853.
101 *PG* 30.7.1853.
102 PWC 1.8.1853.
103 PWC 6.1.1854; 17.7.1854 (Nov. 1853 to Oct. 1862). Constables were also provided with 1 pair of handcuffs, 1 truncheon, 1 coat, 2 pairs trousers, 1 great coat, 1 cape, 1 hat and 2 pairs Blucher boots.
104 *PG* 26.2.1853; Hewitson (1870), p. 334; PWC 6.6.1853.
105 PWC 5.9.1853; *PG* 10.9.1853; *PG* 24.9.1853.
106 *PC* 29.10.1853; *PG* 10.9.1853.
107 *PC* 12.11.1853, 19.11.1853.
108 HO/45/5244^B T. Walmsley to Lord Palmerston 2.3.1854.
109 Mather (1959).
110 Usually 3s 6d per day *PG* 11.3.1854.
111 HO/45/5128 Magistrates of Glossop to Lord Palmerston 22.12.1853.
112 Extra special constables were sworn in on 4 March 1854: HO/45/5244^B Walmsley to Lord Palmerston 3.3.1854.
113 HO/45/5244^B Thomas Dodd to Lord Palmerston 23.4.1854.
114 HO/45/5128 Nath. Eckersley to Lord Palmerston 31.10.1853.
115 HO/45/5128 Mayor to Lord Palmerston 29.6.1853.
116 *PC* 8.10.1853; *PG* 8.10.1853.
117 George Smith's phrasing: *PG* 8.10.1853.
118 PWC 14.11.1853.
119 *PC* 29.10.1853.
120 PWC 2.12.1853.
121 *PC* 19.11.1853.
122 Midwinter, pp. 154–5.
123 HO/45/5128 N. Eckersley to Lord Palmerston 31.10.1853; HO/45/5128 Mayor to Lord Palmerston 11.11.1853.
124 Midwinter, p. 154.
125 HO/45/5244^C 24.4.1854.
126 *PC* 12.11.1853.
127 PWC 18.4.1855.
128 *Hansard* (3rd Series) Vol. 140, 1856, pp. 2128, 2131.
129 Hewitson (1870), p. 330.
130 For the months January to May expenditure increased from £950 18s 4d in 1852 to £1,473 17s 11d in 1854 (PWC 17.7.1854).

	£	s	d
1 Sept. 1851 to 31 Aug. 1852	2,216	17	2
1 Sept. 1852 to 31 Aug. 1853	2,290	3	6
1 Sept. 1853 to 31 Aug. 1854	2,940	12	10

Taken from *Council Proceedings*.
131 HO/4/13, cf. J. Hart, 'Reform of the Borough Police 1835–56', *English Historical Review* (Vol. 70) 1955, p. 418, n. 3.
132 HO/45/5244^B James Lowe to Lord Palmerston 7.3.1854.
133 J.J. Tobias, *Crime and Industrial Society in the Nineteenth Century* (Harmondsworth, 1972), p. 135.
134 J. Clay, *Preston Gaol Chaplain's Reports* 1846–58, p. 33 (L.C.R.O.).

135 HO/45/5244B Cathcart to Lord Palmerston 4.2.1854.
136 A.L. Gallagher, *The Social Control of Working-Class Leisure in Preston, 1850–1875* (Unpublished M.A. Lancaster University, 1975); see also *Report of Select Committee on Public Houses* (Parl. Papers, 1852–3) Vol. XXXVI, pp. 354–75.
137 *DN* 1.11.1853; *RN* 6.11.1853.
138 HO/45/5244B Petition enclosed in a letter from Walmsley to Lord Palmerston 5.5.1854.
139 HO/45/5244B Baxendale to Palmerston 7.3.1854.
140 *PC* 11.2.1854.
141 *PG* 28.1.1854.
142 For some amusing examples of other Lancashire borough police see Midwinter, pp. 156–60.
143 PWC 12.10.1854.
144 Midwinter, p. 160.
145 *PG* 11.3.1854.
146 *PG* 4.3.1854; PWC 2.3.1854.
147 *PG* 4.3.1854.
148 *PG* 18.3.1854.
149 *PG* 4.3.1854.
150 HO/45/5244 (enclosed notes).
151 *PC* 11.3.1854.
152 HO/45/5244B Baxendale to Palmerston.
153 HO/45/5244B Thomas Maudsley to Palmerston 7.3.1854.

Chapter 7 Guardians of the Poor

1 On the political aspects of the Poor Law see D. Fraser, 'The Poor Law as a Political Institution' in D. Fraser (Ed.), *The New Poor Law in the Nineteenth Century* (1976), pp. 111–27.
2 *Economist* 26.11.1853. (This is a reference to the Burnley lock-out.)
3 *Economist* 26.11.1853.
4 Why the problem of Poor Law relief emerged so late in the ten per cent campaign is unclear. Many of the Poor Law Board's records are missing for this period and the Guardian minute books are largely unhelpful. Only in November, when the *Economist* published the correspondence between the Burnley Guardians and the Poor Law Board, was the matter brought to the public's attention.
5 PUZ/1/7 (L.C.R.O.).
6 HO/41/20 Palmerston to Burnley Magistrates 19.10.1853.
7 MH/12/5677 Burnley Union to Poor Law Board 10.10.1853.
8 MH/12/5677 Poor Law Board to Burnley Union 12.11.1853.
9 PUZ/1/7 Burnley Union to Poor Law Board 25.10.1852 (L.C.R.O.).
10 For a general discussion see M.E. Rose, 'The Allowance System under the New Poor Law', *Ec.H.R.* (Vol. 19) 1966, pp. 607–20. The Outdoor Relief Regulation was issued in August 1852 but amended in December 1852 after a storm of protest by the northern Boards of Guardians.
11 MH/12/5677 Burnley Union to Poor Law Board.
12 MH/12/5677 Poor Law Board to Burnley Union 16.11.1853; *Economist* 26.11.1853.
13 Since the guardians were given two to three weeks to send in these applications and since the Board had no right to *ex post facto* disallowance, the guardians had a period of almost a month in which they could grant relief without restriction; see N.C. Edsall, *The Anti-Poor Law Movement, 1834–1844* (Manchester, 1971), p. 256.

14 MH/12/5677.
15 PUZ/1/8 12.11.1853 (L.C.R.O.).
16 MH/12/5677 Burnley Union to Poor Law Board 24.11.1853; PUZ/1/8 24.11.1853 (L.C.R.O.).
17 PUZ/1/8 8.12.1853 (L.C.R.O.).
18 MH/12/5677 Burnley Union to Poor Law Board 9.12.1853.
19 MH/12/5677 see Farnall's notes 9.12.1853, 13.12.1853.
20 MH/12/5677 Burnley Union to Poor Law Board 22.12.1853; PUZ/1/8 22.12.1853 (L.C.R.O.).
21 PUH/1/4 16.12.1853 (L.C.R.O.).
22 Midwinter, pp. 30, 35–6.
23 *PPa* 24.12.1853; PUH/3/3; PUH/1/4 (L.C.R.O.).
24 For a discussion of seven North East Lancashire unions see R. Boyson, 'The New Poor Law in North East Lancashire, 1834–1871', *Trans. Lancs. and Chesh. Antiq. Soc.* (Vol. 112) 1960, pp. 35–7.
25 *PC* 2.10.1852, 16.10.1852.
26 Edsall, pp. 255–6. See also M.E. Rose, 'The New Poor Law in Industrial Areas' in R.M. Hartwell (Ed.), *The Industrial Revolution* (Oxford, 1970), pp. 121–43.
27 *PC* 23.10.1852.
28 *PC* 16.10.1852.
29 Unfortunately, the correspondence between the Preston Union and the Poor Law Board is missing for the period 1853–6. The weekly returns of the number and type (indoor and outdoor) of relief are all that exist and these do not reveal the occupations of those receiving relief. The Guardian minute books are no more helpful since the dispute is barely mentioned. Lowe's brief account (pp. 223–4) suggests that in 'some places neither Farnall nor his advice was received very respectfully'. He claims that the more humane guardians ensured that the operatives were relieved and that the Board refused to implement the labour test. The local press, which religiously reported the Board's Tuesday meetings, present a less favourable picture.
30 *PG* 23.7.1853; *PG* 13.8.1853; *PC* 27.8.1853.
31 PUT/1/18 p. 38 (L.C.R.O.).
32 Farnall was fairly consistent on this point. When Thomas Hoole, a locked-out able bodied cotton spinner, with a wife and five children, was told to apply to Lancaster for non-resident relief he was refused because Farnall told the local poor authorities that 'non-resident outdoor relief in a case like this would in my opinion be highly impolitic. It is impossible to draw any distinction between turnouts and lock-outs at Preston.' MH/12/5893 Note on a letter from Lancaster Union to Poor Law Board 12.12.1853 and Poor Law Board to Lancaster Union 16.12.1853.
33 *PG* 29.10.1853.
34 M.E. Rose (1970), pp. 121–43.
35 *PC* 29.10.1853.
36 *PG* 29.10.1853.
37 *PC* 5.11.1853.
38 *PC* 12.11.1853; *PG* 12.11.1853; *PPi* 12.11.1853.
39 D. Roberts, 'How Cruel was the Victorian Poor Law?', *Hist. J.* (Vol. 6) 1963 claims that Lancashire had some of the worst workhouses, p. 104.
40 *PC* 3.12.1853. Farnall had recommended that at least half of outdoor relief be given in kind: PUT/1/17 p. 266 (L.C.R.O.).
41 PUT/1/17 p. 266 (L.C.R.O.).
42 *PC* 10.12.1853.
43 Within a week 671 were being financed out of union funds. Lowe, p. 221.

44 Very few masters attended Board meetings.
45 *PG* 17.12.1853; *PC* 17.12.1853; *PPi* 17.12.1853. The *Guardian* gives the most extensive coverage of this meeting.
46 W. Proctor, 'Poor Law Administration in Preston Union, 1838–1848', *Trans. Hist. Soc. of Lancs. and Ches.* (Vol. 117) 1965, p. 149.
47 *PC* 16.10.1852.
48 *PC* 2.10.1852.
49 *PG* 29.4.1854.
50 *PG* 17.12.1853.
51 *PG* 10.12.1853; *PG* 21.1.1854; *PG* 11.2.1854.
52 *PG* 7.1.1854.
53 *PC* 7.1.1854. This was carried out: see *6th Annual Report of Poor Law Board* (Parl. Papers, 1854) Vol. XXIX, p. 450; *7th Annual Report of Poor Law Board* (Parl. Papers, 1854–5) Vol. XXIX, p. 76.
54 *PC* 21.12.1854; *PG* 21.1.1854; see above pp. 101, 107.
55 *PC* 14.1.1854; *PG* 14.1.1854.
56 *PC* 21.1.1854.
57 *PG* 11.2.1854; Lowe, p. 233.
58 *PG* 18.2.1854.
59 *PG* 25.2.1854.
60 *PC* 25.2.1854.
61 *PC* 18.2.1854; *PG* 1.4.1854.
62 MH/32/23.
63 *PC* 29.4.1854.
64 *PG* 4.3.1854.
65 *PG* 11.3.1854.
66 *PG* 15.4.1854; *PC* 15.4.1854.
67 *Report from the Select Committee on Poor Removal* (Parl. Papers, 1854–5) Vol. XIII, Appendix 5, p. 339.
68 *PG* 29.4.1854.

Chapter 8 Lord Palmerston

1 *Economist* 26.11.1853.
2 Quoted in J. Ridley, *Lord Palmerston* (1970), p. 414.
3 This point is made by Mather (whose phrasing we use) for the Chartist period; see F.C. Mather, 'Governments and the Chartists' in A. Briggs (Ed.), *Chartist Studies* (1970 Edn.), p. 372. See also Lord Stanley's comment: 'The Preston strike, the chief domestic event of this autumn, came under my notice only in an *indirect* manner', J. Vincent (Ed.), p. 109. (Stress added.)
4 H.C. Bell, 'Palmerston and Parliamentary Representation', *J. Mod. Hist.* (Vol. 4) 1932, p. 193.
5 E. Ashley, *Life and Correspondence: Henry John Temple, Viscount Palmerston*, Vol. 2 (1879), p. 259.
6 *Hansard* (3rd Series) Vol. 136 (1854–5) p. 468.
7 D. Roberts, 'Lord Palmerston at the Home Office', *The Historian* (Vol. 21) 1958–9, p. 79 (Roberts's phrasing).
8 Ridley, p. 414.
9 *Spectator* 31.12.1853.
10 *Morning Post* 26.12.1853.
11 *Times* 16.12.1853.

Notes to pages 150–8

12 See above, chapter 9.
13 Lowe, p. 219.
14 HO/45/5128^{AE} Kinder Smith to Palmerston 21.11.1853.
15 *PPa* 17.12.1853.
16 HO/45/5128^{AE} Palmerston to Memorialists 22.12.1853.
17 *LWN* 1.1.1854.
18 *RN* 1.1.1854.
19 *DN* 28.12.1853, 19.11.1853.
20 *MET* 28.12.1853, 17.12.1853.
21 Sir Robert Ensor, *England, 1870–1914* (Oxford, 1968 Edn.), p. 1.
22 See H.C. Bell.
23 Add. MSS. 43,069 (Aberdeen Papers) Palmerston to Aberdeen 12.2.1854 BM. See also J.B. Conacher, *The Aberdeen Coalition, 1852–1855* (Cambridge, 1968), p. 293.
24 Palmerston to Russell 29.1.1854; cf. G.P. Gooch (Ed.), *The Later Correspondence of Lord John Russell, 1840–1878* Vol. II (1925), pp. 130–1.
25 H.C. Bell, p. 193.
26 For accounts of Palmerston's resignation see B.K. Martin, 'The Resignation of Lord Palmerston in 1853', *Camb. Hist. J.* (1923), pp. 107–12; Conacher, pp. 215–32. Although Sir George Grey agreed to replace Palmerston at the Home Office he never officially took up this position, since Aberdeen had not given Queen Victoria Palmerston's letter of resignation. Palmerston was, therefore, or so it seems, still carrying out his Home Office duties. It is interesting to note that in his letter of acceptance Sir George Grey asked Aberdeen for progress reports on the Eastern and reform question. He did not ask for a similar report on the ten per cent campaign, presumably because he, like his colleagues, was simply not interested in it. Add. MSS. 43,069. Aberdeen to Lord John Russell 20.12.1853 BM.
27 F.B. Smith, *The Making of the Second Reform Bill* (Cambridge, 1966), Ch. 3.
28 PRO/30/22 11B. Bright to Lord John Russell, undated, but in the November/December file. Bright wrote to Cobden on the subject in late November and in all probability wrote to Russell about the same time. Add. MSS. 43,383 Bright to Cobden 28.11.1853 BM.
29 HO/45/5128^{AE} Palmerston to Memorialists 22.12.1853.
30 HO/45/5128 Cathcart to Palmerston 4.12.1853.
31 B. Martin, 'Leonard Horner: a portrait of an Inspector of Factories', *I.R.S.H.* (Vol. 14) 1969, pp. 412–43.
32 *Parl. Papers* Vol. XIX, 1854, pp. 269, 396.
33 *Ibid.* pp. 272–3.
34 *PG* 31.12.1853.
35 HO/45/5244 Palmerston to Board of Trade 6.1.1854.
36 HO/45/5244 Board of Trade to Palmerston 9.1.1854.
37 HO/45/5244 E. Cardwell to Palmerston 13.1.1854. Playfair was an official in the Department of Science and Art, a branch of the Board of Trade.
38 HO/45/5244 Playfair to Cardwell 21.1.1854.
39 HO/45/5244 See Palmerston's dated comment at the end of his copy of the letter from the Board of Trade, dated 9.1.1854.
40 HO/45/5128 Magistrates to Palmerston 22.12.1853.
41 HO/45/5128 undated note.
42 HO/45/5128 John Bottomley (Sergeant) to Palmerston 20.6.1853.
43 HO/45/5128 John Stoves (Mayor) to Palmerston 28.7.1853.
44 HO/45/5128 P.L. Seward (Police) to Palmerston 3.8.1853.

Notes to pages 159–64

45 HO/45/5128 Cathcart to Palmerston 4.12.1853; see also D. Jones, *Chartism and the Chartists* (Harmondsworth, 1975), p. 142.
46 Add. MSS 43,069 Palmerston to Aberdeen 12.2.1854 BM.
47 Conacher, pp. 291–311.
48 HO/45/5244B Cathcart to Palmerston 4.1.1854.
49 Ridley, p. 285.
50 *PG* 11.3.1854, 18.3.1854.
51 HO/45/5244B Robert Baxendale and James Whalley to Palmerston 15.2.1854.
52 HO/43/85/85 Palmerston to Baxendale 18.3.1854.
53 HO/43/85/84 Palmerston to Walmsley 18.3.1854.
54 HO/45/5128 P. Catterall to Palmerston 16.9.1853.
55 HO/45/5244L Palmerston to Mayor of Nottingham 28.8.1854.
56 HO/45/5128 T. Marshall to Palmerston 19.3.1853.
57 HO/45/5128 note by Henry Fitzroy 19.3.1853.
58 HO/41/20 Palmerston to Mayor of Blackburn 19.3.1853; HO/45/5128 Palmerston to Mayor of Blackburn 30.3.1853.
59 See above pp. 98–9, 102.
60 HO/45/5128 Cathcart to Palmerston 4.11.1853, 4.12.1853.
61 HO/45/5128 18.11.1853 note on the reverse of a letter from the Chief Constable of Lancashire; HO/41/20 Palmerston to Mayor of Blackburn 26.11.1853; Palmerston to Mayor of Wigan 5.11.1853.
62 HO/45/5244B Palmerston to Walmsley 3.3.1854.
63 HO/41/20 Palmerston to Walmsley 8.3.1854.
64 HO/45/5244B J. Lowe to Palmerston 7.3.1854.
65 HO/45/5244B note dated 13.3.1854.
66 HO/43/85/84 Waddington to Walmsley 18.3.1854. Palmerston's notes can be found in HO/45/5244B.
67 See Mather (1959) for a general discussion of the continuity of government policy on law and order. See also A.P. Donajgrodzki, 'Sir James Graham at the Home Office', *Hist. J.* (Vol. 20) 1977, pp. 97–120.
68 Add. MSS. 43,069 Palmerston to Aberdeen 10.12.1853 BM.

Chapter 9 The Press

1 P.J. Murphy, 'The Origins of the 1852 Lock-Out in the British Engineering Industry Reconsidered', *I.R.S.H.* (Vol. 23) 1978, pp. 242–66; Fraser, p. 200.
2 For another assessment of strikes and the local press see M. Milne, 'Strikes and Strike Breaking in North East England, 1815–55: the attitude of the local press', *I.R.S.H.* (Vol. 22) 1977, pp. 226–40.
3 *PG* 17.12.1853; *BC* 10.12.1853.
4 *PG* 3.12.1853.
5 *PG* 26.11.1853.
6 See Livesey, *Life and Teachings*, passim. Livesey was a leading figure in the temperance movement and, between 1841 and 1846, he published a newspaper called *The Struggle* to spread the Free Trade gospel.
7 Circulation figures for the year 1853: *Preston Guardian* 323,000; *Preston Chronicle* 98,000; *Preston Pilot* 48,500; *Lancaster Guardian* 44,000; *Lancaster Gazette* 35,000; *Blackburn Standard* 29,000; *Fleetwood Chronicle* (only published in the summer) 8,500; *Ulverston Advertiser* 63,000. Sources: *PC* 15.4.1854; *PG* 5.2.1853.
8 *PG* 29.10.1853.

9 *PG* 17.9.1853.
10 *PG* 26.11.1853, 3.12.1853.
11 *PG* 26.11.1853.
12 *PG* 31.12.1853.
13 *PG* 24.12.1853.
14 *PG* 28.1.1854.
15 *PG* 24.12.1853; *PG* 31.12.1853.
16 *PG* 29.10.1853.
17 *PG* 31.12.1853.
18 Clemesha, p. 223. Dobson was also a tea dealer.
19 *PC* 29.10.1853.
20 *PG* 8.10.1853.
21 *PC* 24.12.1853.
22 *PC* 24.12.1853.
23 *PG* 29.10.1853.
24 *PG* 12.11.1853; *PC* 3.12.1853.
25 *PC* 17.12.1853.
26 *PC* 3.12.1853.
27 *PC* 20.1.1854, 28.1.1854, 11.2.1854. (Original emphasis.)
28 *PG* 28.1.1854.
29 *PG* 4.2.1854.
30 Anon. 11.2.1854 in DDPr 138/87b (L.C.R.O.).
31 *PC* 18.2.1854.
32 *PC* 4.2.1854.
33 *PC* 18.2.1854.
34 *PC* 29.4.1854.
35 *PC* 6.5.1854.
36 *PC* 8.10.1853, 12.11.1853, 11.2.1854.
37 *PC* 20.5.1854.
38 *PPi* 27.8.1853.
39 *PPi* 8.10.1853.
40 *PG* 29.10.1853.
41 *PPi* 29.10.1853.
42 *PPi* 4.2.1853.
43 *PC* 15.10.1853, 7.1.1854.
44 *PG* 29.10.1853, 10.12.1853.
45 *RN* 11.12.1853, 22.1.1854.
46 R. Williams, *The Long Revolution* (Pelican Edn., Harmondsworth, 1971), pp. 186–216.
47 See P. Hollis, *The Pauper Press* (Oxford, 1970); J.A. Epstein, 'Feargus O'Connor and the "Northern Star" ', *I.R.S.H.* (Vol. 21) 1976, pp. 51–97; R.K. Webb, *The British Working Class Reader* (1955); J.H. Weiner, *The War of the Unstamped* (Berkeley, Cal., 1970).
48 *LWN* 1.5.1853.
49 *LWN* 5.6.1853.
50 *LWN* 5.6.1853, 10.7.1853.
51 *LWN* 3.7.1853.
52 *LWN* 31.7.1853.
53 *LWN* 25.9.1853 (our emphasis).
54 *LWN* 23.10.1853 (our emphasis).
55 *LWN* 11.12.1853.
56 *LWN* 19.2.1854.

57 *LWN* 19.2.1854.
58 *LWN* 19.2.1854.
59 *LWN* 19.3.1854.
60 *LWN* 5.6.1854.
61 *LWN* 14.5.1854.
62 *LWN* 4.9.1853.
63 *LWN* 5.2.1854, 19.2.1854.
64 *LWN* 26.3.1854, 2.4.1854, 9.4.1854.
65 *GS* 5.11.1853.
66 *GS* 29.10.1853.
67 *GS* 26.11.1853.
68 *GS* 5.11.1853.
69 *GS* 10.12.1853.
70 *PPa* 24.9.1853.
71 J.T. Ward, *Chartism* (1973), pp. 229–34. See Saville (1952).
72 *PPa* 12.11.1853.
73 See *PC* 8.10.1853; *PG* 15.10.1853; *PPa* 15.10.1853.
74 *PPa* 15.10.1853.
75 *PPa* 17.12.1853.
76 *PPa* 4.2.1854.
77 *PPa* 7.1.1854, 14.1.1854, 29.4.1854, 6.5.1854.
78 *PPa* 14.1.1854.
79 *PPa* 15.4.1854.
80 *PPa* 22.4.1854, 29.4.1854.
81 *PPa* 6.5.1854.
82 Ward (1973), p. 232.
83 *RN* 25.1.1852.
84 *RN* 30.10.1853.
85 *RN* 27.11.1853.
86 *RN* 15.1.1854.
87 *RN* 29.1.1854.
88 *RN* 15.1.1854, 22.1.1854, 29.1.1854.
89 There is no evidence to support the view that the Society of Arts' conference was prompted by Prince Albert. *Reynolds'* merely used the occasion, as it frequently did, for its own purposes. See J. Saville and J.M. Bellamy (Eds.), *Dictionary of Labour Biography* Vol. 3 (1976), pp. 146–57.
90 *RN* 4.12.1853.
91 *RN* 11.12.1853.
92 Fraser, p. 200.
93 *Times* 8.11.1853, 29.12.1853, 4.1.1854, 4.4.1854, 22.4.1854.
94 *Times* 15.3.1854, reporting the meeting at Hoghton.
95 Cf. Lowe *op. cit.* p. 218. See also *Times* 7.10.1853.
96 *Times* 26.10.1853: the *Times* was careful to distinguish between reasonably asking for the ten per cent and 'blasphemously insisting on it as a divine right' 15.3.1854.
97 *Times* 19.10.1853, 10.12.1853.
98 *PC* 29.10.1853, 12.11.1853, 19.11.1853.
99 *PG* 17.12.1853.
100 *PG* 8.4.1854.
101 *DN* 1.11.1853.
102 *DN* 19.11.1853.
103 *DN* 29.11.1853.

244 *Notes to pages 172–80*

104 *DN* 21.1.1854.
105 *DN* 3.5.1854.
106 *MC* 14.1.1854.
107 *MC* 10.1.1854.
108 *MC* 12.11.1853.
109 *PPa* 12.11.1853; H. Scott Gordon, 'The London *Economist* and the High Tide of Laissez-Faire', *J.P.E.* (Vol. 63) 1955, p. 462.
110 *Economist* 24.9.1853.
111 *Economist* 5.11.1853.
112 *Economist* 7.1.1854.
113 *BC* 19.11.1853.
114 *MET* 5.11.1853.
115 *MET* 16.11.1853.
116 *MG* 17.12.1853.
117 *PG* 31.12.1853.
118 *PC* 31.12.1853.
119 *PG* 10.12.1853; *PC* 7.1.1854, 25.2.1854, 1.4.1854.
120 *PC* 25.2.1854, 1.4.1854.
121 *MG* 7.12.1853.
122 *MET* 22.10.1853, 5.10.1853.
123 *BO* 24.11.1853.
124 *LJ* 5.11.1853.
125 *SA* 6.1.1854, 2.12.1853, 11.11.1853; *BS* 26.10.1853, 2.11.1853, 30.11.1853.
126 *LGu* 29.10.1853.
127 *BM* 18.6.1853; *BA* November 1853, December 1853.
128 *LM* 2.5.1854, 9.5.1854, 22.11.1853.
129 *LJ* 5.11.1853; *BC* 19.11.1853.
130 See for example *Bradford Observer* which wanted arbitration to replace trade unions: 15.12.1853 and 20.10.1853.
131 *LM* 28.4.1854.
132 Fraser, p. 205.
133 *Edinburgh Review* (Vol. 100) 1854, pp. 163–92.
134 'To the People of Norfolk', *Cobbett's Weekly Political Register*, LXVIII (1829), p. 559; cf. S. Bennet, 'Catholic Emancipation, "The Quarterly Review" and Britain's Constitutional Revolution', *Victorian Studies* (Vol. 72) 1968–9, p. 283.
135 *Quarterly Review* (Vol. 106) 1859, pp. 485–522.
136 *Blackwood's Magazine* (Vol. 79) 1856, pp. 52–60.
137 *Westminster Review* (Vol. 5) 1854, pp. 119–45.
138 Ashworth (1854), p. 23.

Chapter 10 Defeat (10 February–13 May 1854)

1 *PG* 25.3.1854 (trial report); *BO* 2.3.1854.
2 *PG* 4.3.1854.
3 *PG* 11.3.1854.
4 *PG* 11.3.1854.
5 *MET* 22.3.1854; *LM* 21.3.1854.
6 *PG* 11 and 18.3.1854; *PC* 18.3.1854.
7 *PG* 4.3.1854.
8 *PC* 18.3.1854; *PG* 18.3.1854.
9 *PG* 11.3.1854; *PC* 18.3.1854; *LM* 21.3.1854; Lowe, pp. 239–40.

Notes to pages 180–5

10 *PG* 25.3.1854.
11 *PG* 11.3.1854.
12 *PG* 18.3.1854.
13 *PG* 25.3.1854.
14 *PG* 11.3.1854.
15 *PG* 8.4.1854.
16 *PC* 1.4.1854.
17 *PC* 18.3.1854.
18 See above, pp. 177–9.
19 Thomas Gregson was discharged: Ascroft had been unable to prepare a case against him, though he hinted at its gravity and reserved the right to institute proceedings at a later date.
20 Cowell, Grimshaw and Gallaher, at least, by W.P. Roberts, who aspired to represent all the defendants but was (according to his account) tricked by a Preston solicitor in league with R.B. Cobbett of Manchester. The 'Miners' Attorney-General' claimed that Cowell was on his way to see Roberts in Manchester when he was arrested (*RN* 2.4.1854, 9.4.1854).
21 *PG* 25.3.1854.
22 Lowe, pp. 242–3. Eleven delegates appeared in the dock: to everyone's surprise Gregson had been called to Liverpool on the 27th to stand trial with the rest.
23 *PG* 25.3.1854.
24 *PC* 1.4.1854.
25 *PG* 25.3.1854.
26 *PG* 1.4.1854.
27 *PG* 25.3.1854.
28 *PG* 25.3.1854.
29 R.Y. Hedges and A. Winterbottom, *The Legal History of Trade Unionism* (1930), p. 47.
30 *Ibid.*, p. 50; on these cases see K.W. Wedderburn, *Cases and Materials on Labour Law* (Cambridge, 1967), pp. 372–4. The delegates' defence rested heavily on the argument that no contracts of employment had been entered into by the knobsticks.
31 Wedderburn, p. 383n.
32 *PC* 1.4.1854.
33 *PC* 1.4.1854.
34 Lowe, p. 241.
35 *PG* 25.3.1854.
36 *PC* 1.4.1854; *PG* 8.4.1854.
37 *PC* 1.4.1854.
38 *PG* 8.4.1854.
39 *MET* 25.3.1854 (cited *PG* 1.4.1854).
40 *PG* 25.3.1854.
41 *LGa* 1.4.1854.
42 *PG* 25.3.1854.
43 *PC* 1.4.1854.
44 *PG* and *PC* 1.4.1854; *GS* 22.4.1854.
45 *PG* 1.4.1854.
46 *PG* 25.3.1854.
47 *PG* 22.4.1854. The petition seems to have originated in London, with the Metropolitan Trades' Delegates (*RN* 9.4.1854); signatures were collected in Glasgow by a committee of the local trades (*GS* 22.4.1854). Duncombe's motion for a Select Committee of Inquiry, tabled in April, was withdrawn after the end of the strike (see *PC* 27.5.1854).
48 *PG* 1.4.1854.

49 Lowe, pp. 244–6.
50 *PG* 25.3.1854.
51 *PC* 1.5.1854: text of a letter from J.A. Ewan, secretary of the masters' association, to the *Preston Guardian*.
52 *PC* 1.4.1854 implies the former, *PG* 1.4.1854 states the latter.
53 *PG* 15.4.1854.
54 *PG* 8.4.1854.
55 *PG* 15.4.1854.
56 *PC* 8.4.1854.
57 *PG* 15.4.1854; *LGa* 15.4.1854.
58 *MET* 19.4.1854.
59 *SA* 31.3.1854.
60 *SA* 14.4.1854.
61 *MET* 19.4.1854.
62 *PG* 22.4.1854.
63 *SA* 14.4.1854 and 19.5.1854.
64 *SA* 21.4.1854 and 28.4.1854.
65 *PG* 22.4.1854.
66 *SA* 21.4.1854, 28.4.1854, 5.5.1854, 12.5.1854; *PG* 29.4.1854; Reid (1974), pp. 386–90.
67 *PG* 22.4.1854.
68 *MET* 19.4.1854.
69 *PG* 22.4.1854. This mysterious contribution may possibly have come from Tory-paternalist sources.
70 *PC* 22.4.1854.
71 *PG* 22.4.1854; Amalgamated Committee balance sheet for week ending 16 April; 33rd weekly report of the Cardroom Hands (both in DDPr 138/87b (L.C.R.O.)).
72 *PC* 22.4.1854. (The delegate is, unfortunately, not named.)
73 *MET* 19.4.1854.
74 *PG* 22.4.1854.
75 *PG* and *PC* 22.4.1854.
76 *PC* 22.4.1854 (giving details by numbers of hands, looms and spindles working).
77 *PG* 29.4.1854.
78 *PC* and *PG* 29.4.1854.
79 *PC* and *PG* 29.4.1854.
80 *PC* 6.5.1854; Lowe, p. 248.
81 *PG* 6.5.1854.
82 *PC* 6.5.1854.
83 *PG* 13.5.1854.
84 *PG* 20.5.1854; Spinners' balance sheet, DDPr 138/87b (L.C.R.O.) pp. 274–8.
85 *PG* 13.5.1854, 20.5.1854. True to form, Hornby implemented the reduction a full month after his competitors (*PG* 10.6.1854).
86 *PC* 6.5.1854.
87 *PG* 20.5.1854.
88 *PG* 24.6.1854, 22.7.1854.
89 *PG* 6.5.1854.
90 *PG* 13.5.1854.
91 *PG* 20.5.1854.
92 *PG* 27.5.1854; *PC* 27.5.1854.
93 *PG* 5.8.1854; *SA* 11.8.1854.

Notes to pages 191-6

94 The stormy scenes at the Blackburn meeting on 2 May seem to have been entirely unrelated to this question (see *PC* 6.5.1854; no such incident is reported in *PG* 6.5.1854).
95 *SA* 12.5.1854, 19.5.1854; *PC* 13.5.1854; *MG* 13.5.1854, 20.5.1854.
96 James Lowe, a cautious and dispassionate observer, later concluded after a detailed examination that 'these balance sheets are in the main as correct and as trustworthy as any accounts kept by unskilled men might be expected to be, perhaps more so; that they set forth truthfully all the moneys subscribed to the funds of the Union; that they account for those moneys fairly; and that, although in some cases they conceal the real nature of the expenses, those expenses were natural and necessary, and do not exceed in the aggregate a fair proportion of the sums administered'. (Lowe, p. 252.)
97 *SA* 26.4.1854.
98 *PG* 6.5.1854. At least four manufacturers continued to pay the ten per cent well into May (*PC* 20.5.1854). One of these, Edward Hollins, was to justify a wage reduction *three years later* on the grounds that he had 'forgotten' to take off the ten per cent in 1854! (*PG* 4.4.1857).
99 *PG* 13.5.1854.
100 Placard in DDPr 138/87b (L.C.R.O.).
101 *BS* 20.5.1854; *PC* 20.5.1854.
102 *SA* 21.7.1854, citing *BS* 15.7.1854.
103 *PC* 19.8.1854.
104 Handbill, 'He who allows oppression shares the crime', 18.7.1854, unpaginated section of DDPr 138/87a (L.C.R.O.).
105 *PG* 2.9.1854. On the controversy surrounding the outcome of the Sabden strike, see *PG* 9.9.1854.
106 *PG* 13.5.1854, 20.5.1854; *SA* 12.5.1854.
107 *MG* 13.5.1854.
108 *PC* 3.6.1854; *BA* 3.6.1854, 5.8.1854.
109 *PC* 10.6.1854; *PG* 10.6.1854. This was presumably the 'Preston Weaving Industrial Society' of which the Christian Socialists had such high hopes (*Co-operative Commercial Circular*, September 1854, p. 75, cited Christensen, p. 355, n. 17).
110 *PG* 8.7.1854, 15.7.1854; *PC* 8.7.1854. T.S. Duncombe exerted his influence on the operatives' behalf: see *PPa* 13.5.1854, 27.5.1854; also T.H. Duncombe, *The Life and Correspondence of Thomas Slingsby Duncombe* (1868) II, pp. 109-10.
111 *PC* 7.10.1854; *PG* 7.10.1854. Edward Whittle had by the middle of the month raised only £8 14s 3d towards his share of the bill; he called a meeting of the Blackburn operatives and secured their agreement to a levy of 1d per loom (*BS* 25.10.1854).
112 *PG* 14.10.1854, 11.11.1854.
113 See the placard, 'Cowell Imprisoned', announcing a meeting in the Cockpit on 8 November, DDPr 138/87b (L.C.R.O.); also *BS* 22.11.1854. (Since no mention is made of the Whittles in the *Blackburn Standard*'s report of Cowell's imprisonment, it may be assumed that they had managed to pay their debts).
114 Unattributed press cutting, DDPr 138/87b (L.C.R.O.).
115 *PG* 17.2.1855, 3.3.1855.

Chapter 11 Posterity

1 *PC* 6.5.1854.
2 Add. MSS. 43,653 Cobden to Ashworth 29.11.1853 BM (italics in the original).
3 Add. MSS. 43,653 Cobden to Ashworth 17.6.1854 BM.
4 Add. MSS. 43,653 Cobden to Ashworth 26.8.1854 BM; Boyson (1970), pp. 150-3.

5 Ashworth (1854), p. 16.
6 *Ibid.* p. 29.
7 *Ibid.* p. 27.
8 *Ibid.* p. 30.
9 *Ibid.* pp. 97–8.
10 *Ibid.* p. 98.
11 *Ibid.* pp. 8–9.
12 *Ibid.* p. 6.
13 *Ibid.* p. 58.
14 *Ibid.* p. 95.
15 See generally Fraser, *Trade Unions and Society* and Kay-Shuttleworth's introduction to the Report (pp. vii–xxi).
16 Lowe, p. 208.
17 *Ibid.* p. 233.
18 *Ibid.* p. 212.
19 *Ibid.* p. 212.
20 *Ibid.* p. 215.
21 *Ibid.* p. 214.
22 *Ibid.* p. 215.
23 *Ibid.* p. 242.
24 *Ibid.* p. 237.
25 C. Dickens, *Hard Times* (Harmondsworth, 1969), Introduction by D. Craig; E. Gaskell, *North and South* (Harmondsworth, 1970), Introduction by M. Dodsworth.
26 For a discussion of the problems of serializing the novels and the conflict between Dickens and Gaskell see A.B. Hopkins, *Elizabeth Gaskell: her life and work* (1952), pp. 135–57.
27 *RN* 5.2.1854.
28 H. House, *The Dickens World* (2nd Edn., Oxford, 1969), p. 207.
29 J. Butt and K. Tillotson, *Dickens at Work* (1957), p. 209.
30 *Household Words* 8, 11.2.1854.
31 See *PC* 4.2.1854; *PG* 11.2.1854. See also Dickens's article 'Railway Strikes', *Household Words* 2, 11.1.1851, pp. 361–4 for a more sympathetic view of unions.
32 Dickens, who started to write *Hard Times* in January, never intended writing about the strike, as he knew Gaskell was using the strike in *North and South*: Butt and Tillotson, pp. 209–10.
33 'Stuttering' is Sissy Jupe's word for statistics.
34 There is a vast literature on *Hard Times* and *North and South*. Our discussion is limited to the question of their usefulness as a historical source for the Preston strike. For more general critical comments on the two novels, see F.R. and Q.D. Leavis, *Dickens the Novelist* (1970), pp. 187–212; G. Gissing, *Charles Dickens: a critical study* (1904), pp. 234–59; P. Collins (Ed.), *Dickens: the critical heritage* (1971), pp. 300–55; C. Lansbury, *Elizabeth Gaskell: the novel of social crisis* (1975); W.A. Craik, *Elizabeth Gaskell and the English Provincial Novel* (1975). More generally see R. Williams, *Culture and Society, 1780–1950* (Harmondsworth, 1961); P. Brantlinger, *The Spirit of Reform: British literature and politics, 1832–1867* (Massachusetts, 1977).
35 *MG* 1.2.1854.
36 On this point see K.J. Fielding, 'The Battle for Preston', *Dickensian* (Vol. 50) 1954, pp. 159–62; G. Carnall, 'Dickens, Mrs Gaskell and the Preston Strike' *Victorian Studies* (Vol. 8) 1964–5, pp. 31–48.
37 P. Brantlinger, 'The Case against Trade Unions in Early Victorian Fiction', *Victorian Studies* (Vol. 13) 1969–70, p. 43.

38 It is important to note that Dickens accepted the masters' political economy, and believed that masters and men were interdependent. His criticism of political economy in *Hard Times* stems from the way in which it had been reduced to fact: see House, p. 208.
39 Carnall, p. 48.
40 It allows Margaret and Thornton to make physical contact. See Dodsworth's Introduction, *Gaskell*, pp. 18–19.
41 He does drink, whereas Cowell was a teetotaller.
42 *Hansard* (3rd Series) Vol. 131 (1854), pp. 1222–3.
43 *PG* 24.12.1853; *RN* 6.11.1853.
44 *Hansard* (3rd Series) Vol. 131 (1854), p. 818.
45 *PC* 25.2.1854.
46 *Hansard* (3rd Series) Vol. 131 (1854), p. 823.
47 *Hansard* (3rd Series) Vol. 131 (1854), pp. 831, 833.
48 This was also true of the 1860s. See L. Woodward, *The Age of Reform, 1815–1870* (2nd Edn., Oxford, 1962), p. 161.
49 Add. MSS. 43,653 Ashworth to Cobden 9.1.1854 BM.
50 P.S. Bagwell, *Industrial Relations* (Government and Society in Nineteenth Century Britain) (Athlone, 1974), pp. 26, 109.
51 *Select Committee on Masters and Operatives (Equitable Councils of Conciliation)* (Parl. Papers) Vol. XIII (1856), pp. 19–20, 43–4, 47.
52 See above p. 160.
53 *Select Committee on the best means of Settling Disputes between Masters and Operatives* (Parl. Papers) Vol. XXII (1860).
54 C. Knight, *Knowledge is Power* (new edn., London, 1854).
55 T.J. Dunning, *Trades' Unions and Strikes: their philosophy and intentions* (1860), p. 37.
56 A. Black, *On Wages, Trades' Unions and Strikes* (1859), pp. 23–4.
57 J. Plummer, *Strikes, their Causes and their Evils* (1859).
58 G. Howell, *Labour Legislation, Labour Movements, Labour Leaders* (London, 1902), pp. 101–6.
59 S. and B. Webb, p. 206.
60 Clemesha, p. 230.
61 Hewitson (1883), p. 383; membership had been as high as 3,000 in earlier years. In 1861 both spinners and weavers had a permanent meeting room: *United Kingdom First Annual Trades' Union Directory* (London, 1861; reprinted 1968), p. 81.
62 *PG* 11.4.1857.
63 Banks, pp. 8–10.
64 Hewitson (1883), pp. 179–80.
65 W.A. Jevons, 'Account of the Weavers' Strike at Padiham in 1859' in *Trades' Societies and Strikes*, pp. 433–70.
66 Hewitson (1883), pp. 180–4; 'The Riots in the Cotton Districts', *ILN* 25.5.1878.
67 S. Andrew, *Fifty Years' Cotton Trade* (Oldham, 1887), p. 10.
68 Eccles Shorrock, *History of the Formation of the Blackburn Association ... with the Rise and Fall in the Rate of Wages for Twenty Eight Years* (Manchester, 1880), p. 4. (Copy in L.C.R.O. as DDPr 50/8).
69 G. von Schulze-Gaevernitz, *The Cotton Trade in England* (London, 1895) pp. 200–1.
70 Banks, p. 7.

Epilogue

1 *PG* 14.11.1876 (obituary).

2 *PG* 11.10.1873, 18.10.1873 (obituary).
3 *PG* 29.3.1862 (obituary).
4 *BA* 5.8.1854; *PG* 11.11.1854; *PG* 2.4.1859; *PG* 1.7.1865 (obituary); *Preston Herald* (supplement), 28.6.1865 (obituary).
5 Thomas Banks, *A Short Sketch of the Cotton Trade*.
6 *PG* 12.2.1859, 16.3.1859, 30.4.1859.
7 Reid (1974), p. 424.
8 *PG* 28.3.1857.
9 *PG* 9.4.1859.
10 *PG* 21.3.1857, 24.3.1857, 28.3.1857, 26.3.1859, 23.4.1859.
11 *PG* 14.3.1857, 28.3.1857; *Blackburn Times* 16.9.1871 (obituary).
12 Business card, frontispiece, DDPr 138/87b (L.C.R.O.).
13 *PG* 28.3.1857.
14 *PG* 12.2.1859, 16.3.1859, 26.3.1859, 30.4.1859.
15 R. Sharpe France (Ed.), 'The Diary of John Ward of Clitheroe, Weaver, 1860–4', *Trans. Hist. Soc. of Lancs. and Chesh.* (Vol. 105) 1953, p. 159. The strike was eventually settled by arbitration under a local vicar.
16 *PG* 7.10.1854.
17 Grimshaw to Ahsworth, 2.10.1854, in the unpaginated section of DDPr 138/87a (L.C.R.O.).
18 Note written by Grimshaw (?), Ashworth's comment, both in the unpaginated section of DDPr 138/87a (L.C.R.O.).
19 Reid (1974), p. 456.
20 Mary Ellison, *Support for Secession* (Chicago, 1972), p. 117.
21 Royden Harrison, *Before the Socialists: studies in labour and politics 1861–1881* (1965), p. 66; see also *ibid.*, p. 56, n. 1.
22 Grimshaw to Wilson, April 1864 (Wilson papers, Manchester Public Library; spelling, punctuation etc. are Grimshaw's).

Bibliography

I. Manuscript sources.
II. Parliamentary Papers.
III. Contemporary newspapers.
IV. Contemporary printed works.
V. Secondary printed works.
VI. Unpublished theses.

I. MANUSCRIPT SOURCES

1. Public Record Office

(a) **Home Office papers**
Correspondence and Papers relating to Disturbances:
HO/41/20
HO/43/83
HO/43/85/84
HO/43/85/85
HO/45/2410^A
HO/45/4582
HO/45/5128
HO/45/5128^{AE}
HO/45/5128^E
HO/45/5244
HO/45/5244^B
HO/45/5244^C
HO/45/5244^L
HO/45/5244^R

(b) **Ministry of Health Papers**
Correspondence of Poor Law Unions:
MH/12/5677
MH/12/5893
Papers of Assistant Poor Law Commissioners and Inspectors:
MH/32/22
MH/32/23

(c) **Miscellaneous**
PRO/30/22 (Russell Papers)
PC1/852

2. British Museum

(a) Add. MSS. 43,383. Correspondence between John Bright and Richard Cobden.
(b) Add. MSS. 43,653 and 43,654. Correspondence between Henry Ashworth and Richard Cobden.
(c) Add. MSS. 43,069. Aberdeen Papers.

3. Manchester Public Library

Wilson Papers.

4. Royal Society of Arts

R.S.A. Council Minutes.

5. Midland Bank Ltd.

Preston Banking Co. Records.

6. Lancashire County Record Office

(a) Boards of Guardians
Burnley: PUZ/1/7
             PUZ/1/8
Haslingden: PUH/1/4
             PUH/3/3
Preston: PUT/1/17
             PUT/1/18

(b) Miscellaneous
DDPr 138/86 Financial Report of the Committee of Operatives during the Preston Lockout.
DDPr 138/87a Scrap book: Henry Ashworth (paginated).
DDPr 138/87b Scrap books: Strikes and Preston Lockout. Vol. 1–3 (unpaginated).
DDPr 131/34 Open letter 'To Joseph Gillow Esq.' by 'Consistency'.
QJD 1/217 Riot deposition for Royton, 1848.

7. Preston Town Hall

Preston Watch Committee.

II. PARLIAMENTARY PAPERS

Hansard's Parliamentary Debates, 3rd Series.

PP. 1842 (140) XXI. Report of Factory Inspectors.
PP. 1844 (572) XVII and PP. 1845 (610) XVIII. Reports of the Commissioners for inquiring into the state of Large Towns and Populous Districts.
PP. 1852 (1500) XXI. Report of Factory Inspectors.

Bibliography

PP. 1852-3 (603) XXXVI. Report of the Select Committee appointed to consider the expediency of adopting a more uniform system of Police in England and Wales and Scotland.
PP. 1852-3 (855) XXXVI. Report of the Select Committee on Public Houses.
PP. 1852-3 (1580) XL. Report of Factory Inspectors.
PP. 1854 (1796) XIX. Report of Factory Inspectors.
PP. 1854 (1785) XXIX. 6th Annual Report of the Poor Law Board.
PP. 1854-5 (308) XIII. Report from the Select Committee on Poor Removal.
PP. 1854-5 (1921) XXIV. 7th Annual Report of the Poor Law Board.
PP. 1856 (343) XIII. Report from the Select Committee appointed to enquire into the expediency of establishing equitable tribunals for the amicable adjustment of differences between Masters and Operatives.
PP. 1859 (56 Secs. 2) VII. Report from the Select Committee on Assessing and Collecting the Poor Rates, Highway Rates in respect of Small Tenements.
PP. 1860 (307) XXII. The Report of the Select Committee on the best means of Settling Disputes between Masters and Operatives.

III. CONTEMPORARY NEWSPAPERS

Blackburn Standard
Bolton Chronicle
Bradford Observer
Brighton Gazette
Burnley Advertiser
Burnley Mentor
Daily News
Economist
Examiner
Factory Operative's Guide
Glasgow Sentinel
Illustrated London News
Lancaster Gazette
Lancaster Guardian
Liverpool Albion
Liverpool Journal
Liverpool Mercury
Lloyd's Weekly Newspaper
Manchester Examiner and Times
Manchester Guardian
Morning Chronicle

Morning Herald
Morning Post
New York Daily Tribune
Northern Daily Times
Northern Star
People's Paper
Plymouth, Devonport & Stonehouse Herald
Preston Chronicle
Preston Guardian
Preston Herald
Preston Pilot
Reynolds' Newspaper
Stockport Advertiser
Sussex Herald
Ten Hours Advocate
The Times
Warrington Guardian
Weekly Dispatch
Wigan Examiner
Wigan Observer

Blackwood's Magazine
Edinburgh Review
Spectator
Quarterly Review
Westminster Review

IV. CONTEMPORARY PRINTED WORKS (PRE-1914)

1. Books

Abram, W.A. *A History of Blackburn* (Blackburn, 1877).

254 Bibliography

Aikin, J. *A Description of the Country from 30 to 40 miles round Manchester* (London, 1795).
Andrew, S. *Fifty Years' Cotton Trade* (Oldham, 1887).
Ashley, E. *Life and Correspondence: Henry John Temple, Viscount Palmerston* (London, 1879, 2 vols.).
Ashworth, H. *An Inquiry into the Origin, Progress, and Results of the Strike of the Operative Cotton Spinners of Preston, from October, 1836 to February, 1837* (Manchester, 1838).
Ashworth, H. *The Preston Strike: an enquiry into its causes and consequences* (Manchester, 1854).
Banks, T. *A Short Sketch of the Cotton Trade of Preston for the last 67 Years* (Preston, 1894).
Black, A. *On Wages, Trades' Unions and Strikes* (London, 1859).
Chapman, S.J. *The Lancashire Cotton Industry* (Manchester, 1904).
Clay, Walter Lowe *The Prison Chaplain: a memoir of the Rev. John Clay, B.D.* (Cambridge, 1861).
Clemesha, H.W. *A History of Preston in Amounderness* (Manchester, 1912).
Cobbett, W. *Rural Rides* (new edn, London, 1885).
Defoe, D. *A Tour Through the Whole Island of Great Britain* (new edn, Harmondsworth, 1971).
Dickens, C. *Hard Times* (1854; new edn, Harmondsworth, 1969).
Dobson, W. *The Preston Municipal Elections, 1835–1862* (Preston, 1862).
Duncombe, T.H. *The Life and Correspondence of Thomas Slingsby Duncombe* (London, 1868, 2 vols.).
Dunning, T.J. *Trades' Unions and Strikes: their philosophy and intentions* (London, 1860).
Ellison, T. *The Cotton Trade of Great Britain* (London, 1886; reprinted 1968).
Engels, F. *The Condition of the Working Class in England* (new edn, London, 1969).
Evans, D. Morier *The Commercial Crisis 1847–1848* (London, 1848, 1849; reprinted New York, 1969).
Flinn, M.W. (ed.) *Svedenstierna's Tour of Great Britain, 1802–3* (Newton Abbot, 1973).
Gammage, R.G. *A History of the Chartist Movement* (London, 1854; reprinted 1969).
Gaskell, E. *North and South* (1855; new edn, Harmondsworth, 1970).
Gissing, G. *Charles Dickens: a critical study* (London, 1904).
Hardwick, C. *A History of the Borough of Preston and Its Environs, in the County of Lancashire* (Preston, 1857).
Hewitson, A. *Preston Town Council, or portraits of local legislators* (Preston, 1870).
Hewitson, A. *A History of Preston in the County of Lancashire* (Preston, 1883).
Horsfall, J.B. *Royton and Chadderton: their associations for mental improvement* (Royton, 1854).
Howell, G. *Labour Legislation, Labour Movements, Labour Leaders* (London, 1902).
Hughes, T. 'Account of the Lock-out of Engineers, 1851–2', in National Association for the Promotion of Social Science, *Trades' Societies and Strikes* (London, 1860).
Jevons, W.A. 'Account of the Weavers' Strike at Padiham in 1859' in National Association for the Promotion of Social Science, *Trades' Societies and Strikes* (London, 1860).
Knight, C. *Knowledge is Power* (second edn, London, 1854).
Knight, Rev. G.N. *Lancashire* (London, 1842).
Livesey, J. *The Life and Teachings of Joseph Livesey* (London, 1885).
Lowe, J. 'Account of the Strike and Lock-Out in the Cotton Trade at Preston in 1853' in National Association for the Promotion of Social Science, *Trades' Societies and Strikes* (London, 1860).
Lowenthal, E. *The Ricardian Socialists* (New York, 1911; reprinted 1972).

MacRitchie, Rev. W. *Diary of a Tour Through Great Britain in 1795* (London, 1897).
Mannex and Co. *History, Topography, and Directory of Mid-Lancashire, with an Essay on Geology* (Preston, 1854).
Marx, K. *Capital*, Vol. 1 (London, 1887).
Morley, J. *The Life of Richard Cobden* (London, 1903).
National Association for the Promotion of Social Science *Trades' Societies and Strikes* (London, 1860).
Newbould, T.P. *W.H. Chadwick, the last of the Manchester Chartists* (Manchester, 1910).
Pilkington, W. *Then and Now: Preston's progress for seventy years, 1841–1911* (Preston, 1912).
Plummer, J. *Strikes, their Causes and their Evils* (London, 1859).
'A Preston Manufacturer' [Goodair, J.] *Strikes Prevented* (London and Manchester, 1854).
Preston Pollbook, 1852.
Proceedings of the Council (Preston, 1852–5).
Rebirth of the Trade Union Movement: five pamphlets 1838–1847 (New York, 1972).
Robinson, Samuel *Friendly Letters on the Recent Strikes from a Manufacturer to his own Workpeople* (London, 1854).
Schulze-Gaevernitz, G. von *Cotton Trade in England and on the Continent* (London, 1895).
Shorrock, Eccles *History of the Formation of the Blackburn Association in 1852, and of the North and North-East Lancashire Association, with the Rise and Fall in the Rate of Wages for Twenty Eight Years* (Manchester, 1880).
Smith, Adam, *The Wealth of Nations* (London, 1776; cited from Methuen edn, London, 1961, 2 vols.).
Taylor, W. Cooke *Notes of a Tour in the Manufacturing Districts of Lancashire* (London, 1842; reprinted 1968).
The Trials of Feargus O'Connor and 58 other Chartists on a charge of seditious conspiracy . . . (Manchester, 1843).
Tulket, M. *A Topographical, Statistical and Historical Account of the Borough of Preston* (Preston, 1821).
United Kingdom First Annual Trades' Union Directory (London, 1861; reprinted 1968).
Ure, A. *The Philosophy of Manufactures* (London, 1835).
Walmsley, T. *Reminiscences of the Preston Cockpit and the Old Teetotallers* (Preston, 1892).
Wood, G.H. *The History of Wages in the Cotton Trade During the Past Hundred Years* (London, 1910).

2. Journal articles

Anon. [Dickens, Charles] 'On Strike', *Household Words*, 8 (11 February 1854).
Anon. [Lowe, J.] 'Locked Out', *Household Words*, 8 (10 December 1853).
Chadwick, D. 'On the Rate of Wages in Manchester and Salford, and the Manufacturing Districts of Lancashire, 1839–59', *J. Stat. Soc. of London*, 23 (1860).
Chapman, S.J. 'The Regulation of Wages by List in the Spinning Industry', *Econ. J.*, 9 (1899).
Chapman, S.J. 'Some Policies of the Cotton Spinners' Trade Unions', *Econ. J.*, 10 (1900).
Dickens, C. 'Railway Strikes', *Household Words*, 2 (1851).
Merttens, F. 'The Hours and Cost of Labour in the Cotton Industry at Home and Abroad', *Trans. Manchester Statistical Society*, (1893–4).
'A Prestonian' [Hardwick, C.] 'Lancashire Stump Oratory and Reminiscences of the Labour Battle: Chapter I, The Orchard', *Eliza Cook's Journal*, XI (1854).
Watts, J. 'On Strikes and Their Effects on Wages, Profits and Accumulation', *J. Stat. Soc. of London*, 24 (1861).

V. SECONDARY PRINTED WORKS

1. Books

Anderson, M. *Family Structure in Nineteenth Century Lancashire* (Cambridge, 1971).
Aspinall, A. *The Early English Trade Unions* (London, 1949).
Bagwell, P.S. *Industrial Relations* (Government and Society in Nineteenth Century Britain) (Athlone, 1974).
Beer, M. *A History of British Socialism* (London, 1920, 2 vols.).
Bell, S.P. (ed.) *Victorian Lancashire* (Newton Abbot, 1974).
Berry, A.J. *Proud Preston's Story* (Preston, 1928).
Boyson, Rhodes *The Ashworth Cotton Enterprise: the rise and fall of a family firm 1818–1880* (Oxford, 1970).
Brantlinger, P. *The Spirit of Reform: British literature and politics, 1832–1867* (Cambridge, Mass., 1977).
Briggs, A. *Chartist Studies* (London, second edn, 1970).
Brown, I. 'Dickens as Social Reformer', in Tomlin, R.W.F. (ed.), *Charles Dickens 1812–70* (London, 1969).
Burgess, K. *The Origins of British Industrial Relations* (London, 1975).
Butt, J. and Tillotson, K. *Dickens at Work* (London, 1957).
Bythell, D. *The Handloom Weavers* (Cambridge, 1969).
Challinor, R. and Ripley, B. *The Miners' Association: a trade union in the age of the Chartists* (London, 1968).
Chapman, S.D. *The Cotton Industry in the Industrial Revolution* (London, 1972).
Christensen, T. *Origin and History of Christian Socialism* (Aarhus, 1962).
Church, R.A. *The Great Victorian Boom, 1850–73* (London, 1975).
Cole, G.D.H. *The Life of William Cobbett* (London, 1924).
Cole, G.D.H. *Attempts at General Union 1818–1834* (London, 1953).
Cole, G.D.H. and Filson, D. (eds.) *British Working Class Movements: select documents 1789–1875* (London, 1967).
Collins, P. (ed.) *Dickens: the critical heritage* (London, 1971).
Conacher, J.B. *The Aberdeen Coalition, 1852–1855* (Cambridge, 1968).
Craig, D. Introduction to Dickens, C., *Hard Times* (Penguin edn, Harmondsworth, 1969).
Craik, W.A. *Elizabeth Gaskell and the English Provincial Novel* (London, 1975).
Critchley, T.A. *A History of Police in England and Wales 900–1966* (London, 1967).
Deane, P. and Cole, W.A. *British Economic Growth, 1688–1959* (Cambridge, 1964).
Donajgrodzki, A.P. ' "Social Police" and the Bureaucratic Elite: a vision of order in the age of reform' in Donajgrodzki (ed.) *Social Control in Nineteenth Century Britain* (London, 1977).
Edsall, N.C. *The Anti-Poor Law Movement, 1834–1844* (Manchester, 1971).
Edwards, M.E. *The Growth of British Cotton Trade, 1780–1815* (Manchester, 1967).
Ellison, M. *Support for Secession* (Chicago, 1972).
Ensor, R. *England, 1870–1914* (Oxford, 1968).
Farnie, D.A. *The English Cotton Industry and the World Market, 1815–1896* (Oxford, 1979).
Fitton, R.S. and Wadsworth, A.P. *The Strutts and the Arkwrights* (Manchester, 1958).
Fong, H.D. *Triumph of Factory System in England* (Tientsin, 1930).
Foster, J. *Class Struggle and the Industrial Revolution: early industrial capitalism in three English towns* (London, 1974).
Fraser, D. *Urban Politics in Victorian England* (London, 1976).
Fraser, D. (ed.) *The New Poor Law in the Nineteenth Century* (London, 1976).

Bibliography

Fraser, W.H. *Trade Unions and Society: the struggle for acceptance 1850–1880* (London, 1974).
Gayer, A.D., Rostow, W.W. and Schwartz, A.J. *The Growth and Fluctuation of the British Economy* (Oxford, 1953, 2 vols.).
Gillespie, F.E. *Labor and Politics in England 1850–1867* (Durham, North Carolina, 1927).
Gooch, G.P. (ed.) *The Later Correspondence of Lord John Russell, 1840–1878* (London, 1925, two vols.).
Gray, A. *The Socialist Tradition* (London, 1946).
Hammond, J.L. and B. *The Town Labourer* (London, 1917).
Harrison, Royden *Before the Socialists: studies in labour and politics 1861–1881* (London, 1965).
Hart, J. *The British Police* (London, 1951).
Hartwell, R.M. (ed.) *The Industrial Revolution* (Oxford, 1970).
Hearn, F. *Domination, Legitimation and Resistance: the incorporation of the nineteenth century English working class* (Westport, Connecticut, 1978).
Hedges, R.Y. and Winterbottom, A. *The Legal History of Trade Unionism* (London, 1930).
Henderson, W.O. *The Life of Friedrich Engels* (London, 2 vols, 1976).
Hennock, E.P. *Fit and Proper Persons: ideal and reality in nineteenth-century urban government* (London, 1973).
Hewitt, M. *Wives and Mothers in Victorian Industry* (London, 1958).
Hollis, P. *The Pauper Press* (Oxford, 1970).
Hopkins, A.B. *Elizabeth Gaskell: her life and work* (London, 1952).
Hopwood, E. *A History of the Lancashire Cotton Industry and the Amalgamated Weavers Association* (Manchester, 1969).
House, H. *The Dickens World* (second edn, Oxford, 1969).
Hughes, J.R.T. *Fluctuations in Trade, Industry and Finance: a study of British economic development 1850–1860* (Oxford, 1960).
Hutchison, T.W. *The Cambridge Version of the History of Economics* (mimeo, Birmingham, 1974).
Jefferys, J.B. *The Story of the Engineers, 1800–1945* (new edn, London, 1970).
Jones, D. *Chartism and the Chartists* (Harmondsworth, 1975).
Jones, E.L. *The Development of English Agriculture, 1815–73* (London, 1968).
Kirby, R.G. and Musson, A.E. *The Voice of the People: John Doherty, 1798–1854, Trade Unionist, Radical and Factory Reformer* (Manchester, 1975).
Landes, D. *The Unbound Prometheus* (Cambridge, 1970).
Lansbury, C. *Elizabeth Gaskell: the novel of social crisis* (London, 1975).
Leavis, F.R. and Leavis, Q.D. *Dickens the Novelist* (London, 1970).
Lewenhak, S. *Women and Trade Unions* (London, 1977).
Litchfield, R. Burr 'The Family and the Mill: cotton mill work, family work patterns and fertility in mid-Victorian Stockport', in Wohl, A.S. (ed.) *The Victorian Family: structure and stresses* (London, 1978).
McLellan, D. *Karl Marx: his life and thought* (London, 1973).
Mather, F.C. *Public Order in the Age of the Chartists* (London, 1959).
Mather, F.C. 'Governments and the Chartists', in Briggs, A. (ed.) *Chartist Studies* (London, second edn, 1970).
Mather, F.C. 'The General Strike of 1842: a study in leadership, organisation and the threat of revolution during the Plug Plot disturbances', in Stevenson, J. and Quinault, R. (eds.) *Popular Protest and Public Order* (London, 1974).
Matthews, R.C.O. *A Study in Trade Cycle History: economic fluctuations in Great Britain, 1837–1842* (Cambridge, 1954).

258 Bibliography

Midwinter, E.C. *Social Administration in Lancashire 1830–1860: Poor Law, public health and the police* (Manchester, 1969).
Mitchell, B.R. *Abstract of British Historical Statistics* (Cambridge, 1962).
Musson, A.E. *British Trade Unions, 1800–1875* (London, 1972).
Musson, A.E. *The Growth of British Industry* (Manchester, 1978).
The New Cambridge Modern History: Zenith of European power, 1830–70, Vol. X (Cambridge, 1967).
Perkin, H.J. *The Origins of Modern English Society 1760–1880* (London, 1969).
Plummer, A. *Bronterre: a political biography of Bronterre O'Brien, 1804–1864* (London, 1971).
Pollard, S. *The Genesis of Modern Management* (Harmondsworth, 1969).
Raven, C.E. *Christian Socialism 1848–1854* (London, 1920).
Read, D. *Press and People 1790–1850: opinion in three English cities* (London, 1961).
Ridley, J. *Lord Palmerston* (London, 1970).
Rose, M.E. 'The New Poor Law in Industrial Areas' in Hartwell, R.M. (ed.) *The Industrial Revolution* (Oxford, 1970).
Sandberg, L.G. *Lancashire in Decline* (Columbus, Ohio, 1974).
Saville, J. *Ernest Jones, Chartist* (London, 1952).
Saville, J. 'The Christian Socialists of 1848', in Saville (ed.) *Democracy and the Labour Movement* (London, 1954).
Saville, J. and Bellamy, J.M. (eds.) *Dictionary of Labour Biography* (London, 1972 in progress, five vols. published by 1979).
Schoyen, A.R. *The Chartist Challenge: a portrait of George Julian Harney* (London, 1958).
Shipley, S. *Club Life and Socialism in Mid-Victorian London* (Oxford, 1971).
Simon, Daphne 'Master and Servant', in Saville, John (ed.) *Democracy and the Labour Movement* (London, 1954).
Smelser, N.J. *Social Change in the Industrial Revolution: an application of theory to the Lancashire cotton industry, 1770–1840* (London, 1959).
Smith, F.B. *The Making of the Second Reform Bill* (Cambridge, 1966).
Stevenson, J. and Quinault, R. *Popular Protest and Public Order* (London, 1974).
Tholfsen, T. *Working Class Radicalism in Mid-Victorian England* (London, 1976).
Thomis, M.I. *Responses to Industrialisation: the British experience 1780–1850* (Newton Abbot, 1976).
Thompson, E.P. *The Making of the English Working Class* (Harmondsworth, 1970).
Tobias, J.J. *Crime and Industrial Society in the Nineteenth Century* (Harmondsworth, 1972).
Tomlin, R.W.F. (ed.) *Charles Dickens 1812–70* (London, 1969).
Turner, H.A. *Trade Union Growth, Structure and Policy: a comparative study of the cotton unions* (London, 1962).
Vincent, J.R. *Pollbooks: how Victorians voted* (Cambridge, 1968).
Vincent, J.R. (ed.) *Disraeli, Derby and the Conservative Party: journals and memoirs of Edward Henry, Lord Stanley, 1849–1869* (Brighton, 1978).
Wadsworth, A.P. and Mann, J. de L. *The Cotton Trade and Industrial Lancashire, 1660–1780* (Manchester, 1931).
Ward, J.T. *The Factory Movement, 1830–1855* (London, 1962).
Ward, J.T. *Chartism* (London, 1973).
Webb, R.K. *The British Working Class Reader* (London, 1955).
Webb, S. and B. *History of Trade Unionism* (new edn, London, 1920).
Wedderburn, K.W. *Cases and Materials on Labour Law* (Cambridge, 1967).
Weiner, J.H. *The War of the Unstamped* (Berkeley, Cal., 1970).
Williams, R. *Culture and Society, 1780–1950* (Harmondsworth, 1961).

Williams, R. *The Long Revolution* (Harmondsworth, 1971).
Wohl, A.S. (ed.) *The Victorian Family: structure and stresses* (London, 1978).
Woodward, L. *The Age of Reform, 1815–1870* (second edn, Oxford, 1962).

2. Journal articles

Bell, H.C. 'Palmerston and Parliamentary Representation', *J. Mod. Hist.*, 4 (1932).
Bennet, S. 'Catholic Emancipation, "The Quarterly Review" and Britain's Constitutional Revolution', *Victorian Studies*, 72 (1968–9).
Blaug, M. 'The Productivity of Capital in the Lancashire Cotton Industry during the Nineteenth Century', *Ec. H. R.*, 14 (1961).
Boyson, R. 'The New Poor Law in North East Lancashire, 1834–1871', *Trans. Lancs. and Chesh. Antiq. Soc.*, 112 (1960).
Brantlinger, P. 'The Case Against Trade Unions in Early Victorian Fiction', *Victorian Studies*, 13 (1969–70).
Brigg, M. 'Life in East Lancashire 1856–60: a newly-discovered diary of John O'Neil (John Ward), weaver, of Clitheroe', *Trans. Hist. Soc. of Lancs. and Chesh.*, 120 (1968).
Burgess, K. 'Trade Union Policy and the 1852 Lock-out in the British Engineering Industry', *I.R.S.H.*, 17 (1972).
Carnall, G. 'Dickens, Mrs. Gaskell and the Preston Strike', *Victorian Studies*, 8 (1964–5).
Chapman, S.D. 'Financial Restraints on the Growth of Firms in the Cotton Industry, 1790–1850', *Ec. H. R.*, 32 (1979).
Clements, R.V. 'Trade Unions and Emigration, 1840–80', *Population Studies*, 9 (1955).
Cuca, J.R. 'Industrial Change and Progress of Labour in the English Cotton Industry', *I.R.S.H.*, 22 (1977).
Donajgrodzki, A.P. 'Sir James Graham at the Home Office', *Hist. J.*, 20 (1977).
Dutton, H.I. and King, J.E. 'The Society of Arts and the Preston Strike', *Journal of the Royal Society of Arts* (1979).
Dutton, H.I. and King, J.E. 'The Limits of Paternalism: the cotton tyrants of North Lancashire, 1836–1854', mimeo (1979b).
Epstein, J.A. 'Feargus O'Connor and the "Northern Star" ', *I.R.S.H.*, 21 (1976).
Erickson, C. 'The Encouragement of Emigration by British Trade Unions, 1850–1900', *Population Studies*, 3 (1949).
Fielding, K.J. 'The Battle for Preston', *Dickensian*, 50 (1954).
Fielding, K.J. 'The Preston Strikers', *Dickensian*, 63 (1967).
Fielding, K.J. and Smith, A. ' "Hard Times" and the Factory Controversy: Dickens versus Harriett Martineau', *Nineteenth Century Fiction*, 24 (1969–70).
Foster, J. 'Some Comments on "Class Struggle and the Labour Aristocracy, 1830–60" ', *Social History*, 3 (1976).
France, R. Sharpe (ed.) 'The Diary of John Ward of Clitheroe, Weaver, 1860–64', *Trans. Hist. Soc. of Lancs. and Chesh.*, 105 (1953).
Gatrell, V.A.C. 'Labour, Power and the Size of Firms in Lancashire Cotton in the Second Quarter of the Nineteenth Century', *Ec. H. R.*, 30 (1977).
Gordon, H. Scott 'The London *Economist* and the High Tide of Laissez-Faire', *J.P.E.*, 63 (1955).
Hart, J. 'Reform of the Borough Police 1835–56', *English Historical Review*, 70 (1955).
Hennock, E.P. 'Finance and Politics in Urban Local Government, 1835–1900', *Hist. J.*, 6 (1963).
Hobsbawm, E.J. 'The Machine Breakers', *Past and Present*, 1 (1952).
Jewkes, J. 'The Localization of the Cotton Industry', *Economic History*, 2 (1930).

Johnson, R. 'Educational Policy and Social Control in Early Victorian England', *Past and Present*, 49 (1970).
Jones, D.J.V. 'Chartism in Welsh Communities', *Welsh History Review*, 6 (1972–3).
Joyce, P. 'The Factory Politics of Lancashire in the Later Nineteenth Century', *Hist. J.*, 18 (1975).
King, J.E. 'Perish Commerce! Free Trade and Underconsumption in early British radical economics', *Australian Economic Papers*, forthcoming.
King, J.E. 'Marx as a Historian of Economic Thought', *History of Political Economy*, 11 (1979).
Kingsford, P.W. 'Radical Dandy', *History Today*, 14 (1964).
Lazonick, W. 'Industrial Relations and technical change: the case of the self-acting mule', *Cambridge Journal of Economics*, 3 (1979).
Lloyd-Jones, R. and LeRoux, A.A. 'The Size of Firms in the Cotton Industry: Manchester, 1815–41', *Ec. H. R.*, 33 (1980).
Martin, B. 'Leonard Horner: a portrait of an Inspector of Factories', *I.R.S.H.*, 14 (1969).
Martin, B.K. 'The Resignation of Lord Palmerston in 1853', *Camb. Hist. J.*, 1 (1923).
Milne, M. 'Strikes and Strike Breaking in North East England, 1815–44; the attitude of the local press', *I.R.S.H.*, 22 (1977).
Murphy, P.J. 'The Origins of the 1852 Lock-Out in the British Engineering Industry Reconsidered', *I.R.S.H.*, 23 (1978).
Musson, A.E. 'Class Struggle and the Labour Aristocracy, 1830–60', *Social History*, 3 (1976).
Musson, A.E. 'Industrial Motive Power in the United Kingdom, 1800–1870', *Ec. H. R.*, 29 (1976).
Peyrouten, N. 'Dickens and the Chartists', *Dickensian*, 60 (1964).
Proctor, W. 'Poor Law Administration in Preston Union, 1838–1848', *Trans. Hist. Soc. of Lancs. and Chesh.*, 117 (1965).
Reid, T.D.W. and Reid, N. 'The 1842 "Plug Plot" in Stockport', *I.R.S.H.*, 24 (1979).
Richards, P. 'The State and Early Industrial Capitalism: the case of the handloom weavers', *Past and Present*, 83 (1979).
Roberts, D. 'Lord Palmerston at the Home Office', *The Historian*, 21 (1958–9).
Roberts, D. 'How Cruel was the Victorian Poor Law?', *Hist. J.*, 6 (1963).
Rose, A.G. 'The Plug Riots of 1842 in Lancashire and Cheshire', *Trans. Lancs. and Chesh. Antiq. Soc.*, 67 (1957).
Rose, M.E. 'The Allowance System under the New Poor Law', *Ec. H. R.*, 19 (1966).
Shepherd, M.A. 'The Origins and Incidence of the Term "Labour Aristocracy" ', *Bulletin of the Society for the Study of Labour History*, 37 (1978).
Smith, A. ' "Hard Times" and the "Times" Newspaper', *Dickensian*, 69 (1973).
Taylor, A.J. 'Concentration and Specialization in the Lancashire Cotton Industry, 1825–1850', *Ec. H. R.*, 2 (1949).
Thompson, E.P. 'Rough Music: le charivari anglais', *Annales E.S.C.*, 2 (1972).
Ward-Perkins, C.N. 'The Commercial Crisis of 1847', *Oxford Economic Papers*, 2 (1950).

VI. UNPUBLISHED THESES

Boyle, M.F. *Preston Working Class Radicalism in the 1830s* (B.A. Lancaster, 1977).
Bradshaw, R.P. *The Preston Lock-Out: a case study of a mid-19th century cotton strike and its role in the development of trade union organisation amongst the textile workers* (M.A. Lancaster, 1972).
Farnie, D.A. *The English Cotton Industry, 1850–1896* (M.A. Manchester, 1953).

Bibliography

Gadian, D.S. *A Comparative Study of Popular Movements in North West Industrial Towns, 1830–1850* (Ph.D. Lancaster, 1976).

Gallagher, A.L. *The Social Control of Working-Class Leisure in Preston, 1850–1875* (M.A. Lancaster, 1975).

Reid, C.A.N. *The Chartist Movement in Stockport* (M.A. Hull, 1974).

Tabor, Cheryl R. *The Preston Cotton Unions: an account of their organization and activities, c. 1830–1850* (B.A. Manchester, 1972).

Index

Abbott, William, 178, 182
Aberdeen, Lord, 149, 153–4, 159, 170, 240–1, 252
Abraham, Mr, 146
Abram, W.A., 226, 228, 253
Accrington, 30, 33, 35–6, 57, 64, 98, 178, 192, 230
Acombe, John, 141
Addison, John, 234
Addison, Thomas Batty, 99, 143–7
Aikin, J., 10, 254
Ainsworth, George (operative), 31, 218
Ainsworth, Richard (employer), 234
Ainsworth, William (employer), 24, 42, 78–9, 86–7, 111, 205, 215, 217, 227
Ainsworth and Co., 10, 12, 78
Ainsworth and Paley Junior and Co., 212
Ainsworth, Catterall and Co., 11
Aitken, Mr (of Haslingden), 142
Aitken, William (of Ashton-under-Lyne), 207
Allen, William, 160
Almond, Richard, 108, 114, 228
Amalgamated Committee of Trades and Factory Operatives, Preston, 61, 65, 70–1, 188–9, 191, 223
Amalgamated Committee, Wigan, 104
Ambler, Edward, 135, 146, 185, 190
America, 101, 110–11, 114, 188, 207
American Civil War, 207
Anderson, M., 210–13, 230, 256
Andrew, S., 203, 254
Anti-Corn Law League, *see* Free Trade
'anti-strike committee', 44, 96
Anyon, J., 91
arbitration, 16, 24, 35, 42, 57, 59, 68, 82–4, 96, 107, 112, 151, 168–70, 174–5, 185, 202–3, 206, 244, 250
(*see also* mediation; negotiations)
Arkwright, Daniel, 87, 179, 234
Armstrong, H., 117, 119, 121, 236
Ascroft, Robert, 122, 135, 182–4, 205, 234, 245
Ashford (Kent), 67

Ashley, E., 239, 254
Ashton Marsh (near Preston), 180
Ashton-under-Lyne, 2, 10, 16, 20, 29, 32–3, 63–4, 90, 104, 106, 207, 216
Ashworth, Henry (of Bolton), 11, 21, 27, 82, 89, 95, 111, 175, 195–6, 201–2, 207, 215, 227, 230, 252, 254
Ashworth, Richard (of Walton, near Preston), 97, 143–4, 228
Aspinall, A., 214, 256
Australia, 220
Austria, 111

Bacup, 42, 62–3, 89–90, 98, 104, 115, 155, 193, 205, 222
Bagwell, P.S., 249, 256
Baines, Mr, 190
Bairstow, John, 234
ballads, 43, 100, 125
Bamber Bridge, 97, 114
Banks, Thomas, 51, 160, 193, 204–5, 213, 215, 249, 254
Bannister, Samuel, 130, 214
Barnsley, 67
Bashall, Richard, 28
Bashall, William Junior, 83
Bashall and Boardman, Messrs, 90, 101, 107, 114, 217, 228–9
Batley, 27
Baxendale, Robert, 50, 127, 133, 136, 186, 189, 192–3, 206, 235, 237, 241
Baynes, John, 58
Bedford, 67
Beer, Max, 222, 256
Beevers, Wallace, 3, 60–1
Belfast, 3, 67, 178–9, 182
Belgium, 152
Bell, H.C., 239–40, 259
Bell, S.P., 256
Bellamy, J., 223, 243, 253
Bennet, S., 244, 259
Bennett, Patrick, 126
Bentham (Yorkshire), 50
Bentley, James, 32

Index

Berry, A.J., 223, 256
Bibby, John, 51
Billington, L., 121
Birchall, Robert, 122, 234
Birkenhead, 27
Birley family, 79, 83, 117
Birley, Hugh Hornby (of Manchester), 79
Birley, Robert (of Manchester), 34
Birley, Thomas (of Kirkham), 126
Birley, William (of Preston), 87, 121, 234
Birley Bros. (of Preston), 12, 38, 97, 151, 178, 181
Birmingham, 67, 96, 119
Black, Adam, 202, 254
Black, James, 141–2
Blackburn
  cotton industry, 10, 23–4
  disturbances, 92, 102, 161
  masters' association, 23, 29, 31–2, 91–3, 104, 189, 204
  politics, 47, 59–60, 64, 91–3, 206–7
  strikes, 25, 29–30, 194
  support for Preston strikers, 3–4, 52, 63, 97, 184, 186, 189, 191
  support for Stockport strikers, 3, 32, 35
  ten per cent campaign, 29–31, 34–6, 38, 51–2, 91–3, 104
  trade unions, 16, 24–5, 52, 190, 192, 204, 206–7, 247
  wages, 25, 28, 34, 41, 91, 108, 112, 158, 168, 174, 190
  other references, 41, 45, 85, 97, 130, 132, 178, 191
Blackburn List of Prices, 20, 109, 112, 214
Blackburn Standard, 174, 241
Blackhurst, Thomas, 228
Blacklegs, *see* knobsticks
Blackpool, 37, 92, 204
Blackstone Edge, 158, 180, 188
Blackwood's Magazine, 175
Blakeley Moor, 36, 175, 190
Blanc, Louis, 60
Blaug, M., 211, 259
Board of Trade, 156–7
Bolton, 2, 15–17, 20–2, 28–9, 31–3, 37, 39, 52, 86, 130, 132, 158, 178, 211, 215
Bolton Chronicle, 173–4
bonds, employers, 20, 40, 42, 89–90, 101, 106, 110, 180, 183, 197, 203
Booth, Dr James, 111
Boston Daily Commonwealth, 111
Bowman, John, 25, 50, 70, 107, 160
Bottomley, John, 241
boycotts, *see* exclusive dealing
Boyle, M.F., 215, 260
Boys, W., 91

Boyson, R., 217, 228–9, 238, 247, 256, 259
Bradford, 3, 48, 67, 179, 182, 202
Bradford Observer, 174, 244
Bradley, Henry, 44
Bradshaw, R.P., 260
Braham, Mr, 96
Brantlinger, P., 248, 256, 259
Bray, John Francis, 222
Brickell, Rev., 143
Bridgwater, 67
Brierley, James, 60
Brigg, M., 259
Briggs, A., 239, 256
Bright, John, 47–8, 82–3, 154–5, 168, 201–2, 206–8, 226, 240, 252
Bright, Mr (of Preston), 177–8
Brighton, 67
Brindle (Lancashire), 47
Bristol, 67, 71
Brocklehurst, John, 172, 182, 191, 206
Brown, I., 256
Brown, Robert (surgeon and J.P.), 234
Brown, William (operative), 45, 52, 101, 108, 206
Bryning, Mr, 118
Buchanan, Robert, 168
Buckinghamshire, 115, 177
Builth, 110
Burgess, K., 213–14, 225, 256, 259
Burnley, 10, 20, 30, 32–7, 42–3, 58, 63, 86, 89–90, 98, 105, 108, 138–41, 147, 155, 157, 174, 192–3, 230
Burnley Advertiser, 36, 43, 174
Burnley Co-operative Commercial Association, 105
Burnley Mentor, 27, 43, 83
Bury, 15–16, 28, 33, 42, 63, 80–1, 104–5
Butt, J., 249, 256
Bythell, D., 211, 213

Caird, James, 111
Calvert, J., 91
Calvert, William, 108, 227
Cambridge, 67, 112
Campbell, Lord Justice, 90, 183
Canada, 67
Cardigan, 33
cardroom hands, 2, 15, 33, 35, 37, 39, 42–3, 51, 60–4, 71, 101, 105, 113, 187–9, 212, 224
Cardwell, Edward, 157–8, 240
Cardwell, George, 234
Cardwell, John, 234
Carlisle, 49
Carnall, G., 248–9, 259
Carpenter, Miss, 100
Carr, James, 118–19

Carter, Thomas, 133
Cartwright, Mr, 144
Cathcart, Earl of, 155, 159, 161, 240–1
Catterall, John (operative), 44–5, 219–20
Catterall, John (alderman), 234–5
Catterall, Paul (employer), 84, 87, 102, 227, 234
Catterall, Peter (solicitor), 96, 121, 123–4, 131, 234–5
Chadwick, D., 255
Chadwick, Edwin, 84
Chadwick, William (operative), 30, 52, 101, 110, 191, 221
Chadwick's Orchard, Preston, see Orchard, Preston
Challenger, Alexander, 21
Challinor, R., 218, 224, 228, 256
Chancellor of the Duchy of Lancaster, 123
Chapman, S.D., 210–11, 259
Chapman, S.J., 214, 254–5
Chartism, 19, 24, 47, 50, 52–5, 57–9, 62, 68–9, 79, 111, 129, 135, 158–9, 167, 169, 188, 195, 204–6
Cheadle Heath, 191
Cheetham, John, 1–2, 53
China, unrest in, 13, 95, 142
Chippenham, 67
Chorley, 28, 65, 215, 217, 221
Christensen, T., 219, 223, 247, 256
Christian Socialists, 58, 69, 219, 247
Church (Lancashire), 64
Church, R.A., 212, 256
Clarke, Robert, 166
Clay, Rev. John, 45, 84, 94, 99–100, 132, 226, 236
Clay, W.L., 226–7, 254
Clayton, John, 87
Clayton, William, 234
Clements, R.V., 222, 259
Clemesha, H., 233, 242, 249, 254
coal industry, 98–9
Cobbett, R.B., 245
Cobbett, William, 6, 56, 175, 254
Cobden, Richard, 47–8, 82–3, 168, 195–6, 201, 226, 240, 252
Cockpit, Preston, see Temperance Hall, Preston
Cole, G.D.H., 214, 222, 225, 256
Cole, W.A., 210, 213, 256
collective bargaining, see negotiations
Collins, P., 248, 256
Collinson and Watson, Messrs, 10
Colne, 32, 36, 42
Combination of Workmen Bill, 1853, 68, 167, 229
Combination Repeal Act, 1825, 124
communism, 70, 82, 172, 196

Conacher, J.B., 240–1, 256
conciliation, 174, 202
Confederacy, American, 207
conspiracy, law of, 68, 128, 183–4
Conway, Patrick, 178
Cooke, Thomas, 207
Cooper, George (of Stockport), 28–9, 101, 191–2
Cooper, John (employer, of Preston), 91, 228
co-operation, 41–2, 45, 57–8, 60, 105, 108, 110, 170, 190–3, 195
Coppock, Henry, 35
Corless, William, 190
Corry, George, 90
Cottam (near Preston), 180
Cotton Famine, 84
cotton industry
 after 1854, 203–4
 child labour, 14, 212
 growth of (Lancashire), 7–9
 growth of (Preston), 10–13
 labour force, 14–15, 212
 market conditions, 1846–8, 12, 23–4
 market conditions, 1852, 12, 27
 market conditions, 1853–4, 13–14, 28, 41, 95, 103, 186, 191
 strikes, see strikes
 trade unions, see trade unions
 wages, see wages; wage lists
 women, 14, 17–19, 213
 see also cardroom hands; spinners; weavers
Council, Preston Town, 116–28
Cowell, George
 portrait, 48
 character and temperament, 47–8, 100, 196
 early life, 46
 political activities before 1853, 46–7, 52
 campaigns for ten per cent in summer 1853, 26, 31, 35, 38–9, 160
 prepares for lock-out, 45
 activities during Preston strike, 49–50, 96–7, 100, 102, 105–8, 109–11, 113–15, 177, 180, 183, 187–9
 visits Glasgow, 67
 visits London, 69, 101, 107, 170
 attends Society of Arts conference, 49, 111–12, 169
 attends Labour Parliament, 49, 59–61
 supports Chartists, 55–6, 59–61, 167
 condemns political economy, 56
 opposes Cotton Lords as councillors, 120, 122
 attacks Preston authorities, 120, 125, 135

265 Index

attacks Poor Law Board, 146
criticises Palmerston, 151
attitude to press, 165–7, 172
attacked by press, 49–50, 165–6, 171–3
arrested, March 1854, 181, 245
activities, summer 1854, 192–3
jailed for debt, 1854, 193–4
later life, 206–7
fictional depiction of, 50, 198, 200
other references, 32, 63, 80, 158, 195, 198–200, 205
Craig, D., 248, 256
Craik, W.A., 248, 256
Crankshaw, William, 25
Cranworth, Lord Justice, 183
Craven Heifer Inn, 25
Crawford, Lord, 99
Crediton, 110
Cresswell, Mr Justice, 126, 128, 183
Crewe, 49
crime, decrease in during strike, 132–3
Crimean War, 186
Critchley, J.A., 235, 256
Crook, William, 65
Cuca, J., 213–14, 259

Daily News, 153, 172
Daly, Thomas, 50
Darwen, 24–5, 31–2, 34, 41, 64, 187, 193
Dawson, Hugh Junior, 87, 90, 180
Deane, P., 210, 214, 256
Defoe, Daniel, 6, 254
Delegates' Defence Fund, 185
Derby, 67
Derby, Earl of, 80, 88, 149
Dewsbury, 27
Dickens, Charles, 50, 82, 100, 111, 198–200, 223, 248–9, 254–5
Disraeli, Benjamin, 149
disturbances, public, 39–40, 102, 110, 113, 115, 124–8, 133–4, 160–2, 251
see also police; riots
Dixon, Thomas, 107, 118–20, 135, 144–6
Dobson, Laurence, 143, 165–6, 242
Dobson, W., 233, 254
Dodd, Thomas, 124, 236
Dodsworth, M., 248–9
Doherty, John, 213
Dolphin, James, 178, 182
Donajgrodzki, A.P., 227, 241, 256, 259
Donovan, Daniel, 19
Dowlais, 33
Doyle, Mary, 125
Drummond, H., 201
Dugdale, Thomas, 230
Dukinfield, 86, 104

Duncombe, T.H., 247, 254
Duncombe, Thomas Slingsby, M.P., 136, 185, 229, 245, 247
Dunning, T.J., 202, 254
Dutton, H.I., 232, 259
Dyers, of Manchester, 37, 57, 60, 98

Eastern Question, *see* foreign policy
Eccles, George (operative), 51, 160
Eccles, Richard (employer), 181
Eccles, Messrs, 227
Eckersley, Nathaniel, 228, 230, 236
Eckersley, Messrs, 106, 228
Economist, the, 137–8, 149, 172–3
Edge, Edward, 38, 180
Edinburgh Review, 174–5
Edmundson, Thomas, 52
Edsall, N.C., 237–8, 256
Edwards, M.E., 256
elections, municipal (1853), 96–7, 117–20, 122
Ellison, M., 250, 256
Ellison, T., 212, 254
emigration, 56, 110, 114–15, 147, 207, 220
employers' associations, *see* masters' associations
Engels, F., 6–7, 254
engineering industry, lock-out of 1852, 34, 69, 88–9, 96, 163, 168, 170–1, 203
Ensor, D., 240, 256
Epstein, J.A., 242, 259
Erickson, C., 222, 259
Erle, Mr Justice, 183
Evans, D. Morier, 215, 254
Ewan, J.A., 246
exclusive dealing, 66, 164–6, 203
Exeter, 110

factory movement, *see* Ten Hours movement
Factory Operative's Guide, 53
Fall River, Massachusetts, 67
Farington, 90, 101, 107, 109, 114, 145, 217, 232
Farnall, H.B., 138, 141–3, 145–6, 216, 238
Farnie, D.A., 210–12, 256, 260
Feilden, Montague Joseph, 92–3
Feilden, Sir William, 92
Feilden and Jackson, Messrs, 30
Fellowes, Henry, 43, 51, 206, 221
Feniscowles, 23, 92
Ferrand, William Busfield, 52, 57
fiction, Preston strike in, 198–201
Fielden, John, 47
Fielding, K., 220, 248, 259
Filson, D., 225, 256
Finlen, James, 70, 157, 240
Fish, John Knowles, 187

266 *Index*

Fitton, R.S., 211, 256
Fleetwood, 37, 178, 182
Fletcher, Anne, 51
Fletcher, Margaret, 51–2, 56
Flinn, M.W., 210, 254
Fong, H.D., 256
food riots, 110
foreign competition, 151–2, 197
foreign policy, in 1853–4, 149, 154
Foster, J., 210, 213, 220–3, 256, 259
France, 111
France, R. Sharpe, 250, 259
Fraser, D., 215, 233–4
Fraser, W.H., 214, 226, 229, 248, 257
Free Trade, 31, 56, 78–9, 82–3, 88, 97, 207, 215
Freehold Park, Preston, 180
Friargate, Preston, 39
Fulwood, 180, 184
Furness, J., 87

Gadian, D.S., 261
Galashiels, 67
Gallagher, A.L., 237, 261
Gallaher, Michael, 39, 51, 113, 178, 182, 245
Galloway, George, 125, 177–8, 182
Gammage, R.G., 221–3, 254
Gardner, John (employer), 91
Gardner, John (operative), 51, 178, 182
Gardner, Robert (employer), 23, 80, 91, 217, 227–8
Gardner and Naylor, Messrs, 217
Gardner and Walsh, Messrs, 228
Garnett, George, 207
Gaskell, Mrs, 199–201, 254
Gate, Isaac, 121, 236
Gatrell, V.A.C., 211–12, 259
Gayer, A.D., 212, 229, 257
German, James, 87
German, Thomas, 234
German and Petty, Messrs, 91
Gibbon, Sir John, 130
Gibbon, Joseph, 125–6, 130–2, 134–5
Gillespie, F.E., 223, 225, 257
Gillow, Joseph, 23, 80, 85, 87, 115, 214, 233, 252
Gissing, G., 248, 254
Glasgow, 49, 67, 81, 96, 184, 197, 245
Glasgow Sentinel, 167–9, 228
Glossop, 33, 51, 64, 66, 86, 98, 104, 130–1, 158
Gloucester, 67
Goderich, Viscount, 111
Gooch, G.P., 240, 257
Goodair, John, 25, 45, 80, 84–5, 91, 118–20, 131, 205–6, 212, 216, 234, 236, 255
  see also Napier and Goodair, Messrs
Goodair, Richard, 80, 91
Gordon, H. Scott, 244, 259
Graham, Sir James, 241
Gratrix Bros., Messrs, 90, 109, 114
Gray, A., 222, 257
Gray, John, 222
Great Exhibition of 1851, 51
Great Harwood, 28, 46, 64, 192
Green, F., 70
Greenough, Robert, 193
Greg, W.R., 174
Gregson, John, 206
Gregson, Thomas, 181, 245
Grenfell, C.P., 78–9, 123, 206
Grey, Sir George, 240
Grimshaw, Mortimer
  portrait, 49
  early life, 46
  character and temperament, 47–8, 163, 196
  role in Stockport agitation, 28
  first appearance in Preston, 41
  activities during Preston strike, 4, 14, 48, 66, 107, 111, 115, 125, 156, 159, 179–80, 184, 188–90
  opposes political economy, 56, 207
  supports co-operation, 41, 58, 193
  supports Labour League, 57, 61, 207
  supports Chartism, 58–9
  attends Labour Parliament, 59–61
  attacks Preston authorities, 135, 146
  attacks press, 163, 165, 173
  criticised by press, 165
  arrested, March 1854, 181, 245
  activities in summer 1854, 192–3
  later life, 207–8
  fictional depiction of, 198–200
  other references, 51, 63, 82
Grosvenor, Lord 111

Halifax, 67
Hall, Edwin, 112
Hammond, J.L. and B., 214, 257
Hampson, John, 120
handloom weavers, *see* weavers, handloom
Hansard, 201
Harbury, Benjamin, 52, 221
Hard Times, 198–200
Hardwick, Charles, 46–7, 51, 53, 210–11, 215, 218, 228, 234, 254–5
Hargreaves, James, 141
Harnott, Richard, 66, 190
Harrison, R., 250, 257
Hart, J., 236, 257, 259
Hartlepool, 27

Index

Hartwell, R.M., 238, 257
Haslam, Joseph, 125, 228
Haslam, Messrs, 125, 177
Haslingden, 34, 36, 141–2, 147
Hawick, 67
Hawkins, John, 25, 38, 79, 82, 118, 120, 124–5, 228
Haydock, Peter, 122
Hayes, James, 118–19
Hearn, F., 222, 257
Hedges, R.Y., 245, 257
Hemm, W., 66
Henderson, W.O., 222, 257
Hennock, E.P., 233–4, 257
Hewitson, A., 223–6, 249, 254
Hewitt, M., 230, 257
Heywood (Lancashire), 28, 41, 54, 191
Heywood, Alderman Abel, 184
Heywood, Thomas, 118, 121
Hill, William, 158
Hincksmann and Furness, Messrs, 91
Hindley, 106
Hobabawm, E.J., 214, 259
Hodgskin, Thomas, 111
Hoghton Tower, meeting at, 1–5, 60, 180, 201
Holcroft, James, 16
Hollins, Edward, 79, 90, 108, 114, 123, 133, 203, 217, 232, 247
Hollis, P., 242, 257
Home Office, 116, 123, 130, 132, 134, 138, 150, 154, 158, 240, 251
Home Secretary, *see* Palmerston, Lord
Hood, Thomas, 233
Hoole, Thomas, 238
Hooper, R., 160, 190
Hopkins, A.B., 248, 257
Hopwood, E., 214, 257
Hopwood and Co., 24
Hornby, John, 92
Hornby, William Henry, 32, 36, 92–3, 206, 248
Horner, Leonard, 11–12, 156, 212
Horrocks, John, 10, 77, 79
Horrocks, Richard, 234
Horrocks, Samuel, 77
Horrocks and Jacson, Messrs, 80, 174
Horrockses and Miller, Messrs, 3, 11, 14, 32, 37–8, 44, 77–8, 80, 84, 107–8, 113, 125, 181, 188–9, 193, 212, 227
Horsfall, J.B., 28, 53, 56–8, 163, 192–3, 207, 220, 223, 254
House, H., 248–9, 257
Household Words, 198
Howarth, Giles, 51, 107
Howell, George, 203, 254
Howitt, Mr, 144

Hughes, J.R.T., 212, 229, 257
Hughes, Thomas, 225, 254
Hugo, Victor, 60
Hull, 33, 67, 120, 181
Humber, John, 79, 87, 121, 134, 235–6
Humber, William, 79, 121, 234
Humber Bros., Messrs, 38
Hume, Joseph, 79, 96, 201
Humphreys, Price, 50, 60
Humphries, Edward, 202
Hungarian nationalism, 47, 50, 52
Huntingdon, Mr, 113
Hutchison, T.W., 222, 257
Hyde, 64, 86, 104, 187

India, markets in, 12–13, 95
intimidation, 25, 35, 64–5, 112–13, 124, 160, 173, 183
Ipswich, 27, 67
Ireland, 115, 179

Jacson, C.R., 80, 137, 234
Jefferys, J.B., 225, 257
Jevons, W.A., 249, 254
Jewkes, J., 211, 259
Johnson, R., 227, 260
Jones, D.J.V., 222, 241, 257, 259
Jones, E.L., 211, 257
Jones, Ernest, 4, 49, 55–60, 70, 106, 151, 158–9, 169–70, 205
Joyce, P., 228, 260

Kay-Shuttleworth, Sir J.P., 84, 139, 157, 248
Kelly, Mr, 177–8
Kendal, 50
Kennington Common, 159
Kershaw and Co., Messrs, 216
Kettle, Sir Rupert, 203
King, J.E., 222, 232, 259–60
Kingsford, P.W., 260
Kingsley, Charles, 223
Kirby, R.G., 213–15, 257
Kirkham, 79, 92
Knight, Charles, 202, 254
Knight, Rev. G.N., 210, 254
knobsticks, 3, 22, 35, 99, 106–7, 109, 113–15, 123–8, 134, 136, 160, 177–81, 188–9, 191, 204, 231, 245
Knowles, J., 121
Kossuth, L., 52
Kydd, Samuel, 57, 111–12

Labour League, *see* Lancashire, Yorkshire and Cheshire Labour League
Labour Parliament, 49, 59–61, 106, 158, 169–70, 198

268 *Index*

labour test, 139–44, 147
Lancashire Reform Union, 206
Lancashire, Yorkshire and Cheshire Labour League, 52–4, 57, 61, 207
Lancaster, 43, 101, 130, 132, 178, 194, 238
Lancaster Gazette, 241
Lancaster Guardian, 174, 241
Lancaster, William, 228
Lambert, Mrs, 181
Landes, D., 210, 257
Lang, John, 52, 178, 182, 228
Lansbury, C., 257
Lawless, Mr, 190
Lawson, Birley and Co., 216
Lazonick, W., 212, 260
Leavis, F.R. and Q.D., 248, 257
Leeds, 89, 119
Leicester, 67
Leigh (Lancashire), 28
Leigh, Adam, 87
Leigh, James, 87
Leigh, Messrs J. and A., 38, 125–6
LeRoux, A.A., 260
Lewenhak, S., 257
Lincoln, Abraham, 207
Linlithgow, 33
Litchfield, R. Burr, 213, 257
Literary and Philosophical Institution, Preston, 87
'Little Charter' movement, 79
Liverpool, 27, 33, 37, 71, 96, 132, 184
Liverpool Assizes, 126, 128, 182
Liverpool Journal, 174
Liverpool Mercury, 174
Liverpool Trades' Guardians Association, 66, 191
Livesey, Joseph, 163, 220, 226, 254
Livesey, R.N., 118
Lloyd, Edward, 167
Lloyd-Jones, R., 260
Lloyd's Weekly Newspaper, 153, 167–8, 232
lock-outs
  Blackburn (threatened, 1853), 31–2
  Burnley (1853), 42–3, 58, 89, 98, 102–4
  Bury (1853–4), 89, 104–5
  engineering industry (1852), 34, 69, 88–9, 96, 163, 168, 171, 200, 203
  Preston (1853–4), 40, 94–115
  Wigan (1853), 89, 104–6
  see also strikes; ten per cent campaign
London, 33, 49, 51, 54–5, 59, 67–70, 81, 101, 107, 111–12, 184, 245
Louis Philippe of France, 150
Lowe, James, 50, 126–7, 151, 161, 195, 211–12, 215, 224, 227, 229–32,
240, 243–7, 254–5
Lowe, Robert, 234
Lowenthal, E., 222, 254
Ludlow, J.M., 223
Lytham, 205

Madisson, Mr, 112
magistrates, 41, 43, 78–9, 122–8, 181–3, 185
  see also disturbances; riots
Malthus, T.R., 56
Manchester, 2, 15–20, 22–3, 27, 29–30, 33–4, 37, 50, 54, 57–60, 62–3, 66, 71, 89, 91, 108–9, 125, 130, 132, 143, 181–2, 184, 190, 198–9, 207, 211
Manchester Chamber of Commerce, 50, 111
Manchester Commercial Association, 111
Manchester Courier, 157
Manchester Examiner and Times, 153, 157, 173–4, 184, 207
Manchester Guardian, 36, 50, 157, 164, 173–4, 207
Mann, J. de L., 210, 213, 258
Mannex and Co., 227–8, 255
Manufacturers' Defence Fund, 81–2, 203, 232
Marsden, Richard, 24–5, 227
Marsh, Preston, 45, 58, 96, 101, 193
Martin, B., 240, 260
Martin, B. Kingsley, 240, 260
Martineau, Harriet, 174
Marx, Karl, 56, 60, 222, 255
Mass Movement, 4, 59–61, 70, 158, 169–70
Master and Servant laws, 22, 39
masters' associations
  Ashton, 90
  Bacup, 90, 104–5
  Blackburn, 23, 29, 31–2, 91–3, 104, 189, 204
  Bolton, 28
  Burnley, 42–3, 90, 102–5
  Bury, 105
  early, 20–1
  Lancashire federation, 33–4, 81–2, 86, 88–9, 108–9, 159
  Manchester, 23, 86
  Padiham, 105, 203
  Preston, *see* Preston Masters' Association
  Stockport, 20–1, 26, 29–30, 33, 35, 104, 186
  Wigan, 90, 105–6
  see also bonds; lock-outs; ten per cent campaign
Mather, F.C., 214–15, 217, 222, 233, 235–6, 241, 257
Mathews, John, 41, 53–4, 56, 59–60, 70, 101, 107, 187, 191, 206

269 Index

Matthews, R.C.O., 211–12, 257
Maudley, C.F., 212
Maudsley, Thomas, 237
Maurice, Rev. F.D., 111, 223
mayor of Preston
  in 1845, 78
  in 1853–4, 96, 121–2, 124, 127
McClure, Robert, 216
MacDonald, Alexander, 168
McGuffog, William, 87
MacLean, John, 60, 65, 223
McLellan, D., 222, 257
M'Quire, Mr, 60
MacRitchie, Rev. William, 6, 255
mediation, 43, 45, 82–3, 96, 111–12, 153, 155–61, 165–6, 171–2, 174, 185, 201, 227
  see also arbitration; negotiations
mediation committee, 185
Mehemet Ali, 150
memorials, *see* petitions
Merthyr Tydfil, 222
Merttens, F., 255
metropolitan police, 126, 134, 161
Metropolitan Trades' Delegates, 68–70, 151, 245
Mexico, 152
middle-class opinion, 32–3, 99, 107, 112, 127, 135, 185
Midwinter, E., 235–7, 258
Mill, John Stuart, 56
Miller, Henry, 37, 87
Miller, Thomas Junior, 3, 37, 39, 42, 45, 77–9, 87, 110, 112, 137, 193, 205, 234
Miller, Thomas Senior, 11, 45, 77
Mills, James, 221
Mills, John, 53
Milne, M., 241, 260
Mitchel, John, 53
Mitchell, B.R., 213, 258
Mitchell, Joseph, 179
Monk, Thomas, 122–3, 128, 234
Morley, J., 226, 255
Morning Chronicle, 171–2
Morning Herald, 171
Morning Post, 154
Moss, Jack, 25
Mossley, 216
Mounsey, James, 234
Municipal Corporations Act, 1835, 116–17, 129
Murphy, P.J. 241, 260
Murphy's Temperance Hotel, 101
Musson, A.E., 210–11, 213–15, 222, 257–8, 260
Myres, Miles, 118–19, 234, 236

Napier and Goodair, Messrs, 32, 46, 91, 192, 217
National Association for the Promotion of Social Science, 197, 255
National Association of United Trades for the Protection of Labour, 19, 24–5, 57, 68–70, 101, 202
Naylor, Thomas, 25, 86, 178–9
negotiations, 21, 33, 42, 96, 108, 151, 165, 167, 185, 190
  see also arbitration; mediation
New Edgly Mill, 95
New York Daily Tribune, 222
Newbould, T.P., 221, 255
Newcastle-upon-Tyne, 67
Newsham, Henry, 44
Newton, William, 56, 68–9, 112, 160, 183, 225
Newton Abbot, 67
North and South, 198–201
Northern Liberator, 167
Northern Star, 167
Northamptonshire, 203
Norwich, 67
Nottingham, 67
Nottingham, John, 25

Oastler, Richard, 47, 57
O'Brien, James Bronterre, 68–9
O'Connor, Feargus, 68, 173, 214, 218
Oldham, 2, 10, 15, 17, 20, 24, 31–3, 53, 55, 59, 130, 143, 191, 203, 215
Orchard, Preston, 34–5, 37, 41, 44, 52, 96, 101, 110–11, 120, 124–5, 165, 177, 179–80, 193
Orrell, R., 114, 228
overlookers, 43, 105, 227
over-production, 56, 86, 204
Owen, Robert, 18, 111
Owen, William, 167
Oxford Road Twist Co., 207

Padiham, 32–5, 41, 43, 57, 63, 68, 98, 102, 104–5, 155, 189, 203, 222, 230
Page, Rev. S.F., 43
Pakington, Sir John, 229
Paley, John Junior, 22, 24, 78–9, 87, 137, 215, 234–5
Paley, John Senior, 12, 79, 87, 212, 234
Paley, William, 91, 121
Paley, Messrs, 227
Palmerston, Lord, 102, 120, 123–8, 133, 136, 149–62, 169, 202, 230, 232, 234, 237
Parliament, discussion of strike in, 210–12
Parliamentary reform, 149, 153–4, 156, 159, 170

Parliamentary reform (*cont.*)
 see also Chartism
Park, Thomas, 125
Parker, James, 117, 119, 121, 234
Parker, R. Townley, MP, 42, 96
Parker, S., 145
Parkinson, William, 51, 178, 181
Parr, Rev. J.O., 42, 45, 144, 185
Pateley Bridge, 79
Paternalism, by employers, 84–5, 92–3
Payment of Wages Bill, 1854, 201
Pedder, Richard, 128, 234–5
Peel, William, 70
People's Charter, see Chartism
People's Paper, 68, 70, 151, 167, 169–70, 173, 232
Perkin, H.J., 222, 258
Peterloo, 195
petitions, 128, 136, 150–3, 169, 185
Peyrouten, N., 260
piecers, 15, 17, 37
piecework prices, see wage lists
Pilkington, James (employer, of Blackburn), 92
Pilkington, W. (piecer and author, of Preston), 212–13, 255
Pilkington, Mr (Poor Law Guardian, of Preston), 144–6
Playfair, William, 157–8, 240
Plummer, A., 225, 258
Plummer, John, 203, 255
Plymouth, 96, 130
police, 2, 33, 36–7, 116, 120, 125–6, 128–36, 160–1, 185, 193, 233
political economy, 55–7, 83, 85, 110, 149, 151–3, 157, 161–2, 166, 168–9, 172–5, 207, 249
Pollard, S., 213, 258
Pool, Thomas, 126
Poor Law Amendment Act, 1834, 143–4
Poor Law Board, 138–41, 144–7, 170
poor relief
 in Burnley, 138–41, 147
 in Haslingden, 141–2, 147
 in Preston, 143–8
 other references, 23, 27, 115
Portsea, 67
Postlethwaite, James, 51, 96
Potteries' Examiner, 167
Pratt, Tidd, 193
press, local, 163–7, 173–4
press, national, 112, 171–5
press, working-class, 112, 167–71
Preston
 Chartism, 222
 civil authorities, 33, 36–7, 41, 43, 77–80, 116–36, 160–2, 179, 181–3, 185, 193, 197
 cotton manufacturers, 77–80, 87–8, 117–19, 121–3, 129
 disturbances, 39–40, 113, 115, 124–8, 133–4, 161
 early development of, 6–7
 growth of cotton industry in, 10–13
 importance of Indian and Chinese markets to, 13
 living conditions, 7, 23, 99–100
 Masters' Association, see Preston Masters' Association
 Operative Reform Association, 78
 Orchard, see Orchard, Preston
 politics, 77–80, 87–8, 91–2, 116–23, 146, 205–6
 poor relief, 23, 143–8
 Ratepayers' Association, see Preston Ratepayers' Association
 riots, 21–2
 strikes, 21–2, 25–6, 27–45, 94–115, 177–94, 203
 Ten Hours movement, 23, 47, 50–1, 78, 80, 88, 227
 ten per cent campaign, 28, 31–2, 34–5, 37–45, 80–2, 94–102, 106–15, 124–7, 132–6, 147, 150–3, 155, 157–8, 177–94
 Theatre, 107, 185
 trade unions, 21–6, 61–2, 65, 192–3, 203–5, 249
 wages, see wages
 weather in 1853–4, 109, 113
Preston Banking Company, 88, 226, 252
Preston Chronicle, 123, 131, 143, 157, 164–6, 241
Preston Guardian, 23, 28, 38, 55, 123, 125, 127–8, 136, 157, 163–6, 241
Preston Masters' Association, 20–2, 28–9, 40, 42, 44, 83–91, 97–8, 102, 108–9, 111, 118, 121–2, 124, 135, 144, 155, 163, 171, 180, 183, 188–9, 196–7, 205, 228
Preston Pilot, 164, 166–7, 241
Preston Ratepayers' Association, 117–20, 128, 135, 145–6, 179–80, 185
Preston Weaving Industrial Society, 247
price of food, 95, 110, 229
Prideaux, G.W., 70
Priestly, Mr, 142
Prince Albert, 170, 243
Proctor, W., 239, 260
prosecution of delegates, 128, 166, 181–5, 193
protectionism, 56–7, 68, 97, 159
Proudhon, P.-J., 60
provocation by police, 2, 41, 99, 113, 115,

Index

129, 133–5, 160, 179–80
Pryme, Professor, 112

Quarterly Review, 175
Queen Victoria, 149, 154, 240
Quinault, R., 214, 258

R. v Duffield, 183
R. v Rowlands, 183
R. v Selsby and others, 183
Radcliffe, 26, 50
Raven, C.R., 219, 258
Raw, J., 118, 236
Rayner, William, 128
Read, D., 258
Rebecca notices, 110, 195
'Reconciliation Committee', 190
Redmayne, Mr, 206
Reid, C.A.N., 214, 217, 221, 246, 250, 260–1
Reid, D., 214, 260
Reynolds, G.W.R., 167, 225
Reynolds' Newspaper, 153, 167, 170–1, 173
Rhodes, Thomas, 41, 52, 60, 96, 101, 166, 183, 191, 206
Ribbleton Moor, 180
Ricardian Socialists, 56
Ricardo, David, 56
Richards, P., 260
Richardson, Robert, 51, 206
Richardson and Whitworth, Messrs, 89, 113
Richmond, George, 51, 101
Ridley, J., 239, 241, 258
Rigby, Henry, 184
Rigby, Mr, 190
Riley, Christopher, 178, 182
Rio de Janeiro, 67
Riot Act, read in Preston, 126–7, 136, 160–1, 197
riots
 in Blackburn, 102, 132, 161, 203, 235
 in Devon, 110
 in Kidderminster, 131
 in Manchester, 37, 214
 in Preston, 21–2
 in Wigan, 98–9, 131–2, 161, 235
 see also disturbances
Ripley, B., 218, 224, 228, 256
Rishton Moor, 3
Roberts, D., 238–9, 260
Roberts, William Prowting, 35, 64, 183–4, 192, 245
Robinson, Samuel, 82, 84–5, 255
Rochdale, 20, 142, 188, 206
Rodgett, Edward, 117–18, 120, 123
Rodgett, Miles Junior, 37, 79, 114

Rodgett, Miles Senior, 87, 228
Rodgett, Messrs, 217
Rodgett Bros., Messrs, 100, 228
Rose, A.G., 215, 218, 222, 260
Rose, M.E., 238, 258, 260
Rossendale, 42, 63, 98
Rostow, W.W., 212, 229, 257
Royal Society of Arts, *see* Society of Arts
Royton, 28, 40, 53, 193, 219, 252
Russell, Lord John, 24, 149–50, 153, 159, 240
Russia, 95

Sabden, 192–3, 247
St Petersburg, 222
Salford, 130
Salt, Robert, 118–19
Sandberg, L., 212, 258
Satterthwaite, Michael, 120, 146
Saville, J., 219, 222–3, 253
Say's Law, 56
Schoyen, A.R., 225, 258
Schultze-Gaevernitz, G. von, 249, 255
Schwartz, A.J., 212, 229, 257
Scotland, 16, 190
Seed, Henry, 229
Seed, James, 87
Seed, William, 90, 109
self-help, 58, 145
Sergeant, John, 39, 51, 160, 206
Settle, 37
Seward, P., 240
Sharples and Wilding, Messrs, 90, 177
Shaw, William, 87, 90, 234
Sheffield, 48, 67, 71, 96, 107
Shepherd, M.A., 225, 260
Shipley, S., 225, 258
Shorrock, Eccles, 204, 255
short-time working
 in 1847–8, 12, 23
 in 1853–4, 103–4, 155, 186, 190
short-time movement, *see* Ten Hours movement
Simon, D., 219, 258
Sinope, massacre of, 154
Slater, R., 228
Slater and Pollard, Messrs (of Burnley), 42, 98
Slater and Smith, Messrs (of Preston), 91
Small Tenements Rating Act, 1850, 119
Smelser, N., 213–14, 221, 258
Smethurst, Messrs, 217
Smethwick, 67
Smiles, Samuel, 79
Smith, Adam, 56, 87, 255
Smith, Anne, 47, 259–60
Smith, F.B., 240, 258

Smith, George (employer, of Preston), 79–80, 122, 131, 134, 236
Smith, Kinder (operative, of Oldham), 53, 163, 184, 186, 192, 223, 240
Smith, Samuel (employer, of Preston), 91, 121
Smith, Thomas (operative, of Stockport), 52, 191
socialism, 84, 112
  see also communism
Society of Arts, 49, 111–12, 168–70, 243, 252
South Shields, 27, 33
special constables, 130–1, 134
Spencer, Alderman, 131, 234–5
spinners, 14–15, 17–22, 24, 26, 28–33, 35, 37–9, 42, 44, 51, 58, 60–5, 71, 81, 96–7, 101, 104, 109, 112–13, 115, 125, 127, 173, 177–8, 185–91, 203, 215, 224, 249
Stafford, 67
Staffordshire, 201, 203
Stalybridge, 32, 64, 158
'Steeple Jack', 37
Stephens, Rev. Joseph Rayner, 47, 57
Stevenson, J., 214, 258
Stockport
  labour force, 14
  masters' association, 20–1, 26, 29–33, 35, 89, 104, 186
  strike of 1853, 3, 28–36, 43, 52, 82, 101, 167
  strike of 1854, 128, 170, 186–9
  ten per cent campaign, 28–36, 41–2, 46, 61–2, 186–9
  wages, 20, 24, 28–9, 174, 216
  other references, 10, 37–8, 64, 80, 97, 106, 110, 132, 191–2, 211
Stockport Advertiser, 174
Stockton-on-Tees, 67
Stoke-on-Trent, 67
Stoves, John, 240
Strickland, Sir George, MP, 42, 51, 78–80, 107, 160, 201, 227
strikebreakers, *see* knobsticks
strikes
  before 1853, 16–18, 21–2, 24–6, 29, 54–5, 79, 86, 122, 132, 195, 202–3
  in 1853 (Preston), 27–45, 94–115
  in 1853 (Stockport), 28–36, 82, 167
  in 1853 (other towns), 27, 31, 33, 36–7, 42
  in 1854 (Preston), 94–115, 177–95
  in 1854 (Sabden), 192–3
  in 1854 (Stockport), 186–9
  in 1854 (other towns), 194
  after 1854, 203–4, 206

see also knobsticks; lock-outs; ten per cent campaign
Strikes Prevented (by John Goodair), 85, 227
Sturgeon, Charles, 69–70
subscriptions to strike funds, 4, 32, 34–5, 37, 39, 41, 43, 62–7, 70–1, 97–8, 101–2, 108, 114–15, 170, 173, 184–6, 188–9, 191–2, 204
Sunderland, 27
Svedenstierna, E., 6
Swainson family, 79, 117
Swainson, Charles, 77, 79, 117–20
Swainson, Edward, 87
Swainson, John Junior, 38–9, 87, 90, 180, 183
Swainson Bros., Messrs, 109, 180
Swainson and Birley, Messrs, 11–12, 37–8, 113, 188, 212
Swansea, 33
Swindon, 67
Swinglehurst, Edward, 24, 37, 41, 45, 50, 52–3, 59, 115, 124, 135, 146, 160, 165, 179

Tabor, C.R., 215, 261
Taiping revolt, 13–14
Talfourd, Sir Thomas, 84–5
tape-machine sizers, 224
Taunton, 110
Taylor, A.J., 211, 260
Taylor, W. Cooke, 82, 255
Taylor, William, 227
Teer, John, 58, 60, 223
teetotallism, 43, 46, 50
Temperance Hall, Preston, 24–5, 31–2, 39, 41, 43, 111, 113, 125, 247
Ten Hours movement, 23, 29, 46–7, 50–2, 57, 78, 80, 88, 92, 169, 207, 227
ten per cent campaign
  cardroom hands in, 33, 35, 37, 39, 42–3, 51, 60–4, 71, 101, 105, 113, 187–9, 234
  origins of (1846–8), 23–6
  revives (1853), 27
  spinners in, 28–33, 35, 37–9, 42, 44, 51, 58, 60–5, 71, 81, 96–7, 101, 104, 109, 112–13, 115, 125, 127, 173, 177–8, 185–91, 224
  throstle-spinners in, 62–3, 71, 96–7
  weavers in, 28–39, 41–5, 46–65, 71, 78, 90, 96–104, 107–15, 124–5, 141, 151, 169, 179–81, 184–93, 218, 223–4
  in Accrington, 30, 35, 98, 104
  in Blackburn, 29–31, 34–6, 38, 51–2, 91–3, 104

Index

in Bolton, 29–30, 37, 218
in Burnley, 30, 32, 35–7, 42–3, 98, 102–5, 155
in Colne, 36
in Darwen, 31
in Haslingden, 36
in Manchester, 37, 98
in Padiham, 32, 36, 98, 155
in Preston, 28, 31–2, 34–5, 37–45, 80–2, 94, 102, 106–15, 124–7, 132–6, 147, 150–3, 155, 157–8, 177–98
in Stockport, 28–36, 61–2, 186–9
in Wigan, 37, 42, 63, 98–9, 104–6
see also amalgamated committee; strikes; subscriptions
Thackery, Thomas, 216
Theatre, Preston, 107, 185
Tholfsen, T.R., 222, 258
Thomis, M.I., 226, 258
Thompson, E.P., 213–14, 260
Thompson, Mr, 118
Thompson, William, 222
Threlfall, Richard Junior, 117, 119, 122, 236
Threlfall, Richard Senior, 25–6, 38, 86–7, 181
Threlfall, William, 121
throstle-spinners, 14, 62–3, 71, 96–7, 113
Tillotson, K., 248, 256
Times, the, 86–7, 171–2
Tobias, J.L., 236, 258
Tonge, Thomas, 191
Todmorden, 86
Tolpuddle, 195
Tomlin, R.W.F., 258
trade unions
after 1854, 203–5
cardroom hands, 15, 61–3
craft unions, 43, 49, 59, 65–71, 96, 101, 106–7, 184, 190
early (Lancashire), 14–20, 213
early (Preston), 21–6
employers' attitude towards, 40, 81–5, 89, 91, 93, 98, 103–4, 196, 226
handloom weavers, 15–17, 21
middle-class attitude to, 163–76, 197–203
piecers, 15
powerloom weavers, 14–15, 19–26, 52–3, 61–3, 189–90, 192–3, 203, 206–7, 249
spinners, 14–15, 17–22, 26, 61–4, 86, 185, 204–5, 249
see also lock-outs; Metropolitan Trades' Delegates; National Association of United Trades; strikes

Tremenheere, Hugh, 84
Truck System, 57, 115, 201
Tsar Nicholas of Russia, 150
Tulket, Marmaduke, 210–11, 255
Turkey, 95
Turner, H.A., 213–15, 258
Turner, James Aspinall, 111
Tyrell, Sir John, 97

Ulverston Advertiser, 241
underconsumption, theory of, 56, 86, 204
unions, *see* trade unions
Ure, A., 213, 255

Vincent, J.R., 226, 239, 258

Waddington, H. (government official), 234, 241
Waddington, James (operative), 2, 51, 115, 178, 181, 184, 190, 221
Wadman, H.B., 51, 113
Wadsworth, A.P. 210–11, 213, 256, 258
wage lists, 19–20, 22, 33–4, 36, 39, 112, 203
wages
reductions in 1842, 19
reductions in 1847–8, 23–5, 196
in Preston, 2, 4, 10–11, 21–2, 24–6, 31, 34, 38, 41, 45, 81, 83, 91, 97–8, 102, 108–9, 112, 129–30, 151, 157–8, 193, 203, 216, 247
in Stockport, 20, 24, 28–9, 174, 216
Walker, Robert (operative), 52
Walker, Thomas (tobacconist), 121
Walling, Rev. W., 44
Walmsley, Richard (policeman), 125
Walmsley, T. (author), 220, 255
Walmsley, Thomas (mayor of Preston, 1853–4), 122, 126–9, 131, 135, 234, 241
Walton (near Preston), 28, 144, 146, 189, 193, 228
Walton, William, 41, 45, 52, 96
Wapping, 181
Ward, J.T., 221–2, 228, 243, 258
Ward, John (of Clitheroe), 206
Ward, Mr (of Preston), 144
Ward-Perkins, C.N., 215, 260
Warrington, 47, 53, 58, 132, 198, 223
Watch Committee, Preston, 116, 120, 128–35, 233, 252
see also police
Watson, Councillor, 236
Watts, J., 236
weavers, handloom, 8, 14–17, 20–1, 24, 97, 121, 141, 145
weavers, powerloom, 14–15, 19–21, 24–6,

weavers, powerloom (*cont.*)
   28–39, 41–5, 46–54, 56–65, 71, 78, 90, 96–104, 107–15, 124–5, 141, 151, 169, 179–81, 184–93, 203–4, 206, 218, 223–4, 249
Webb, R.K., 242, 258
Webb, S. and B., 54, 203, 213–14, 225, 258
Wedderburn, K.W., 245, 258
Weiner, J.H., 242, 258
Westminster Review, 175
Westray, John, 60
Whalley (near Blackburn), 206
Whalley, James, 51, 136, 235, 241
Whittaker, T., 126
Whittle, Edward 'Ned', 20, 52–3, 59, 62, 64, 108, 160, 190, 193, 206, 247
Whittle, Edwin, 193
Whitworth, Henry, 89
Wigan, 27, 33, 37, 42, 63, 79, 89–90, 104–7, 130, 132, 142, 158, 161, 235
Wilkinson, Henry, 37
Williams, R., 242, 248, 258–9
Williamson, J., 91
Wilmslow, 82
Wilson, George (of Manchester), 207, 252
Wilson, Mr (of Wigan), 228

Wilton, Earl of, 108
Winckley Square, Preston, 87, 205
Winter, Thomas, 160, 202
Winterbottom, A., 245, 257
Wohl, A.S., 259
Wolverhampton, 67
women
   in cotton industry, 14, 17–19, 213
   in Preston strike, 51–2, 94
Wood, Sir Charles, 207
Wood, G.H., 214, 217, 255
Wood, Luke, 3, 52, 101, 115, 125, 177, 182, 187, 191, 230
Woodford, Capt. John, 128, 132
Woodhead, Dennis, 128
Woodhouse, J., 118
Woodplumpton, 144
Woodward, L., 249, 259
Worden, R., 228
workhouses, 143–6
Worswick, Robert, 3, 53
Wright, Rev. J.H.C., 35–6
Wright, James Duncan, *see* 'Steeple Jack'

Yates, R., 118–19, 121
Young, James, 2, 60

Printed in Great Britain
by Amazon